Vision and Method in Historical Sociology

Some of the most important questions of the social sciences in the twentieth century have been posed by scholars pursuing investigations at the intersections of social theory and history viewed on a grand scale. What research agendas have these investigators followed? How have their basic assumptions about society, history, and the purposes of scholarship informed the questions they have asked, and the kinds of answers they have offered? How have they used various sources of evidence about the past to pursue case studies or comparisons among groups, periods, nations, or civilizations? These are some of the issues addressed by the essays collected in *Vision and Method in Historical Sociology*.

The nine core essays of the book focus on the careers and contributions on nine major scholars: Marc Bloch, Karl Polanyi, S. N. Eisenstadt, Reinhard Bendix, Perry Anderson, E. P. Thompson, Charles Tilly, Immanuel Wallerstein, and Barrington Moore, Jr. These essays, written by younger scholars who are themselves involved in historical sociology or social history, convey a vivid sense of the vision and values each major scholar brings (or brought) to his work. In addition, the essays analyze and evaluate the research designs and methods used in the most important works of each scholar.

The 1970s and 1980s are proving to be a period of rapid growth and renewal for historical sociology. The introduction and conclusion to this volume discuss the long-running tradition of historically grounded research in sociology, while the conclusion also provides a detailed discussion and comparison of three recurrent strategies for bringing historical evidence and theoretical ideas to bear upon one another. Finally, an annotated bibliography on methods of comparative and historical sociology is also offered as an aid to ongoing research and teaching.

Informative, thought-provoking, and unusually practical, *Vision and Method in Historical Sociology* offers fascinating and relevant reading to sociologists, social historians, historically oriented political economists and anthropologists – and, indeed, to anyone who wants to learn more about the ideas and methods of some of the best-known scholars in the modern social sciences.

Vision and Method in Historical Sociology

Edited by Theda Skocpol
Harvard University

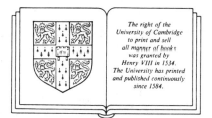

The right of the
University of Cambridge
to print and sell
all manner of books
was granted by
Henry VIII in 1534.
The University has printed
and published continuously
since 1584.

Cambridge University Press
Cambridge
New York   New Rochelle
Sydney   Melbourne

Published by the Press Syndicate of the University of Cambridge
The Pitt Building, Trumpington Street, Cambridge CB2 1RP
32 East 57th Street, New York, NY 10022 USA
10 Stamford Road, Oakleigh, Melbourne 3166, Australia

First published 1984
Reprinted 1985, 1986, 1987, 1989

Printed in the United States of America

Library of Congress Cataloging in Publication Data

Main entry under title:

Vision and method in historical sociology.

Based on the proceedings of the Conference on Methods
of Historical Social Analysis, held in Cambridge,
Mass., October 1979.

Bibliography: p.
1. Historical sociology – Congresses.   2. Historical
sociology – Methodology – Congresses.   I. Skocpol, Theda.
II. Conference on Methods of Historical Social Analysis
(1979 : Cambridge, Mass.)
HM104. V57   1984   301'.0722   84–7013
ISBN 0 521 22928 6 hard covers
ISBN 0 521 29724 9 paperback

FOR OUR TEACHERS, INCLUDING OUR STUDENTS

Contents

Contents

Preface

On a gorgeously colorful October weekend in 1979, about a dozen historical sociologists, along with a couple of sociologically acclimated social historians, gathered in Cambridge, Massachusetts. We assembled for three intensive days of discussion about the ideas and methods embodied in the work of major historical sociologists, including several – Reinhard Bendix, Barrington Moore, Jr., Charles Tilly, and Immanuel Wallerstein – who had been the teachers of conference participants. Everyone, including myself as the organizer of this Conference on Methods of Historical Social Analysis, approached the event with considerable skepticism about its likelihood of success.

Papers had been prepared and circulated in advance. Each author had been asked to probe the major works of a single senior scholar, considering the nature of the questions posed; the ways in which theoretical ideas and historical evidence were brought to bear upon one another in answering those questions; the use of comparisons across historical cases; and, more generally, the strategies each scholar had devised to design historical investigations and communicate them to relevant audiences. Although the papers were to focus on sets of works by individuals, they were also supposed to avoid overpersonalizing the issues. Neither biography nor sheer intellectual history was the aim, for I had commissioned these essays to further methodological reflection among a growing network of young historical sociologists. The idea was to examine closely – and compare – the methodologies used in excellent, substantive examples of research and writing by important scholars not already so remote or canonized as Max Weber, Alexis de Tocqueville, or Karl Marx. The payoff, I hoped, would come not only in the edited collection of essays to follow the conference but also in the greater self-consciousness we participants would bring to our own ongoing scholarship – and, perhaps even more important, to our teaching of the growing numbers of still younger sociologists who now undertake research in historical sociology.

But would it work? On the eve of the conference, it was not at all clear. The draft essays were the usual mixed bag of conference papers: some very strong; others weak or not to the point; and one (a crucial paper) canceled at the last minute and therefore missing altogether. More worrisome still were other dangers. It looked as if conference participants might fall to quarreling on behalf of their respective teachers. We all wondered whether each session might not revolve simply around assessments of the individual scholars' substantive arguments. Indeed, from the moment of his arrival, one especially articulate participant repeatedly proclaimed that "historical sociology has no methods!"

In the event, all of the possible troubles happened to some degree, yet on the whole the conference was an exhilarating and intense intellectual experience – so agreed even the most skeptical participants in its aftermath. Discussants in each session did a beautiful job of criticizing each paper and of using its materials to bring out larger points about the purposes, the successes, and the limitations of the work of the major scholar. Telling comparisons were made of each scholar's approach to that of others. Methodologies were indeed clarified – with "methodology" understood not as a set of neutral techniques, but as the interrelations of substantive problems, sources of evidence, and larger assumptions about society, history, and the purposes of scholarship. Session discussions ranged widely and built on one another. After the conference, I was able to provide detailed advice on revisions to the authors, and many of them worked quickly to prepare qualitatively better essays out of the insights generated in the collective discussions.

During the last few years, in the span between the 1979 conference and the completion of this book, several sophisticated commentaries on methods of historical sociology have appeared. Arthur Stinchcombe's *Theoretical Methods in Social History*, Charles Tilly's *As Sociology Meets History*, and Philip Abrams's posthumously published *Historical Sociology* all help to define what is distinctive about historically oriented sociological research and open for debate a whole range of issues about the uses of theory, evidence, and analytic devices, including comparisons. What is more, they do this by focusing to significant degrees on current research practice, rather than dwelling solely on nineteenth-century classical authors. Had these fine books already been available at the time I conceived the plan for this volume I might not have seen a need for it. By now, however, I am glad this book has happened, for

its chapters add new perspectives to the still nascent reflective literature about the ways in which historical sociology has been – and could
be – practiced in our time.

Because this collection is organized around the work of individuals,
a sense comes through of the vision and values each scholar personally brings, or brought, to his work. Surely, I now realize, this is all to
the good. It conveys what a serious business this kind of scholarship
can be – compelling enough to claim whole lifetimes of effort from
people who really want to understand the shaping of significant aspects of the modern world and its antecedents. Besides, methodological discussions all too often portray research in an antiseptic, deper-
sonalized manner, belying the obvious and consequential truth that
scholarship is always done by real people with axes to grind and
projects to pursue.

The volume also has a personal flavor to it in a second sense: Each
chapter reveals one or two younger scholars characterizing and evaluating the work of an older scholar. (The age differences are, of course,
average and relative. A bit plaintively, Charles Tilly queried, "How did
Dietrich sneak into the youngsters' tent?," pointing out that he and
Dietrich Rueschemeyer are the same age. Moreover, Perry Anderson is
chronologically and generationally the peer of some of the authors in the
volume.) Naturally, each chapter embodies a distinctive point of view,
influenced by the kind of work and the aspirations for scholarship that
its author brings to the task. The arguments would certainly have been
different had different authors been involved, and this suggests an obvious point worth underlining: In no sense are these definitive evaluations
of the achievements of Marc Bloch, Karl Polanyi, S. N. Eisenstadt, Reinhard Bendix, Perry Anderson, E. P. Thompson, Charles Tilly, Immanuel
Wallerstein, or Barrington Moore, Jr. They are simply genuine, thoughtful discussions by people who themselves do historical sociology. Reading and comparing these essays ought to inspire not fixed judgments
but reexaminations of the important works discussed and, above all,
new efforts to practice historical sociology at the level of excellence
achieved by every one of the major scholars surveyed here.

A word of explanation is in order about the particular scholars selected for discussion in this book. Some readers may think that major
works by sociologists such as Seymour Martin Lipset, Kai Erikson,
Gerhard Lenski, Joseph Ben-David, Alvin Gouldner, Robert Bellah,
Morris Janowitz, Daniel Bell, and others might entitle them to a place
in a volume about historical sociology. Others will wonder why, if
nonsociologists by discipline were included, Marc Bloch was chosen

rather than say, Fernand Braudel, or Karl Polanyi and E. P. Thompson rather than any number of other equally relevant scholars. In response, I can only admit that I chose the scholars included here partly by guessing that Eisenstadt, Bendix, Moore, Wallerstein, and Tilly are so prominently and automatically identified as major historical sociologists – rather than as political sociologists, theorists, or sociologists of religion and so forth – that they simply had to be in the book. Beyond that, I proceeded by selecting other figures, including nonsociologists, whose works could be fruitfully compared to the works of the other scholars, and who have so positively influenced younger historical sociologists that I could readily find excellent authors willing to write engagingly about them. In short, beyond the "indispensable" five, I mostly let the willingness of good authors to come forward determine the four additional scholars to be included in a book that, for reasons of length, needed no more than nine core chapters. The result, I believe, is a set of essays that complement one another in many fascinating ways. But I will not pretend to comprehensiveness, or try to disguise a certain degree of arbitrariness in deciding which historical sociologists and other, sociologically relevant, historical social analysts to include and which, by default, to omit.

In addition to the nine chapters on the work of the scholars chosen for inclusion here, the introductory and concluding chapters discuss the long-standing tradition of historically grounded research in sociology and identify alternative strategies for bringing historical evidence and theoretical ideas to bear upon one another. These research strategies continue to be used to address a wide range of significant problems in what is proving to be a golden period of historical sociology in the 1970s and 1980s. Thus *Vision and Method in Historical Sociology* looks not only to past accomplishments but also to the present and future of an energetic and growing set of endeavors. An Annotated Bibliography on Methods of Comparative and Historical Sociology is likewise offered as an aid to ongoing research and pedagogy.

The conference that laid the basis for this volume was partly funded by an advance from Cambridge University Press, partly by a small grant from the Millard Fillmore Fund, and partly by a Problems of the Discipline Grant from the American Sociological Association. The authors and I are indebted to these funding sources for their support, and we also appreciate the editorial help and patience of Susan Allen-Mills at the New York office of Cambridge University Press. The following participants in the 1979 conference made many helpful contributions:

Victoria Bonnell, Walter Goldfrank, Bruce Johnson, Michael Hechter, and Jonathan Wiener. During the time the book was being prepared, I benefited greatly from stays at the Institute for Advanced Study in Princeton. David Brain at Harvard University did library research for this project at the time of the 1979 conference, and during 1982–83 Elisabeth Clemens at the University of Chicago provided skillful editorial assistance and made useful suggestions about themes to be covered in the Introduction and Conclusion. Bill Skocpol helped in countless ways from the intellectual to the practical. Further acknowledgments are recorded just before the notes accompanying each part of the book. Altogether, many people contributed to the completion of this project, and we are grateful to every one of them.

East Windsor, New Jersey   T.S.
and Chicago, Illinois

1. Sociology's Historical Imagination

THEDA SKOCPOL

> Every social science – or better, every well considered social study –
> requires an historical scope of conception and a full use of historical
> materials.
>
> C. Wright Mills[1]

In a basic sense, sociology has always been a historically grounded and
oriented enterprise. As wise commentators have pointed out again and
again, all of the modern social sciences, and especially sociology, were
originally efforts to come to grips with the roots and unprecedented
effects of capitalist commercialization and industrialization in Europe.
What accounted for the special dynamism of Europe compared to other
civilizations, of some parts of Europe compared to others? How were
social inequalities, political conflicts, moral values, and human lives
affected by the unprecedented changes in economic life? Would industrializing capitalist societies break asunder or generate new forms of
solidarity and satisfaction for their members? How would changes proceed in the rest of the world under the impact of European expansion?
The major works of those who would come to be seen as the founders
of modern sociology, especially the works of Karl Marx, Alexis de
Tocqueville, Emile Durkheim, and Max Weber, all grappled with such
questions.[2] To varying degrees, all offered concepts and explanations
meant to be used in truly historical analyses of social structures and
social change.

Truly historical sociological studies have some or all of the following
characteristics. Most basically, they ask questions about social structures or processes understood to be concretely situated in time and
space. Second, they address processes over time, and take temporal
sequences seriously in accounting for outcomes. Third, most historical
analyses attend to the interplay of meaningful actions and structural
contexts, in order to make sense of the unfolding of unintended as well
as intended outcomes in individual lives and social transformations.
Finally, historical sociological studies highlight the *particular* and *varying* features of specific kinds of social structures and patterns of
change. Along with temporal processes and contexts, social and cultural differences are intrinsically of interest to historically oriented
sociologists. For them, the world's past is not seen as a unified devel-

1

opmental story or as a set of standardized sequences. Instead, it is understood that groups or organizations have chosen, or stumbled into, varying paths in the past. Earlier "choices," in turn, both limit and open up alternative possibilities for further change, leading toward no predetermined end.

To be sure, some of sociology's founders focused more closely than others on explaining particular sequences of historical events. And some founders, or their followers, turned more readily than others to the fashioning of transhistorical generalizations and teleological schemas. Thus, strictly speaking, Tocqueville and Weber – and Marx in his essays on current events – were more "historical" in the senses I have listed than Durkheim, or Marx in his more philosophical writings. Yet each of the founders was so committed to making sense of the key changes and contrasts of his own epoch that he was a historically oriented social analyst according to at least some of the basic criteria just mentioned.[3] None of the founders ever got entirely carried away by a philosophy of universal evolution, by formal conceptualization, or by theoretical abstraction for its own sake. Each devoted himself again and again to situating and explaining modern European social structures and processes of change.

The Partial Eclipse of Historical Sociology

Despite its roots in the works of the founders, by the time sociology became fully institutionalized as an academic discipline in the United States after World War II, its historical orientation and sensibilities were partially eclipsed. Important scholars such as Robert Bellah, Reinhard Bendix, and Seymour Martin Lipset continued to do historical work in the direct tradition of the founders,[4] but the most prestigious theoretical and empirical paradigms broke with the tradition. The antihistoricism of "grand theory" and "abstracted empiricism" was lamented by C. Wright Mills in *The Sociological Imagination*, his passionate dissent from establishment trends in American sociology of the 1950s.[5] Although Mills pointed out that qualitative investigations of social problems could exhibit equal disregard for temporal and structural contexts, empiricist antihistoricism was chiefly exemplified in Mills's account by quantitative studies of specific social patterns, in which U.S. realities of the moment were naively treated out of context as proxies for all of human social life. At the opposite, though complementary, extreme of the sociological practice of his day, the antihistoricism of grand theory was for Mills supremely epitomized in Talcott Parsons's

The Social System, published in 1951.[6] That prestigious work set forth a grid of abstract categories through which all aspects of social life, regardless of times and places, could be classified and supposedly explained in the same, universal theoretical terms.

The Social System elaborated a theoretical edifice overwhelmingly devoted to accounting for societal equilibria, with only passing nods to phenomena of social change. Yet Parsons himself was too great a theorist, and structural functionalism too ambitious as a world view and a scholarly approach, not to take on more directly issues of societal transformation. Evolutionist theories of "development" or "modernization" proliferated in the later 1950s and in the 1960s, all of them treating "societal differentiation" as the master key to classifying and ordering all types of societies and accounting for transformations from traditional to modern social orders.[7] Given the hegemony of the United States in the international order it shaped after World War II, and given the Cold War rivalry between the United States and the Soviet Union, it was perhaps not surprising that these theories of societal change as modernization mapped standardized lines of change along which all normally developing nations would sooner or later move. In due course, they would supposedly come to resemble what the United States was happily conceptualized to be in the 1950s and early 1960s: economically expanding and innovative, highly educated and achievement-oriented, politically pluralistic, and pragmatically nonideological.

Meanwhile, in the Soviet Union, Stalinist readings of Marxist grand theory had already established a twisted mirror image of this evolutionist scheme. In the Soviet version of modernization, economic progress inevitably drove all nations through fixed stages.[8] Each stage was a mode of production with its own characteristic technological level and associated patterns of class domination and class conflict. Nations would move through successive stages toward a classless "socialist" order and would ultimately arrive at a conflict-free "Communist" utopia.

This is not the place to discuss in detail how and why. Yet between the 1950s and the 1980s, the implicit world views embodied in both static and developmentalist versions of structural functionalism were rendered less meaningful by the reverberations of political conflicts inside the United States and across the globe. Economic-determinist and linear evolutionist readings of Marxism also lost any appeal they once held for most Western intellectuals. Meanwhile, however, different versions of Marxist ideas, stressing class consciousness, historical process, and the roles of varying cultural and political structures, became attractive to

3

younger scholars looking for ways to criticize social scientific orthodoxies. Not only did the historically oriented Western Marxist theorist Antonio Gramsci gain enormously in visibility and popularity, Marx's own writings were also selectively reexamined to plumb their resources for handling issues of consciousness and political struggle.[9]

During this same period, the ideas of Alexis de Tocqueville and (especially) Max Weber have also sparked renewed interest for students of social change and comparative social structures. Simply put, people have turned to the particular works or readings of classical sociologists that could best help them reintroduce concerns for sociocultural variety, temporal process, concrete events, and the dialectic of meaningful actions and structural determinants into macrosociological explanations and research. For these purposes, the methodological ideas and historical works of Max Weber are especially relevant, so it is hardly surprising that the small coterie of sociologists who, in 1982 and 1983, launched a new section of the American Sociological Association dedicated to fostering Comparative and Historical Sociology devoted their early efforts to reconsiderations of themes from Weber's scholarly corpus.

Are Revivals of the Classics the Essence?

If reconsiderations of Weber were the essence of the increasing interest in historically oriented theorizing and research in contemporary sociology, this interest could be treated simply as an intellectual revival. The renewed interest in Weber's historical writings could be seen as accompanied by, and furthering, a de-Parsonizing of our understanding of Weber's ideas, essentially the kind of project to which Anthony Giddens and Randall Collins have devoted significant efforts.[10] We could speak of an era of Weberian historical interpretation taking over the baton of macrosociological explanation from Durkheim and Parsons, on the one hand, and snatching it from the waiting arms of various neo-Marxists, on the other. And that would be that.

There are able commentators who advocate this way of understanding what the spreading interest in historical work in sociology is all about.[11] Others would respond to this identification of historical sociology with Weber's legacy by constructing Durkheimian or Marxian historical sociologies as alternatives or supplements.[12] In my view historical sociology is better understood as a continuing, ever-renewed tradition of research devoted to understanding the nature and effects of large-scale structures and fundamental processes of change. Compelling desires to answer historically grounded questions, not classical theoretical paradigms, are the driving force. To be sure, there have always been, and always will be, sociologists who do not ask or seek to answer historically grounded, macroscopic questions. Although none can afford to ignore structural and historical contexts, all sociologists need not investigate directly matters such as the origins and development of capitalism and nation-states; the spread of ideologies and religions; the causes and consequences of revolutions; and the relationship of ongoing economic and geopolitical transformations to the fates of communities, groups, and types of organizations. Moreover, there certainly have been moments when many scholars interested in macroscopic questions attempted antihistorical modes of addressing them. The brief credibility of Parsonian structural functionalism as an all-encompassing theory of society was one such moment.

But the realities of modern social life are so fundamentally rooted in ongoing conflicts and changes in communities, regions, nations, and the world as a whole, that sociologists have never stopped – and will never want to stop – fashioning fresh theories and interpretations that highlight the variety of social structures, the epochal constraints and alternative possibilities for change, the intersections of structural contexts and group experiences, and the unfolding of events and actions over time. Indeed, historically oriented analyses in sociology are bound to be especially attractive in periods such as our own, when for the world as a whole – for the leaders and victors in earlier phases of economic development and geopolitical conflict, as well as for the peripheral and newly industrializing nations – there are such obvious uncertainties about the continuation of existing trends and relationships into the future. Broadly conceived historical analyses promise possibilities for understanding how past patterns and alternative trajectories might be relevant, or irrelevant, for present choices. Thus excellent historical sociology can actually speak more meaningfully to real-life concerns than narrowly focused empiricist studies that pride themselves on their "policy relevance."[13]

Research Agendas in Historical Sociology

The classical questions and answers of Weber, Marx, Tocqueville, Durkheim, and others naturally live on in the ongoing enterprise of historical sociology. This happens partly because the founders' answers to the important questions they asked about their own and earlier times were not always correct or complete. Even more it happens because the ideas of the founders rightly continue to serve as fruitful benchmarks for much sociological theorizing. Yet it is a sign of the continuing vitality of historical sociology in the twentieth century, right down to the present, that new questions and ideas, beyond the letter if not the spirit of the founders, are always being addressed by sociologists with comparable vision and will to understand social structures and transformations from the vantage points of their own times and places.

The nine scholars whose working lives and major projects constitute the focus of the chapters in this book all operate on terrain shared with the founders. Most of the major works of the scholars discussed here, from Marc Bloch's *Feudal Society* and *French Rural History* to Barrington Moore's *Social Origins of Dictatorship and Democracy*, and from Karl Polanyi's *The Great Transformation* to Immanuel Wallerstein's *The Modern World-System*, continue to explore the antecedents, nature, and consequences of the original capitalist and democratic revolutions of Europe.[14] The specific problems addressed, however, are often distinct from those of the founders, and fresh answers are certainly offered.

English industrialization, the French Revolution, and German bureaucratization were, one might say, the events and processes that preoccupied the founders. Their basic shared concern was to conceptualize the distinctiveness and dynamics of capitalist industrialism and democracy in contrast to other orders of social life. Among the scholars surveyed here, Reinhard Bendix, Perry Anderson, E. P. Thompson, and Charles Tilly draw both their questions and their answers almost entirely from this classical agenda. Bendix and Anderson build on Weber's arguments about bureaucratization and transformations of political regimes. Thompson reworks the quintessential Marxian ideas about industrialization and the formation of the working class in England. Tilly probes the tensions between the explanations offered by Durkheim and Marx for the changing forms of group conflict that accompanied European revolutions, statemaking, and capitalistic development. Even so, each of these contemporary historical sociologists offers new blends of, or counterpoints to, the classical arguments. And each deploys his own distinctive methods for mediating between theories and historical facts.

Beyond these four, the twentieth-century scholars break new ground in their questions as well as arguments and ways of arriving at them. Karl Polanyi's *The Great Transformation* deals not only with the establishment of capitalist market society in England but also with the national and international crises of the market order from the early to

6

middle twentieth century. Marc Bloch's historical agenda focuses mainly on European and French feudal patterns as worthy of explanation in their own right. In three very different ways, S. N. Eisenstadt, Immanuel Wallerstein, and Barrington Moore, Jr., seek to encompass and explain in the same conceptual terms broad swatches of non-Western along with Western history. Eisenstadt's most important book, *The Political Systems of Empires*, analyzes the emergence and long-term fates of historical bureaucratic empires throughout world history. Wallerstein explores the origins, structure, history, and projected future demise of the capitalist world economy. Moore probes the patterns and moral significance of the alternative paths that agrarian states have traversed into the modern world. These grand subject matters have pushed Eisenstadt, Wallerstein, and Moore well beyond Marx's and (even) Weber's strategies of using the non-West mainly to validate by contrast arguments about the special dynamism of the West.

The chapters to come take very seriously the particular problems explored by the nine scholars, for their arguments and methods certainly cannot be understood apart from the questions they address and their individual reasons for caring to ask those questions. So the authors probe their subjects in different ways, not only because authors write from their own individual points of view, but more fundamentally because each major historical sociologist is (or was) concerned with a distinctive set of problems, forming his own special lifelong research agenda. Still, some important common themes emerge, telling us about the special qualities shared by these scholars and the similar theoretical and methodological challenges all of them have faced in their research and writing.

Vantage Points for Thinking Big

In the twentieth century, the Western social sciences have been centered in universities and professional associations. Both research and teaching have been, as they say, institutionalized in an array of specialized disciplines, and often in very narrowly or technically focused compartments within those academic disciplines. Even so, major unspecialized works by every single one of the nine men examined here have been celebrated in the institutional worlds of academic social science. Professional associations have awarded their highest prizes to books by Bendix, Eisenstadt, Anderson, Wallerstein, and Moore, and both graduate and undergraduate reading lists have, again and again, given pride of place to Bloch's *Feudal Society*, Polanyi's *The Great Trans-*

formation, Eisenstadt's *The Political Systems of Empires,* Bendix's *Work and Authority in Industry,* Anderson's *Lineages of the Absolutist State,* Thompson's *The Making of the English Working Class,* Tilly's *The Vendée* and many theoretical or quantitative articles, Wallerstein's *The Modern World-System,* and Moore's *Social Origins of Dictatorship and Democracy.*

What is more, many of these scholars have sought and attained great institutional influence within academia: Bloch helped to found the internationally prestigious French *Annales* school and attained the most coveted prize in French academic life, a professorial chair in Paris. Eisenstadt holds Germanic sway at the Hebrew University, has been visiting professor at the Western world's most prestigious universities, and participates in every important international conference conceivably related to his breathtakingly broad interests. Bendix, a professor at the University of California, Berkeley, is honored by established sociologists, political scientists, and historians alike, and gained sufficient professional visibility to be elected president of the American Sociological Association. Tilly has attracted large amounts of research funding over the years, built a major research center at the University of Michigan, and serves as a professional gatekeeper in three or four disciplines. Wallerstein enjoys broad international prestige comparable to Eisenstadt's, and has managed to embody his world-system perspective in a research center and journal at the State University of New York at Binghamton, in yearly conferences at revolving university locations around the United States, and in a section of the American Sociological Association that controls several sessions for every year's annual meeting.

Despite these evidences of mainstream academic and professional attainments, every one of our nine scholars has been in some sense marginal or opposed to orthodox academic ways of doing things. Their marginality or opposition has been intimately related, as both cause and effect, to their ability to ask bigger questions than most social scientists ever dream of posing. In turn, asking big questions has led them toward the various blends of general theorizing, totalizing or comparative historical analysis, and sensitivity to contextual details and temporal processes that make their scholarly achievements so compelling.

The connection between genuinely oppositional marginality to mainstream academia and asking big questions and devising unorthodox ways to pursue the answers is most obvious – and certainly most clearly highlighted in the subsequent chapters – for those scholars who have also been politically engaged leftists. Karl Polanyi was and Perry Anderson, E. P. Thompson, and Immanuel Wallerstein all are committed socialists of one variety or another, although, significantly, none of these four has been permanently associated with any established Communist or Socialist party. Polanyi, according to Block and Somers, wrote *The Great Transformation*, "the book that brought together all of the themes of a lifetime" for this humanist socialist, as a "conscious political intervention . . . to influence the shape of the post–World War II world."[15] And Polanyi completed this masterwork *before* he moved into a more specialized academic niche in economic anthropology.

Anderson has not pursued a regular academic career in any sense. As Fulbrook and I stress, he has formulated his "totalizing" questions and answers in historical sociology in close conjunction with his effort to reorient revolutionary socialist intellectual life in Britain through the *New Left Review*. Similarly, as Kay Timberger elaborates, E. P. Thompson did not become a historian through graduate work at a university. He has conceived all of his major scholarly projects not in the course of a regular professorial career but through involvements in adult worker education and the Communist Historians' Group of 1946–56, followed by participation in the British New Left after his break with the Communist Party, and culminating, now, in his plunge back into the crusade for nuclear disarmament. In general, this trajectory has left Thompson free to pursue intensely felt, politically relevant subjects with polemic gusto and insouciance, defying narrow academic conventions. *The Making of the English Working Class* reflects this freedom in both its grand design and its detailed arguments.

Unlike Polanyi, Anderson, and Thompson, Immanuel Wallerstein *has* pursued an academic career; thus his situation is perhaps the most revealing tale of marginality among the leftists. Wallerstein's intention in conceptualizing and studying the modern world system of capitalism has been, Ragin and Chirot maintain, fundamentally political. They tell the fascinating story of Wallerstein's step-by-step movement away from modernization theory and empiricism, toward the more holistic and historical approach embodied in the world-system perspective. For his Ph.D. and his first books, Wallerstein studied the early hopes and later travails of decolonized African nations; thereafter he experienced some of the most intense battles of the American student rebellion of the 1960s. Simultanously, he moved from the role of loyal Columbia graduate student into the uncomfortable position of a young associate professor who (from the point of view of the Columbia establishment) sympathized too much with student New Leftists. Thus, at the very intellectual juncture when he arrived at his vision of the world system, launched his own major historical projects, and "set himself the task of becoming the academic spokesman and promoter of the vision of world history that lay behind the Third World's revolutionary ideologies," Wallerstein's collegial life at Columbia became "increasingly unpleasant" and he relinquished his tenure there. Since 1975, the perhaps inevitable relationship between Wallerstein's politically leftist big thinking and his marginality to the most orthodox centers of academic and professional life has been aptly expressed by his semiperipheral empire building through the Braudel Center at Binghamton and through the Political Economy of the World System Section of the American Sociological Association.

In some ways, the issue of how distance is gained from academic orthodoxies becomes even more interesting when we turn from those scholars who have explicitly combined scholarship and leftist politics to those whose extraacademic involvements, while often important (think of Bloch's work in the Resistance), have come in forms more acceptable to their respective national academic establishments. Participating in government service or military activities during legitimate national emergencies, or engaging in intellectual journalism and the giving of speeches on issues of current interest to educated publics are, after all, entirely respectable forms of academic political involvement. No doubt they are conducive to a certain breadth of scholarly vision, but they hardly give us a sufficient view of the special critical vantage points attained by Bloch, Eisenstadt, Bendix, Tilly, and Moore. Varying factors, it seems to me, came into play for each of these scholars.

The careers of Marc Bloch and Charles Tilly reveal the special concomitants of unusual thinking for two scholars who eventually became very successful shapers of collective research agendas at the centers of established academia. Bloch finally "arrived" at a professorship in Paris, where he had originally received his graduate education. But his highly unorthodox ideas about methods of historiography, and his unusually cosmopolitan and transnational sense of the scope appropriate to the study of medieval Europe, germinated while this man from a Jewish family with roots in Alsace was a professor at the University of Strasbourg, an Alsatian university considered quite peripheral in the French system, as it had been earlier in the German system. Bloch, moreover, drew (selectively and cautiously, as Chirot shows) on sociological ideas to broaden his agenda of historical questions and explanations.

Decades later in the United States, as Lynn Hunt skillfully argues, Charles Tilly would fashion an unusually broad and temporally deep agenda for his historical sociology by simultaneously using archival methods to do French history and quantitative statistical techniques to test sociological hypotheses and develop an innovative theory of collective political violence. Moreover, while Tilly's eventual research base was at a major American university and in a leading sociology department, his blend of French history and quantitative sociology relegated him to a minor department for his first job, after he did graduate work at Harvard during the era of Talcott Parsons's dominance, not under Parsons but under George Homans and Barrington Moore. (Later on, Harvard brought Tilly back as a nontenured professor, but then, to its later chagrin, failed to retain him with tenure.) Tilly has been the closest to a straightforward academic among all of the scholars assessed in this book. Yet his attempt from the very beginning of his intellectual career to combine issues and methods central to more than one discipline has kept him at the disciplinary margins of both sociology and history, even as it simultaneously allowed him to put himself and his students at some of the most innovative cutting edges in the American social sciences of the last two decades.

Hamilton and Rueschemeyer tell us practically nothing about the biographies and careers of Eisenstadt and Bendix, preferring to concentrate on the critical intellectual stances these men developed toward structural functionalism, the paradigm that dominated American macrosociology for their intellectual generation. Both Eisenstadt and Bendix have certainly become established professors, yet they drew upon Weber's concepts and comparative historical studies to criticize Talcott Parsons. In seeking the roots of their critical stances, I do not think we should ignore the fact that both came from European Jewish backgrounds. Like the other Central European, Polanyi, Eisenstadt and Bendix were émigrés from what was, before World War II, the most civilized arena of high culture in the West. Both also received very cosmopolitan and wide-ranging European-style higher educations. Eisenstadt and Bendix therefore carried their own understandings of European ideas and history into international sociological debates. Moreover, Eisenstadt's major permanent university position has been in Israel, that remarkable home of intellectuals who are at once extraordinarily cosmopolitan and attuned to Western orthodoxies and inescapably aware that not all of world history happens in big, core nations.

Barrington Moore, finally, was never an international emigrant, but he became, in a sense, another sort of émigré. Drawing on the kind of self-confidence bred by a privileged background, by a secure association with elite universities, and by an education in the classics, including Greek and Latin, Moore became an internal émigré away from the distractions of career building in American academia, deliberately giving up the professional influence he might have had if he had been willing to chair departments, build his own research center, promote the careers of his students, and shape the agendas of journals and professional associations. Although he taught at Harvard and was based in that university's Russian Research Center until his recent retirement, Moore quit the Social Relations Department many years ago and thereafter became only nominally affiliated with the Government Department. Moore's one sustained commitment to collegial pedagogy at Harvard was in the Social Studies Program, an elite interdisciplinary honors program dedicated (like the course in which many of the program's founders taught, "Soc. Sci. 2" in the College at the University of Chicago) to teaching the classics of modern social theory: Marx, Weber, Durkheim, and Freud. Beyond this, Moore has always insisted on a fiercely private life.

Moore's scholarly agenda, as Dennis Smith shows, has been as remarkable for its sustained pursuit of consistent intellectual and moral concerns as for its breadth. Moore's books are written in profound solitude – for example, on a yacht in the waters off Maine – with criticism only from Elizabeth Moore and a very few friends or associates. Thinking of himself as an intellectual artisan in an era of bureaucratized research, Moore has worked singly or in small groups only with carefully selected graduate and undergraduate students. He has conveyed to them, not a theory or a method, but his own exacting standards of scholarly craftsmanship and his sense that the unflinching pursuit of answers to large, humanly significant questions is all that really matters in the life of the mind.

Historical Critiques of Functionalism, Economism, and Evolutionism

Thinking big and approaching social analysis historically need not go together, of course. During the decades when our nine scholars have been at work, the grand paradigms of Parsonian structural functionalism, liberal economics, and economic-determinist Marxism, along with their applications to problems of development through modernization theories and Marxist evolutionism, have dominated much of academic discourse about societal structures and socioeconomic change. Again and again in the chapters to come, we see how all of the major scholars discussed here have shaped their arguments partly or overwhelmingly in critical response to the abstract generalizations offered by proponents of one or more of these perspectives. For many of these scholars, the very shape of their historical studies seems to have been significantly determined by dialogues with existing grand theories. For others, concern with historical problems as such has been primary, and their critical dialogues with the general theories have been correspondingly more nuanced.

The chapters on Eisenstadt, Bendix, Anderson, and Thompson provide a fascinating set of insights into the parallel ways in which these scholars have attempted to introduce historical variety and particularity into grand theories. Eisenstadt and Bendix orient themselves to structural functionalism, while Anderson and Thompson are engaged in critiques of Marxist economism and evolutionism. What I find especially interesting is not the similarities within these pairs but the parallels between Eisenstadt and Anderson on the one hand and Bendix and Thompson on the other.

Eisenstadt and Anderson are friendly critics of structural functionalism and Marxism, respectively. Each is determined to use the basic theoretical perspective to explain large-scale structures and long-term developments, and each is equally committed to using the variety of the world-historical record to criticize overly general readings of the theory. Not incidentally, Eisenstadt chooses to conceptualize and explain "historical bureaucratic empires," which fit poorly into a simple modernization framework opposing traditional to modern societies. Similarly, Anderson tackles "the absolutist state," which has been a source of controversy for Marxists unable to decide whether it was feudal or capitalist.

Both scholars proceed to conceptualize the particular historical periods and political regimes that interest them as what Gary Hamilton aptly calls "configurations in history." These are systemic constructs, defined for Eisenstadt in terms of "levels of differentiation" and "modes of societal integration," and defined for Anderson as "modes of production" and patterns of "class dominance and class struggle." Having done this conceptual work, it becomes possible to account for aspects of world history in terms of the structures and dynamics posited by functionalism or Marxist theory. Eisenstadt accounts for a major type of sociopolitical regime, the bureaucratic empire. Anderson accounts for the central, dynamic trajectory of Western European history in contrast to other histories. Neither Eisenstadt nor Anderson, however, claims that all of world history can be encompassed in a single scheme of societal stages or a single master logic of change.

In large part because both are unusually sensitive to subjective meanings and cultural variety in history, Reinhard Bendix and E. P. Thompson are more skeptical than Eisenstadt and Anderson of the utility of structural functionalist and Marxist theories for explaining historical patterns. I would argue, nevertheless, that Bendix and Thompson remain just as closely oriented to the respective grand theories. They proceed by bouncing particular historical cases off theoretical concepts rather than by finding clever new ways to make basic structural functionalist and Marxist concepts and propositions work to explain societal types and long-term change.

Bendix's work has become, as Dietrich Rueschemeyer shows, increasingly concerned simply with descriptively contrasting historical cases to one another. According to Bendix, structural functionalist and modernization theories overgeneralize patterns of structure and change by applying concepts (often abstract versions of Weber's concepts) that are ethnocentric and that inevitably fail to capture the full particularity of any country's history, even within the West. Bendix therefore advocates turning theoretical ideas into ideal types – optimally, into polar pairs of "contrast conceptions," such as "contractual authority" versus personal "fealty." Such concepts can then be used as benchmarks to help in the accurate characterization of historical instances. In this way, Bendix avoids overgeneralization – and indeed downplays explanation as such – in favor of the use of theoretical ideas purely as sensitizing devices for case-by-case historical discussions.

In remarkably analogous ways, E. P. Thompson uses theoretical ideas as benchmarks in his study, *The Making of the English Working Class*. Economic-determinist notions of class, or narrowly economic arguments about how working people were supposedly affected by industrialization, are introduced by Thompson to dramatize their failure to capture the cultural, political, and subjective dimensions of the events through which the English working class both was made and made itself. Thompson does not try to displace old general theories with a more rigorous new one, for he views even his own favored theoretical concepts as "elastic" devices for illuminating the particulars of each historical instance. "They do not impose a rule, but they hasten and facilitate the interrogation of the evidence, even though it is often found that each case departs, in this or that particular, from the rule."[16] Likewise, Kay Trimberger's discussion of Thompson's "dialectical" arguments reminds one of Bendix's preference for using contrast conceptions to sensitize himself to combinations of opposite tendencies in particular instances.

Thus Eisenstadt and Anderson, on the one hand, and Bendix and Thompson, on the other, have reacted in alternative ways to the challenges of bringing existing grand theories and historical variety to bear upon one another. Notice, however, that all four of these scholars have remained closely engaged in their respective dialogues with the grand theories. They have been so closely engaged in these dialogues, in fact, that the arguments they have developed about historical problems have either been specifications and reworkings of structural functionalist and Marxist ideas or else assertions that the complexity, particularity, and subjective meaningfulness of historical instances cannot be adequately encompassed by the grand theories in question. None of these scholars, I would maintain, has used the confrontation of existing theories and history to generate a new set of explanatory generalizations.

Immanuel Wallerstein and Charles Tilly have been just as closely engaged in critical dialogues with existing grand theories as the four scholars just discussed. Yet these historical sociologists indubitably *have* used the confrontation of theory and history to generate new theoretical arguments.

Wallerstein has used historical critiques of modernization theories and Marxist evolutionism almost single-mindedly for the purpose of devising a new grand paradigm to displace the discredited old ones. This is the picture that comes through in Ragin and Chirot's thoughtful discussion of Wallerstein's historical sociology of the capitalist world system. Determined to displace generalizing theories that conceptualize social change as a series of stages through which all nations pass, and yet not willing to surrender to purely idiographic history or journalism, Wallerstein posited the capitalist world system as a single totality. This totality is to be understood simultaneously through theorizing about its structure and dynamics and through tracing the history of the system as a whole from its emergence in early modern times through the present. According to Wallerstein, the varied histories of regions, nations, classes, and peoples also need to be fully explored in all of their concreteness and variety, but not by using the methods of cross-national causal analysis associated in his mind with modernization theory. Instead, investigations and comparisons of these histories serve, as Ragin and Chirot put it, "to illustrate general features of the world system" as a whole. For Wallerstein, the antinomies between theoretical generalization and historical analysis are overcome once and for all through the world-system perspective.

The primary thread of Charles Tilly's historical sociology over the last two decades can be understood as an argument with Durkheim and with his modern intellectual successors, the structural functionalists and "relative deprivation" theorists. The argument is over the connections between such long-term processes as commercialization, industrialization, urbanization, and the rise of national states and the changing forms and objectives of collective action, including violent actions. Like Wallerstein, in other words, Tilly has been disputing the standard sociological wisdom of his time. But he has certainly gone about this task in a different way. Instead of positing a new grand theoretical paradigm and doing historical reinterpretations in terms of its conceptual dictates, Tilly has, as Lynn Hunt recounts, assembled quantitative data bases for long stretches of historical time, especially French historical time. He has then bombarded the data bases with alternative causal hypotheses, some of them purportedly deduced from Durkheimian and modernization premises, others developed from the "political mobilization" model for explaining collective action devised by Tilly himself (partly on the basis of Marxist premises).

Especially in the last few years, Tilly has also carried on more of a grand theoretical battle – a battle of labels and concepts, at least – with modernization theories. He has begun to insist that there is no such thing as social change in general, whether for nations or for world systems. Rather, there are epochal processes, such as the processes of statemaking and capitalist accumulation that have remade the modern world in the last several hundred years. The historical sociologist's task is to analyze the relationships between these epochal processes and to probe their consequences for forms of group action.[17] Thus far, however, Tilly himself has only attempted this for one national history. He has not actually generalized about macroscopic structures or trends through comparative-historical analyses, in ways comparable to his use of intranational comparison of groups, regions, and time periods to arrive at generalizations about the causes of collective action.

If we look back over the six scholars we have just surveyed, it is striking how thoroughly the historical work of all of them has been permeated by their arguments with structural functionalists and modernization theorists, or with economic-determinist and evolutionist Marxists. In varying ways, all of these historical sociologists have been theory driven. This is perhaps clearest for Eisenstadt, Anderson, and Wallerstein. But I think it also holds for the others, even though the modes they respectively chose for arguing with existing grand theories spurred Tilly to do quantitative data analysis and drove Bendix and Thompson to renounce the very goal of explanatory generalization in favor of meaningful characterizations and interpretations of particular histories. Anderson, Bendix, Eisenstadt, Thompson, Tilly, and Wallerstein alike have all pursued their historical studies in close, albeit critical, relationship to the dominant macrotheoretical paradigms of contemporary sociology.

Developing Explanations for Historical Patterns

Critical dialogues with ahistorical grand theories are also important in the work of Karl Polanyi, Marc Bloch, and Barrington Moore, Jr. Yet each of these three scholars primarily practices historical social analysis in what I would call a *problem-oriented* way. The primary aim is not to rework or reveal the inapplicability of an existing theoretical perspective, nor is it to generate an alternative paradigm to displace such a perspective. Rather, the primary aim is to make sense of historical patterns, using in the process whatever theoretical resources seem useful and valid.

Much of Karl Polanyi's scholarship, Block and Somers explain, was devoted to criticizing the overgeneralizations of liberal economics or the economic determinism of certain Marxists and to developing, instead, concepts that would allow analysis of historically varying economic institutions in the entire societal contexts in which they functioned. In *The Great Transformation,* however, the work that Block and Somers call Polanyi's most important contribution to historical sociology, the object of explanation was a specific world-historical process, the emergence and eventual crisis of nineteenth-century capitalist "market society," centered in Britain. Not unlike Wallerstein, although on a different scale, Polanyi was faced with the challenge of explaining a single case, a single totality of structure and process. Block and Somers tell us that Polanyi used a "metaphor of organic misdevelopment" to help him conceptualize the emergence and development-into-crisis of market society. Yet, they point out, Polanyi constantly moved back and forth from the metaphor to concrete causal arguments referring to particular sequences of historical events in Britain and on the international scene. For he knew (in Block and Somers's words) that "metaphor can only operate as an heuristic; it cannot be used to carry the argument," as Wallerstein's world-system model all too often seems to do. This contrast between Wallerstein and Polanyi is easily understandable, however, when we realize that Wallerstein's goal is the development of an overarching paradigm to displace modernization theory, while Polanyi's goal in *The Great Transformation* was to make unified sense of a concrete set of institutions and events.

Marc Bloch and Barrington Moore, the first and last scholars discussed in the chapters of this volume, seem to me quite similar to

Polanyi, and especially similar to one another, in the spirit and methods of their historical work. Both are theoretically well informed and eclectic: Chirot points out that Bloch knew and drew on the sociological ideas of the Durkheim school, as well as Marxian ideas about classes. Smith tells us of Moore's willingness to borrow ideas from structural functionalism and from evolutionism, as well as (more obviously) from Marx and Weber. Like all of the other scholars, moreover, Bloch and Moore are critical of overly abstract and single-factor-determinist theories. Yet neither spends very much effort arguing with, or trying to displace, such theories. Instead, both are more committed to making sense of important historical realities; for the most part, they simply ignore totally unhelpful theories, no matter how fashionable. To help devise good questions to put to history, as well as good answers to explore with various kinds of evidence, both Bloch and Moore accept the aid of whatever theoretical propositions they can borrow from others or devise themselves in the ongoing course of their historical investigations. Both use comparative historical analysis as one of their primary techniques for examining hypotheses and exploring patterns of historical causation.

Bloch's commitment, Chirot writes, "was to tell us what had happened and to explain why." As a historian, his interest lay in understanding medieval European society as a significant totality, finding the temporal and spatial boundaries within which relatively enduring and regular patterns of economic, social, political and cultural life had prevailed. In Bloch's view, the task of theories was "only to help the historian look for better evidence about the past," including evidence from sources not usually tapped by historians. Comparisons among regional or national patterns could be just as useful for rejecting bogus general explanations and getting an accurate sense of causal sequences particular to given cases, as for generating valid causal generalizations that might apply to more than one instance.

As a sociologist rather than a historian by discipline, Barrington Moore is naturally more interested than Bloch in using historical evidence to develop general arguments. He seeks generalizations, for example, about alternative "routes" for agrarian states to the modern world and about human reactions to unjust social situations. But even when he poses a rather abstract issue for investigation, such as the second one just mentioned, Moore always moves quickly into concrete historical instances. Like Bloch, he teases his sense of particular and general causal connections out of explorations of case histories and out of comparisons of relevant aspects of similar and different cases. In

Social Origins of Dictatorship and Democracy, Dennis Smith points out, "Moore's discussion of each national case is punctuated with detailed and subtle cross-references to other societies. These references are brought in not as a mere adornment but as essential material for an argument being constructed before the reader's eyes." When Moore runs up against a particularly difficult case from the point of view of his own emerging general argument, he spends extra time on it – for example, with India in *Social Origins* – rather than downplaying or ignoring it, as other analysts might do.

Both Bloch and Moore are more interested in the use or development of explanatory generalizations than are Bendix or Thompson, yet the possible theoretical gains from their kind of approach may seem much more modest and restricted than those attained by, say, Wallerstein or Eisenstadt. This appearance could be misleading. Daniel Chirot argues that Marc Bloch was able to suggest "an important general rule of social change" through his comparative study of what may seem a very arcane historical problem: intra-European variations of beliefs about "the royal touch," the capacity attributed to kings to heal diseases. Although Bloch's argument "has not lent itself to flashy theory construction," it is, Chirot argues, the most "scrupulous study of a case of the routinization of charisma." Chirot emphasizes that the generalizable results of this study can "allow those who study other periods and times to ask interesting questions and suggest tentative answers." This, surely, is what any good macrosociological theory should do. It may be all that it can ever reasonably aspire to do.

In the final reckoning, problem-oriented historical sociologists like Marc Bloch and Barrington Moore may tell us even more about social structures and social change than do historical sociologists who rework, or argue with, overarching theoretical paradigms. That is my sense of one of the most important lessons to be learned from comparing the achievements of the scholars discussed in this book. While reading through the following chapters, however, each reader will have repeated opportunities to consider for himself or herself how fruitful theorizing and convincing historical analysis are best combined. Whatever varying assessments one may make of their strengths and shortcomings, each of the extraordinary scholars we are about to meet has unflinchingly faced this challenge. Each one, too, has met the challenge with notable success. Together, they have immeasurably enriched the enduring tradition of sociological research based on "an historical scope of conception and a full use of historical materials."

Theda Skocpol

Notes

1. C. Wright Mills, *The Sociological Imagination* (New York: Oxford University Press, 1959), p. 145.
2. See the discussions in Anthony Giddens, *Capitalism and Modern Social Theory* (Cambridge, U.K., and New York: Cambridge University Press, 1971); Philip Abrams, *Historical Sociology* (Ithaca, N.Y.: Cornell University Press, 1982), chaps 1–4; Robert Nisbet, *The Sociological Tradition* (New York: Basic Books, 1966); Gianfranco Poggi, *Images of Society: Essays on the Sociological Theories of Tocqueville, Marx, and Durkheim* (Stanford, Calif.: Stanford University Press, 1972); and Neil J. Smelser and R. Stephen Warner, *Sociological Theory: Historical and Formal* (Morristown, N.J.: General Learning Press, 1976), pt. 1.
3. Durkheim is the founder most often considered ahistorical, but see Robert Bellah, "Durkheim and History," *American Sociological Review* 24(4) (1959):447–61. For discussions of the other founders as historically oriented analysts, see especially Melvin Richter, "Comparative Political Analysis in Montesquieu and De Tocqueville," *Comparative Politics* 1 (1969):129–60; Neil Smelser, "Alexis De Tocqueville as Comparative Analyst," in *Comparative Methods in Sociology*, ed. Ivan Vallier (Berkeley: University of California Press, 1971), pp. 19–48; R. Stephen Warner, "The Methodology of Marx's Comparative Analysis of Modes of Production," in *Comparative Methods*, ed. I. Vallier, pp. 49–74; Leonard Krieger, "The Uses of Marx for History," *Political Science Quarterly* 75 (1960):355–78; E. J. Hobsbawm, "Karl Marx's Contribution to Historiography," in *Ideology in Social Science: Readings in Critical Social Theory*, ed. Robin Blackburn (New York: Vintage Books, 1973), pp. 265–83; Reinhard Bendix, *Max Weber: An Intellectual Portrait* (Garden City, N.Y.: Doubleday Anchor, 1960); Gunther Roth, "Max Weber's Comparative Approach and Historical Typology," in *Comparative Methods*, ed. I. Vallier, pp. 75–96; and David Zaret, "From Weber to Parsons and Schutz: The Eclipse of History in Modern Social Theory," *American Journal of Sociology* 85(5) (1980):1180–1201.
4. See Robert N. Bellah, *Tokugawa Religion: The Values of Pre-Industrial Japan* (Boston: Beacon Press, 1970; orig. 1957); Reinhard Bendix, *Work and Authority in Industry* (Berkeley: University of California Press, 1974; orig. 1956); and Seymour Martin Lipset, *Agrarian Socialism* (Berkeley: University of California Press, 1950).
5. Mills, *Sociological Imagination*, chaps. 2 and 3.
6. Talcott Parsons, *The Social System* (Glencoe, Ill. Free Press, 1951).
7. For major examples, see Neil J. Smelser, "Mechanisms of Change and Adjustment to Change," in *Industrialization and Society*, ed. Bert F. Hoselitz and Wilbert E. Moore (The Hague, Mouton, 1963), pp. 32–54; Marion J. Levy, Jr., *Modernization and the Structure of Societies* (Princeton, N.J.: Princeton University Press, 1966); Talcott Parsons, "Evolutionary Universals," *American Sociological Review* 29 (1964):339–57; Talcott Parsons, *Societies: Evolutionary and Comparative Perspectives* (Englewood Cliffs, N.J.: Prentice-Hall, 1966); Karl W. Deutsch, "Social Mobilization and Political Development," *American Political Science Review* 55 (1961):493–514; Gabriel A. Almond, "A Developmental Approach to Political Systems," *World Politics* 16 (1965):183–214; and Gabriel A. Almond and G. Bingham Powell, Jr., *Comparative Politics: A Developmental Approach* (Boston: Little, Brown, 1966).
8. An orthodox statement of Soviet "modernization" theory appears in Joseph

Stalin, *Dialectical and Historical Materialism* (New York: International Publishers, 1940); reprinted in *The Essential Stalin: Major Theoretical Writings, 1905–52*, ed. Bruce Franklin (Garden City, N.Y.: Doubleday Anchor, 1972). For an early precursor, see Nikolai Bukharin, *Historical Materialism* (Ann Arbor: University of Michigan Press, 1969; orig. 1921).

9. Perry Anderson's *Considerations on Western Marxism* (London: New Left Books, 1976) discusses the development of Western Marxist theories in the twentieth century. For one of the most popular of all Western Marxist texts, see Antonio Gramsci, *Selections from the Prison Notebooks*, trans. Quentin Hoare and Geoffrey N. Smith (New York: International Publishers, 1971). On the revival of Marxist ideas among young sociologists, see Michael Burawoy, "Introduction: The Resurgence of Marxism in American Sociology," in *Marxist Inquiries: Studies of Labor, Class, and States*, supp. to vol. 88 of *American Journal of Sociology*, ed. Michael Burawoy and Theda Skocpol (Chicago: University of Chicago Press, 1982), pp. 1–30.

10. See Giddens, *Capitalism and Modern Social Theory;* Randall Collins, "Weber's Last Theory of Capitalism: A Systematization," *American Sociological Review* 45(6) (1980):925–42; and Randall Collins, *Conflict Sociology: Toward an Explanatory Science* (New York: Academic Press, 1975).

11. See especially Charles Ragin and David Zaret, "Theory and Method in Comparative Research: Two Strategies," *Social Forces* 61(3) (1983):731–54. I discuss Ragin and Zaret's position further in the concluding chapter of this volume.

12. In effect, Robert Bellah and those working with him are currently pursuing a kind of Durkheimian historical sociology, and Jeffrey Alexander's *Theoretical Logic in Sociology*, 4 vols. (Berkeley: University of California Press, 1982–84) may be laying the basis for another version of this kind of enterprise. Marxian historical sociologies have been cogently advocated by, among others, Eric J. Hobsbawm, "From Social History to the History of Society," *Historical Studies Today, Daedalus* 100 (1971):20–45; and Gareth Stedman Jones, "From Historical Sociology to Theoretical History," *British Journal of Sociology* 27(3) (1976):295–304. Some people might consider Charles Tilly and his collaborators to be practitioners of a certain kind of Marxian historical sociology.

13. For example, Charles Sabel's historical sociology of industrial relations from the nineteenth century to the present offers a vivid sense of alternative policy possibilities in the present for the advanced capitalist democracies, including the United States. See Charles Sabel, *Work and Politics: The Division of Labor in Industry* (Cambridge, U.K., and New York: Cambridge University Press, 1982) and Michael Piore and Charles Sabel, *The Second Industrial Divide* (New York: Basic Books, forthcoming).

14. Full citations for the books I mention are given in the notes and bibliographies of the chapters dealing with each respective author.

15. For this quotation from the chapter on Polanyi by Block and Somers, as for other quotations from the chapters to follow, I see no need to give a formal citation.

16. E. P. Thompson, "The Poverty of Theory," in *The Poverty of Theory and Other Essays* (London: Merlin Press, 1978), p. 237.

17. See especially Charles Tilly, *Big Structures, Large Processes, Huge Comparisons* (New York: Russell Sage Foundation, forthcoming).

2. The Social and Historical Landscape of Marc Bloch

DANIEL CHIROT

In the 1970s the work of the French *Annales* school (so named after their journal, *Annales: Economies, Sociétiés, Civilisations*) finally achieved a well-deserved fame in American social science. It is not that it was previously obscure, but it had only been the knowledgeable specialists of European history who had appreciated it. The growth of historical work in sociology has greatly increased the prestige of the *Annalistes*, and Immanuel Wallerstein has even gone so far as to name his research establishment at the State University of New York the Fernand Braudel Center. Braudel has been the reigning senior member of the *Annales* since the death of Lucien Febvre, whose student he was.

The fame of Braudel and Emmanuel Le Roy Ladurie, the heir apparent, has spread far beyond the academies, and their works are translated as high-priced trade books for a general intellectual audience. In France, they are best-sellers.

The movement, for that is what the *Annales* group became, was begun by Lucien Febvre and Marc Bloch in the 1920s, when they both taught at the University of Strasbourg. Even more than Febvre, Bloch's two decades of unsurpassed scholarship and publication established the intellectual foundations and fame of the *Annales*.

Forty years before it became fashionable to combine history, sociology, anthropology, and economics, Marc Bloch was doing it. His work, and that of his direct followers, has been so influential that Bloch might be considered one of the fathers of contemporary historical sociology.

Bloch's three most important books were primarily about the Western European Middle Ages. *The Royal Touch*, published in 1924, studied beliefs in the magical healing touch of the French and English kings, which lasted from about the eleventh century until the eighteenth. *French Rural History*, which first appeared in 1931, was his most innova-

tive study. In it, he laid the basis for modern comparative rural historical research throughout the world. Both his substantive conclusions
and the means by which he reached them, using recent maps and
existing field shapes to complement old documents, have provided a
model for followers. *Feudal Society*, which was published as two volumes, in 1939 and 1940, was his most synthetic, generalizing work,
and it has been his most widely read book.

Bloch's last two books, *Strange Defeat* and *The Historian's Craft*, were
written during World War II. One was about the war, and the second,
unfinished, work consisted of his thoughts about historiography. All of
these, and many lesser books and articles, have been translated into
English. Bloch's influence can be seen in the works of Wallerstein,
Perry Anderson, Charles Tilly, and Barrington Moore, as well as in the
research and writing of dozens of other historical sociologists. His importance continues to grow as the factual detail and method of his
works impress new generations of historical thinkers.

Five aspects of Marc Bloch's work should interest those studying
methods of social historical writing. Reading Bloch is, naturally, more
enjoyable and rewarding than reading an essay about his work, and
discussing the content of his research is more instructive than analyzing his methodological approach. But there are certainly social historians who might profit from the lessons of Bloch, yet might not wish to
immerse themselves in the Western European Middle Ages. For them,
his methods and rationale for writing history are worth describing and
explaining.

Only four of the sets of points are genuinely methodological: the
temporal and social units of analysis he used, the types of evidence he
examined and the questions he asked of his evidence, his use of the
comparative method, and finally, the role he assigned to social theory.
The fifth, but not the least interesting, issue raised by Bloch's work
concerns the importance of history itself. Why write it at all?

In his last book, *The Historian's Craft*,[1] written in Vichy France during
1941–42, at a time of national and personal disaster, he spent many
pages justifying historical research. It might have seemed impractical
and irrelevant to the immediate political concerns of the time, but not
to Bloch. Using the example of his own work, that of his colleagues,
particularly Lucien Febvre, and of other historians, he explained how
history ought to be studied, and why. The justification and methodology of his life's work were so intimately connected that they can hardly
be considered apart. But just as an "apology" for a career is more
dignified if it follows a series of completed works, so will I reserve this

Daniel Chirot

part of Bloch's thought for the conclusion of this chapter, after I have covered the four methodological topics that were crucial to this work.

Temporal and Social Units of Analysis

An old convention sets historical time by reigns, by the political rise and fall of dynasties or empires, and by startling, key events that are assumed to have transformed the political situation of societies. Units of analysis tend to be politically determined as well. States, nations, and administrative boundaries of all sorts tell historians how to choose the physical limits of their topic. This is acceptable only if such limits are not taken too seriously. No one would be startled, wrote Bloch, somewhat archly, by an economic history of the reign of Louis XV. Why, then would convention not accept a "diplomatic history of Europe from Newton to Einstein?"[2]

For Bloch there were two kinds of useful historical periods, generations and civilizations. "Civilization" referred to the total material, psychological, and structural components of a society, which changed very slowly compared to the change experienced by succeeding generations.[3] *Feudal Society* was a history of a major civilization, with two distinct periods within it. It offered the reader an outline of what should be studied to understand so large, complex, and changing a unit of history.

First, there was the historical environment, in this case, the atmosphere of disorder and fear created by the Moslem, Hungarian, and Scandinavian invasions and raids in Western Europe in the ninth and tenth centuries. The long period of insecurity forced ties of dependency on the people. If either existing states or family and tribal structures had been stronger, they might have been able to protect individuals; that they were not produced the kind of personal hierarchy of dependence that later came to be known as feudalism.[4]

The second dimension of a civilization was its cultural environment, including the available technology. Communications, attitudes toward nature, religion, intellectual activities, and law were the main cultural components of Bloch's scaffold in *Feudal Society*. He would have placed a greater emphasis on agricultural technology if he had not already published *French Rural History*, which was a discussion of the agrarian basis of feudal society.[5]

Events took place in a singular context, and similar kinds of invasions and insecurities as those that beset Western Europe occurred repeatedly in other times and places without necessarily producing

24

feudalism. It was the particular context, the physical and geographic as well as the cultural milieu in which these events took place, that created feudal civilization. The farming and military technologies of the early Middle Ages both reduced and defined the possible adaptations made by Europeans to the invasions and to the internal collapse of their states. The very formation of a class of hereditary nobles occurred because of the expense of outfitting mounted warriors, the limited size of the surplus extractable from agriculture, the poor communications that hindered trade, and the physical nature of Europe. One should not, therefore, be surprised that feudal society took different forms in parts of Europe that differed strongly from the area where it was strongest. It never took hold, for example, in Sweden, or in mountainous Switzerland.[6]

Where extended families or their equivalent were stronger than in Western Europe, for example in the Balkans, prolonged periods of invasion and insecurity created societies that were not at all feudal.[7] Nor is it difficult to show that the nature of class relations changed markedly and became more rigid after the original impetus to the creation of feudal society, insecurity, lessened. Then it became a matter of an elite class trying to retain its position against challenges to its supremacy that could never have been mounted in the ninth or tenth centuries. The second feudal age, starting in the eleventh century, was virtually a different civilization from the first, which had its roots in late Merovingian and Carolingian times.[8]

Bloch never claimed that all of feudal civilization was uniform, only that there were common elements. Only when these uniformities were well understood did it become possible to explain differences within a civilization. The same scaffolding that held up Bloch's model of feudalism could then be used to show how ultimately France, Germany, England, Italy, and Spain had developed somewhat differently.

In England, for example, the unique feature of national development was the creation of a united feudal monarchy after the Norman conquest. This endowed the English feudal state with a much stronger administrative apparatus than those that existed at the time on the continent, and this, in turn, led to a somewhat different form of feudalism than elsewhere. In Germany, on the other hand, it was not so much the different sequence of events as the more primitive and more tribal nature of society at the start of the feudal period that set that country off on a slower evolution than France. The reverse was true of Italy, where Roman society, administration, and communications never disintegrated as fully as in Gaul. Spain, of course, experienced the most dramatically different sequence of events and changes after the destruction of the proto-feudal Visigothic state. Yet all of these places had enough in common, both in terms of context and events, to share a broadly similar civilization.[9]

Feudal Society emphasized the diversity of important influences on social life. The mode of feeling and thought of a civilization, religious attitudes, folk traditions, and legal heritage played major roles, and Bloch made no attempt to impose the primacy of material factors over spiritual ones. Only after he had established the essential traits of the civilization he was studying (we might say parameters) did he, in the second volume, engage in the analysis of class structures, conflicts, and political change. A reader can note, in *Feudal Society*, how un-Marxist (but not in the least anti-Marxist) Bloch's analysis was. Class and class conflict were far from being his central organizing principles. Nor were they the primary motive force of change. In another context, Bloch wrote:

> I have a very great admiration for the works of Karl Marx. As a man he was, I fear, quite intolerable, and his philosophy is certainly a good deal less original than some people like to think. But never was there a more powerful analyst of the social problem. . . . But is that any reason for establishing his teaching as the touch-stone of all knowledge?[10]

The reader can see, in *Feudal Society*, how Bloch decided to set the temporal and social limits of his subject of study. If the defining characteristic of feudal ties of dependency was a response to the insecurity of the invasions, then they marked the start of the civilization. If weak family and tribal ties, weak states, and a weak economy combined with the need to outfit expensive mounted warriors, then the areas with these conditions were within feudal Europe and others were not. In other words, thorough knowledge of the subject revealed a set of conjunctions, conditions that occurred more or less simultaneously, to create a type of society that would persist for a long time.

In *French Rural History* Bloch set his temporal and social limits rather differently than in *Feudal Society* because his subject was somewhat different. He divided Western Europe into what could almost be called agrarian civilizations. He recognized that France as such was not the proper unit of study, because it had three different types of field systems: the open fields of the north characterized by long, narrow plots, the small hedge-enclosed *bocages* fields of Brittany and the Massif Central, and the enclosed, irregular, puzzle-shaped fields of the south. (The second was really a fairly recent and minor variant of the third.)

Much of the difference between the two main types of field shape, the first and the third, could be explained by the existence of a true, or wheeled, mouldboard plow in the north and the old Roman, or scratch, plow in the south. It was not, however, merely a matter of plows, or of simple causality.

But do these material considerations explain everything? The temptation is certainly great to unroll a causal chain from a technological invention. The true plow made fields long [because of its restricted turning radius that made short fields inefficient]; these, in turn, strengthened the hold of collective organization [because of the requirement for large teams of animals to pull the heavy plows, and of the need for a coordinated, village-wide rotation pattern]. From a plow wheel added on to a plowshare there flows an entire social structure. Let us beware: to reason like this would be to forget the thousand resources of human ingenuity. The plow, no doubt, made fields long. It did not make them narrow. There is no *a priori* reason that would have prevented the inhabitants from dividing their territory into a small number of large parcels, each one of which could have been wide as well as long. Instead of having each owner control many thin strips, they could have made it so that each one owned a few larger, and more squared fields. In fact, such a configuration seems to have been avoided rather than sought out. By dispersing one's fields, one could hope to equalize luck; each inhabitant could have a share of the various types of available soils; each would have the same chance of surviving the natural and man-made afflictions that beset the land – hail, plant diseases, devastations – which often hit a village's territory unevenly, and spared some parts. These ideas, which were so deeply anchored in the peasants' mentality that they still oppose rational redistribution of parcels today, worked on the distribution of fields in the areas of irregularly shaped [southern] fields just as much as in those of the long [northern] fields. But in the former, where they used the scratch plow (*araire*), to make fields smaller, and to keep them of convenient width, one only had to reduce their length. The use of the true plow (*charrue*) made it impossible to proceed this way. Where it was used, therefore, they had to avoid shortening the length of the parcels, while still making them smaller, so they had to make them thin. This obliged them to group parcels into regular bands, otherwise – absurd idea – they would have had to cross each other! This way of grouping parcels, however, presupposed a certain understanding on the part of the inhabitants, and their acquiescence to collective constraints. This was so much the case that one could almost say, just about entirely reversing the previous deduction, that without communal habits, the adoption of the true plow would have been impossible. But undoubtedly, it is very difficult, in a history which we recreate through conjectures, to accurately weigh cause and effect. Let us therefore limit our ambition and note that as far back as we can see, the true plow, mother of the long fields, and the practice of a strongly collective life were associated to define, very clearly, an agrarian civilization. The absence of these two traits defined an entirely different type of civilization.[11]

Fully developed feudal civilization of the type found in northern France, western Germany, and much of England rested on the open field system of agriculture, which in turn depended on collective cooperation within villages. The collective arrangements of the open-field villages, however, probably antedated feudalism, and they certainly persisted after it ended as a social and political form of organization. Bloch therefore set the close of his period of study in *French Rural History* much later, when the rights of common pasturing were abandoned. That marked the end of the old agrarian civilization and the introduction of the new, capitalist type of farming. Similar changes took place in other parts of open-field Europe as well (in England they were particularly easy to date because they were carried out by acts of Parliament), and even though they were gradual, they were decisive in creating new kinds of rural societies. In France, the French Revolution codified the changes and accelerated them as they continued to work their way through the most backward parts of France even in the nineteenth century. But neither the Revolution nor the nineteenth century marked the essential boundary, which had come some time before.[12]

It would be difficult to exaggerate the implication of Bloch's delineation of the temporal boundaries of this change, because any interpretation of the economic effects of the Revolution and of France's industrialization depends on the correct assignment of a time period for this gradual transformation.

As for the start of the period he examined in *French Rural History*, Bloch admitted that some of the roots of field systems probably lay in pre-Roman, perhaps even in pre-Celtic, times. There was, however, a natural point of division between the ancient and the medieval world, marked by the depopulation of late Roman times and the collapse of the Carolingian effort to reclaim abandoned lands during the ninth and tenth centuries. The start of the great clearings in about 1050, which coincided with what Bloch was later to call the start of the second feudal age, was the real starting point for this study.[13]

How can the contemporary social historian use Bloch's example to set temporal and social limits to his or her material? There are no fixed rules. One must first understand a great deal about the subject, and then pick the essential traits that define the civilization being studied. These traits, which consist of a set of conjunctions of different factors, mark both the limits of any type of society and the period during which it exists. Within that time and social space, it then becomes possible to erect a scaffold, a kind of model of the society, with fairly precise rules that hold up for a long time.

But what about the social historian who studies much shorter and limited topics than civilizations? Here Bloch was not much help because he rarely forgot that the true object of his work was a vast period that he studied on a continental scale.

Lucien Febvre used the notion of generations far more than Bloch, but in his methodological writing, as well as in the autobiographical comments he made, Bloch showed that he thought of generations as an appropriate unit of short-term historical analysis.[14] In particular, he felt that he was a member of the "Dreyfusard" generation, the French intellectuals marked by the debate that revolved around that prolonged scandal, the political upheaval it provoked, and the triumph of liberalism that ended it. Those born only a few years after Bloch were less loyal to the Third Republic and less liberal. Bloch felt strongly that this was an example of how central common experiences and points of reference could be in shaping an individual's thought. He did not deny that class, education, region of birth, and other chance factors were also important, but he claimed that there was this extra dimension that historians might use to periodize their studies.

Evidence

Because he is so well known as someone who analyzed field patterns to unlock the secrets of medieval societies, it is easy to forget that Marc Bloch was also a great analyst of conventional documents and written sources.

An interesting example was his imaginative use of medieval epics. He found that even though their form was broadly similar in much of Western Europe during the late eleventh and twelfth centuries, their

contents were not. The French drew their inspiration from mythologized events in the eighth and ninth centuries, while the Germans
went back to folk tales of the fourth to sixth. In Castile, quite to the
contrary, the epics were about very recent, almost contemporary
events; in Italy, there were no standard medieval epics.[15] This disparity
revealed deep differences between these lands. In Germany, which
was influenced by old tribal mores much later than the lands earlier
ruled by Rome, folk mythology remained much more lively well into
the feudal period, which corresponded to a generally tardy feudaliza-
tion. In Italy, where literacy was never lost, nobles and courts continued to use Latin literature. Castile, which was a brand-new creation,
had no past to mythologize, except for the recent adventures of the
reconquest. France was in an intermediary position, though there were
important differences between the north and the south. Nor were
these variations throughout Europe limited to literature. Economies,
degrees of urbanization, legal structures, and languages were all more
or less correlated with the seemingly superficial but actually important
differences in epic tradition.

In *Feudal Society* Bloch listed the kinds of evidence suitable for historical analysis. Every aspect of social life was included: official documents, place names, field shapes, customs, collectively held psychological attitudes (if these could be guessed), coins, trade records, and
architectural styles were fair game. Evidence from the modern period,
well after the end of the Middle Ages, was as important to his conclusions as evidence from the period he was studying. Totally definitive
conclusions, however, were not possible, because sources never gave
complete enough explanations. For him, history "has still all the excitement of an unfinished excavation."[16]

In *French Rural History* Bloch entirely abandoned the concept of linear
history, and wrote, instead, from the present or near past into the
distant past, and back toward the present. Because the book was primarily a history of field shapes and the changing social and technological adaptations made by French agriculture, he saw no need to proceed
conventionally. The best evidence about such matters existed in the
eighteenth, nineteenth, and in some cases, twentieth centuries when
reliable maps and, more recently, aerial photographs, were available.
The open fields that predominated north of the Loire River and the
puzzle-shaped fields to the south represented distinct ways of farming
and of organizing social life. They had probably originated in very
ancient usages that could not be readily discerned in documents. Contemporary or near contemporary evidence allowed Bloch to trace his

way back through the confusing documentary remnants of the past and to interpret them better than if he had tried to reason from the past toward the present. This method did not always work, because even in the past, there had been occasional abrupt changes. In Brittany, for example, the hedges surrounding fields seemed to Bloch to have appeared as recently as the sixteenth century. But it was at least more fruitful to begin this way, with the most recent good evidence, than by searching for elusive and hypothetical origins of present phenomena in the past.[17]

In his review of *French Rural History*, printed as an introduction to the later editions of the book, Lucien Febvre wrote that Bloch had originated the method of reading the past from the present, and that he had been the first to understand that peasants did not cultivate their land with charters because of his unorthodox approach to time. Other great historians, according to Febvre, had been armchair archivists, unfamiliar with peasant techniques or with the physical constraints of the land because they had not gone out to look at present peasant life. Because they did not look around them, these traditional historians had failed to note the variety of field shapes in Europe, or to draw proper conclusions.[18]

This conclusion was not entirely correct. Bloch himself ignored the important earlier work of Lefebvre des Noëttes, *L'attelage, le cheval de selle à travers les ages. Contribution à l'histoire de l'esclavage.*[19] This was a book that was methodologically far ahead of its time. The author actually built animal harnesses from old illustrations, tried them out, and found convincing explanations about the great technological progress made during the Middle Ages. Bloch was aware of, and cited earlier works about, the relationship between field shapes and social organization, such as those by Maitland and Meitzen.[20] But Bloch certainly advanced, if he did not entirely create, a new method of studying the past without regard to the strict linear concept of time that had guided previous studies. Bloch's style has dominated rural historical research ever since the 1930s.

Even in *French Rural History*, where he paid so much attention to nonwritten sources, Bloch used extensive documentary analysis. He knew as well as any good historian how to apply the rules of logical criticism to documents. His reasoning about critical analysis, of which he was proud, was acute, but neither outstandingly innovative nor central to the way in which he felt that his and Febvre's historical styles were different from those used by conventional historians. Nevertheless, the ability to critically evaluate conventional written sources was the bread and butter of historical work. One had to do it well to be a minimally acceptable historian.[21] Neither Bloch nor Febvre ever imagined that the *Annales'* contribution should be to claim historical insight without being able to meet, at the very least, the standard qualifications demanded of all members of the craft. They felt that good history should go beyond this, but not to the detriment of what had already been achieved in developing a sound historical method.

One of the major innovations of the *Annales* school was its use of geographic evidence. The inspiration for this came from Vidal de la Blache.[22] In an essay about Bloch written after his death, Febvre recalled the liberating effect of geography on those of Bloch's generation who learned from this master. Not only did Vidal de la Blache promote geography to a position of honor among the social scientific disciplines, but in the gloomy classrooms of the turn of the century, "geography was fresh air, the walk in the countryside, a return with an armful of flowers, the eyes stripped of soot, the brain refreshed, and a taste of reality biting into the abstract."[23] In another essay about Bloch, Henry Baulig wrote, "Spatially, the comparative method has at its disposal a choice instrument, the map. Marc Bloch kept on asking for maps of things, of customs, of words."[24]

Geography was something that Bloch felt, an intimate association between people and the land, observed first-hand by walking the countryside, and analyzed in terms of the necessary adaptation of society to its physical circumstances, as well as the transformation of the land itself by human action. His feeling for France's geography was part of his patriotism as well as of his analytical framework. One is struck, in *Feudal Society* and in *French Rural History*, with how often Bloch returned to examples from the Ile-de-France, the subject of his first book, and the part of France he knew best as a student.

Geography was much more than a physical given; there was little in the French countryside that was not the result of centuries, sometimes millenia, of human action. The interaction between the physical context of a place, human social organization, and the ways in which these two modify each other (what sociologists now call human ecology) not only preoccupied Bloch and Febvre but became the basis for the work of their two best students, André Déléage and Fernand Braudel.[25] The latter made human ecology the key to his notion of the "long term" in history, and therefore an explanation of the many persistences in social life over centuries.[26]

Ultimately, reading geographic evidence was, for Bloch, very similar to reading documentary materials. Simple causal statements were eschewed in favor of careful weighing of all the relevant factors. It would be as wrong to call him a geographic determinist on the basis of *French Rural History* as to read his earlier *Serfs and Kings* or *The Royal Touch* and conclude that he was a mere analyst of conventional archives. Evidence as such was important, but only if the proper questions could be asked of it.

Living, as we do, in an age when archaeologists grow their own wild wheat to find evidence about the Mesolithic, and when historians use anything from oral tradition to counting tree rings to date events, it is difficult to find Bloch's use of various bits of information startling. The key is this: Bloch felt that the problems being researched, the questions being posed, should determine the kinds of evidence to be used. Whereas the conventional social scientists of his day, and of ours, formulate problems according to the evidence available to them, Bloch reversed that order, and contributed significantly to the great opening of materials, the spread of types of admissible evidence that have since been the hallmark of the *Annales* school.

The Comparative Method

In a self-confident and perhaps slightly arrogant little monograph published in 1913, *The Ile de-France, The Country Around Paris*, he counseled local historians to forsake the mere collection of random facts. To avoid antiquarianism, he told them to read broader studies and to understand whole regions. They might, in this way, learn about the most important questions to be asked of their evidence, and contribute material to the first-rate historians whose work depended in part on the minutely detailed researches of these dedicated amateurs.[27] (I have heard sociologists telling historians the same things – learn to be comparative in order to ask good questions so that we may use your tedious, if necessary, work to our own ends.)

Bloch's instructions were explicit: "co-ordinate and compare the results of these enquiries, recognize the likenesses, explain and reject the anomalies, and discern the essential facts among the infinite number of regional varieties."[28]

As the scope of Bloch's thinking spread beyond France to the whole of Europe, he continued to emphasize the importance of comparative history. In 1928 he wrote:

> A humanist education had accustomed us to picture Rome and Greece as too like ourselves; but the comparative method in the hands of ethnographers has restored to us with a kind of mental

shock this sense of difference, the exotic element, which is the indispensable condition for a balanced understanding of the past.[29]

The main point of conducting comparative history, then, was simply to look at less familiar situations to clear the mind of anachronistic misconceptions, which were a constant threat to historical research. Familiarity with a past period could lead all too easily to imposition of modern standards, but a good look at many other histories, as well as comparative ethnographic data, lessened that danger.

The analysis of similarities between cases was interesting, said Bloch, especially because it prevented historians "from following certain paths that are mere blind alleys." As an example he gave the nearly simultaneous rise of estates (*Stände* in Germany, *Cortes* in Spain, *Parliamenti* in Italy, Parliament in England, *Etats* in France) throughout Western Europe and the creation of political structures in which power was divided between the kings and these states (*Ständestaat*). Local studies or national histories of the sort that emphasize the causes of such formations miss the point, because there was nothing specifically English or French or German about this development. Rather it corresponded to a continental trend, which must be explained as such.[30]

Differences were even more interesting for Bloch. They could allow the analyst to distinguish what had caused the differences. In his essay on comparative history, however, the first point about analysis of differences Bloch emphasized was that "first of all, it is essential to clear ground of false similarities, which are often merely homonymous. And some of them can be very insidious."[31]

In his study of the magical healing powers exercised through touch by the kings of France and England during the Middle Ages, Bloch cited Frazer's *The Golden Bough* and other sources that told of similar powers found among chiefs and kings throughout the world.[32] Bloch therefore knew that there was nothing unique about the Capetian and Norman dynasties that initiated the practice of the royal touch in their countries. Or was there? Were all the royal houses in Europe endowed with such powers? Aside from the occasional saintly king here and there the answer was no! Only in France and England was this power thoroughly routinized and practiced for so many centuries, eight in the former and six in the latter country.

Frazer had compared Polynesian to English monarchy, and generalized from the case he knew better, in the Pacific. There, chiefs could either cause or cure certain diseases. Therefore, Frazer, who knew that scrofula, the illness supposedly cured by the English kings, was called "the King's Evil," concluded that the monarch could cause as well as heal scrofula. He was wrong, if logical. "Let us beware," warned Bloch, "of committing . . . the error of transporting the Antipodes in their entirety to Paris or London."[33] The comparative method could neither verify details about a place nor impose the mores of one society on those of another.

Internal comparisons between European dynasties, particularly the French and English royal houses, unlocked the explanation of the royal touch. In France, the practice began with the Capetians, who had usurped the throne from the Carolingians and needed to bolster their weak legitimacy. About one century later, the same magical power was claimed by Normans who had overthrown the Anglo-Saxon line in England. To make their healing powers seem stronger, they even claimed to have inherited them from Edward the Confessor, thereby trying to persuade the people that the bloodlines between the old and the new dynasties were so tight as to confer hereditary magical abilities. It is doubtful that Edward himself had claimed to have the royal touch, but this imaginative forgery took hold in the popular imagination. The Middle Ages were rich in similarly wonderful, politically motivated fraud. Later, other European dynasties tried to claim the same magical healing capacities for themselves, but they failed. All over Western Europe people believed in the established, traditional power of the French and English kings to effect a cure for scrofula. But by the time imitators came along, the church was strong enough to expose them as frauds acting for clear political motives.[34]

There was a subtle interplay of general and particular history in *The Royal Touch*. A certain general mentality, or way of thinking about the world (Bloch used the term *collective consciousness* or perception) was required to establish the royal charisma of touch. It had to be established beforehand that the monarchy was somewhat sacred (and this long antedated the Capetians), and belief in the royal touch depended on certain attitudes toward magic, healing, and disease. After the general spirit of the times had begun to change, however, well-established charisma could retain its power for a long time, even if it ceased to be possible for new examples of the same type to establish themselves. In England, the charismatic touch persisted beyond the Reformation into the late seventeenth century, at a time when it would have been absurd for a new dynasty to claim the power. The Hanoverians, who replaced the last Stuart, made no attempt whatsoever to retain it. In France, because dynastic change occurred later, the power remained active well into the eighteenth century, even though French intellectuals and the kings themselves, particularly Louis XV, thought it somewhat silly. Charles X tried to revive the power in 1825, but it was too late, and he dropped the practice. By then, of course, it was not only faith in the royal touch that had disappeared but the essential legitimacy of the dynasty itself.[35]

By using a comparative approach and listing the significant differences between the royal touch in France and England, Bloch established an important general rule of social change. Ideologies, beliefs, and superstitions have their time. Coincidental events, such as immediate political needs or dynastic changes, can determine whether or not particular collective perceptions become fixed in the popular mind. Once in place, they can outlive their time, but this does not mean that late attempts to begin the same tradition would succeed. Suggestive as this may be, and meticulously documented as Bloch made it, its general value is only to allow those who study other periods and times to ask interesting questions and suggest tentative answers. This may be why this most scrupulous study of a case of the routinization of charisma has not lent itself to flashy theory construction, and so remains less cited than other, less careful works on this topic.

I do not want to suggest that Bloch was skeptical of comparative history. On the contrary, in all of his books, including *The Royal Touch*, he stressed its importance. In *The Historian's Craft* he wrote that the failure to be comparative produced "grim esoterism . . . dreary textbooks which bad teaching practices have put in place of true synthesis." The damage done by this narrow-minded traditionalism was immense. It left the reading public and intellectuals in particular open to politically motivated lies about the past. "They [the dreary textbooks] conspire to surrender the mass of defenseless readers to the false brilliance of a bogus history, in which lack of seriousness, picturesque rubbish and political prejudices are supposed to be redeemed by shameless self-assurance: thus Maurras, Bainville, or Plekhanov affirm that which Fustel de Coulanges or Pirenne would have doubted."[36]

Most of Bloch's polemical ire was directed against the traditional historians, though he left the bulk of the propagandistic work in favor of comparative social and economic history to his colleague, Lucien Febvre.[37] In the late twentieth century, sociologists who write history need not be warned about errors of old-fashioned history. Our stock-in-trade is the broad comparative generalization, not the pedantic attention to detail and the fear of sweeping theoretical conclusions. There is little point, then, in stressing Bloch's main arguments to demolish, once again, his moribund foes. It is salutary to remember, however, just why he was so upset with the dullness and pedantry of the traditional historians. They left the way open to deceitful, pseudo-historical generalizers whose superficial brilliance could then be used for noxious political ends.

Social Theory

In a talk he once gave on economic theory, Bloch remarked, "The science of economic phenomena can only be a science of observation. We say that it cannot be satisfied with deductions based on *a priori* givens . . . Logical reasoning, in the science which we are trying to elaborate, intervenes only to classify and interpret facts. Hypotheses must always be refreshed by contact with experience." He then held Adam Smith and Karl Marx up as examples of good economic historians in their times.[38]

Everyone can agree with this statement, even those who refuse to understand its meaning. Other remarks made by Bloch can help make the point more distinctive than it seems to be at first sight.

In *The Historian's Craft* Bloch discussed sociology by explaining how, in the generations just prior to his, the Comtian view of physical science had mesmerized intellectuals. The result, in historical writing, was a bifurcation.

> [Some] were willing to abandon, as outside a true science of man, a great many eminently human realities which appeared to them stubbornly insusceptible to rational comprehension. This residue they scornfully called mere events or happenstance. It was also a good part of the most intimate and individual side of life. Such was, in sum, the position of the sociological school founded by Durkheim . . . To this great scientific effort our studies are vastly indebted. It has taught us to analyze more profoundly, to grasp our problems more firmly, and even I dare say, to think less shoddily. It will be spoken of here only with infinite gratitude and respect. If it seems sterile now, that is only the price that all intellectual movements must pay, sooner or later, for their moments of fertility.[39]

The second branch consisted of those so discouraged by the possibility of turning history into science that they retreated to saying that writing it was merely an aesthetic pursuit. Bloch disliked this position, and felt that history could be made more rigorous and useful.

Once again, as in many debates, he took a position in the middle of the argument. He admired the construction of social theories practiced by the sociologists (that is, chiefly Durkheim and his school), and he was much inspired by them, particularly in *The Royal Touch*. He found them overused, however, and tending toward sterility by the late 1930s. He understood the rationale of those who had given up, but he had far less sympathy for them than he did for the sociologists.

Throughout *The Royal Touch* there is much Durkheimian phraseology ("conscience collective," "social facts.") It is therefore curious to note that even in the early 1920s Bloch did not use Durkheim as a sociologist might have. Bloch advanced no comprehensive theory of society, nor did he consider his research as any kind of attempt to test Durkheim's theories. The goal was to tell us what had happened and to explain why. Rather than concluding with a demonstration of the universality of the phenomenon, he chose to emphasize its singularity.

> In political matters the way of acting and feeling of the majority of Frenchmen in the time of Louis XIV is surprising, and even shocking to us; the same holds for a part of English opinion under the Stuarts. We understand poorly the idolatry of kings and the monarchy; it is difficult for us not to interpret it unreasonably, as the effect of who knows what kind of abject servility. This problem we have, on an important issue, of penetrating into the mentality of a period with whose literary tradition we are so very familiar is caused, possibly, by our having over-studied its conceptions with respect to government only in the works of its major theoreticians. Absolutism is a sort of religion. Is it not true that to know a religion only by its theologians is to ignore its living sources?[40]

What Durkheimian theory had told Bloch was that a people's collective consciousness was a deep-seated phenomenon that could not be understood without resort to the study of mass ideology. That approach to the problem by a historian was new. What Bloch did not take from Durkheim was the notion that there ought to be a series of propositions drawn from the theory and that these ought to be tested in some way to construct a better general theory of religion, magic, or charisma. In other words, theory's task was only to help the historian look for better evidence about the past.

As we have already seen in the discussion of comparative history in *The Royal Touch*, Bloch was able to suggest a general rule about social ideologies and the time periods in which they may gain acceptance, as well as about their survival beyond their times. But these were far from being general theories, only helpful ideas for the further study of analogous phenomena.

In the last two decades of his life, after the publication of *The Royal Touch*, Bloch came to consider himself an economic rather than a general historian, and his chair in Paris, to which he went in 1936, was specifically in that domain. His treatment of theory in his two major later books, therefore, may be more indicative of his final position. Actually, however, there was more continuity in his treatment of theory than in the questions he chose to study, or the content of the theories he used.

An unstated but important orienting assumption lay embedded in Bloch's writings: Social groups and individuals do everything in their power to maximize their chances of survival, and in the long run, their calculated attempts to spread, and thereby lessen their risks, are rational. Rationality lies more in the eye of the beholder than in the actor, and in this instance, Bloch's belief in it as a guiding principle of human behavior meant simply that the calculations that led to behavior were comprehensible, as efficacious as possible under the circumstances, and that, consequently, they were subject to logical explanations by historians. The entire notion of the long-run changes in behavior was important to that of economic rationality, because it could take some time for a society to learn how to adapt to its circumstances, especially when rapid change had occurred. This theoretical belief, however, was so patently obvious to Bloch that he felt it would be useless to write it down; he merely used it to guide his thinking and research and did not try to subject it to any proof.

The long paragraph I quoted earlier from *French Rural History* that describes the different types of field systems and agrarian civilizations that existed in France is worth rereading. It contains the theory of risk minimization that guided Bloch's notions of social adaptation to and interaction with the environment. It also shows how he felt about the relative impossibility of finding first causes of complex social phenomena. It is valuable for its cautionary epistemological note, that neither material nor cultural factors make much sense alone. The point of the application of a historian's theoretical intuition to the study of social adaptation was to increase understanding of how a civilization worked.

Another illustration of Bloch's use of theory as a means but not as an end in itself can be found in his description of the deep social changes that occurred during the second feudal period. In *French Rural History*, he observed:

> One would be giving a fairly correct image of eleventh century society by representing it, essentially, as a series of vertical constructions; it was fragmented into an infinity of groups gathered

tightly around their chiefs, who were themselves dependent on other chiefs: groups of serfs or tenants, vassal households. From the middle of the twelfth century, or thereabouts, an opposite way of organizing people occurs, by horizontal layers. Large administrative units—principalities, a monarchic state—encompass and stifle the small lordships. Hierarchical classes, chiefly the nobility, form themselves and become strong. The commune—usually urban, but sometimes extending to rural collectivities—gives itself this most revolutionary institution as its basis: the oath among equals of mutual support replaces the old vow of obedience given by the subordinate to his master. And everywhere the sense of bonds between men loses strength.[41]

This was the origin of the Western European social classes that were to form the basis of a Marxist analysis of society. Bloch, as I said earlier, admired Marx, but hardly thought that his analysis of class had anything universally valid about it. In fact, the society of the first feudal age was not organized by class. Knowledge of Marx's theory of class organization enabled Bloch to perceive the distinction between the second and first periods of feudalism. The differences between rich and poor, powerful and weak, had always existed. But it was the mark of a profound and discontinuous transformation when people began to organize themselves on that basis. The social change, in this case, preceded and rendered possible the eventual transition to capitalism for which Marxist methods of analysis are valid.[42]

The most important characteristic of Bloch's theoretical orientation, and that of the entire *Annales* school, has been its rejection of any single organizing principle. Neither class and class struggle, geography, collective psychology, kinship patterns, technology, nor political events necessarily overwhelmed the others. All contributed to the shape of civilizations, and to changing them, without being sufficiently powerful to undo everything else.

Febvre's student, Braudel, carried this tendency even further by refusing, in his study of the Mediterranean, to organize his thoughts in any but the loosest and almost random sort of format. There is much that is instructive in Braudel, but there is no theory of society or of history other than a statement that everything is important, and in the long run, things change rather slowly. The broad range of writing and research by today's leading representative of the Bloch-Febvre-Braudel tradition, Emmanuel Le Roy Ladurie, confirms this tendency, and his recent, widely acclaimed book, *Montaillou*, is almost antitheoretical in its attempt to portray all of one small place at one time.[43]

Is there a contradiction between this result and Bloch's earliest, arrogant demand in *The Ile-de-France* that other historians let important theoretical considerations guide their research? More than a quarter of a century of experience taught him a good bit, but there is no serious contradiction in any case, because Bloch never abandoned his belief that there were guiding forces in social life and that some questions were more important than others. Those with a good intuitive grasp of a period and place were able to construct a theoretical model and to use it to evaluate evidence, ask new questions, and improve the model. That models were of limited value, good for a civilization at most, often for more limited topics alone, was understood. Once such a model was in place, however, it could be very useful, as long as it was not abused.

It must be stressed, in passing, that this awareness of theoretical limitations, the mixing of various kinds of evidence to produce a satisfactory image of a period, and the demands of accuracy required Bloch to have an exceptionally lucid and colorful writing style. His theoretical models were frail constructions that disintegrated even as they sailed; by its nature change destroyed the validity of the model explaining it. To launch them at all and keep them floating for a while took great linguistic as well as scientific skill. This remains as true among today's *Annalistes* as it was for Bloch.

Bloch was neither antitheoretical nor atheoretical. Social theory had a major, essential role to play in historical work. The final result of any major inquiry had to be a set of generalizations that would perfect the model most suitable for a particular situation, as well as the elaboration of rules about social behavior that could help all historians, of all times and places, with interesting comparative notions. Toward the end of *Feudal Society*, he made some suggestive remarks about Japan, as if to say, use my book to increase your powers of imagination.[44]

It seems to me that this is not what sociologists think of when they discuss the importance of theory. They are still, as they were in Bloch's time, caught up in Comtian ideas about the physical sciences, which limits their range as well as the utility of their theories. As far as historical work is concerned, the attempt to prove universal laws by ranging through great sweeps of time around the globe is the reverse of what Bloch intended.

Apology for History

In a little book written in the fall of 1940, just after the Germans had conquered France, at a time of right-wing obscurantism, rising anti-

Semitism, and persecution of those who still believed, as Bloch did, in the essential goodness of the liberal vision, he analyzed the reasons for that catastrophe.[45] As a man marked for trouble (his family were Alsatian Jews who had fled Alsace after the Franco-Prussian War), his first sentence was, "Will these pages ever be published? – I cannot tell." Rather than yielding to discouragement, he applied his historical mind to the events of that year, both because he felt that he had been a witness to something important and because he knew that his sense of social and economic change would help him understand better than most others.

This is not the place to discuss the vast literature about the fall of France in 1940. It is, however, important to note that at the time, explanations tended to focus on the general degeneracy of French society, its internal divisions between an unrealistic left and a bitter, anachronistic right, its industrial weakness compared to Germany, and its demographic shortages. (There is no need to repeat the charges of the left that there was treason by the right, and of the right that the British had double-crossed France, or that a Communist fifth column impeded the war effort. Such charges were widely believed, but they had so little substance as to bear no analysis.)

A month after the event, before he or anyone else had had time to examine any of the relevant documents, Bloch saw the real reason. The French general staff had not learned the lesson of motorized transport. The original strategic mistake of allowing armies to be trapped in Belgium was vastly compounded by the repeated failure to order tactical retreats in sufficient depth. Nor was there the slightest awareness that motorized transport required good, safe roads, which were exceedingly vulnerable to guerrilla attack. Bloch saw these things not from the point of view of an aging reserve captain called to duty in 1939 and involved in the Belgian debacle, which he was, but as a historian.[46]

All the other charges about the weaknesses of France were somewhat correct, wrote Bloch in the later parts of the book, but none of them explained the rapid collapse of the army. They explained, rather, something that was only beginning to take shape as he wrote, a collaborationist attitude among the majority of the French, an unwillingness to resist once the official war had been lost, and a grotesque attempt to find scapegoats. But if the army, which was well equipped though poorly administered and led, had stood its ground, the catastrophe would not have occurred.

The fault lay largely in a method of teaching strategy and tactics that was too historically oriented, or rather, too heavily based on the notion that the past can teach us how to behave in the present. This was false history, claimed Bloch, because it failed to take into account the essential changes of the twentieth century. In any case, as he had said before, and was to say again in *The Historian's Craft,* history is the science of change. Napoleonic military history was primarily useful because it could teach officers how different warfare had become in the early nineteenth century from what it had been in the eighteenth and show how long it took for other European powers to catch on to that fact. Napoleonic history had little to say about modern warfare.[47] That was the whole point of studying history, to show how change had occurred.

Bloch was contemptuous of those who believed that a knowledge of the past was a guide to the future, but he was even harsher toward those who mythologized the past. Vichy's social policy claimed that a return "back to the land" would purify France. Nonsense, said Bloch, because the idyllic, docile peasant life of the French right had never existed.[48] History ought to disabuse readers of silly notions about the past.

If history was not to be a guide to the future, what useful purpose could it serve? For one thing, Bloch's almost instantaneous perception of what had really gone wrong with the French army showed that historical training was useful for understanding any social situation, past or present. Those accustomed to building social models, even if they applied their skills to exotic times and places, developed a sense of how to repeat the procedure for new occasions and civilizations. For another, there are general rules that, while not forming closed or rigid theories, serve as guides to an understanding of human behavior. One of Bloch's most perceptive observations, and it was a peculiar one for such a political moderate, was that revolutions have the great merit of bringing the young to power and so refresh a social system. Even the Nazis had done this, while the French had done the reverse, bringing to power a generation of the past.[49]

Bloch was to state these things more clearly in his last book. In it he was to observe, some two years before he was shot by the Germans for being in the Resistance, how valuable historical training could be. The critical method of examining historical documents, of evaluating evidence, of asking good questions of a social situation, should become part of everyone's education, and not be restricted to historians. Those of us who teach sociology and history might ask ourselves if Bloch's program is being followed today. I almost hesitate to quote him; his statement will strike many contemporary sophisticates as naive and foolishly sentimental. But it was, after all, part of the concluding remarks of a great career.

> It is a scandal that in our own age, which is more than ever exposed to the poisons of fraud and false rumor, the critical method is so completely absent from our school programs. It has ceased to be the mere humble auxiliary to exercises of the study. Henceforth, far wider horizons open before it, and history may reckon among its most certain glories that, by this elaboration of its technique, it has pioneered for mankind a new path to truth and, hence, to justice.[50]

Notes

1. It is a bit odd that the titles of three of Bloch's major works have been incompletely translated into their English versions. Perhaps this is because Anglo-Saxons demand more precision than the French, or catchier titles. The unfinished manuscript of this book was *Apologie pour l'histoire ou métier d'historien* (Justification for history or the historian's craft). This was the way it was first published in Paris, in 1949. The English translation, however, cut the title in two (New York: Knopf, 1953).
2. Bloch, *The Historian's Craft*, trans. P. Putnam, p. 183.
3. Ibid., pp. 183, 187–89.
4. Bloch, *Feudal Society*, trans. L. A. Manyon (Chicago: University of Chicago Press, 1961), pp. 3–56, 123–75. *La société féodale* was originally published in Paris.
5. Ibid., pp. 59–120.
6. An interesting account of why feudalism was unable to establish itself in Switzerland's high mountains is found in Benjamin R. Barber's *The Death of Communal Liberty* (Princeton, N.J.: Princeton University Press, 1974).
7. This is one of the better insights in Perry Anderson's *Lineages of the Absolutist State* (London: New Left Books, 1974), pp. 361–94.
8. *Feudal Society*, pp. 52–71, 283–331.
9. Ibid., pp. 176–89; 329–31; 421–37.
10. Bloch, *Strange Defeat*, trans. G. Hopkins (London: Oxford University Press, 1949), p. 152. The manuscript was written in 1940, and first published in Paris as *L'étrange défaite, temoignage écrit en 1940*, in 1946.
11. First published in Oslo, this work was called *Les caractères originaux de l'histoire rurale française* (The unique traits of French rural history) (hereafter *Les caractères originaux*). *French Rural History: An Essay on Its Basic Characteristics*, trans J. Sondheimer (Berkeley: University of California Press, 1966). I am using an extensively annotated edition by Robert Dauvergne (Paris: Armand Colin, 1960–61), pp. 56–57.
12. Bloch, *Les caractères originaux*, pp. 202–51.
13. Ibid., pp. 3–6.
14. Bloch, *The Historian's Craft*, p. 183. See Febvre's *Le problème de l'incroyance au XVIe siècle: la religion de Rabelais* (Paris, 1942). On generations, see H. Stuart Hughes, *The Obstructed Path: French Social Thought in the Years of Desperation* (New York: Harper Torchbooks, 1969), p. 33.
15. Bloch, *Feudal Society*, pp. 92–102.
16. Ibid. p. 52.

17. Bloch, *Les caractères originaux*, pp. x–xiv, 30–63.
18. Ibid. pp. iv–vi.
19. Paris, 1931 (revised edition of a work published in 1924).
20. F. W. Maitland, *Domesday Book and Beyond* (Cambridge, 1921). A. Meitzen, *Siedlung und Agrarwesen der Wastgermanen und Ostgermanen, der Kelten, Finnen und Slawen* (Berlin, 1895).
21. *The Historian's Craft,* pp. 110–37.
22. See Lucien Febvre's review of Vidal de la Blache's geography textbook, 1923, republished in *Pour une histoire à part entière* (Paris: S.E.V.P.E.N., 1962), a collection of Febvre's essays, pp. 147–66.
23. Lucien Febvre, "Marc Bloch et Strasbourg," in his essays, *Combats pour l'histoire* (Paris: Armand Colin, 1953), p. 398.
24. "Marc Bloch, géographe," in *Annales d'Histoire Sociale*, vol. 2 (*Hommages à Marc Bloch*), 1945, p. 6.
25. See André Déléage, *La vie rurale en Bourgogne jusqu'au début du XIe siècle* (Mâcon, 1941). Déléage was killed in 1944. On Braudel, see below.
26. Fernand Braudel, "Time, History, and the Social Sciences," in *The Varieties of History*, 2 ed., ed. Fritz Stern (New York: Vintage, 1973), particularly pp. 411–12.
27. *L'Ile-de-France (les pays autour de Paris)* was first published in Paris. I am using the English translation by J.E. Anderson (Ithaca: Cornell University Press, 1971), pp. 60–63; 110–23.
28. Ibid., pp. 119–20.
29. "Pour une histoire comparée des sociétés Européennes" was first published in 1928. The quote is from an English translation, "A contribution toward a comparative history of European societies," in *Land and Work in Medieval Europe, Selected Papers of Marc Bloch*, trans. J. E. Anderson (New York: Harper Torchbooks, 1969), p. 47. The essay exists in French in *Mélanges historiques*, 2 vols. (Paris: S.E.V.P.E.N., 1963).
30. "A contribution toward a comparative history . . .," p. 56.
31. Ibid., p. 58.
32. Bloch, *Les rois thaumaturges* (Strasbourg: Istra, 1924). The word exists in English – thaumaturgy means the performance of miracles or wonders. The English translation of the book, however, calls it *The Royal Touch*, trans. J. E. Anderson (London; Routledge & Kegan Paul, 1973).
33. *Les rois thaumaturges*, pp. 53–54.
34. Ibid., pp. 27–86; 156.
35. Ibid., pp. 376, 381, 387–99, 402–05.
36. *The Historian's Craft*, p. 87. Maurras was founder and Bainville an important member of the *Action Française*, a royalist, right-wing, but intellectually oriented political group that became firmly collaborationist with the Germans during the war. The others presumably need no introduction. On Bloch's appreciation of Pirenne, see Lucien Febvre's introduction to *The Historian's Craft*, p. xiii.
37. Lucien Febvre, *Combats pour l'histoire* (Paris, 1953).
38. "Que demander à l'histoire," in *Mélanges historiques*, vol. 1, p. 4. The talk was first published in 1937.
39. *Craft*, pp. 14–15.
40. *Les rois thaumaturges*, pp. 344–45.
41. *Les caractères originaux*, p. 109.
42. Ibid. pp. 189–200.
43. Fernand Braudel, *The Mediterranean and the Mediterranean World in the Age of Philip II*, trans. S. Reynolds (New York: Harper & Row, 1972–73). The book

was originally published in 1949, and a revised edition appeared in 1966. Emmanuel Le Roy Ladurie, *Montaillou: The Promised Land of Error*, trans. B. Bray (New York: Braziller, 1978). Originally this was *Montaillou, village occitan de 1294 à 1324* (Paris, 1975).

44. *Feudal Society*, pp. 446–47.
45. *Strange Defeat*.
46. Ibid., pp. 37–51.
47. Ibid., pp. 117–118.
48. Ibid., p. 147.
49. Ibid., p. 161.
50. *The Historian's Craft*, pp. 136–37.

*Selected Bibliography of Works in English
by Marc Bloch and the Annales*

Bloch, Marc. *The Royal Touch*. 1924. Translated by J. F. Anderson. London: Routledge & Kegan Paul, 1973.

Bloch, Marc. *French Rural History: An Essay on Its Basic Characteristics*. 1931. Translated by J. Sondheimer. Berkeley: University of California Press, 1966.

Bloch, Marc. *Feudal Society*. 1939–40. Translated by L. A. Manyon. Chicago: University of Chicago Press, 1961.

Bloch, Marc. *Strange Defeat*. 1946. Translated by G. Hopkins. London: Oxford University Press, 1949.

Bloch, Marc. *The Historian's Craft*. 1949. Translated by P. Putnam. New York: Knopf, 1953.

Bloch, Marc. *Land and Work in Medieval Europe: Selected Papers by Marc Bloch*. Translated by J. E. Anderson. New York: Harper Torchbooks, 1969.

Bloch, Marc. *Slavery and Serfdom in the Middle Ages. Selected Papers by Marc Bloch*. Translated by W. R. Beer. Berkeley: University of California Press, 1975.

Braudel, Fernand. *The Mediterranean and the Mediterranean World in the Age of Philip II*. 1949, 1966. Translated by S. Reynolds. New York: Harper & Row, 1972–73.

Duby, Georges. *Rural Economy and Country Life in the Medieval West*. 1962. Translated by C. Postan. Columbia: University of South Carolina Press, 1968.

Febvre, Lucien. *A New Kind of History: From the Writings of Febvre*. 1962. Translated by K. Folca. London: Routledge & Kegan Paul, 1973.

Febvre, Lucien. *Life in Renaissance France* (essays). Translated by M. Rothstein. Cambridge, Mass: Harvard University Press, 1977.

Le Roy Ladurie, Emmanuel. *The Peasants of Languedoc*. 1966. Translated by J. Day. Urbana: University of Illinois Press, 1974.

Le Roy Ladurie, Emmanuel. *Times of Feast, Times of Famine: A History of Climate Since the Year 1000*. 1967. Translated by B. Bray. Garden City, N.Y.: Doubleday, 1971.

Le Roy Ladurie, Emmanuel. *The Territory of the Historian*. 1973. Translated by B. and S. Reynolds. Hassocks, Sussex: Harvester Press, 1979.

Le Roy Ladurie, Emmanuel. *Montaillou: The Promised Land of Error*. 1975. Translated by B. Bray. New York: Braziller, 1978.

3. Beyond the Economistic Fallacy: The Holistic Social Science of Karl Polanyi

FRED BLOCK and MARGARET R. SOMERS

Karl Polanyi's intellectual work stands among the most significant and original contributions to social science scholarship in the period since the end of World War I. In particular, his book *The Great Transformation*[1] is now widely recognized to be a classic of sociological thought. Although Polanyi was influenced by the major figures of nineteenth- and early twentieth-century sociology, his work cannot easily be classified within one or another of the major social science traditions. There are echoes throughout *The Great Transformation* of Marx, Weber, Durkheim, and other classical thinkers, but Polanyi was not a direct disciple of any of these theorists. In fact, in anthropology, where Polanyi's influence has been greatest, the uniqueness of his contribution is suggested by the recognition of a distinctly Polanyian paradigm in economic anthropology that stands in conflict with both Marxist and substantivist traditions.[2]

Significantly, such a paradigm or tradition cannot be located in the other disciplines that were central to Polanyi's work – history, economics, and sociology. While his ideas have influenced subgroups within each of these disciplines, there has been no recognizable attempt to carry out a Polanyian research program in any of them, and for a long period there was almost no secondary literature on Polanyi. In recent years, however, there are distinct signs of a Polanyi revival in these disciplines; his work is cited more frequently and the quantity of secondary literature is expanding.[3] The reasons for this revival of interest in Polanyi are not difficult to discern: *The Great Transformation* and Polanyi's central theoretical concerns resonate with contemporary intellectual sensibilities in several unique ways.

Above all, *The Great Transformation* tells of the conflict between the imperatives of a capitalist world economy and the pursuit of social welfare within nation-states. Polanyi's account of the 1920s and 1930s analyzes the incompatibility of international capitalist arrangements with both democracy and the social reforms that had been won by the European working classes. This argument speaks directly to the concerns of the present period, in which the conflict between "legitimation and accumulation," "the limits of legitimacy," and the "crisis of democracy" have become central themes of social sciences;[4] once again there appears to be a contradiction between the imperatives of the capitalist world system and the achievements of democratic politics within nation-states.

Moreover, in this current period, there has been a great revival of the theory of the free market. In response to the obvious inadequacies of Keynesian strategies of economic management, some economists and politicians have returned to the nineteenth-century belief in the "magic of the market," arguing that economic problems can be solved through a systematic reduction in the role of government. For those who are skeptical of these arguments, Polanyi is a crucial resource because his work took shape as a critique of earlier efforts to justify noninterference in the market. The figures Polanyi was polemicizing against – Hayek and von Mises – are the intellectual idols of the present generation of free marketeers, and Polanyi's critique of their ideas is perhaps the most devastating ever produced in that it demonstrates the fundamental flaws and contradictions in the idea of self-regulating markets.

Finally, Polanyi's work is appealing to contemporary critical intellectuals who are influenced by the Marxist tradition and concerned with transcending its limits. Polanyi sought to develop a distinctive theoretical and political position – a non-Marxist socialism that was uncompromising in its opposition to capitalist institutions and in its demand for individual freedom. While in his lifetime his position was clearly a lonely one, he anticipated many of the themes that have become central to current debates within Marxist and post-Marxist circles. Most fundamentally, Polanyi recognized that Marxism was critically flawed by the "economistic fallacy" – the attribution to the economy of a privileged analytic and historical status relative to all other spheres of human behavior.

In this chapter, we will elaborate on these aspects of Polanyi's contemporary relevance. However, our central concern is to demonstrate that Polanyi's work is also of critical importance to methods of comparative and historical analysis. The two issues are closely linked – the fact that Polanyi's work is attuned to contemporary concerns makes it urgent that we learn how he sought historical answers to the questions he posed. Before proceeding to this task, it is necessary to establish the context in which Polanyi worked and to lay out the basic arguments of *The Great Transformation*.

Polanyi's Life

There exists no full biography of Karl Polanyi, but such a project would certainly be worthy of the efforts of the most skillful intellectual historian. Polanyi's life spans five countries, he wrote in three languages, and he was actively engaged in political events from the reform politics of pre–World War I Hungary to the North American peace movement of the 1960s. Together with his wife, Ilona Duczynska, his personal networks extended from the major figures of the classical period of European communism to dissident Hungarian intellectuals active in the 1950s and 1960s. In short, to sort out the people and events that Polanyi influenced, or was influenced by, would require a broad canvas that encompassed many of the central events and ideas of the twentieth century.

For our purposes, a brief glimpse at Polanyi's life will have to suffice.[5] He was born in Hungary in 1886 to a remarkable family. His brother, Michael Polanyi, is internationally known, first as a scientist and then as a philosopher. Their father was a Hungarian Jew who had converted to Christianity and had become wealthy as a builder of railroads, only to lose his fortune at the turn of the century. Polanyi's Russian mother, a strong intellectual, hosted a salon that became an intellectual center in prewar Budapest. As a student, Karl was an active member of the Galileo Circle, a group of intellectuals committed to the liberating potential of social science and planning in vigorous opposition to "clericalism, corruption, against the privileged, against bureaucracy – against the morass that is ever-present and pervasive in this semi-feudal country."[6]

Polanyi's ideas can be traced to the formative period of Hungarian history from 1908 to 1918, in which a generation of middle-class intellectuals was radicalized by the stagnation of the Austro-Hungarian Empire and ultimately by the barbarity of World War I. Polanyi was typical of this generation in that he was not drawn toward the Socialist Party, despite an intense sympathy for the working class that led him and other members of the Galileo Circle to participate in worker education projects. The Socialists were unattractive because their adherence to the deterministic Marxism of the Second International made them

Fred Block, Margaret Somers

relatively cautious and conservative. Moreover, the Socialists were unwilling to espouse the cause of the Hungarian peasantry; despite the size of the rural population, they dismissed the problems of the peasantry with phrases about the idiocy of rural life.

In particular, Polanyi passionately rejected the Second International's belief in the inevitability of progress as a consequence of predetermined stages of historical development. Central to him and others of his generation was the idea that progress could only come through conscious human action based on moral principles. The contrast between his view and that of the Socialists is encapsulated in Polanyi's memorial address for the poet Endre Ady, who was a personal symbol of the younger generation's hopes for a renewal of the Hungarian nation: "The truth is 'that the bird soars despite rather than because of the law of gravity' and 'that society soars to stages embodying ever loftier ideals despite rather than because of material interests.' "[7]

Only months after these words were spoken the hopes for Hungarian renewal were dashed. With the end of World War I, power passed from the Empire to the Karolyi regime, a coalition government dominated by the Socialists. Polanyi was associated with the Radical Party of Oscar Jaszi, which was a part of the coalition, but his and other reformist hopes came to nothing as external pressures and internal disagreements blocked effective action. Dissatisfaction with political stalemate led many to turn to the newly formed Hungarian Communist Party, which recruited many radicalized middle-class intellectuals. The pressure from the left led the bulk of the Socialists to join with the Communists in creating the Hungarian Soviet Republic under the leadership of Béla Kun. But the Béla Kun regime, in the absence of support from the Soviet Union, collapsed under both internal and external pressures, and the right seized power.

While Polanyi was initially sympathetic to Hungarian bolshevism, his abrupt departure for Vienna while Béla Kun was still in power suggests that he anticipated imminent disaster. He would not return to Hungary except for a visit toward the end of his life. In Vienna, he worked as a journalist for *Oesterreschische Volkswirt*, a position that allowed him to study closely the turbulent political and economic events of the 1920s. In Vienna he met his wife, Ilona Duczynska, who had been an active participant in the Béla Kun regime and had been forced to flee from the White Terror that followed the revolutionary regime's collapse.

As the political situation in Vienna turned to the right in the early 1930s, Polanyi emigrated to England, where he eventually found a job in worker education. In England he became associated with a group of Christian Socialists and Quakers and collaborated with them on a book, *Christianity and the Social Revolution*. His own essay in that book, "The Essence of Fascism," prefigured some of the arguments in *The Great Transformation* in pointing to the reduction of human beings to mere products within the structure of the corporatist Fascist state. In 1940, caught in the United States during the blitzkrieg, Polanyi was able to get a teaching job at Bennington, where he crystallized his thoughts and wrote *The Great Transformation*. After the war, Polanyi was invited to Columbia to teach economic history, a position that he retained until 1953, when he retired to Canada, where Ilona had settled because McCarthyism had prohibited her from living in the United States.

During the Columbia years and in Canada, Polanyi's research shifted from the history of capitalist society to the analysis of archaic and primitive economies. A collaborative research project at Columbia led to the publication of *Trade and Markets in the Early Empires* in 1957. With the exception of a number of essays, the rest of Polanyi's work was published after his death in 1964. A research monograph, *Dahomey and the Slave Trade*, was published in 1966, and in 1968 George Dalton collected a number of the published essays, chapters from the three books, and some unpublished material in a volume called *Primitive, Archaic, and Modern Economies*. Finally, in 1974, Harry Pearson published an unfinished manuscript, *The Livelihood of Man*, containing both general material on Polanyi's theory of society and economy and an extensive analysis of ancient Greece.

Polanyi's interest in primitive and archaic economies grew directly out of the analysis of nineteenth-century market society. In *The Great Transformation* he sought to demonstrate that the market had played a subordinate role before the rise of capitalism and argued that previous scholarship, particularly of the ancient world, had erred fundamentally in interpreting the role of markets in those societies by using theoretical categories derived from modern capitalism. Despite his devastating criticism of a market-dominated society, Polanyi was never interested in generating visions of a return to a preindustrial past; his concern was to conceptualize and realize social arrangements that would reconcile technology and human needs, freedom and social order. This commitment was reaffirmed in a little-known collection of writings of Hungarian poets, *The Plough and the Pen*, which he edited with his wife, Ilona, shortly after the Hungarian revolution of 1956. This commitment was reaffirmed as well in his final project, the launching of the socialist journal *Co-Existence*, which absorbed much of his energy in the final years of his life. The page proofs of the first issue arrived the day Polanyi died.

The Great Transformation

While there can be little doubt that Polanyi's work in anthropology and classical studies has had far more influence on subsequent scholarship, *The Great Transformation* remains his major achievement – it is the only book-length manuscript he brought to completion and it develops all of the themes that were pursued in his later work. As befitting a scholar with such an irregular career, Polanyi wrote the summary work, the book that brought together all of the themes of a lifetime, at the beginning of his academic career, not the end. Hence, it is appropriate to focus our analysis on *The Great Transformation*.

Polanyi wrote *The Great Transformation* as a conscious political intervention; his hope was to influence the shape of the post–World War II world. Fascism and the war had brought about the collapse of "civilization as we have known it," but this catastrophe had occurred behind the backs – without the comprehension – of the historical actors. Without an understanding of what had happened, there was little reason to believe that barbarism and war could be avoided in the future. While it was on the continent that the weaknesses of the market caused the most tragic damage, Polanyi was persuaded that the long-run factors that had caused the wreck of civilization must be analyzed in the birthplace of the Industrial Revolution – England.[8] Polanyi sought to point the way toward a more humane and rational structure for the postwar world by illuminating the origins of fascism and World War II in the rise of the self-regulating market. This developmental project structured his entire approach.

Polanyi's passionate hatred of market society and his hope for a socialist alternative provides the driving force of the analysis of *The Great Transformation*. But he was not willing simply to extend and elaborate the arguments that were dominant in the socialist tradition, either on the Communist left or the Social Democratic right. His differences with both of these traditions were profound, and he sought instead to rebuild the socialist analysis of capitalism from its very foundations. This led him to reanalyze precapitalist societies and to reappropriate such pre-Marxist theorists as Aristotle, Hegel, and Robert Owen. The audacity and originality of Polanyi's effort to reconstruct the socialist critique of capitalism gives his work its lasting power.

The distinctiveness of Polanyi's approach is most clearly indicated in the final pages of *The Great Transformation,* in which he poses

> three constitutive facts in the consciousness of Western man: knowledge of death, knowledge of freedom, knowledge of society. The first, according to Jewish legend, was revealed in the Old Testament story. The second was revealed through the discovery of the uniqueness of the person in the teachings of Jesus as recorded in the New Testament. The third revelation came to us through living in an industrial society.[9]

In each case, understanding and acceptance of knowledge is the basis for human freedom. In particular, "Uncomplaining acceptance of the reality of society gives man indomitable courage and strength to remove all removable injustice and unfreedom."[10] In short, Polanyi sought a third way between the utopianism of those who imagined that issues of political power and social conflict would automatically disappear as a result of a revolutionary transformation and the resignation of those who believed that it was futile to take radical action to create a better society.

The Great Transformation is the account of the rise and fall of market society. There are two critical transformations: the emergence of market society out of mercantilism and the collapse of market society into fascism and world war. Polanyi's political purpose led him to develop his analysis of the second transformation more fully than the first, but there are lacunae in both analyses. Nevertheless, the two parts of the argument command attention both for Polanyi's critiques of competing interpretations and for his understanding of large-scale historical change.

Polanyi begins by insisting that England's transition from a commercialized mercantilist society to market society was neither inevitable nor the result of an evolutionary process. He challenges the prevailing wisdom that saw the emergence of nineteenth-century capitalism as the result of the steady expansion of market activity from the Middle Ages onward. Instead, Polanyi points out that while markets were numerous and important from the sixteenth century on, there was no sign of the coming of control by markets over society. On the contrary, regulation of these markets by the state limited their impact. Both long-distance and local trade within mercantilism were regulated either by the state or by town burghers, who strongly opposed the creation of national markets.[11]

In opposition to the familiar evolutionary view, Polanyi argues that the emergence of national markets did not result from the gradual extension of local or long-distance trading, but from deliberate mercan-

Fred Block, Margaret Somers

tilist state policy.[12] The creation of national markets was the by-product of state building strategies that saw economic development as a foundation for state strength. But even the creation of national markets fell short of the full development of market society, since that required still another disjuncture – the commodification of land, money, and labor. Polanyi analyzes the commodification of labor in his discussion of England's Speenhamland Act.[13]

In the last quarter of the eighteenth century, rural England was suddenly beset by a disturbing and acute increase in pauperism. Fear of pauper rebelliousness was intense among the landed classes, but it coexisted with a concern for the potential depopulation of the countryside as higher wages in the emerging rural-industrial villages attracted the pauperized country people. Although it was not understood at the time, pauperism was a product of a marked increase in both the extent and volatility of England's world trade. The volatility was most intensely experienced in the countryside as rural unemployment was set side by side with severe dislocations of both village and town occupations, and, when the economic downturns reduced commercial and manufacturing employment, the laboring poor were left only to drift back to their country parishes for survival. The eradication of the family plot had done away with any vestiges of unemployment insurance for the unemployed, so that even those employed in rural industry had no means of security other than the fate of the pauper. For Polanyi, pauperism was only the overt sign of the dislocations soon to explode with the onset of the Industrial Revolution and the market economy. Yet the outcome was not inevitable; expanding trade and markets would not autonomously make a qualitative leap into a market society. Only conscious political intervention could bring about this historically unique event. This analytic perspective underlies Polanyi's focus on Speenhamland.

In 1795, the Act of Settlement of 1662 was partially repealed to release labor from the need to find employment only in the home parish. Under the pressure of the needs of industry, "parish serfdom" was abolished and the physical mobility of the laborer was restored, enabling the establishment of a labor market on a national scale for the first time in history. In the very same year, however, a new practice of Poor Relief was introduced, known as the Speenhamland Act. It was an institution reflecting the principle of the "right to live" through the establishment of a system of grants-in-aid of wages based on the going price of bread; family allowances were appended to this and it was to be given as outdoor relief, rather than through commitment to the

54

workhouse. The intent was to generate employment in the Speenhamland countryside and simultaneously prevent itinerant pauperism, as
relief was limited to the local parish.[14] It was an act *in response* to the
structural problems of pauperism and to the first political act of intervention, the repeal of the Settlement Law, which threatened to unleash
the blockages to a free labor market.

Speenhamland was a success in maintaining the local political power
of the landed classes and in retarding the inauguration of full-fledged
capitalism through the blocking of the release of labor. But for the lives
of the poor and the multitudes of rural tenant rate payers, the consequences were devastating. Wages crashed beneath subsistence because
employers had no incentives to pay decent levels when the parish was
obligated to keep their workers alive at bare subsistence. While squires
took on the role of the benevolent almsgivers in their positions as
political rulers, they benefited from virtual gang labor while the taxes
to support labor came only from the pockets of the occupying propri-
etors or the rural middle class.

Speenhamland, a system supposedly organized to support the poor,
was in fact benefiting the employers by using public funds to subsidize
their labor costs. In some areas only those who were on the rates had a
chance of employment and those who tried to keep off the rates and
earn a living on their own were hard pressed to find a job. The consequence was a vast demoralization of the poor as the able-bodied laboring poor became indistinguishable from paupers – all being forced onto
the rates. Incentives to work were undermined and the dignity of the
English worker was stripped away by this method of welfare, which
crystallized in one system the mutual incompatibility and unworkabil-
ity of the protectionist "right to live" with the wage system of the labor
market – two contradictory impulses that prefigured the entire development of the nineteenth century.[15]

This incompatible duality must be stressed in Polanyi's discussion of
Speenhamland. It is not protection per se that he criticizes, but the
configuration of this particular institution. Not only was aid-in-wages a
particularly insidious mechanism in its depressant effects on wages,
equally serious was the passage in 1799 and 1801 of the anti-Combina-
tion Laws, preventing workers from gaining their status as workers able
to collectively resist and bargain for power within the system through
the mechanism of true unionism. While the protectionist principle attempted to protect workers from the dangers of the market, the wage
system compelled them to gain a living by selling their labor, without
the possibility of labor finding its own value due to aid-in-wages. Thus a

new class of employers had been created with no corresponding class of employees that could constitute itself as a class; the laws against trade unions were the final structural obstacle to workers' capacity to force up wages for the employed.

Speenhamland was repealed in 1834, according to Polanyi as a result of the political victory in 1832 of the new industrial middle class armed not only with new legislative power but also with "scientific" laws of Malthusian population theory.[16] The Poor Law Reform eliminated outdoor relief to the unemployed and forced those displaced in the countryside into the hated workhouse as the only alternative to the despised factories. This was the full institutionalization of labor as a commodity in that workers now had only themselves to sell in order to survive. The right to live outside the wage system no longer existed as the "social net" disappeared in favor of allowing the market, not the state, to allow wages to find their proper level; industrial capital was now in its true inaugural moment.

Polanyi was no romantic; he was not contrasting the virtue of Speenhamland to the vice of market capitalism that was to ensue. Indeed, his assessment of Speenhamland's impact on social life is unequivocally negative, despite the subsequent catastrophic impact of its repeal, the resulting forced urban migration, and the unprecedented "scientific cruelty" of the New Poor Law. A plague on both houses, he charges: "If Speenhamland meant the rot of immobility, now the peril was that of death through exposure."[17]

Polanyi places great emphasis on the Speenhamland interlude for several reasons. First, Speenhamland illustrates the nonevolutionary and discontinuous nature of market development. The rise of the labor market did not occur automatically – it had to be institutionalized by the political intervention of the Poor Law Reform. This emphasis on the role of the state in the unleashing of market forces is essential to Polanyi's argument about the historical novelty of the nineteenth-century market economy and its concomitant ideological distortions. The road to the free market was paved with continuous political manipulation, whether the state was actively involved in removing old restrictive regulations, as in the case of Speenhamland, or building new political administrative bodies to bolster the factors of production of the new market economy, as in the administrative mechanisms of the New Poor Law. The political mechanizations surrounding the Speenhamland interlude – its institutionalization, its dynamics, and its final repeal – all serve to demonstrate the degree to which the "natural" self-regulating market was politically constructed in its origins.

Second, Polanyi argues that the experience of and the debates around Speenhamland established the fundamental assumptions of liberal ideology. The reform of the Poor Law occurred when "economic liberalism burst forth as a crusading passion, and *laissez-faire* became a militant creed."[18] Polanyi's goal was to show that the fundamental assumptions that continued to shape economic thought in the 1930s and 1940s dated from that century-old passion. Once this was done, he could demonstrate that those assumptions had been fundamentally mistaken from the start. For this reason he had to return to Speenhamland and the birth of the "liberal creed." There was nothing more central for Polanyi than these three points: that the ideology of economic liberalism was pervasive, that it was fundamentally mistaken, and that it had become "one of the main obstacles to the solution of the problems of our civilization."[19]

To make this point persuasively, he also used Speenhamland to argue that the effort to create a free market for labor was doomed to failure because of the contradiction between arrangements that sought to protect human labor and the wage system that made no adjustment for social needs. For Polanyi, market society is impossible without the full commodification of labor that the Poor Law Reform created. Hence, the commodification of labor is the paradigm of market society; the attempt to transform human beings into commodities is the core, and the core weakness, of market society. It is the core weakness because no sooner was market society institutionalized than a powerful counter-movement began – the effort to protect society from the market. Precisely because the commodification of labor represents such a fundamental threat to the fabric of human society, it set in motion an irresistible counter-pressure for the protection of society. In contrast to the calculated efforts of industrialists and state builders to create a market society, Polanyi argues that the counter-movement was spontaneous, unplanned, and came from all sectors of society in response to the devastating impact of the market.[20] Through comparative historical analysis, he shows that despite the radically different ideological configuration of governments, all European countries, including England, passed through a period of free trade and laissez-faire followed immediately by a period of interventionist legislation concerning public health, factory conditions, social insurance, trade associations, public utilities, and so on, reflecting the essential contradictions of industrial development within a free-market system. Polanyi describes the opposing principles of market society and the protectionist counter-movement in the following terms:

The one was the principle of economic liberalism, aiming at the establishment of a self-regulating market, relying on the support of the trading classes, and using largely *laissez-faire* and free trade as its methods; the other was the principle of social protection aiming at the conservation of man and nature as well as productive organization, relying on the varying support of those most immediately affected by the deleterious action of the market – primarily, but not exclusively, the working and the landed classes – and using protective legislation, restrictive associations, and other instruments of intervention as its methods.[21]

The successive victories of this counter-movement impaired the effectiveness of a self-regulating market, or the unimpeded supremacy of the market over people, resulting in even deeper economic disorders and even stronger movements for protection. Behind the backs of all concerned, these processes gradually undermined the basis of nineteenth-century stability, leading to World War I and the seemingly sudden collapse of civilization. The 1920s and 1930s were a new period of stalemate, similar to the institutional contradictions of Speenhamland, during which a new order struggled to be born.

While he does not mention it directly, Polanyi's argument draws heavily on Keynes's critique of classical economics. Within that classical economic tradition – the theory of the self-regulating market – there is no problem of maintaining demand because shifts in factor prices, including the price of labor, will restore equilibrium and high levels of investment. But as Keynes insisted,[22] working class organization significantly diminished the flexibility of wages, so that the equilibrating mechanism no longer worked. Without that mechanism, investments were likely to be withheld and the problem of inadequate demand became chronic. In sum, the progressive strengthening of the working class from the 1830s to the 1920s served to diminish the curative powers of capitalism's periodic economic crises, leading to progressively more serious economic downturns, culminating in the Great Depression of the 1930s. Polanyi criticizes those who deny that social legislation and trade unions have interfered with the mobility of labor and the flexibility of wages, insisting that such a position implies "that those institutions have entirely failed in their purpose, which was exactly that of interfering with the laws of supply and demand in respect to human labor, and removing it from the orbit of the market."[23]

Polanyi's discussions of the protection of land and money are parallel to his discussion of labor. Drawing on the historical experience of Germany, he argues that the major mechanisms for protecting the land were agricultural tariffs that aided the peasantry by slowing competitive food imports. This, too, hampered the equilibrating mechanisms of the self-regulating market, while also enhancing the political position of those traditional social groups – the old landed classes, the church, and the army – that supported agricultural protection. Precisely because the protection of the land was a general social interest, these groups were given a mission that allowed them to preserve their influence, enabling them later to be available to provide reactionary solutions when the collapse of liberal society occurred.

Whereas the protection of labor and the land were associated primarily with anticapitalist social groups, the movement for the protection of money was a concern of all social groups and classes. Monetary protection took the form of the growing importance of national central banking as a mechanism to protect nations from the vagaries of the world market. The gold standard was the lynchpin of the self-regulating market because it ensured equilibrium in international payments. When a nation was spending more than it was earning, gold would flow out and the money supply and the level of economic activity would diminish, which in turn would lead through price and demand effects to higher exports and lower imports, and a restoration of balance.

The problem was that as the nineteenth century wore on, there was a decline in the willingness of all groups in society to accept the periodic economic downturns and resulting crises of the credit system that were imposed by this mechanism. Workers agitated against unemployment, capitalists against a fragile banking system, and farmers against falling prices. The result was a series of gradual measures to insulate the national economy from the world market. The growing resort to trade protectionism from the 1870s on also falls into this category, but Polanyi's emphasis is on those measures that tended to decrease the impact of gold movements on the domestic supply of money. The growth and elaboration of central banking created a variety of means by which the impact of international forces was lessened, and Polanyi insisted: "Central banking reduced the automatism of the gold standard to a mere pretense. It meant a centrally managed currency; manipulation was substituted for the self-regulating mechanism of supplying credit, even though the device was not always deliberate and conscious."[24]

This protection of money had two important consequences. First, reducing the automatism of the gold standard reduced the gold standard's capacity to operate as an equilibrating mechanism. Another key link in the theory and practice of market self-regulation was impaired, so the fragility of the market system increased. Second, the creation of central banking tended to solidify the nation as a cohesive unit whose economic interests were in conflict with those of other nations. The effort to protect the national market from the world market led directly to efforts to manipulate that market in one nation's favor. "The import tariffs of one country hampered the exports of another and forced it to seek for markets in politically unprotected regions."[25] The result was economic imperialism as the European nations rushed, in the last part of the nineteenth century, to secure control over Africa and Asia as a means of exporting domestic economic strains. The more serious the economic pressures on each nation, the more intense the interimperialist rivalries. Hence, in Polanyi's view, imperialism is the international protectionist institution par excellence, in both its attempt to combat market strains and in its destructive impact.

World War I was the result of these intensifying international conflicts. Throughout the second half of the nineteenth century, high finance – the international banking community – had served successfully as a peace interest. Whenever the European powers moved close to a general war, the bankers mobilized to mediate the conflict, since such a war would endanger their position and profits. However, as the interimperialist conflicts grew more intense, the effectiveness of this peace interest diminished. Furthermore, the freezing of Europe into two hostile alliances meant that it was no longer possible to avoid war through a system of shifting alliances. Polanyi suggests that the actual timing of World War I was contingent on a variety of factors, but its ultimate occurrence was inevitable as an expression of the contradictions of nineteenth-century civilization.

Because the war was not understood as the final crisis of the self-regulating market, every effort was made to reestablish the key institutions of nineteenth-century civilization in the post–World War I world. In particular, a doomed effort was made to restore the gold standard despite the reality that the war had swept away its main bulwark– Britain's international hegemony. Polanyi notes, however, that this restoration was not simply the work of the political right, but that leftists from the Bolsheviks to the Social Democrats were also unable to imagine a world without the gold standard.

This restoration in a context where the gold standard could not possibly work resulted in a fundamental conflict between parliamentary democracy and capitalism. The working class through electoral politics sought to further protect itself from the market through the passage of various forms of social legislation. But this social spending came into conflict with the needs of each capitalist economy to maintain its international competitiveness and its capacity to respond to international market pressures. The result was a period of intense stalemate. The working class lacked the strength and perhaps the imagination to push for a genuine alternative to capitalism; all it could do was weaken capitalism by pressing for an extension of protection. The capitalists were unable to effectively resist these pressures within parliamentary rule, but this meant that they were also unable to make capitalism work.

This period of paralysis gave way to the stock market crash and the world depression. In the midst of the depression, Fascist movements provided a real although barbaric solution to the contradictions of market society. The solution "can be described as a reform of market economy achieved at the price of the extirpation of all democratic institutions, both in the industrial and in the political realm."[26] Fascism also broke with the gold standard system by substituting political controls for the market in managing international economic transactions. For Polanyi, the power and dynamism of Fascist movements was not a function of their capacity to recruit supporters but rather a result of their ability to provide a solution to the impasse of liberal capitalism. Writing of Hitler's accession to power, Polanyi argued that "to imagine that it was the strength of the movement which created situations such as these, and not to see that it was the situation that gave birth in this case to the movement, is to miss the outstanding lesson of the last decades."[27] While Polanyi recognizes that fascism took different forms in different societies, he insists that it was ultimately an international movement that was rooted in the structure of the world economy.

Those nations that did not become Fascist responded to the pressures of the 1930s in one of two other ways. Polanyi saw the New Deal as representing another paradigmatic solution to the impasse of market capitalism, one that retained democracy but instituted a number of measures to insulate the national economy from the world market, such as Roosevelt's decision to abandon the gold standard. While Polanyi is not explicit on this point, his view of the New Deal rests on the assumption that the reform measures of the 1930s represented the beginning of a transition to social arrangements under which the market would again be subordinated to social relations. In short, rather than seeing the New Deal leading to a reinvigorated liberal capitalism, he views it as the beginning of a transition to socialism.[28] The other paradigmatic response to the crisis of the 1930s was that of the Soviet Union, which Polanyi insists only actually became socialist with Stalin's decision to build "socialism in one country" – a decision that Polanyi links to the crisis of the world economy.

For Polanyi, it was self-evident that these diverse responses to the crisis of market society could not coexist for long without war. Hence, World War II was a direct outcome of the breakdown of market society. Unless this lesson was fully understood, Polanyi believed that the post–World War II period would be as disastrous as the interwar period.

Polanyi's Underlying Concepts

To fully understand Polanyi's contribution, it is necessary to go beyond this brief summary of the major arguments of *The Great Transformation* to grasp the conceptual framework upon which Polanyi constructs his specific historical analyses. The foundation on which all his concepts rests is the idea of totality, a social whole that provides the necessary context for grasping particular social dynamics. Polanyi's emphasis on totality parallels Lukács, but in contrast to Lukács's penchant for abstraction, Polanyi attempts to give the concept a concrete meaning.[29] As with Marc Bloch's notion of "totalizing history,"[30] Polanyi seeks to demonstrate the structural relationship among all parts of the social whole, while rejecting the genetic determinacy of any one aspect. In this orientation, Polanyi saw himself continuing the tradition of Aristotle: "In terms, then, of our modern speech Aristotle's approach to human affairs was sociological. In mapping out a field of study he would relate all questions of institutional origins and function to the totality of society.[31] Polanyi's intellectual commitment to holism is evident in his specific views of the relationship between the social and the economic, the nature of market society, the role of social classes, and the position of the state in society.

Polanyi's entire critique of market society rests on his belief in the dominance of the social. He considers the procedure of analyzing people's interests in terms of a distinction between material and ideal concerns to be fundamentally misguided. For Polanyi, all human behavior is socially shaped and defined; whether a person is trying to make money or achieve inner peace, the source of the action is in a set of socially created definitions that make one or the other goal appear rational or desirable. The proper distinction is not between different types of interests, but among different social arrangements that generate different belief systems and different structural possibilities. In striking contrast to those theorists who begin from the individual actor in developing theories of "economic man" or "rational man," Polanyi's starting point is society, and for him any analysis of individuals in isolation from society is merely fanciful.

This focus on social arrangements and the way in which they generate different types of human behavior leads directly to Polanyi's critique of what he saw as the economic determinism of both liberalism and orthodox Marxism. For Polanyi, nineteenth-century society was unique in the way that economic imperatives had become dominant in shaping human life. In earlier societies, the economy – the arrangement for ensuring humanity's livelihood – was embedded in social relation, subordinated to religion, politics, and other social arrangements.[32] In opposition to Adam Smith, Polanyi stressed that the orientation toward individual *economic* gains played only a minor role in these earlier societies. Only in the nineteenth-century self-regulating market did economic self-interest become the dominant principle of social life, and both liberalism and Marxism made the ahistorical error of assuming that what was dominant in that society had been dominant throughout human history.

Polanyi called this mistake "the economistic fallacy," a distortion in thought that paralleled the distortion of a society in which the market had become dominant. His attack on this fallacy led him to his extensive study of nonmarket societies to substantiate his argument for the historical specificity of market society. Even to embark on such a project, however, Polanyi was forced to make a critical distinction between two different meanings of the word *economic*. The formal definition refers solely to the process of economizing scarce means to make the most efficient use of what is available for particular ends. The substantive definition is "an instituted process of interaction between man and his environment" through which material needs are met. The point is that as long as analysts use the first definition, they will find in precapitalist societies the same basic dynamics that exist in capitalist societies. Only with the second definition is it possible to escape the tendency to project what presently exists back into the past. The substantive definition of the economy necessarily serves to place the economic back in the context of the social whole:

> The human economy then is embedded and enmeshed in institutions, economic and non-economic. The inclusion of the non-economic is vital. For religion and government may be as important for the structure and functioning of the economy as monetary institutions or the availability of tools and machines themselves that lighten the toil of labour.[33]

As for the "natural economic" motivations ascribed to people by liberalism, Polanyi decries hunger and gain as no more economic than love or hate:

> Single out whatever motive you please, and organize production in such a manner as to make that motive that individual's incentive to produce, and you will have induced a picture of man as altogether absorbed by that particular motive. Let that motive be religious, political or aesthetic; let it be pride, prejudice, love, or envy, and man will appear as essentially religious, political, aesthetic, proud, prejudiced in love or envy. Other motives, in contrast, will appear distant and shadowy since they cannot be relied upon to operate in the vital business of production. The particular motive selected will represent "real" man.

> As a matter of fact, human beings will labor for a large variety of reasons as long as things are arranged accordingly.[34]

Only in a market society could this economistic view of people prevail precisely because it had established a set of institutional mechanisms of production that made human survival depend on economic drives. If so-called economic motives were natural to people, Polanyi suggests, we would have to judge all early and primitive society as thoroughly unnatural.

Polanyi's belief in the dominance of the social also led him to the conclusion that a society that elevated economic motivation to absolute priority could not survive. For this reason, he insists that the nineteenth-century self-regulating market was a utopian experiment that was destined to fail. This is one of Polanyi's most important insights, and it provides the basis for his argument concerning the protectionist counter-movement. Pure human greed, left to its own devices, would place no limit on competition, Polanyi argues, and the result would be a destruction of both society and environment. Workers would be exploited beyond the point where they could even reproduce themselves, food would be systematically adulterated to expand profit margins, and the environment would be devastated by pollution and the unrestricted use of resources. Moreover, even before these catastrophes, a society in which each individual pursued only his or her economic self-interest would be unable to maintain the shared meanings and understanding that are necessary for human group life. As with Durkheim's emphasis on the noncontractual basis of contract, Polanyi saw that market transactions depended on collective goods such as trust and regulation that could not possibly be provided by market processes.

For this reason the protectionist counter-movement was irresistible; it was the response of the endangered human species to the threatened destruction of society caused by the unregulated market. Yet once protectionist measures began, it was only a matter of time before the equilibrating mechanisms that ideally operated in a purely self-regulating system would be fatally impaired. In sum, the utopianism of economic liberalism sought to suspend the dominance of the social, but this dominance was reasserted in the protectionist counter-movement.

The second concept that is shaped by Polanyi's holism is the notion of market society itself. For Polanyi, the distinction between the existence of markets in society and the existence of a market society is fundamental. The followers of the economistic fallacy consistently jump from the fact that markets existed in a particular society to the conclusion that the laws of supply and demand operated as they do in contemporary capitalism. But Polanyi devoted much effort to showing that markets could operate on very different principles. In many pre-capitalist societies prices were administratively set, so that supply and demand played a marginal role at best. Moreover, even when price-making markets existed, as during mercantilism, the systematic regulation of those markets meant that markets played a subordinate role in social life. Hence, market society was created only in the nineteenth century when these restrictions were eliminated and land, labor, and money were commodified. The issue is not the existence of markets, but the way in which markets are inserted into the social whole. The category of market society is used only to describe that social whole in which the market principle extends to and organizes land, labor, and money and structures society around the principle that these are true, not fictitious, commodities.

The concept of market society also has a spatial dimension for Polanyi; analysis of particular societies has to take place within the broadest relevant context – the capitalist world economy. Polanyi was among the first to recognize that the international context was of critical importance for understanding developments within particular nations. But Polanyi understands the international dimension as more than simply a world market in which nations compete. He recognizes that on the international level, just as on the national level, market society requires an institutional order to function. In other words, unstructured international economic competition would lead simply to a continuing state of war. For this reason, analysis of world capitalism requires a focus on the international economic regime that sets the rules within which economic competition takes place. The gold standard system that plays a central role in the unfolding of his story was such an international regime.

The third important aspect of Polanyi's holism is his unique view of the role of social classes in history. Polanyi repeatedly uses the standard Marxist class categories such as bourgeoisie and working class, but he does not accept the Marxist practice of treating these classes – in themselves – as the subjects of history. Neither does he, after the fashion of the Althusserians, see classes as mere "bearers" of social structure. Instead, social classes are provided with opportunities by the development of society as a whole, and their capacity to respond to these opportunities depends on their ability to propose solutions to problems that are in the interests of society as a whole. Polanyi organizes his argument not around the story of classes themselves, but around the three social substances – land, labor, and money – addressed by classes as part of the protectionist movement.

Since Polanyi rejects the view that individuals are motivated solely by self-interest, he considers no mistake to be greater than to define classes as aggregates of economic interests. On the contrary, classes are social constructions; they represent collective responses to changes in the organization of society. In particular, Polanyi insists that reducing the working class to its economic situation and interest distorts the entire history of its political development.

Polanyi's critique of the economism of class analysis originates from his argument that cultural disaster is more significant than economic exploitation. Addressing the liberal defenders of the Industrial Revolution who use economic statistics indicating improvement in the standard of living to dispel charges of exploitation, Polanyi characterizes their position: "How could there be social catastrophe where there was undoubtedly economic improvement?"[35] Here, setting the stage for an entire generation of social historians yet to come – E. P. Thompson being the most important – [36] Polanyi uses anthropological evidence to demonstrate that social calamities are primarily cultural, not economic, phenomena, and as such cannot be measured by income figures or population statistics. He argues that cultural catastrophes involving broad strata of common people are infrequent occurrences and that the cataclysm of the Industrial Revolution was an exceptional landslide in the history of classes, one that within less than half a century transformed vast masses of the inhabitants of the English countryside from settled folk into unprotected market commodities. If the infrequency of so dramatic an event makes it difficult to grasp, Polanyi makes it easier by drawing an analogy between the imposition of market society and the impact of colonialism on peoples of the Third World. He argues that, in both situations, "not economic exploitation, as often assumed, but the disintegration of the cultural environment of the victim is then the cause of the degradation."[37]

For this reason, Polanyi sees classes as cultural, not economic, institutions, constituted primarily to redress the cultural devastation created by market society. Polanyi viewed the goals for which individuals will strive as culturally determined over and above crude economic necessity, and the entire counter-movement for protection is primarily a cultural and social phenomenon, and only secondly an economic one. For this reason, it represented not just a different class interest from that of the market, but a fundamentally different *principle* from the economic one. In this struggle, for greater protection from the market, the working class found unlikely allies and was effective precisely because it was able to represent the general needs of society against the market. This lengthy quotation conveys Polanyi's views on this issue:

> Once we are rid of the obsession that only sectional, never general, interest can become effective, as well as of the twin prejudice of restricting the interests of human groups to their monetary income, the breadth and comprehensiveness of the protectionist movement lose their mystery. While monetary interests are necessarily voiced solely by the persons to whom they pertain, other interests have a wider constituency. They affect individuals in innumerable ways as neighbors, professional persons, consumers, pedestrians, commuters, sportsmen, hikers, gardeners, patients, mothers, or lovers – and are accordingly capable of representation by almost any type of territorial or functional association such as churches, townships, fraternal lodges, clubs, trade unions, or most commonly, political parties based on broad principles of adherence. An all too narrow conception of interests must in effect lead to a warped vision of social and political history, and no purely monetary definition of interests can leave room for that vital need for social protection, the representation of which commonly falls to the persons in charge of the general interests of the community – under modern conditions, the government of the day. Precisely because not the economic but the social interests of different cross sections of the population were threatened by the market, persons belonging to various economic strata unconsciously joined forces to meet the danger.[38]

In sum, classes play a key historical role, but it is not a role that can be understood in terms of economic self-interest.[39]

Finally, Polanyi's theory of the state also reflects his commitment to holism. As one would expect from his view of social classes, he rejects the Marxist tendency to explain state policies in terms of economic interests. Instead, he inclines toward a Hegelian view of a "universal" state that acts to preserve society by transcending conflictual, particular interests in favor of general ones. However, there is more to Polanyi's view than this; he argues that the very success of the protectionist counter-movement led directly to disaster. In other words, state action was not able to produce the functional outcome that one expects from such a Hegelian conception of the state.

The added complexity to Polanyi's view rests on the insight that the self-regulating market created a peculiar situation in which development was caught in the contradictory conflict of two sets of "general" interests. On the one hand, the working class, landed classes, and others who pushed for social protection were acting on behalf of social organization and natural resources, and the state was responsive to their pressures. On the other hand, that very market they were exposing, as oppressive as it may have been, was now the material foundation of the society; survival of the new civilization – shaped and organized by market principles – depended on the survival of the market. Market interests had also become general interests and the state had little choice but to respond to these interests as well.

Thereby the state acted in the interests of society as a whole when it passed protective legislation, and yet the same was true when it passed promarket laws; it clearly did not "belong" to either of these forces. The state was necessarily both a universal, representing the interests of society against the market, and a class state, pursuing the agendas of the capitalist class, since the reproduction of capitalist relations was necessary to preserve society. The state became, in short, the crystallization of the contradictory impulses of nineteenth-century development.

This formulation of Polanyi's anticipates much current discussion that stresses that the state is pulled in contradictory directions by the imperatives of private accumulation and the imperatives of democratic legitimation.[40] As in Polanyi's view, this argument locates the determinants of state action in terms of the logic of the society as a whole, rather than in terms of some particular interests. However, Polanyi's concept of the protection of society has more analytic power than the notion of legitimation; the latter can easily be understood narrowly in terms of the subjective perceptions of the citizenry. Polanyi's concept conveys more powerfully the precariousness of market social arrangements that constantly impel new kinds of state action to stabilize economy and society.

Polanyi's view of the state rests on an insight that is in fundamental conflict with the liberal tradition. While liberalism emerged historically in opposition to an oppressive state and retained a fundamental suspicion toward politics, Polanyi viewed politics, including the exercise of power, as fundamentally constitutive of human societies and necessary for social order and progress. The distinctiveness of Polanyi's approach is clearest in his treatment of the ancient irrigational empires of Babylonia and Assyria. While the historiography influenced by liberalism assimilated these societies to the category of "tyrannical administrative bureaucracy," Polanyi's view is very different. He argues that these empires prospered through a political decision to sanction gainless transactions regulated by the king and the law. The spread of such transactions "multiplie[d] manyfold the productivity of labor in a flood-controlled agriculture." Polanyi continues:

> The absence, or at least the very subordinate role, of markets did not imply ponderous administrative methods tightly held in the hands of a central bureaucracy. On the contrary, gainless transactions and regulated dispositions, as legitimized by law, opened up, as we have seen, a sphere of personal freedom formerly unknown in the economic life of man.[41]

It is difficult to imagine a view of politics and the state that is further removed from the liberal tradition.

Polanyi's Methodological Contributions

Polanyi's effort to develop a holistic approach to historical analysis represents his most significant contribution to historical and comparative analysis. The formulations that were discussed in the previous section constitute a significant legacy to contemporary scholarship. Yet there are also other methodological principles that can be extracted from Polanyi's writings that bear on the vexed questions of historical and comparative analysis. The discussion that follows will touch on three of these: the centrality of institutional analysis, the role of metaphor, and the management of multiple levels of analysis. In addition, the discussion will touch upon one key weakness in Polanyi's approach: the limitations of his analyses of nonmarket societies.

Since Polanyi's primary task was to develop a method that avoided the assumption that all societies operated on the same economic principles, he chose to focus his analysis at the level of concrete institutions.

He saw this as the best way to avoid the conscious or unconscious introductions of theories of motivation that could lead the analyst to findings that simply confirmed his or her initial biases. For example, many theorists had approached primitive societies with the question of how these people economized given the existence of scarce resources, but for Polanyi this question assumed a motivation that might not be there. Polanyi's contrasting approach would be to ask what are the institutional arrangements by which this particular society ensures its own livelihood.

The focus on concrete institutions has another advantage – it allows Polanyi to distinguish different subtypes of a particular institution. Hence, as mentioned earlier, Polanyi does not jump to conclusions just because markets existed in a particular society; he carefully differentiates among the different kinds of markets, showing how some were price making while others operated within a system of administered prices. Similarly, Polanyi shows that money fulfills different functions in diverse societies.

For one with Polanyi's interest in holism, an exclusive concentration on concrete institutions has its limits. Polanyi needed to develop concepts that would allow him to talk about societies as a whole, but without reintroducing the biases of motivational analysis. For this reason, he developed his classification of the forms of integration of human economies – reciprocity, redistribution, and exchange.[42] Each of these is a mode by which individual social units are linked together to form a social whole. Different forms of integration can coexist within the same society, but generally societies can be characterized by the form of integration that is dominant. Furthermore, Polanyi remarks:

> It would be a mistake rigidly to identify the dominance of exchange with the nineteenth century economy of the West. More than once in the course of human history have markets played a significant part in integrating the economy, although never on a territorial scale, nor with a comprehensiveness even faintly comparable to that of the nineteenth-century West.[43]

Although this schema is on a different level of analysis than concrete economic institutions, its referent is still a concrete institutional issue – how do different societies integrate economic subunits. While there are certain affinities between this approach of Polanyi's and functionalist analysis, in which the question asked is how different societies satisfy certain universal needs,[44] there are also important differences. Polanyi clearly feared that the attempt to produce a catalog of "functional requisites" for human societies would simply reintroduce the biases of motivational analysis. Therefore he limited his list to the two that seemed intuitively necessary – arrangements to ensure the "livelihood of man" and arrangements to ensure some degree of integration of subunits. In both cases, the answers that Polanyi found could be expressed in terms of specific institutional arrangements rather than abstract functions that then had to be correlated with particular institutional arrangements.

Polanyi's comparisons across societies are always focused on the different means by which societies manage similar problems. This allows Polanyi to demonstrate the previously hidden links between seemingly diverse phenomena. Hence, redistribution, reciprocity, and exchange are comparable responses to the problem of integration. Or fascism, the New Deal, and socialism are comparable responses to the problems created for national societies by the collapse of the world market. In a sense, this procedure of Polanyi anticipates such contemporary work as that of Barrington Moore and Alexander Gerschenkron.[45] These theorists proceed to comparison by asking how different societies manage a particular problem, such as how to generate the savings necessary for industrialization. In sum, Polanyi's institutional focus allows him to distinguish arrangements that appear to be the same and to compare those that do not seem to be comparable.

A second important aspect of Polanyi's method is his use of metaphor. The most spectacular aspect of *The Great Transformation* is its effort to explain the rise of fascism in terms of the emergence of industrial capitalism that occurred more than one hundred years earlier. This connection is expressed in terms of a metaphor of organic misdevelopment; the ultimate collapse of market society was the working out of fundamental strains that were inherent in market society from the beginning. The acorn was flawed, and that is why the seemingly mighty oak of nineteenth-century society crashed so dramatically and so suddenly. Moreover, when Polanyi expresses this idea in his own language – the collapse occurred because society had to save itself from the market – there is more than a hint of reification. The abstract entity, society, appears to have a life of its own and acts against another abstract entity, the market. Measured against the standards of contemporary scholarship in which the hypostasizing of entities and the resort to theories of organic development or misdevelopment are often seen as cardinal sins, Polanyi's argument appears to be seriously flawed.

Yet such a view misses what is most powerful and useful in Polanyi's argument: the way he moves back and forth between metaphor or metatheory and a series of concrete causal arguments. In analyzing large-scale historical change, the use of metaphors such as those of organic development or misdevelopment is indispensable. The indispensability does not rest on the fact that development is immanent in history, but that the effort to make sense of large-scale historical change requires frameworks that are able to link together a variety of concrete processes. For such frameworks to be intelligible, they must rest on analogies with familiar organic or mechanical processes.[46]

From this standpoint, the effort to rid historical analysis of metaphors is deeply mistaken, but there is an important truth in the debunking of metaphor. Quite simply, the metaphor can only operate as a heuristic; it cannot be used to carry the argument. Specific causal arguments must be invoked to explain each step in the process; the analyst cannot rely on such assertions as that evolution or systems maintenance requires certain outcomes without giving concrete causal explanations of those developments. In short, analysis must operate on two levels. The first is the level of metaphor and hypostasization, providing a summary of the major historical dynamics that are being analyzed. The second is a set of causal arguments based on institutional and class forces, explaining the various processes of institutional transformation.

One measure of a piece of historical analysis is the skill with which the analyst moves between these levels, and in this respect Polanyi is exemplary. The metaphoric structure gives the book its power, but Polanyi does not rest on the metaphor for explanation. As the following passage indicates, Polanyi was acutely aware of the need to fill in the metaphor with a set of concrete historical arguments:

> A civilization was being disrupted by the blind action of soulless institutions the only purpose of which was the automatic increase of material welfare.

> But how did the inevitable actually happen? How was it translated into the political events which are the core of history? Into this final phase of the fall of market economy the conflict of class forces entered decisively.[47]

Polanyi fills out his analysis of the protectionist counter-movement with a discussion of concrete historical actors and of the very specific dynamics that their actions set in motion. He can be faulted, of course, on the accuracy of some of his historical arguments and for an occasional lack of clarity when he fails to emphasize which are the most important processes, but he does not allow the metaphor to substitute for history.

The third dimension of Polanyi's method to be considered is the way in which he manages multiple levels of analysis. Because of his aware-ness of the importance of the world economy, he incorporates that level of analysis, while also considering the actions of states and the conflicts among classes and other social groups within societies. These three levels of analysis have been the subject of much discussion since the publication of Immanuel Wallerstein's *The Modern World-System*.[48] This is not purely coincidental, as Wallerstein acknowledges Polanyi to be one of the major inspirations for his world-system theory. There are many important differences, however, between Polanyi's formulations and those of Wallerstein's, of which two are particularly relevant here.

First, Wallerstein tends to define the global level of analysis primarily in terms of a world market in which nations compete. He pays far less attention than does Polanyi to the institutional arrangements, such as the gold standard system, by which that world market is organized. This omission makes it harder for Wallerstein to integrate international politics into his analysis of the world market, since the strength or weakness of international economic regimes is closely linked to the balance of political and military power among states. Second, as a number of his critics have noted, Wallerstein tends to collapse the three different levels of analysis into one; at times, both class relations and state action are seen as determined by the dynamics of the world system.[49] On the other hand, some of Wallerstein's critics make the opposite error – they tend to collapse both world economy and state action into class relations, which are seen as determining.[50] Polanyi, in contrast, makes a significant effort to grasp the interrelations among the three levels without collapsing any one into another.

Polanyi does this by using an implicit concept of opportunity struc-tures. His historical argument suggests that particular moments in the organization of the international economic regime provide particular kinds of opportunities for states to act, and the degree of freedom or unfreedom open to the state, in turn, shapes what is possible for class struggle. One example is found in his analysis of the 1920s. The resto-ration of the gold standard after World War I created a conjuncture in which there were opportunities for creative response by national gov-ernments. There was little choice but to obey the rules of the game, but this obedience ensured the frustration of working class goals, resulting in political stalemate.

The situation changed dramatically with the coming of the world depression in the 1930s. The failure of the gold standard mechanism created a more open international opportunity structure, which Hitler was quick to use to his advantage. Polanyi writes: "Germany at first reaped the advantages of those who kill that which is doomed to die. Her start lasted as long as the liquidation of the outworn system of the nineteenth century permitted her to keep in the lead."[51] Germany, as well as Japan and Italy, gained advantage from breaking with the nineteenth-century rules of the game before the rest of the world had come to understand their obsolescence. Precisely this opportunity to experiment with economic autarchy and an aggressive foreign policy gave Fascist movements their power. While Polanyi insists that the Fascist impulse was international, it is logical that it should achieve state power in those dissatisfied powers that had the most reason to oppose the existing international rules of the game.[52]

Hence, the three levels of analysis are linked by two different opportunity structures. There is a global opportunity structure that shapes what is possible for particular governments. This set of limits, in turn, creates a national opportunity structure that shapes what social groups or class forces will be most effective in influencing state policy. This implicit framework leaves unresolved the critical question of whether the opportunity structures are completely determining or if it were possible, for example, in a period such as the 1920s for a more imaginative working-class movement to have created new opportunities. Still, this framework suggests a method by which the three levels of analysis can be managed without losing a sense of the analytic autonomy of each level.

In fact, the opportunity structure argument is also helpful in explaining Polanyi's project in writing *The Great Transformation* and in accounting for the failure of that project. *The Great Transformation* was aimed primarily at the British working class that Polanyi had come to know in his years as a worker educator. Polanyi clearly believed that the end of the war would once again create an open international opportunity structure and that Britain could be particularly influential in responding to that new structure. This meant, in turn, that the British working class had the opportunity to push Britain toward democratic socialism and a definitive break with the gold standard. Polanyi correctly perceived that such a move by Britain would have a major impact on the European continent and through much of Africa and Asia.

Polanyi assumed that the United States would continue on its New Deal course, remaining relatively indifferent to the development of the world economy. This was where Polanyi was wrong; U.S. policy makers came out of the war determined to restore an open world economy based on the principles of a self-regulating market. Given U.S. military and economic strength, this fundamentally altered the international opportunity structure and served to block any impulses in Britain toward socialism or new international economic arrangements.[53] Polanyi quickly recognized the changing reality, and in his essay "Our Obsolete Market Mentality," published in 1947, he pleaded for a shift in American policy away from the restoration of a self-regulating world economy.[54]

There is much to Polanyi's method that is still of great use, but it is also important to note one central weakness. Although Polanyi is able to understand important aspects of nonmarket societies by contrasting them with market societies, his concepts have little analytic power for understanding the dynamic processes within nonmarket societies. The contrast is particularly striking because the conflict between self-regulating markets and social protection makes his analysis of capitalism especially attuned to processes of change. One is struck, for example, in reading his study of Dahomey, that he provides little analysis of internal change processes beyond descriptive references to the centralization of political-military power by particular families.

To be sure, his intellectual project lay elsewhere; he was more concerned to show that a society like Dahomey was able to contain and control the destructive impact of international trade than to explain its own internal dynamics. But this theoretical weakness in the face of nonmarket societies also meant that he had little effective grasp on the internal dynamics of societies like the Soviet Union. Once a society decided to resubmerge the market in social relations, Polanyi had little to say other than to insist on the moral and social imperatives of democracy and the retention of individual freedom. In this respect Polanyi shared much in common with the Marxist tradition's analytic weakness in the face of postcapitalist societies.

Polanyi's Relationship to Marxism

In other respects, however, Polanyi diverges sharply from Marxism. He devotes an entire chapter of *The Great Transformation* to an incisive attack on the economic determinism of Marxism, and the book is sprinkled with references to the economistic errors of both liberalism and Marxism. Moreover, Polanyi takes pains at a number of points to develop interpretations that are at odds with dominant Marxist ones, as in his analysis of high finance as a peace interest, in obvious conflict to Lenin's emphasis on the responsibility of finance capital for war.[55] The roots of these criticisms are both political and intellectual. Polanyi's intellectual development took shape in the context of active opposition to first the Hungarian Social Democrats and then to the Hungarian Communist Party. While a devoted supporter of working-class emancipation, Polanyi did not limit his vision of the social revolution to the proletariat; he considered the peasantry an equally important force for liberating change.

Nevertheless, Polanyi's writing can only be understood as a continuation and development of certain ideas within the Marxist tradition. Polanyi was aware of the fundamental tension in Marx's work between a societal approach, which recognized the dominance of the social, and an economistic one, which sought to locate determining economic laws.[56] While fiercely critical of the latter tendency in Marx and the Marxist tradition, the former view was the foundation on which Polanyi was building. Hence, Polanyi's analysis of the dominance of the market in capitalism can be understood as an elaboration of Marx's discussion in *Capital* of the fetishism of commodities.[57]

Polanyi's understanding of Marx clearly owed much to the work of his countryman George Lukács. Through Lukács Polanyi had access to a Hegelianized Marxism that attempted to combat the economic determinism of the Second International.[58] The influence is clearest in Polanyi's emphasis on totality – the social whole conceived in terms of relations – a central concept for Lukács. Polanyi also followed Lukács in seeking to historicize historical materialism. Lukács insisted that while Marx's emphasis on economic factors was completely necessary for understanding capitalism, a similar mode of analysis was inappropriate for precapitalist societies. To pursue such an analysis serves, in fact, to project capitalism back through all history and make its transcendence impossible. Lukács wrote of vulgar Marxism that "by elevating the laws of development specific to capitalist societies to the status of universal laws it lays the theoretical foundations essential to its aim of conferring immortality upon capitalist society in practice."[59] This insight was central to Polanyi, whose life work was devoted to showing the radical discontinuity between precapitalist and capitalist society and the inapplicability of modern economic categories for understanding those societies.

Furthermore, in arguing that the commodification of labor is the paradigm of market society, Polanyi was also drawing on Lukács. For Lukács, the transformation of the social character of humans and their environment into commodities is a process of reification – the transformation of humans and social relations into things. Since humans compose the basis of society, the reification of labor is the germinal moment and the subsequent prototype for all forms of reification in society: The "destiny of the worker becomes the general destiny of the entire society."[60] Similarly, because philosophy is social in character, reified society gives way to reification in thought crystallized in the general dominance of appearance over reality, of the commodity form over the social. For Lukács, as for Polanyi, both the Marxism of the Second International and classical economic thought succumbed to this reification. Instead of the narrow economistic focus on appearances, Lukács posits the total ensemble of social relations as his conceptual focus, and only this perspective on totality can break reified thought.[61]

In light of the Lukácsian influence on Polanyi, the common Marxist dismissal of Polanyi as a mere circulationist appears misguided.[62] Marxists use this term of abuse for theorists who fail to recognize the primacy of production and instead see the exchange and circulation of commodities as of primary importance, and some Marxists have reasoned that since Polanyi places so much emphasis on markets, he must be a circulationist. But if the commodification of labor is the paradigm of market society, Polanyi can hardly be accused of ignoring the centrality of the relations of production. In fact, in a discussion of the forms of integration, Polanyi observes: "We need only fix our attention on the role of land and labor in society – the two elements on which the dominance of the forms of integration essentially depend."[63] In short, Polanyi's focus is consistently on the institutional forms through which production is organized.

Although Polanyi followed Lukács on a number of critical points, there are also important divergences. Polanyi rejected Lukács's views on the role of the working class as a universal revolutionary force that embodied rationality in history. Moreover, Polanyi distanced himself from Lukács and from the entire Marxist tradition in his handling of the relationship between forces of production and social relations of production. To avoid the evolutionism that he detested, Polanyi carefully avoided any implications that a particular stage in the development of the productive forces was a precondition for alternative types of social arrangements.[64]

Polanyi sought instead to ground the possibility of socialism not in the development of productive forces, but in humanity's historic capacity to subordinate the economy to social relations. If market society was, as he insisted, a deviation in human history, then socialism would simply mark a return to the dominant practice of subordinating the market to social control. In this context, it becomes easier to understand why Polanyi devoted his career after *The Great Transformation* to the analysis of premarket societies. The social arrangements of premarket societies were the obvious place to begin to lay the theoretical foundations for a postmarket socialist society.

Despite this emphasis, Polanyi was well aware that the emergence of nineteenth-century society was inextricably linked to the Industrial Revolution itself. "But how shall this Revolution itself be defined? . . . We submit [that there was] one basic change, the establishment of market economy, and that the nature of this institution cannot be fully grasped unless the impact of the machine on a commercial society is realized."[65] This created an intellectual problem that neither Polanyi nor any other theorist has been able to resolve satisfactorily. On the one hand, he rejects the view that the development of productive forces is the major element in historical change. On the other hand, it seems incontrovertible that nineteenth-century development is shaped by the technological innovations of the Industrial Revolution. What then is the relationship between technological change and broader social change and what connections are there between technologies and possibilities for different kinds of social arrangements? Polanyi does not offer answers, but he seems to draw on both determinist and antideterminist lines of arguments at different points.

Conclusion

If Polanyi is ambiguous in his attempt to situate the role of technological innovation in the emergence of capitalism, he is unequivocal about his central concern in *The Great Transformation* – the cause of the destruction of nineteenth-century civilization. Against all alternative explanations, Polanyi insists that the disintegration was a result of the protective measures that "society adopted in order not to be, in its turn, annihilated by the action of the self-regulating market."[66] Polanyi, in sum, looks to the conflictual dynamics of social and economic *institutions* to explain both the construction and subsequent destruction of market society.

Polanyi's institutional focus leads directly to his conviction that power and compulsion are part of the elementary requirements of any organized social life. He does not avoid the implications of this position; for him, it is hopelessly inadequate to assert that the coming of socialism will solve the problems of politics and bureaucracy. Politics and the state cannot just wither away. The achievement of human freedom will require conscious action to restrain the necessary but dangerous exercise of political power: "The true answer to the threat of bureaucracy as a source of abuse of power is to create spheres of arbitrary freedom protected by unbreakable rules. For, however generously devolution of power is practised, there will be strengthening of power at the center, and, therefore, danger to individual freedom."[67] This insistence on the need for conscious action to subordinate both the market and the state to society grew directly out of the commitment, formed in his youth, to a politics based on a moral vision of how people should live.

> Socialism is, essentially, the tendency inherent in an industrial civilization to transcend the self-regulating market by consciously subordinating it to a democratic society . . . From the point of view of the community as a whole, socialism is merely the continuation of that endeavor to make society a distinctly human relationship of persons which in Western Europe was always associated with Christian traditions.[68]

What was most important for Polanyi was that society overcome the illusion fostered by both Marxism and liberalism that the difficult problems of human governance could magically be solved either through the end of scarcity or the self-regulating market. On the contrary, as he states in the final passage of *The Great Transformation*:

> As long as man is true to his task of creating more abundant freedom for all, he need not fear that either power or planning will turn against him and destroy the freedom he is building by their instrumentality. This is the meaning of freedom in a complex society; it gives us all the certainty we need.[69]

In a letter written "to the love of his early youth" in 1958, Polanyi, after mentioning his "martyrdom of isolation," suggests that "one more decade – and I would stand vindicated in my lifetime."[70] In a way, the remark was prophetic in that 1968 was the year of the May events in France, of the Tet offensive in Vietnam, and of the most dramatic indications of crisis in the post–World War II international economic regime. Once again market society was under serious attack and its central institutions were in crisis. Although these events confirmed Polanyi's diagnosis of the fragility of market society, it has taken still another decade before Polanyi's intellectual contribution has begun to receive the recognition that it deserves. Yet those who now turn to Polanyi's writings should recognize that even beyond his diagnosis of the contradictions of market society and his contributions to the reconstruction of radical theory, he also has much to contribute to the comparative and historical study of societies. In particular, his work constitutes one of the most sustained efforts to develop a holistic method for comparative-historical analysis. As such, it remains an indispensable reference point for future work.

Fred Block, Margaret Somers

Notes

A number of people helped save us from grievous errors by providing information on Polanyi's life and on Hungarian history. These people include Istvan Eorsi, Gyorgy Litvan, Gyorgy Markus, Gabor Vermes, and Hans and Eva Zeisel. In addition, many others read earlier versions of this manuscript and made valuable comments: Giovanni Arrighi, Daniel Bell, George Dalton, Larry Hirschhorn, E. J. Hobsbawm, Peter Lange, Anthony Leeds, Gyorgy Markus, Larry Miller, John Myles, Harry Pearson, and Theda Skocpol. Since we did not always follow the proffered advice, we alone are responsible for shortcomings that remain.

1. Originally published in 1944, references are to the Beacon Press edition, 1957. Hereafter cited as *Transformation*.
2. See, for example, George Dalton and Jasper Kocke, "The Work of the Polanyi Group: Past, Present, and Future," paper delivered at Indiana University Conference on Economic Anthropology, April 1981; and S. C. Humphries, "History, Economics and Anthropology: The Work of Karl Polanyi," *History and Theory* 8(2) (1969):165–212.
3. The major secondary works are listed in the bibliography.
4. This literature is reviewed and extended in Alan Wolfe, *The Limits of Legitimacy* (New York: Free Press, 1977).
5. The biographical data are pieced together from Lee Congdon, "Karl Polanyi in Hungary, 1900–1919," *Journal of Contemporary History* 11 (1976):167–83; Ilona Duczynska, "Karl Polanyi: Notes on His Life," in Karl Polanyi, *The Livelihood of Man* (New York: Academic Press, 1977); Kari Levitt, "Karl Polanyi and *Co-Existence*," *Co-Existence* 2 (November 1964):113–21; Hans Zeisel, "Karl Polanyi," in *International Encyclopedia of the Social Sciences* (New York: Macmillan, 1968); and personal communications from G. Markus, Hans and Eva Zeisel, and G. Litvan. Note that the chapter on the Polanyis in Peter Drucker, *Adventures of a Bystander* (New York: Harper & Row, 1979), while vastly entertaining, is inaccurate on a number of points.
6. Duczynska, "Karl Polanyi," p. xi.
7. Polanyi as quoted in Congdon, "Karl Polanyi in Hungary," p. 179.
8. His wife wrote: "It is given to the best among men somewhere to let down the roots of a sacred hate in the course of their lives. This happened to Polanyi in England. At later stages, in the United States, it merely grew in intensity. His hatred was directed against market society and its effects, which divested man of his human shape." Duczynska, "Karl Polanyi," p. xiv.
9. Polanyi, *Transformation*, p. 258A.
10. Ibid., p. 258B.
11. See Polanyi, *Transformation*, pp. 274–79. Also relevant is Ira Katznelson, "Community, Capitalist Development, and the Emergence of Class," *Politics & Society* 9(2) (1979):203–37.
12. In emphasizing the ways in which medieval towns were part and parcel of feudalism and not an opposition force, Polanyi anticipated much contemporary Marxist discussion of the transition question. In particular, see Perry Anderson, *Lineages of the Absolutist State* (London: New Left Books, 1974), and John Merrington, "Town and Country in the Transition to Capitalism," *New Left Review* 93 (September–October 1975):71–92. However, it must also be acknowledged that Polanyi fails to provide a satisfactory account of the transition to capitalism because he touches only briefly on the

interconnections among state policy, capitalist interests, and changes in the organization of production.

13. Polanyi, *Transformation*, pp. 77–85.
14. There is extensive debate among historians as to the geographical scope of the allowance system. John and Barbara Hammond argued for the wide diffusion of the Speenhamland system; they were clearly a strong influence on Polanyi. See John and Barbara Hammond, *The Village Labourer*, vols. 1 and 2 (London: Longmans, Green, 1948; orig. 1911). For a full discussion and appraisal of the opposing arguments, see J. D. Marshall, *The Old Poor Law* (London: Macmillan Press, 1968).
15. There is also widespread disagreement in the historical literature on the issue of Speenhamland's impact. Mark Blaug, for example, argues that Speenhamland was a rational device for maintaining the surplus rural population. "The Myth of the Old Poor Law and the Making of the New," *Journal of Economic History* 23 (1963):151–84. Eric Hobsbawm and George Rude, *Captain Swing* (London: Lawrence and Wishart, 1969) dispute this view. See also Polanyi's appendixes 9 and 10, *Transformation*, pp. 286–88, 289–90.
16. For a revisionist interpretation of the New Poor Law as legislation constructed to maintain the traditional power of the landed classes, see Anthony Brundage, *The Making of the New Poor Law* (New Brunswick, N.J.: Rutgers University Press, 1979), and "The English Poor Law of 1834 and the Cohesion of Agricultural Society," *Agricultural History* 48 (July 1974):405–17. For a parallel reinterpretation of the 1832 Reform Bill, see D. C. Moore, *The Politics of Deference* (London: Harvester Press, 1976).
17. Polanyi, *Transformation*, p. 83.
18. Ibid., p. 137.
19. Polanyi, *The Livelihood of Man*, p. xvii. Hereafter cited as *Livelihood*.
20. Polanyi's emphatic discussion of the unplanned nature of the protectionist movement is animated by his opposition to the dominant paradigm of classical liberalism as stated in A. V. Dicey, *Lectures on the Relation Between Law and Public Opinion in England During the Nineteenth Century* (London: Macmillan Press, 1940; orig. 1905) where it is argued that a "collectivist conspiracy" undermined the free market.
21. Polanyi, *Transformation*, p. 132.
22. John Maynard Keynes, *Economic Consequences of Sterling Parity* (New York: Harcourt, 1925).
23. Polanyi, *Transformation*, p. 177.
24. Ibid., p. 195.
25. Ibid., p. 217.
26. Ibid., p. 237.
27. Ibid., p. 239.
28. This was, of course, one of Polanyi's most serious errors–his failure to anticipate that limited forms of Keynesian intervention could stabilize market societies. However, the current crisis of Keynesian policies suggests the possibility that over the long term, Polanyi might have been correct.
29. George Lukács, *History and Class Consciousness* (Cambridge, Mass.: MIT Press, 1971). See also Andrew Feenberg, *Lukács, Marx and the Sources of Critical Theory* (Totowa, N.J.: Rowman and Littlefield, 1981). On holism as an explanatory strategy in the social sciences, see Paul Diesing, *Patterns of Discovery in the Social Sciences* (Chicago: Aldine, 1971).
30. Marc Bloch, *Feudal Society*, trans. L. A. Manyon (Chicago: University of Chicago, 1961); Lucien Febvre, *A New Kind of History*, ed. Peter Burke, trans. K. Folca (New York: Harper & Row, 1973).

Fred Block, Margaret Somers

31. Polanyi, *Primitive, Archaic, and Modern Economies* (New York: Doubleday Anchor, 1968), p. 96. Hereafter cited as *Primitive, Archaic*.
32. Polanyi's views on this issue are stated most forcefully in *The Livelihood of Man*, pp. 5–56.
33. Karl Polanyi, Conrad Arsenberg, and Henry Pearson, eds., *Trade and Market in the Early Empires* (Glencoe, Ill.: Free Press, 1957), p. 250.
34. Polanyi, *Primitive, Archaic*, p. 68.
35. Polanyi, *Transformation*, p. 157.
36. E. P. Thompson, *The Making of the English Working Class* (New York: Vintage, 1966). To be sure, both Thompson and Polanyi were influenced by the Hammonds.
37. Polanyi, *Transformation*, p. 157 and appendix 11, pp. 290–94.
38. Ibid., pp. 154–55.
39. See Margaret Somers, "Political Structure, Proto-Industrialization and Family Economy: The Institutional Basis of Class Formation in Early Nineteenth Century England" (Center for European Studies, Harvard University).
40. See Wolfe, *Limits of Legitimacy*, and James O'Connor, *The Fiscal Crisis of the State* (New York: St. Martin's Press, 1973).
41. Polanyi, *Livelihood*, p. 74.
42. Polanyi, *Transformation*, chap. 4, and *Livelihood*, pp. 35–43.
43. Polanyi, *Livelihood*, p. 43.
44. See, for example, Talcott Parson, *Societies* (Englewood Cliffs, N.J.: Prentice-Hall, 1970).
45. Barrington Moore, *Social Origins of Dictatorship and Democracy* (Boston: Beacon Press, 1966); Alexander Gerschenkron, *Economic Backwardness in Historical Perspective* (Cambridge, Mass.: Harvard University Press, 1962).
46. Northrop Frye, in commenting on Spengler and Toynbee, remarks that "every historical overview of this kind . . . is and has to be metaphorical." "*The* Decline of the West by Oswald Spengler," *Daedalus* (Winter 1973):11. See also the discussion in Arthur Stinchcombe, *Theoretical Methods in Social History* (New York: Academic Press, 1978).
47. Polanyi, *Transformation*, p. 219.
48. Immanuel Wallerstein, *The Modern World-System: Capitalist Agriculture and the Origins of the European World-Economy in the Sixteenth Century* (New York: Academic Press, 1974). Wallerstein's co-worker, Terence Hopkins, was strongly influenced by Polanyi at Columbia.
49. For such criticisms, see Theda Skocpol, "Wallerstein's World System," *American Journal of Sociology* 82 (March 1977):1075–90; Aristide R. Zolberg, "Origins of the Modern World System: A Missing Link," paper presented at the American Political Science Association meetings, August 1979; Peter Gourevitch, "The International System and Regime Formation: A Critical Review of Anderson and Wallerstein," *Comparative Politics* 10:4 (April 1978):419–38; Margaret Somers, "Modes of Production, Social Formations and the State: The Historiography of Perry Anderson and Immanuel Wallerstein," paper presented at the American Political Science Association meetings, August 1979.
50. Robert Brenner, "Origins of Capitalist Development: A Critique of Neo-Smithian Marxism," *New Left Review* 104 (July–August 1977):25–93.
51. Polanyi, *Transformation*, p. 246.
52. It could be argued, however, that in emphasizing the role of international opportunity structure, Polanyi fails to give adequate attention to the peculiarities of national developments in the triumph of fascism in certain countries.

See Alexander Gerschenkron, *Bread and Democracy in Germany* (New York: Howard Fertig, 1966); *Economic Backwardness;* and Moore, *Social Origins.*
53. This is the argument of Fred Block, *The Origins of International Economic Disorder* (Berkeley: University of California Press, 1977).
54. This essay is reprinted in Polanyi, *Primitive, Archaic,* pp. 59–77.
55. Polanyi, *Transformation,* pp. 11–16; V. I. Lenin, *Imperialism* (New York: International Publishers, 1939; orig. 1917). An effort to resolve the conflict between their two positions is made in Fred Block, "Cooperation and Conflict in the Capitalist World Economy," *Marxist Perspectives* 5 (Spring 1979):78–91.
56. See Polanyi, *Primitive, Archaic,* pp. 133–34.
57. Polanyi chose, however, not to define his project in those terms. He wrote: "Marx's assertion of the fetish character of the value of commodities refers to the exchange value of genuine commodities and has nothing in common with the fictitious commodities mentioned in the text." Polanyi, *Transformation,* p. 72.
58. Polanyi and Lukács were acquaintances, and Polanyi had read Lukács's *History and Class Consciousness.* Congdon, "Polanyi in Hungary," p. 183, and personal communication with G. Markus.
59. Lukács, *Class Consciousness,* p. 54.
60. Ibid., p. 265.
61. See Feenberg, *Lukács, Marx,* and Andrew Arato and Paul Breines, *The Young Lukács and the Origins of Western Marxism* (New York: Seabury Press, 1979).
62. The circulationist charge is made by Lucette Valensi, "Economic Anthropology and History: The Work of Karl Polanyi," in *Research in Economic Anthropology* 4 (1981), but the charge is effectively refuted by George Dalton in his "Comment" in the same volume.
63. Polanyi, *Livelihood,* p. 43.
64. Polanyi explicitly renounces a "stage theory" of history: "No 'stages theory' is here implied; a pattern may appear, disappear, and recur again at a later phase of the society's growth." Ibid., p. 308. George Dalton, in his "Comment," notes: "Polanyi, unlike Marx, has nothing at all to say about the deep causes of sequential change: no stages, no evolution, no propelling mechanisms transforming one epoch into another. The closest he comes to considering such dynamic matters is to suggest, as a program of research, the two broad problems that absorbed him: to investigate the place of economy in society, and to investigate historically how domestic market exchange, market foreign trade, and market money came to penetrate and transform their non-market antecedents."
65. Polanyi, *Transformation,* p. 40.
66. Ibid., p. 249.
67. Ibid., p. 255.
68. Ibid., p. 234.
69. Ibid., p. 258B.
70. Polanyi, *Livelihood,* p. xx.

Bibliography

POLANYI'S WORK

"The Essence of Fascism." In *Christianity and the Social Revolution,* edited by J. Lewis, K. Polanyi, and D. K. Kitchin. New York: Scribner, 1936.
The Great Transformation. 1944. Rev. ed. Boston: Beacon Press, 1957.

Fred Block, Margaret Somers

"Our Obsolete Market Mentality." *Commentary* 3 (February 1947):109–17. Reprinted in *Primitive, Archaic and Modern Economies.*
Trade and Market in the Early Empires, edited with Conrad Arensberg and Harry Pearson. Glencoe, Ill.: Free Press, 1957.
The Plough and the Pen: Writings from Hungary, 1930–1956, edited with Ilona Duczynska. London: Owen, 1963.
Dahomey and the Slave Trade. Seattle: University of Washington Press, 1966.
Primitive, Archaic and Modern Economies. 1968. Rev. ed. Boston: Beacon Press, 1971.
The Livelihood of Man. New York: Academic Press, 1977.

SECONDARY WORK

Congdon, Lee. "Karl Polanyi in Hungary, 1900–1919." *Journal of Contemporary History* 11 (1976):167–83.
Dalton, George. "Introduction." In Karl Polanyi, *Primitive, Archaic and Modern Economies.* Boston: Beacon Press, 1971.
Dalton, George, ed. "Symposium: Economic Anthropology and History: The Work of Karl Polanyi." In *Research in Economic Anthropology* 4 (1981).
Dalton, George, and Jasper Kocke. "The Work of the Polanyi Group: Past, Present, and Future." Paper delivered at Indiana University Conference on Economic Anthropology, April 1981.
Hechter, Michael. "Karl Polanyi's Social Theory: A Critique." *Politics & Society* 10(4)(1981):399–430.
Humphreys, S. C. "History, Economics and Anthropology: The Work of Karl Polanyi." *History and Theory* 8(2)(1969):165–212.
Kindleberger, Charles P. "*The Great Transformation* by Karl Polanyi." *Daedalus* (Winter 1973):45–53.
Levitt, Kari. "Karl Polanyi and Co-Existence." *Co-Existence* 2 (November 1964): 113–21.
North, Douglass C. "Markets and Other Allocation Systems in History: The Challenge of Karl Polanyi." *Journal of European Economic History* 6(3) (Winter 1977):703–16.
Pearson, Harry. "Editor's Introduction." In Karl Polanyi, *The Livelihood of Man.* New York: Academic Press, 1977.
Sievers, A. M. *Has Market Society Collapsed? A Critique of Karl Polanyi's New Economics.* New York: Columbia University Press, 1949.
Stanfield, J. Ron. "The Institutional Economics of Karl Polanyi." *Journal of Economic Issues* 14(3) (September 1980):593–614.
Szecsi, Maria. "Looking Back on *The Great Transformation.*" *Monthly Review* 30(8) (January 1979):34–45.
Zeisel, Hans. "Karl Polanyi." *International Encyclopedia of the Social Sciences.* New York: Macmillan, 1968.

4. Configurations in History: The Historical Sociology of S. N. Eisenstadt

GARY G. HAMILTON

At the time of its publication in 1963, *The Political Systems of Empires* seemed almost the sole occupant of that area we now recognize, without literary grace, as macrocomparative historical sociology.[1] To be sure, Reinhard Bendix's *Work and Authority in Industry* came earlier and certainly had historical and comparative dimensions.[2] At that time, however, it appeared more as a contribution to "the sociology of knowledge and the sociology of work relations" than as a comparative analysis of historical change.[3] Also present was Wittfogel's influential and much criticized book, *Oriental Despotism*, and Coulborn's more appreciated and more limited edition, *Feudalism in History*.[4] Although both were comparative and historical, neither resonated with the historical vision nor possessed the comparative breadth of *Political Systems*. E. P. Thompson's *The Making of the English Working Class* also appeared in 1963, but did not draw sociologists to it until several years later; even then it was (and continues to be) viewed as a historical instead of a sociological analysis – a mistake that could not be made about *Political Systems*.[5] In 1963, Bendix's *Nation-building and Citizenship* and Tilly's *The Vendee* lay one year in the future; Moore's *Social Origins of Dictatorship and Democracy* and Parsons's *Societies: Comparative and Evolutionary Perspectives* three years in the future; Wallerstein's *The Modern World-System* and Anderson's *Passages from Antiquity to Feudalism* eleven years in the future.[6] When it appeared, *Political Systems* provided that generation of sociologists and historians with a singular and almost dramatic reintroduction to something old: the sociology of history. Indeed, in 1963, as one reviewer wrote, *Political Systems* was "the most successful historical-sociological study to appear since [those of] Max Weber."[7]

Gary G. Hamilton

In the first few years after its publication, *Political Systems* was among the most important books in sociology, and its author, S. N. Eisenstadt, among the most prominent sociologists. *Political Systems*, of course, remains important today, as does Eisenstadt himself. But in the intervening years, between 1963 and now, historical sociology has changed its theoretical preferences, moving from the structural functionalism of the 1950s and early 1960s to the world systems and other neo-Marxian perspectives of the 1970s and 1980s. The result has been a decline in the influence of Eisenstadt's writings, not only of *Political Systems* but of his more recent ones as well.

In fact, when one reads an Eisenstadt work today, one has the uneasy feeling of its being outdated. First, the jargon – the vocabulary and grammar of structural functionalism – does not seem to work anymore. The words and phrasings of this language seem better suited for use, in Carl Becker's term, in an earlier climate of opinion, a taken-for-granted world of sociological discourse, which is now no longer taken for granted.[8] In the 1970s historical sociologists learned a new perspective and a new language – different words with equally "uncertain meanings which, having from constant repetition lost their metaphorical significance, are unconsciously mistaken for objective reality."[9] Shaped by the vision and language of an earlier time, Eisenstadt's writings are difficult to understand in today's climate.

Next is the level of analysis. Although his recent works emphasize the continuity of historical sociology between the 1960s and the 1970s, Eisenstadt's writings reside in the abstract problematics of structural functionalism, with its emphases on values, on systemic characteristics, on differentiation.[10] These issues are analyzed at societal and transsocietal levels, as in the lengthy debates on traditional, modernizing, and modern societies. But with a new language and perspective has come a different set of observations and a different set of problems for investigation. A generation educated in Moore's class analysis of the paths to dictatorship and democracy or in Wallerstein's look at the long sixteenth century finds that Eisenstadt strangely lacks a grounded sense of history. In an Eisenstadt look at revolutions, there is no blood being spilled; at class conflicts, no suffering; at great ideas, no thinkers. History, for Eisenstadt, is placed at the level of abstractions; events, people, motivations, all seem to be viewed from a great distance, through the conceptual windows of "differentiated institutions," "crystallized roles," or "cultural orientations." Being unfamiliar with his language and ignorant of the issues he is addressing, today's readers feel uncomfortable with the writings of S. N. Eisenstadt.

More, however, is involved in a sociology of history than simply a theoretical perspective. True, such a perspective greatly influences the end result: the analysis of history. But it is also true that, whatever the perspective used, any sociologist of history must make decisions about fashioning causal explanations, about determining historical meanings and historical facts, and about designing a comparative methodology. These decisions have ontological and epistemological groundings, and on the same grounds different theoretical perspectives may be used to construct distinctive interpretations of history. Moreover, theories may locate the questions that need to be addressed and even provide the language in which to answer them, as well as parts of the answers. But theories in themselves do not confront history, analysts do that. Just as one does not necessarily judge a house by the tools and materials with which it was built, even though both certainly influence what was built, one should not judge an analysis of history solely by the perspective used to build an understanding of history. Used badly, a structural functional perspective, like Weberian and neo-Marxian ones, produces nonsense. Used well, they all contribute to our understanding of the past as well as the present. S. N. Eisenstadt is very good at what he does. Without a doubt he gives us the best portrayal of history from a structural functional point of view that is currently available.

In this chapter I will not engage in yet another critique of structural functionalism. This has been done by others and, in any event, would not aid in our understanding the contribution that Eisenstadt does in fact make to a sociology of history.[11] Instead I want to discuss the underlying dimensions of Eisenstadt's writings – the philosophy of history, the comparative framework, the interpenetration of method and theory – that appear throughout his work. These dimensions are, of course, influenced by structural functionalism, but not exclusively so. In varying degrees, all theoretical perspectives are flexible; they allow partisans considerable latitude to develop their own predilections. Consider, for instance, the wide range of positions that individuals take under the rubric of Marxian sociology, while still considering themselves faithful to that tradition. Structural functionalism is no different, and Eisenstadt's stand in relation to this intellectual tradition reveals as much about his own vision of history as about something fundamental in the nature of structural functionalism. This essay is a discussion of Eisenstadt's attempt to construct a sociology of history in its own right, as it is distinct from but related to structural functionalism.

To this end I divide the following chapter into three sections. In the first section, I discuss the careful manner in which Eisenstadt positions

Gary G. Hamilton

his work in relation to the writings of others. Among other things, this positioning lays an ontological foundation for his sociology of history. In the second and longest section, I give an interpretive analysis of this sociology: classifying, theorizing, and interpreting historical configurations. Here I note the interrelation between Eisenstadt's comparative methodology and his theories of history. These interrelations establish a scaffolding from which Eisenstadt fashions a historical analysis. In the final section, I evaluate Eisenstadt's sociology of history within the context of other sociologies of history, particularly a Marxian one. In this section I describe some of the logical and empirical difficulties of configurational analysis, as well as some specific shortcomings that I see in Eistenstadt's work.

Positioning

Social scientific writing, many observe, is grounded in philosophic assumptions about the nature of knowledge and social reality. Gouldner, for one, calls these "domain assumptions" and "world hypotheses."[12] In a different sense, Foucault labels them "épisteme."[13] Whatever the term used, these assumptions supposedly exist apart from the act of doing social science; they are a priori. Philosophical assumptions are simply there, in a person's life experiences, in Weltanschauungen, in the taken-for-granted world of scientific discourse. They do not determine theory; they inform it, by shaping the mentalities of those who in turn create theory. Passively standing in a received world, social scientists are the unwitting representatives of their era, their class, or their discipline.

While it is undoubtedly true that many philosophic assumptions stand a priori to scholarly work, this valuable insight should not lessen our appreciation of the equally subtle, yet active ways that scholars themselves contrive their theoretical and methodological stands. These contrivances depend less on those taken-for-granted assumptions common to a discipline (or subdiscipline) than on a scholar's actual choices about locating his or her own vision in relation to the views of others, so as to communicate that vision logically and forcefully to an often unknown and potentially critical audience. In making these choices, scholars seek to justify their conception of knowledge, to legitimize it as a valid form of scholarly discourse.[14] These are active, not passive, decisions and are often made with some recognition (although, one must argue, never a full recognition) of their philosophic consequences. Remember, for instance, Weber's tortured methodological

88

writings or Marx's "warm-ups" for *Capital* or Durkheim's reflections on Rousseau and Montesquieu.[15] These writing are, in effect, position papers – attempts to ferret through the works of others to locate one's own position.

Eisenstadt, like most modern scholars, continually defines his own views by bouncing them off the works of others. Superficially, this sort of positioning appears to be a mundane exercise, a format requirement of modern scholarship with its obligatory first chapter "reviews of the literature." But to many writers, Eisenstadt among them, positioning is serious business, in part because it occurs at two interrelated levels. One level indeed assumes the spirit of a literature review, with the purpose of revealing where a particular piece of work fits within and advances the knowledge of a substantive specialty. Although related to substance, the second level of positioning probes the more abstract problems of analysis: the ontological and epistemological structuring of a scholarly argument.[16] At this level scholars attempt to delineate essential qualities of the topic being discussed and the methods by which these qualities can be known. Eisenstadt engages in both types of positioning.

In terms of the first level, few modern scholars can match Eisenstadt's breadth of substantive interests. In the more than thirty years since his first publication, Eisenstadt has written major works on migration, stratification, political structure and organization, modernization, traditional societies, sociological theory, social change, and revolutions.[17] Each of these works, in addition to his many edited books and articles, features extensive surveys of the relevant literature. These surveys are important because they provide the data, or at least sources for the data, from which Eisenstadt constructs a secondary, sociological analysis of the specific topic. Most of the literature he surveys he treats casually, neither describing the works at length nor discussing the major arguments concerning substantive interpretations found within them.[18] Instead, Eisenstadt places his substantive contribution on a more abstract plane, that of general configurational analysis, such as interpreting the nature of imperial political institutions or the nature of modernizing regimes. Accordingly, he holds himself apart from the detailed substance of cases and their inherent controversies; out of a literature survey, he draws the more general and hence the more agreed-upon features of his topic; and from these features, he fashions his sociological and historical conclusions.

Eisenstadt's aloofness from the topical literature results, in part, from his positioning at the second level. Although diverse in his sociological

Gary G. Hamilton

interests, Eisenstadt is consistent on the premises of his sociological arguments.[19] In his early works, these premises are largely implied; but from the mid-1960s on, as he and other structural functionalist writers come under attack, Eisenstadt devotes many of his major writings to a clarification of his position.[20] Sometimes this effort is an implicit one, as when he writes about the history and direction of sociological theory.[21] More often, it is a straightforward, earnest attempt to block out his ontological location and to forge a link with others similarly located, even though they may be found on the other side of the theoretical spectrum, in Marxian sociology, for instance.[22]

Eisenstadt marks off his position with care. His work, he says, stands in strong opposition to two interpretive traditions: evolutionism and historicism.[23] Eisenstadt spends more time explaining his opposition to evolutionism than he does to historicism, partly because his own position is much closer to this tradition and is, in fact, often mistaken for it. To Eisenstadt, evolutionism, as an interpretation of social change, places the theories of change logically prior to the analysis of facts. Evolutionists use general causes and general trends to explain concrete instances of change, wherever and whenever the instances occur.[24] By employing the universal to explain the particular, evolutionists, Eisenstadt charges, confuse general tendencies with the actual causes of change.[25]

According to Eisenstadt, evolutionism stumbles on two assumptions that adherents of this position typically make.[26] First is the assumption that change follows universally predictable patterns that inherently manifest themselves within all societies. To this assumption Eisenstadt replies that change is indeed ubiquitous, but its direction and nature are not universal or explained by general principles and first causes. Change is always tied to concrete circumstances as defined within a particular society.[27] Second is the assumption that with its emphasis on universal traits and tendencies, evolutionary interpretations do not specify the particular characteristics of societies or the mechanisms of particular changes. Because everything is illustrative of the same general processes, there is no need to distinguish differences among phenomena.[28] In reply to this assumption, Eisenstadt notes that the historical record shows great variability, which can neither be explained satisfactorily by universals nor be explained without precise specification of particular societies, and of institutions and changes internal to these societies.

Eisenstadt's opposition to evolutionism must be read, in part, as a critique of structural functionalism itself.[29] Working within, as well as

90

in tension with, this theoretical perspective, Eisenstadt argues for a shift of emphasis away from examining the general attributes of societies (e.g., functional prerequisites and pattern variables) toward specifying the systemic qualities of particular types of societies. This is a subtle shift, but one having important consequences, as I will describe. In effect, Eisenstadt suggests that structural functionalism contains the appropriate classificatory concepts needed to delineate naturally occurring types of societies, such as historical, bureaucratic empires, the topic of *Political Systems*.[30] But such historical configurations can only emerge from a structural functional analysis if the universalistic implications of this tradition are downplayed. By the time Eisenstadt wrote *Political Systems* he no longer used Talcott Parsons's AGIL scheme and had reduced the status of Parsons's pattern variables to sensitizing concepts.[31] From 1965 on, Eisenstadt no longer cites Parsons as a means to justify his own work, as he had earlier. Politely acknowledging Parsons's contribution to a systemic analysis, Eisenstadt shifts to Max Weber as the principle source to legitimize his vision of society.

Eisenstadt takes an equally strong stand against historicism. Historicism is the interpretive tradition that stresses the uniqueness of historical outcomes, the inability of general theory to explain these outcomes, and the active role of analysts in manufacturing historical meanings.[32] Instead of arguing at length against this perspective, Eisenstadt is inclined to dismiss it, as being obviously incorrect. At one point, he asks, "Is it possible to explain systematically the variety of structural forms which accompany the process of modernization or does one have to accept some historian's dictum of the total uniqueness and incomparability of any situation?"[33] Without qualification, Eisenstadt sides with the possibility of systematically and theoretically explaining historical variations. To Eisenstadt, societies possess systemic qualities that are real and describable. The nature of a society and of change in that society are taken into account. To ignore these qualities, as by implication a historicist would do, is analogous to a biologist who studies animal behavior without the aid of species classification.

Eisenstadt contrasts his position with the historicist stance of Reinhard Bendix, a stance that he labels the "ecological group" approach. In reference to Bendix's critique of modernization theory, Eisenstadt charges that Bendix, among others, conceptualizes change as not having "any definite universal systemic, symbolic or structural characteristics: it is basically a specific, one-time historical process."[34] "In some cases," he further elaborates, "as in the work of Bendix, these criticisms have . . . converged with a total denial of the system approach to society – producing instead a view of society as an (ecological) conglomeration of continuously competing groups and units."[35] In another work, he observes: "In the works of Bendix . . . the ecologic 'group' approach basically denies the existence of a systemic social division of labor, with its implications of systemic properties and needs of social life, stressing instead ecological coexistence and competition among different groups."[36] From Bendix's point of view, Eisenstadt maintains, history is solely determined by struggles among groups, by accidents, and by situational adjustments; history is formless, seamless, uninterpretable. Missing from this characterization are the essentials of societies and of change: History and change are not random or limitless; both are functions of the irreducible systemic qualities of historical configurations – of those phenomena that occur naturally in history and represent a distinctive clustering of variables.

In suggesting that Parsons errs on the side of evolutionism and Bendix on the side of historicism, Eisenstadt clears the way for his own appropriation of the work of Max Weber. Both Parsons and Bendix are well-known scholars of Weber's sociology and had for many years debated over the proper interpretation of Weber's works. Eisenstadt does not acknowledge this debate. But he does mention, with approval, Parsons's synthesis of Weber's and Durkheim's theories of action, noting that Parsons "opened" Weber's work to a systemic interpretation.[37] He also implies, however, that Parsons's own systemic interpretations went too far toward stressing the universal qualities of social systems rather than specifying crucial differences among them.[38] Eisenstadt's critique of Bendix's interpretations of Weber is accomplished in one sentence. After outlining the systemic qualities in Weber's work and charging the ecological groups with denying the existence of such qualities in societies, Eisenstadt states, "The 'ecological group' model has been most fully developed in the works of Reinhard Bendix, *who attributes his approach to Weber.*"[39] Obviously, Bendix's claim to be a bearer of Weber's sociology, according to Eisenstadt, is illegitimate. Not Parsons, not Bendix, but rather Eisenstadt is the genuine heir of the Weberian legacy.

By positioning himself between Parsons and Bendix and in direct descent from Weber, Eisenstadt not only places his own special demands on Weberian sociology but also locates the ontological position from which he builds a sociology of history. We can understand this position as one of "typological realism." This position is contained in his attempt to develop concepts of social formations (e.g., roles, institutions, societies) that embody concrete phenomena in their essential reality.

These historically real concepts differ from those concepts that either Parsons or Bendix have developed in relation to their study of Weber. On one hand, in *The Structure of Social Action*, Parsons criticizes Weber's use of ideal types.[40] These "useful fictions," as Parsons calls them, have an inappropriate epistemological grounding for their use in building a social science.[41] Instead, Parsons favors concepts having "analytical realism," meaning that "the general concepts of science [should not be] fictional but [should] adequately 'grasp' aspects of the objective external world."[42] Analytically real concepts, however, do not refer to social formations, no matter how conceived. Rather they refer to "*general attributes* of concrete phenomena," and not to the phenomena themselves.[43] Parsons illustrates these concepts with two examples: mass in relation to a body and rationality in relation to an act. Parsons adds that it is nonsensical to think of analytical elements (mass or rationality) as existing by themselves (without a body or an act).[44] Eisenstadt shifts his conceptual focus from general attributes to the concrete phenomena themselves – to social bodies and social acts.

On the other hand, Bendix holds with and even extends Weber's view that sociological concepts must necessarily be "abstractions from observations of behavior and from historical evidence" that " 'freeze' the fluidity of social life."[45] According to Bendix, these ideal types of concepts depart from reality and should not be mistaken for it. Their only purpose is to be useful in the analysis of social action, which is constantly changing. Eisenstadt rejects ideal types in favor of real types – concepts that do not freeze action but rather contain within them the dynamics of action itself. In Eisenstadt's words, his approach points to "the systemic nature of societies, the multiplicity of dimensions of social systems and of forces that generate different complexes of these dimensions, as well as the openness of situations of change."[46] His concepts attempt to embody this approach by tapping the essential qualities of social systems as they exist in nature. This is the goal of configurational analysis.

For the sake of greater clarity, Eisenstadt's position can be characterized as having its roots in an Aristotelian ontology. At one point, Eisenstadt explicitly acknowledges this linkage: "[The] recognition . . . of the great variety of types of social order or of societies . . . at least in the analysis of political orders, is present in Aristotelian thought, as is the attempt to relate different political orders to different types of individual moral postures and civic attitudes. In these two respects, modern sociological analysis is very much in the Aristotelian tradition."[47] The logic deriving from this position can be summarized as follows: Empirical reality is complex and diverse, but close observation reveals the existence of independent and recurring configurations. Such configurations have an essence, so to speak, because they represent a clustering of variables that gives a configuration a wholly distinctive, irreducible form. Like animal life, social life exists in natural forms. Like biologists, sociologists, through the application of consistent criteria, must isolate and classify these forms before attempting a theoretical analysis. Ideally, then, an analyst, using the correct criteria of classification, should be able to examine empirical facts to arrive at a classification of real types. Once these types are defined, the analyst can theorize about the behavior of specific types. Understanding the behavior of a specific type, the analyst is then able to interpret the behavior of individual examples of that type. With this logic and procedure Eisenstadt analyzes history, attempting all the while to distinguish between the forms and flux contained therein.

About whether it is possible to examine history and society in this fashion, Eisenstadt simply comments, "The proof of the pudding is, of course, in the eating – it is only through attempts at the construction of such types, at different levels of abstraction, that the limits of the usefulness of the comparative approach and the possibility of subsuming these types under general laws can be discerned."[48] The next section looks at the pudding, at Eisenstadt's classification of history and theories about historical configurations as well as historical interpretations based on them. The final section will evaluate its palatability.

Configurational Analysis

The centerpiece of Eisenstadt's sociology of history is what I call configurational analysis. This is a common sort of analysis in sociology, not at all confined to historical sociology. The importance of Eisenstadt's use of this approach is not only that he carries it to its logical extremes, but that he does so in the context of trying to explain historical change. Simply put, configurational analysis is the attempt to isolate and describe the essential qualities of patterned actions that are assumed to occur naturally. The analysis is ideally encompassed in three steps. First is the differentiation of a bounded pattern of action (a configuration) from other similar but different patterns; this step is the process of classification. Second is the internal examination of the pattern with the goal of developing generalizations about its essential characteristics; this step creates a theory about the form and nature of the pattern. Third is the analytic use of this pattern to predict and explain any empirical case that can be similarly classified; this step is empirical interpretation. Throughout, configurations are the fulcrum of analysis. They are the objects of classification, the subjects of theory, and the sources of empirical interpretations.

I will examine each of these steps in turn as they are manifest in two of Eisenstadt's most ambitious works, *The Political Systems of Empires* and *Revolution and the Transformation of Societies*. Besides providing good illustrations of Eisenstadt's configurational analysis, both books represent Eisenstadt's serious attempt to deal with historical complexity – with continuity, diversity, and change. The complexity emerges in *Political Systems* as Eisenstadt isolates a type of societal configuration, historical bureaucratic empire, from other types of societies. The significance of such bureaucratic empires is that they stand between distinctly traditional and distinctly modern societies, but do not represent an evolutionary process whereby the traditional evolves into the modern. Instead, they represent the development of societies with centralized political regimes. Such societies were historically widespread, both temporally and spatially. They waxed and they waned, but in retrospect they contained the first institutionalized instance of something that would become centrally important in modern societies: autonomous political institutions. *Political Systems* is a sociological account of the creation, maintenance, and disintegration of the premodern state.

In *Revolution* Eisenstadt analyzes nothing less than the nature of historical change itself. Ostensibly focusing on modern revolutions (what has been called "true" or "total" revolutions), this book contains the conceptual framework to judge the meaning of modern change and the locations in which such changes are likely to occur against the backdrop of the characteristics of premodern changes. Again, Eisenstadt's message is antievolutionist; modern patterns of change constitute a distinct break from the diversity of premodern patterns and cannot be explained in terms of general impulses emanating from within traditional societies. Instead, modern patterns must be understood as a historical "mutation," which once having occurred became a continuing and decisive force in the modern times. Revolutions are both a cause and a consequence of this mutation.

In these as well as his other works, Eisenstadt writes about historical complexity. He makes this more than any other feature of history the focus of his analysis. By what criteria and by what logical procedure does he render historical complexity available to our understanding of the past and to our interpretation of the present?

Gary G. Hamilton

Classifying

According to Eisenstadt's reading of history, a simple understanding of the past or of the present is always misleading and is never merely concise. As he says in connection with his interpretations of revolutions, "A closer look at the data indicates a more complex picture."[49] Despite the complexity of history, meaningful patterns can be discerned through the appropriate use of the comparative method. Only by drawing comparisons can one pattern be isolated from other patterns. The focus of a comparative analysis should be the delineation of similarities and differences among units – be these units societies or individuals or something more intangible, such as ideas or change. By controlling the unit of observation and then categorizing the differences among those units, Eisenstadt equates comparison with classification.[50]

Eisenstadt recognizes, however, that there are difficulties in using comparisons for this purpose. "The basic problem in comparative studies is not whether it is possible to construct . . . types according to any relevant criteria, but whether it is at all worthwhile to do so."[51] He lists two measures of a worthwhile typology. First, a typology must be based on a delineation of "common characteristics . . . among various societies."[52] But with only this test, he notes, a typology may be an artifact of one's definitions and not reflect genuine similarities and differences among societies. A second measure is needed.

> The more important test of the worthiness . . . is . . . whether common features delineate characteristics which are important for the understanding of the working of these types – *as special, institutionalized systems, with boundary-maintenance and systemic problems of their own which differ from those of other systems.* [This] test is greatly dependent on the degree to which it is possible to discern both the societal conditions common to different societies under which each type of institutional system develops and becomes crystallized and the conditions of their change and transformation.[53]

In other words, typologies should define configurations – the boundaries of patterns as well as their inner workings and dynamics – in a way that distinguishes them from other configurations. By emphasizing systemic qualities of types, Eisenstadt implies that the validity of a classification relies less on definitional (theoretical) precision than on historical evidence.

As I suggest in the previous section, Eisenstadt here is staking an ontological claim: There are configurations in history and these configurations have systemic properties. The discovery (for indeed it is a

96

process of discovery) of these configurations depends on the conceptual tools that one uses to mine history. Much of Eisenstadt's writings about his positioning revolve around a basic point: For the task of finding and specifying configurations, not all conceptual tools work equally well. The historicist's concepts have an antisystemic bias and are of little use. The universalistic concepts of structural functionalism are serviceable if only because they are based on a recognition that societies operate on systemic principles. Marxian concepts, too, would work, because they contain systemic implications as well.[54] All of these concepts, however, have to be turned toward the task of specification, toward the discovery and delineation of configurations.

In *Political Systems*, Eisenstadt shows how the process of specification works. He states his two basic assumptions on the first page. The first assumption relates to a universalistic assessment of history: "The political system is a basic part of any society's organization."[55] His second assumption points to the necessity to specify as a means to understand historical variation: "Different types of political systems develop and function under specific social conditions, and the continuity of any political system is also related to such specific conditions."[56] Specification thus proceeds on the logic that that which is common to all units of analysis and is empirically observable and systemically important in them is an appropriate starting point for building a typology. Accordingly, Eisenstadt outlines the basic characteristics of all political systems as well as their relationship with other institutions in society and then uses these characteristics as variables to locate empirical clusters that would indicate potentially valid (historically real) types of political systems.

Deriving these characteristics from structural functional writers, he reasons as follows:[57] (1) All political activities are organized in roles, but the extent to which this occurs, as well as the extent to which political roles are differentiated from other types of roles, varies among societies. (2) All political activities are institutionalized, but the degree and manner of this institutionalization varies; some societies have special organizations to attend to special types of political activities, such as legislative, administrative, judicial, and party activities, whereas other societies have these activities embedded in other institutions, such as those relating to family and other types of ascriptive groups. (3) All political systems have goals, but these goals differ according to their content, to whose interests they serve, to the criteria governing their definition, and to the degree that different groups in society participate in their definition. (4) All political systems attempt to legitimate their exercise of power, but they differ by "the type of legitimation sanctioning a given political system and its rulers."[58]

Using these criteria as a means of specification, but noting that "theoretically, the possible interrelations between these variables are manifold," Eisenstadt concludes that "several major types [of political systems] stand out in the history of the development of human society."[59] Among the seven types of polities he lists is the object of analysis in this book – "centralized historical bureaucratic empires."[60] The essence of this historical configuration is "the *limited autonomy* of the political sphere."[61] This essential feature is revealed in four ways. First, rulers have the capability to set their own political goals. Second, the political sphere contains specialized political roles, such as those of bureaucratic and administrative officials. Third, rulers attempt to centralize the political sphere into a more consolidated unit. And fourth, specific administrative organizations (e.g., bureaucracies) develop, as do arenas (e.g., grand councils and parliaments) of political struggle.

Taking his first step in specifying a type of political system, Eisenstadt spends the rest of the book substantiating its historical validity. This task is accomplished through the use of typological comparisons. He lists the historical cases that would seem to possess these defining features and notes that the cases also share other empirically discernible fundamental characteristics that differ from historical cases exemplifying other political systems.[62] Eisenstadt divides the book into two parts, the first dealing with the similarities among these cases in the development of configurational patterns and the second with the similarities among the cases in the maintenance of these patterns. Eisenstadt attempts to balance the comparisons of similarities with comparisons of differences between these cases of bureaucratic empires and those cases falling into related but clearly distinct categories. He refers to the latter as control groups. "The analysis here includes several societies . . . that, because they shared some, but only some, characteristics of the bureaucratic societies, served as control groups with regard to the hypothesis about the conditions of institutionalization of the political systems of the historical bureaucratic societies."[63]

Eisenstadt uses such control groups to accomplish two purposes. First, contrast cases help substantiate that bureaucratic empires are an empirically valid historical configuration. What is not a bureaucratic empire accents what is.[64] But there is a second and more significant purpose, a theoretical one. Eisenstadt cites contrast cases as evidence that configurations are systemic in nature but are not at the same time on a natural evolutionary track. For example, he discusses the failure of the Carolingian Empire and Mongol Empire to become bureaucratic empires, even though in both cases strong rulers gave these societies "a marked orientation" in that direction. In both, the historical conditions were insufficient for the creation of the *system* of bureaucratic empires: "The ruler's attempts to establish a centralized polity . . . did not become fully institutionalized: Polities of this kind generally 'regressed,' so to speak, into types of 'precentralized' polities – patrimonial empires, dual-conquest empires, or feudal states."[65]

On the whole, however, Eisenstadt has little use for contrast cases. His purpose in *Political Systems,* as well as in his other writings, is to analyze what a configuration is rather than what it is not. For this purpose, he must compare those cases that serve as examples of the type. As I will discuss, such comparisons of similarity have more theoretical than classificatory significance.

In *Revolution and the Transformations of Societies,* as in *Political Systems,* Eisenstadt offers classification as a means to begin analyzing history and specifically revolution. In this book, however, the typological entry into history is accomplished through a classification of change, instead of societies or some institutional part of societies. Here, too, he argues that complexity requires classification: History "testifies to a universal societal predisposition to change."[66] Not all change is alike, however. "Even a superficial look at the history of human societies as presented by the evolutionists indicates that their approach is simplistic, that far-reaching changes that historical and even primitive societies have experienced cannot be accounted for by their assumptions."[67] At the same time, change is not limitless. "Just as the themes of protest are not randomly distributed but are systematically related to the parameters of the social order and its cultural traditions, so movements of protest within any society are systematically related to its basic organizational parameters."[68] Like societies and institutions, maintains Eisenstadt, change has configurational natures. *Revolutions* is a study of those configurations, an analysis of "some basic patterns of societal conflict, contradiction, and change especially from the point of view of our interest in understanding the specificity of the types of social change subsumed under the rubric of 'modern revolution.' "[69]

Eisenstadt isolates three overarching types of changes that occur in historical societies. These types ideally provide the contrast needed to reveal the nature of modern change, as well as the systemic, nonevolutionary characteristics of change in general. First, there are the "patterns of segregative change."[70] He notes that these patterns occur in different types of historical societies, such as patrimonial regimes, nomadic kingdoms, and a few centralized kingdoms. Citing several historical examples for each type of society, he argues that change in these cases follows the systemic contours of these types of societies. These contours reveal a dissociation or segregation of institutional spheres; change occurred within spheres rather than among them, so that whatever changes did occur they rarely influenced the stability of the configuration. Thus sectarian movements or even rebellions against a particular ruler would be unlikely to take on transformational qualities, which would result in a configurational change of the society itself.

A second type of change is what Eisenstadt calls the "coalescent pattern of change."[71] This pattern is also common to several different types of societies, in particular bureaucratic empires and feudal regimes containing imperial elements. Giving historical examples for these types as well, Eisenstadt argues that coalescent change reflects the systemic parameters of the type of society in which it occurs. These parameters are set by the overlapping of institutional spheres; religious, economic, and social groups and institutions are interconnected within the political framework. Thus a protest movement that begins in one sphere, for instance a sectarian movement, would naturally converge on the political center and involve other nonreligious and nonpolitical groups in that society. Change in these types of societies would "coalesce" in political institutions and would have the potential for dramatic conflict. Typical among such conflicts are dynastic rebellions resulting in the overthrow of the state apparatus and its replacement by different political institutions and possibly different symbolic legitimations for political order. Yet even with so violent a change, Eisenstadt argues, the systemic qualities of these forms of society in premodern times "did not burst beyond the limits of traditionality."[72] Revolutionary change did not arise naturally from coalescent patterns.

The third type of historical change Eistenstadt labels the "pattern of exceptional change."[73] Just as the term implies, this type of change refers to those exceptions to the rule, such as the Greek and Roman city-states and the Near Eastern tribal societies out of which Judaism and Islam grew. In these cases, rapid change arose out of deep-rooted social conflicts that became translated into political struggle in such a way that the political order was reconceptualized "in a new type of political symbolism." Although rapid and historically decisive, such changes were seldom institutionalized into a stable societal system. Revolutionary change did not arise from this source either.

Having grouped the complexity of premodern change into three major patterns, Eisenstadt analyzes their internal varations and potentials at some length. He concludes that what is known as revolutionary change has no place in any of these categories. "Modern revolutionary symbolism and movements, as well as associated processes of change, stand in sharp contrast to the traditional patterns we have been discussing."[74] Modern revolutions belong to a new and different type of change, one characterized by, among other things, a "transformation of the fundamental premises of the social and cultural order" and a "restructuring of the relationship between the center and the periphery."[75] The ideas of equality, freedom, and participation created new modes of interaction that increased activity in and among all spheres of life. In short, revolutionary change created a new type of society. Within this new type, the family was no longer isolated from the legal framework, economics from politics, religion from secular beliefs. Each sphere of life intertwined with all other spheres and converged on the political center to sustain its functions and to redress its discontents. "Out of these processes of revolution there developed unique types of societal transformation and ultimately a new civilization: the civilization of modernity."[76] Against these four basic types of change (three traditional patterns and one modern pattern) Eisenstadt analyzes societal changes in the world today – their conditions, their variations, and their consequences.

Whether he is classifying societies, institutions, social changes, or something else, Eisenstadt proceeds on the assumption that historical complexity is a patterned complexity. Classifications must capture those patterns, and comparisons of difference (i.e., typological comparison) provide the way to do that. Comparisons are the net by which the elusive configurations of history are trapped for close observation. At one point, in *Political Systems,* Eisenstadt reflects on this procedure:

> Are we justified in grouping these various historically and geographically separate and distinct societies under one heading, and claiming that they constitute or belong to one type? Obviously, many differences must exist between these different societies – differences in historical and geographical backgrounds and in cultural traditions. And yet, from the point of view of comparative sociological analysis, they seem to belong to one type evincing some basic common characteristics. These common characteristics do not, of course, eliminate the cultural and historical differences between them – but at least some of these differences can most profitably be regarded as variations of these common qualities, or as factors which influence such variations; and they can be most fruitfully analyzed as such.[77]

Gary G. Hamilton

Here as elsewhere, Eisenstadt maintains that, if a historically valid configuration is discovered, the differences among the historical examples of that configuration are variations on a theme. In making this claim, Eisenstadt is, in effect, arguing that historical complexity comes in two varieties: the greater complexities arising from the differences among configurations and the lesser complexities arising from differences within configurations. Classifying is designed to deal with the greater complexities, with those basic differences among configurations. This is an exercise in distinguishing between apples and oranges – between those things that can be compared at only the most general level, and never in depth. Theorizing, the second step in configurational analysis, aims at the discovery of the essence of the configuration, and thus is most concerned with lesser complexities – the "little" differences in history that reveal the underlying rules.

Theorizing

How do theories about history relate to classifications of history? How is it possible to build theories from classifications? Does not the very process of classification directly influence the nature of the resulting theories?

On the surface, none of these questions poses much difficulty for Eisenstadt. In fact, his answers, largely implicit in his writings, provide the core of his sociology of history. As he states in several locations, only when historical variation has been categorized can generalizations about history emerge. Only when one knows what is there in history can one tell what it means. Naturally theories arise from classifications because, if well done, those classifications embody historical reality. To build a theoretical understanding of history is the reason that Eisenstadt develops typologies in the first place. In the final section, I will evaluate Eisenstadt's attempts to build theories of history. For the present I will suspend judgment, in an effort to convey in a brief space Eisenstadt's method for developing theories as well as some examples of the theories he makes.

Eisenstadt begins *Political Systems* with a statement of purpose: "Its main objective is the comparative analysis of a certain common type of political system [bureaucratic empires] that can be found in different societies, and it seeks to find some patterns or laws in the structures and development of such political systems."[78] He pursues this objective throughout the study. After isolating bureaucratic empires as a type of political system, Eisenstadt develops hypotheses designed to

102

probe its very nature. Eisenstadt lists two principal hypotheses and a series of corollary ones in his second chapter, after his discussion of the fundamental characteristics of bureaucratic empires, and continually refers to the process of verification of these hypotheses throughout the remainder of his book.

At what are these hypotheses aimed? Both hypotheses point to the specification of "the conditions under which the political systems of the centralized bureaucratic empires develop, become institutionalized, and are maintained."[79] In other words, given the fundamental characteristics of bureaucratic empires, which constitute the *essence* of this historical form, Eisenstadt wants hypotheses about how this essence arises out of a historical past in which it is not present and how it remains stable despite varying circumstances. The first hypothesis probes the contribution of the political sphere to the development and maintenance of the system; he hypothesizes that a necessary condition of bureaucratic empires is the ruler's "aspirations and activities" that promote a degree of political autonomy from other societal institutions.[80] The second hypothesis deals with the contribution of "non-political institutions, in the fields of economic and cultural activity or social organization and stratification" to the same ends.[81] Here he hypothesizes that two conditions were necessary for the historical appearance and continuation of this configuration: first, a level of differentiation "within *all* institutional spheres of society" promoting specialized activity, and second, an availability of "free-floating resources" (e.g., revenues, symbols, workers) that could be used by a ruler.[82]

Eisenstadt clearly recognizes that the verification of such hypotheses requires the study of internal variation, which in turn requires, as I will discuss, more typologies and hence more comparative analysis. But the study of variation internal to a type is a study of dynamics, not of morphology, although morphological elements naturally enter in. At the forefront in the study of dynamics is the question of similarities. What do all the cases within a type have in common with regard to the hypotheses being tested? If the cases have been accurately classified, there must be striking similarities that override the differences among them, differences that in the end can be seen as minor variations on major themes. Insofar as the similarities exist, this further supports the empirical validity of the type as well as revealing its essential dynamics. Eisenstadt organizes each chapter of *Political Empires* around an aspect of the hypotheses, and within each chapter he presents brief case studies of the principal examples of bureaucratic empires to show their similarities in regard to that aspect. He usually concludes each chapter with a summary of the basic similarities, but always reminds the reader that differences also exist and that some of these differences may be consequential.

Given the hypotheses and the procedure, what sorts of theories emerge from Eisenstadt's analysis of bureaucratic empires? The principal theory, undergirding all of the other ones, is quite simply that the *system* of bureaucratic empires depends on the simultaneous presence of the conditions outlined in the two hypotheses: (1) a degree of political autonomy for the ruler and (2) a "certain level of differentiation and free-floating resources in all the major spheres of the society." "Only when these two conditions obtained concurrently – even if developed to different degrees – was it possible for the basic premises of the political systems of the historical bureaucratic societies to evolve constantly and to be institutionalized, in the forms of a centralized polity, organs of political struggles, and bureaucratic administration."[83]

In what sense is this a theory? It is not a secular theory, in the sense of offering an explanation for a particular event. Instead it is a configurational theory; it resides above the level of historical details. The theory itself states that the essential characteristics of the configuration only appear when these two conditions are met. Eisenstadt's brief use of contrast cases aims at showing that the configuration does not appear when one of the conditions is not present. More importantly, however, he shows through the study of internal variation that the two conditions can be met in many *types* of ways. Different historically specific patterns produce the same configurational pattern. Different types of exchange mechanisms produce economic specialists (e.g., merchants, brokers, consumers, and producers) and free economic resources.[84] Different types of religious organizations and ideologies similarly produce their own specialists and free ideological resources, which the ruler can manipulate as sources of political legitimation.[85] Likewise, rulers, having many different types of political objectives, attempt to create equivalent situations of political autonomy.[86] They favor different types of taxation,[87] use different types of armies,[88] promote different types of laws,[89] and in general advocate different types of policies toward gaining control of the free-floating resources while simultaneously denying their use to different types of competing elites.[90] Despite all these and many other differences for which Eisenstadt outlines and develops typologies, the same outcome prevails: the development and perpetuation of the necessary and sufficient conditions for bureaucratic empires to exist as a configurational entity.

Once both conditions are present, in the proper degrees and forms, the system of bureaucratic empires "crystallizes."[91] From the *flux* of history emerges a *form* of history. Once a form is "institutionalized," it takes on systemic qualities, with self-reinforcing patterns that maintain its internal functions and protect its boundaries; the form, so to speak, lives in history. Rulers, merchants, theologians, elites, and bureaucrats are caught in a system of their own making; their decisions and actions are shaped by its parameters. But these parameters, according to Eisenstadt, do not imply a simple value consensus or produce a harmonious society. Instead, the parameters provide the ground rules, the norms, for political struggle.[92] More important, they give rise to basic contradictions within the system of bureaucratic empires, contradictions between the rulers' needs for resources and their abilities to obtain them over time.[93]

The continuous and patterned tensions between competing groups over the use of resources lead to several patterns of change.[94] The direction of these changes, however, is not fixed. Rather, the potential for change lodged within the patterns of bureaucratic empires holds open the fate of any one society. A society's system of bureaucratic empire may disintegrate and move to a simpler form; it may continue as it has, by balancing the contradictory elements; or it may be pushed forward to a more complex type of political system, the modern one. In none of these fates, however, are contradictions internal to societies ultimately resolved: "These tensions continue and no solution of them can be accepted as final and unchangeable."[95]

In schematic outline, this is Eisenstadt's theory of bureaucratic empires. It is a theory about a configuration in history. Like any good Aristotelian theory, it aims at understanding the nature of the beast – how it comes into being, becomes stable, and changes.

In *Revolution*, Eisenstadt pushes configurational analysis to its theoretical limits. As in *Political Systems*, Eisenstadt's objective is to analyze the dynamics of a configuration in history. In this book, however, the configuration is a type of change. "Under what conditions and in what historical circumstances do revolutions and revolutionary transformations occur?"[96] Besides being of interest in the context of the literature on revolutions, this question goes to the heart of Eisenstadt's sociology of history. This is a question not just about revolutions, but more particularly about transformations.

Transformation is the term Eisenstadt uses to describe a change in configurations. A society is transformed when its systemic patterns change from being of one type of society to that of another type. To explain transformations is the crucial test of Eisenstadt's configurational analysis. As I have shown, this mode of analysis attempts to

Gary G. Hamilton

locate and describe stable types of societies. In the context of history, however, specific societies change. For instance, particular societies may have left their tribal origins to become, in a matter of centuries, industrial nations. If history reveals the existence of relatively stable configurations, how does one describe and explain changes in those configurations in particular areas? One way to do this, of course, is to propose an evolutionary sequence of configurations. Eisenstadt is opposed to this solution, for the reasons I have outlined above. He is equally opposed to any form of analysis that would downplay or deny the existence of these configurations. He is caught in a dilemma, and in *Revolution* he offers his most encompassing attempt to resolve this particular theoretical challenge.

Superficially, Eisenstadt's solution to this dilemma is simple – too simple, because, as I will discuss in the conclusion, it involves some methodological problems that are difficult, if not impossible, to solve. In *Revolution*, Eisenstadt propounds a theory of history that is firmly grounded in configurational analysis. Although portions of this theory are found in his early works, even those preceding *Political Systems*,[97] in *Revolution* it is most explicit.

History, in the sense of changing configurational patterns, is the result of neither evolutionary forces nor historical accidents.[98] But change does come in patterns. These patterns are complex and hence change must be broken into different types, each of which has essential characteristics. Because types of changes are themselves varied, both in their appearances and in their consequences, they cannot be studied apart from the societies in which they are found. This is the case, argues Eisenstadt, because change is directed by and rooted in the systemic nature of societies. Even so, each society institutionalizes its configurational system in slightly different ways. Each society works out the potential of a configuration, and attempts to institutionalize that potential in a concrete form. Change arises from the specific modes of institutionalization and not simply from the configurations. In this sense, Eisenstadt maintains that *minor variations* on major configurational themes determine the specific directions of change, and consequently of history itself. Configurations in history do not line up in a necessary sequence, such that all societies move in an orderly fashion from one development stage to another. Instead, the minor variations supply the specific dynamics for societal transformations and determine the direction and content of change. Therefore, the direction of change is always open and varies considerably even among societies having the same configurational pattern.[99]

In this manner, Eisenstadt suggests, revolutionary change must be viewed. Revolutionary change is a transformative change that carries societies from premodern configurational patterns into the civilization of modernity. This type of change, however, is not inherent in the dynamics of premodern societies of whatever type. Instead, it arose as a minor variation of the system of bureaucratic empires. Revolutionary change is a "mutation."[100] Eisenstadt locates the beginnings of this mutation in sixteenth- and seventeenth-century Western Europe. "The principal participants were *traditional* [rulers]," whose primary goals were to generate and control resources, and whose attempts to force closure in regard to these resources helped generate new social, economic, and religious groups.[101] Within these groups, which were linked more closely than ever to a political center, opposition grew, creating the conditions for a transformation into a historically unique configuration. The "breakthroughs" appeared in the symbols and ideologies of revolution as well as in its basic organizational principles. These started "in the Revolt of the Netherlands and intensified in the Great Rebellion in England. They were more fully elaborated in the ideology of the American Revolution and they crystallized in the French Revolution."[102] The crystallization of revolution marks the establishment of a new configuration in history: "the civilization of modernity."

This new course in history became open to other societies that had transformative potential – those traditional societies having a coalescent pattern of change. In fact, such societies were forcibly turned toward this path by the dynamic created by a transformed Western Europe and United States. Carried with missionary fervor by the West, world capitalism and world ideologies interrupted the continuity of all varieties of traditional societies, forcing those societies to alter or adjust to the new configurational patterns of modernization and modern society.[103] Societies exhibiting coalescent patterns of change, such as Russia and China, altered their traditional patterns by means of a revolutionary transformation. Those societies characterized by a segregative pattern of change, such as most Latin American and South Asian countries, did not respond to Western influence with a transformative change, but rather reformulated traditional patterns, becoming what Eisenstadt calls neo-patrimonial societies.[104] Regardless of the type of change that occurred, each society crystallized the potential of its respective configuration in its own fashion, which in turn structured the specific direction of change for that society. Although similar in form, societies remain diverse in practice. Modernity does not breed conformity. Change is always open.

This brief interpretive rendering of Eisenstadt's historical theories shows that they are about configurations and not events. As developed in both *Political Systems* and *Revolution* as well as his other works, these theories strike a precarious balance between the stability of forms and the openness of change. On one hand, stability is manifest in change, because change is part of the orderly behavior of forms. Says Eisenstadt, "[Changes are] inherent in, and part and parcel of, the structural characteristics and political process of the society in which they occurred."[105] On the other hand, Eisenstadt suggests that the direction of change, and ultimately the transformation of societies, is determined by the idiosyncratic ways a particular society institutionalizes or fails to institutionalize configurational patterns. In any one society, its system of bureaucratic empire may falter and the society revert to simpler form. Or its process of modernization may break down.[106] Or conditions may push the society to a more complex form, perhaps by revolutionary means. Whatever happens, the configurations are there in history, as more or less stable systemic patterns, and specific societies move into and out of those patterns according to the manner in which the potentials of societies are crystallized in action.

Interpreting

The last step in configurational analysis is the interpretation of specific cases. After developing a theory of a configuration, how then does Eisenstadt interpret historical examples of that configuration? To what extent do his classifications of societies aid his interpretation of events occurring in any one society?

Whether they appreciate his writings or not, reviewers of his works uniformly agree that Eisenstadt engages in very little historical analysis.[107] For instance, one reviewer, Charles Tilly, compares the argument developed in *Revolution* with his great-uncle's Marbelator.

> You put a small marble in the slot at the top, and the ball began its antic trip through the machine. It clicked and whirred across bridges, down steps, and around corners, sometimes speeding and sometime dawdling, often veering into the depths of the runways only to shoot out unexpectedly at a lower level. But when it rolled from the bottom chute, the marble was still the same glass ball that went in. *Revolution and the Transformation of Societies* is an abstract Marbelator – a simple, familiar argument careening through a vast conceptual contraption.[108]

Like those of many others, Tilly's critique centers on the absence of case detail. Eisenstadt "offers neither a systematic body of evidence nor a sustained analysis of any particular revolution."[109] Therefore, charges Tilly, Eisenstadt's books do not increase our understanding of empirical events.[110]

Eisenstadt's critics are correct; one does not read an Eisenstadt book or article to learn about the substance of historical events. One encounters no historical narratives and no attempts at locating historical causation in the course of particular actions. Nor does one confront a rigorous effort at formulating universal history, in the mode of Immanuel Wallerstein's *The Modern World-System*. This is not to say, however, that Eisenstadt offers no historical interpretations. Quite the contrary is true; his writings are filled with them. But all of them are summary interpretations of historical evidence or interpretations of how particular cases should be classified.

In *Political Systems*, short case studies appear in most substantive chapters. For instance, when discussing the social organization of bureaucratic empires, Eisenstadt devotes two pages to the Byzantine Empire, three to the T'ang dynasty in China, two to the Spanish-American Empire, and one to the European countries in the Age of Absolutism.[111] In each case study, he summarizes the conclusions found in the work of historians and directs these conclusions to the analytic substance of the chapter. In the case of Absolutist Europe, for instance, he notes that "one trend was evident throughout the seventeenth and eighteenth centuries: the growth in the numbers and influence of the urban middle class."[112] There is nothing surprising or original in this or any other case study; they are merely summaries, and always phrased abstractly. Moreover, one has no sense of being offered a testable hypothesis that could be applied to one of the historical cases. In fact, a reader who is not familiar with the historical case material might well get the impression that the major interpretive problems in the historical literature had all been solved.

This impression is certainly conveyed in Eisenstadt's analytic appendix. Almost one hundred pages in length, the appendix contains twenty-three tables in which Eisenstadt rates each historical case according to the main variables of bureaucratic empires. For some variables he gives cases numerical scores. For instance, one learns that the "autonomy of political goals of rulers" in Absolutist France, during the reign of Louis XIV, had a score of five on a scale of one to ten, one being "almost total dependence" and ten "great independence."[113] During the reign of Louis XV, however, the same variable had a score of three.[114] How Eisenstadt arrives at these scores is not clear.[115] What is clear, however, is that by these tables Eisenstadt wants to verify the conditional existence of bureaucratic empires as well as their internal variations. As he puts it, "Tabular presentation may well serve to bring some order into what might otherwise easily become an impressionistic evaluation."[116] Without some knowledge of the cases, one might impute a degree of certitude to what in fact must be considered a highly impressionistic scoring system.

Fortunately, however, what value *Political Systems* contains is not found in the analytic appendix or in the interpretation of case material. Eisenstadt *does not* offer this work or any of his other works, with the possible exception of his studies of Israeli society, as "an original contribution to an analysis of any society."[117] To look for such a contribution is to come away disappointed. Instead, Eisenstadt envisions his contribution to be one of general sociology, of the development of general theories about history and social formations. It is on these grounds that I will evaluate his work, not on the grounds that he does not make an original contribution to our understanding of particular cases.

Eisenstadt's Sociology of History: An Assessment

The preceding section schematically traces the objectives, methods, and theories of Eisenstadt's historical sociology. These center on what I have called configurational analysis. As I have implied above, the logic of configurational analysis is analogous, but by no means identical, to the logic used by biologists to examine species behavior. It is also analogous to the logic used by chemists to analyze substances. These three areas of investigation, as well as others that could be suggested, have in common the attempt to examine natural forms. Although Eisenstadt occasionally borrows concepts from both biology and chemistry, he does not use explicit analogies as a mode of explanation. At this point, let me draw out the analogy to biology more clearly, for it is on the basis of the general logic of this approach that I will evaluate Eisenstadt's sociology of history.

Whether studying monkeys or amoebae, specialists of animal life attempt to define the parameters of behavior, as well as the internal functioning, of a form of life.[118] The understanding of animal behavior is couched within the understanding of that species as a unified form of existence. Such unified forms always united a multiplicity of parts. As the philosopher of biological sciences, Marjorie Grene, points out, the unified whole and the multiplicity of parts necessarily exhibit " 'double determinateness,' the whole depending on the parts as conditions of its existence, but the parts existing as parts only as so constituted by the unifying principle of the whole. Thus in themselves, at least in living nature, all entities exist on at least two levels at once."[119] Theories about biological entities are typically theories of double determinateness, and such theories necessarily create a functional nexus between the unified whole and the contributing parts.

When explaining the specific actions of one animal, specialists use two distinct sets of causal factors. First, they examine the actions in terms of how an animal of that species acts. For example, the animal barks because it is a dog; barking is in the nature of dogs, as well as being functional to that nature. Second, they examine those situational factors of the setting that would account for such species-specific actions; the dog barks because a stranger approaches. The first set of factors is ahistorical, applicable to any animal of that species regardless of time and place. The second set is specifically historical and situational. To explain the multiplicity of animal species, biologists typically point to the second set as being decisive; historical and situational circumstances structure the process of natural selection and change by mutation. Even though the general direction of evolution has been toward more complex wholes and more specialized parts, the operation of evolution is worked out situationally and always results in the development of another unified whole.

Eisenstadt's historical sociology parallels this logic of analysis. His specific focus is on the double determinateness of particular social forms, that is, on the conditions for the existence of unified historical configurations, on the principles that structure the relation among parts, and on the function of parts in maintaining the principles of the whole. Bureaucratic empires, revolutionary change, or any type of social form exists simultaneously at two levels: the crystallized whole and the institutionalized parts, both of which are functionally intertwined. In terms of the biological analogy, Eisenstadt's historical sociology deals almost exclusively with the first set of causal factors, the behavior of forms. This is a distinctly sociological enterprise, and is essentially ahistorical. Eisenstadt is, of course, aware of the importance of the second set of causal factors, the historical and situational influences, but his writings do not emphasize these. He also downplays, but certainly does not ignore, the processes of social evolution and the general attributes of all social systems. His chief interest, to which all else takes second place, is the identification and analysis of unified social wholes.

With this emphasis, he differs from the Parsonian interpretation of structural functionalism. Parsons's main works in the general area of historical sociology stress the evolutionary process, primarily a theory of differentiation, and the general attributes of social systems (e.g., the functional prerequisites). Parsons slights the notion of a multiplicity of social forms and does not develop his sociology as a means to analyze an array of distinct, unified wholes. Yet, despite the differences between Eisenstadt's and Parsons's analytic approaches, Eisenstadt continues to use a Parsonian interpretation of society to analyze the double determinateness of social forms, albeit in a reconstructed way. For instance, Eisenstadt repeatedly applied Parsons's theory of evolution (i.e., resources that are released from ascriptive bonds through entrepreneurial efforts are reinstutionalized at more universalized and specialized levels) to explain the transformation of parts in the creation of new social configurations.[120] Although he employs a variant of structural functional theory, his analysis remains in tension with it.

From 1973 on, Eisenstadt begins to write about the similarities between his interpretation of structural functionalism and the neo-Marxian interpretations of societies.

> The major analytic contribution of the more "open" Marxist approaches was their emphasis on the relationship between power elements and the systemic characteristics of social order; on the basic laws . . . which regulate the structure of the system; on the systemic nature of conflict, in the sense of systemic contradiction in the dynamics of social systems; and on the historicity of such dynamics.[121]

> Of special interest . . . is the recent emphasis in Marxist or Marxist-inspired analyses on international systems in general, particularly the modern capitalist or imperialist system. These analyses use general systemic qualities of supranational entities to explain the dynamic of concrete societies.[122]

Eisenstadt is critical of Marxist sociology as well, but his critique, unlike his critiques of evolutionism and historicism, centers on his desire for Marxists to expand their insights from an exclusive concentration on the economic sphere to an incorporation of other institutional spheres. Eisenstadt believes this expansion is now occurring: "The most important opening on the part of the Marxists was the recognition that the internal structure of society was given not only in its relation to economic power but in the deeper structure which – even when defined as mode of production – could not be subsumed under any single institutional determinant, and which probably had multiple facets and principles."[123]

Indeed, a similarity exists between Marx's sociology and Eisenstadt's version of structural functionalism, but it is more an ontological than a theoretical similarity. Both interpretations emphasize the reality of configurations, and both reject a strictly evolutionary point of view but remain in tension with it. Marx himself defined his approach as an "analysis of forms" and directed his more scientific efforts at the factors of double determinateness in economic configurations.[124] Like Eisenstadt, Marx wanted "natural laws" of these configurations. Theoretically, of course, Eisenstadt and Marx are far apart. Eisenstadt tends to locate the essential characteristics of societies in political institutions, where Marx stressed the primacy of economic institutions. More recent Marxist writers, however, are closing this gap by writing about the institutional linkages among spheres and by emphasizing the partial autonomy of the political state.[125] These writings are heading toward a rapprochement with structural functionalism, a trend that might lead to a greater appreciation of Eisenstadt's writings.

Whether a rapprochement is in the offing or not, Eisenstadt's sociology of history is worth evaluating seriously, not only in its own right but also as an example of a sociological approach to history that Eisenstadt shares with others. A complete evaluation on both scores is impossible in this location. In the remaining space I want to discuss what appear to me to be some of the general hazards of the overall approach, as well as some specific shortcomings of Eisenstadt's work.

The general hazards can be viewed as distinct sets of challenges that are present at each step in configurational analysis. Of the three, the challenge of classification is the most serious, because with this approach classifying operates on the assumption that real configurations can be found in history. The first challenge can be phrased as a question. In a world of complexity and variation, is it possible to define genuine similarities among societies or some aspect thereof? In sociological analysis, this question goes beyond the more biological question, Is a white crow a crow? Social and historical facts *are not* directly observable; the size and shape of a society, an institution, a mode of production, an idea, or a role cannot be seen and measured as well or as accurately as can a crow of whatever color. Lacking the ability directly and empirically to observe a *form* of history or society, configurational analysts must attempt to locate the genuine similarities by using classificatory concepts. On this point Eisenstadt would undoubtedly agree with Marx: "In the analysis of . . . forms . . . neither microscopes nor chemical reagents are of use. The force of abstraction must replace them both."[126] Therefore, the challenge of classification is to locate the concepts that enable one to find and describe configurations that actually exist in nature.

113

Where is one to find such concepts and what sort of concepts are they? Eisenstadt uses Parsonian concepts. Marx was more eclectic, borrowing concepts from Hegel and the British economists, among others. Regardless of where they were found, the concepts determined what features of society were to be preserved as significant similarities and what other features could be regarded as inconsequential differences. In other words, classificatory concepts are predeterminations and necessarily interpenetrate with one's theoretical framework.

Unlike a microscope, abstractions are not inductive devices by which one explores a natural world. Instead, their logical structure is deductive; intertwined with theory, they deductively establish which and in what manner features of society contain the unifying principles of the whole. Hence, the empirical status of the forms derived from configurational analysis differs from that guiding a biological analysis of animal life or a chemical analysis of substances. In *Political Systems* Eisenstadt says there are seven main types of political systems. Is this an empirical statement or an assertion arrived at by way of a theory of classification? Similarly, is Marx's classification of the modes of production empirical or theoretical? Both would imply that they are empirical; in Eisenstadt's chemical language, only so many forms crystallize out of a historical solution. These classifications are empirical only insofar as they derive from a theoretical framework that pinpoints "genuine" criteria of specification, whereas in biology and chemistry, the forms of life and of substance exist independently of the theories used to explain them. Thus the theories can be tested for how well they explain the forms. This is impossible in configurational analysis, because to do so is tautological; the theory predetermines the forms and the forms necessarily support the theory. Whether configurations actually exist in history is certainly a debatable question, a question that is not to be answered through the force of abstraction. The interpenetration of theory and classification creates a tautological loop that is probably impossible to circumvent in configurational analysis.

The challenge of theorizing about configurations once they are defined is also difficult. Assume, for the moment, that genuine criteria of classification exist and that real societal configurations can be identified. Given this assumption, a student of social forms must meet two challenges of theorizing. The first is to formulate a theory of double determinateness and the second is to develop a theory of transformational change. The first is a logical requirement of any analysis that concentrates on unified wholes, whatever the discipline. The second is a logical requirement of configurational analysis when a temporal dimension is added.

The first challenge of theorizing is also better understood as a question. Given that social configurations exist, what are their unifying principles and what parts or combination of parts serve as the necessary and sufficient conditions for the existence of the whole? Eisenstadt's theory of bureaucratic empires is totally an attempt to answer these two questions, and his effort to do so consists of analyzing all the historical cases that he places into this category of political systems. Marx took a different and more historically specific strategy in developing his theory of the capitalist mode of production.

> The physicist either observes physical phenomena where they occur in their most typical form and freest from disturbing influences or, wherever possible, he makes experiments under conditions that assure the occurrence of the phenomena in their normality. In this work, I have to examine the capitalist mode of production, and the conditions of production and exchange corresponding to that mode. Up to the present time their classic ground is England. That is the reason why England is used as the chief illustration in the development of my theoretical ideas.[127]

Whether drawn from one case or many cases, the end product of theorizing is to be a theory of a unified whole that exists apart from situational influences. In other words, a theory of a configuration must strive for a level of generality that cuts it loose from empirical cases. The same theory must apply to any example of that configuration, regardless of time and space.

This kind of theory necessarily possesses several features.[128] It is a theory of double determinateness, which has functionalist implications; the parts function to preserve the singularity of the whole and the principles of the whole function to establish the particular arrangement of the parts. It is endogenic; relations between the whole and parts are self-maintaining, regardless of whether the internal processes of a social form work toward equilibrium or toward transformational change. Finally, causal explanations based on a configurational theory are always, in some sense, teleological; they are arguments based on the design of the social form. The causes for monopolization in capitalist societies or bureaucratization in bureaucratic empires are analogous to those explaining the barking of a dog: They are in the nature of the entity and functional to it.

The danger of a theory of double determinateness is the likely possibility of one's sacrificing historical specificity for an internally consistent model by which everything and hence nothing can be explained. In other words, by what criteria can one distinguish between the "natural" behavior of a form and situationally specific behavior? The abstractness and ambiguity of configurational theories allow for no clear distinction between the two, with the result that historically specific events tend to be explained teleologically, as a natural consequence of the entity itself.

This danger is magnified by the second challenge of theorizing – to develop a theory of transformational change. A constant tension exists in configurational analysis between the flux of historical examples and the stability of historical forms. Being based on the actuality of forms, configurational analysis of history not only involves theorizing about those forms but also involves explaining how any particular society is transformed from one form to another. A theorist must ask, Where are the mechanisms of transformation located: in the workings of the configuration or in the specificity of the historical environment? At what point is the essence of one historical form replaced by the essence of another historical form? These are logically troublesome questions, which configurational theorists are forced to resolve theoretically instead of empirically. The reason is simple enough. The lack of independence between forms and theory makes it difficult to specify environmental and situational components of configurational behavior, which in turn makes it difficult to distinguish between "normal" change and transformational change. For the sake of logical completeness, among other reasons, most theorists locate the mechanism of transformation within a theory of double determinateness.

Marx, of course, found these mechanisms of transformation in the contradictions between the relations and forces of production and suggested that at the historical moment when these contradictions become too severe a revolution would provide the means of transformation. Eisenstadt, too, postulates that contradictions are present in all types of societies, and that these are both normal aspects of configurational behavior and the motors of transformational change. But Eisenstadt wants the direction of change to be open and therefore stresses the decisiveness of situational factors in determining change. Despite his recognition of situational variability, Eisenstadt, however, never leaves a configurational mode of analysis. Instead, in his abstract and ambiguous way of writing, he tends to expand the typologies that explain internal variation of a type to fit the number of cases he examines. In so doing, he hopelessly intermixes configurational and situational factors and provides no way to distinguish between them. As a consequence, his ahistorical analysis absorbs situational factors, making them as much a result of the configuration as factors influencing its development. Therefore, regardless of his words to the contrary, the direction of change in Eisenstadt's analysis is not open; it is imprinted in the systemic patterns of a society's adaptation to a configuration. The mechanisms of transformation are hence not historical or situational, but remain lodged within the workings of the unified whole. Although his writings are often ambiguous, Eisenstadt, like Marx, would seem to explain transformations teleologically, as a function of the inherent contradictions within social forms.

The first two steps in configurational analysis, classifying and theorizing, rely heavily on the assumptions that social forms do, in fact, exist in nature and that one's theoretical framework is sufficient to locate and describe their essential reality. As I have suggested, both assumptions involve logical as well as empirical obstacles that are difficult if not impossible to overcome.

Despite these difficulties, however, I believe that configurational analysis is an invaluable tool in the analysis of history. The diversity of historical events and outcomes, the disquieting of the feeling that history may repeat itself, and the uncertainty of the world today require an understanding of the past that goes beyond a simple recounting of chronology. Configurational analysis allows an entry into the past that takes whole societies, eras, and even civilizations as the unit of observation. It is a descriptive form of analysis, by which an observer uses a predeterminative theoretical framework to abstract patterns from concrete events and to make sense of those patterns in terms of the societies in which they occur. Its importance to a sociological understanding of history lies in the descriptive, almost paradigmatic, force of the societal models that emerge by using this approach. For me, the value of the models is not that they present an essential reality but rather that they are useful fictions. Configurational models are never anything other than partial and faulty portrayals of a historical past. Yet they do provide a means by which an aspect of past actions can be tentatively interpreted for our present understanding. In making this claim, I am, of course, supporting Weber's claim that ideal types are ontologically a better way to enter history, and in making this claim, I am also suggesting that the most important challenge of configurational analysis is the challenge of interpreting.

The danger of using configurational analysis to interpret history is, as Bendix suggests, to make the abstractions more real than the actions and events from which they are drawn.[129] This is the fallacy of misplaced concreteness. Indeed, in configurational analysis it is always tempting to make the abstraction explain historical outcomes without ever seriously confronting the historical evidence. Eisenstadt succumbs to this temptation. Eisenstadt's model of bureaucratic empires is forceful, more so than the other models he develops, but even here he does not exploit its descriptive power in an empirical analysis. He does not use any of his models to disentangle the complexity of events; rather, he elevates historical complexity to the level of configurations. History becomes a function of complex configurations. It is certain that Eisenstadt is very sensitive to the diversity of historical causes: to the role of ideas and material interest, to the importance of consensus and conflict, and to the interplay between continuity and change. But he tries to place all of these factors into his configurational models in an effort to capture reality in the abstract. This weakens the descriptive force of his models because it drives them to such abstract heights that they are no longer useful as interpretive devices.

By contrast, the more one-sided focus of many Marxian configurations increases their usefulness by providing an explicit path to sets of empirical issues about history.[130] The temptation to use abstracted social forms as the explanation for such events as revolutions and economic crises is, of course, present in Marxian sociology. Also present is the temptation to make the models ever more encompassing and, in fact, to confine scholarly discourse to a discussion of models. Many succumb to both temptations, but even so there remains an empirical bent in Marxian sociology that is underdeveloped in structural functionalism.

The importance of Eisenstadt's sociology of history is his attempt to give structural functionalism the same bent. For me, however, he did not go far enough. By reifying Weber's ideal types, Eisenstadt makes his typologies stand for historical reality; as such they become the goal of analysis. For interpreting historical and situational causes, Weber's approach is the better one. Weber's typologies were to be the points of departure to "gaining insight . . . into the causal 'significance' of individual components of the events." Such typologies act as "control groups" – simplistic fabrications *against* which one disentangles actions and outcomes.[131] That such ideal types are fictitious does not deny the organizational, even the systemlike, qualities of societies. Rather, ideal types acknowledge these qualities while simultaneously acknowledging that they cannot be encompassed by any number of models. Most important, however, ideal types, although they may suggest systemic and functional aspects of society, also allow for the recognition that action and structure are two aspects of the same reality. With this recognition comes the realization that action and structure, being the

118

same thing, cannot be used to explain one another. Instead, causal explanations should aim for adequacy at the level of actor meanings.[132] To fashion such explanations is the most important challenge of configurational analysis; it is a challenge yet to be fully met.

Notes

Besides the contributors to this volume, who discussed and gave suggestions on an early draft of this essay, I want to thank a number of people who read or commented on the early draft, this revised draft, or both: Nicole Biggart, Leon Mayhew, Benjamin Orlove, Guenther Roth, Judith Stacey, and John Walton. I especially want to thank Theda Skocpol, whose lengthy comments on the first draft led to the present version.

 1. S. N. Eisenstadt, *The Political Systems of Empires* (New York: Free Press, 1963). Hereafter cited in the text as *Political Systems.*
 2. Reinhard Bendix, *Work and Authority in Industry* (New York: Wiley, 1956).
 3. Edward Gross, "Review of Work and Authority in Industry," *American Sociological Review* 21 (1956): 789–91.
 4. Karl Wittfogel, *Oriental Despotism* (New Haven, Conn.: Yale University Press, 1957); R. Coulborn, ed., *Feudalism in History* (Princeton, N.J.: Princeton University Press, 1956).
 5. E. P. Thompson, *The Making of the English Working Class* (New York: Vintage Books, 1963).
 6. Reinhard Bendix, *Nation-building and Citizenship* (New York: Wiley, 1964); Charles Tilly, *The Vendée* (Cambridge, Mass.: Harvard University Press, 1964); Barrington Moore, Jr., *Social Origins of Dictatorship and Democracy* (Boston: Beacon Press, 1966); Talcott Parsons, *Societies: Evolutionary and Comparative Perspectives* (Englewood Cliffs, N.J.: Prentice-Hall, 1966); Immanuel Wallerstein, *The Modern World-System* (New York: Academic Press, 1974); Perry Anderson, *Passages from Antiquity to Feudalism* (London: New Left Books, 1974).
 7. Gabriel Almond, "Review of Political Systems of Empires," *American Sociological Review* 29 (1964): 418. This assessment was also reached by Guenther Roth in his review of *Political Systems, American Journal of Sociology* 71 (1966): 722–23.
 8. Carl Becker, *The Heavenly City of the Eighteenth Century Philosophers* (New Haven, Conn.: Yale University Press, 1932).
 9. Ibid., p. 47.
10. For a recent example of these emphases, see Eisenstadt, "Cultural Orientations, Institutional Entrepreneurs, and Social Change: Comparative Analysis of Traditional Civilizations," *American Journal of Sociology* 85 (1980): 849–69.
11. Among the most useful of the numerous critiques of structural functionalism is Anthony D. Smith, *The Concept of Social Change* (London: Routledge & Kegan Paul, 1973); Alvin Gouldner, *The Coming Crisis of Western Sociology* (New York: Basic Books, 1970); and Richard J. Bernstein, *The Restructuring of Social and Political Theory* (Philadelphia: University of Pennsylvania Press, 1978).
12. Gouldner, *Western Sociology,* pp. 30–31.
13. Michel Foucault, *The Order of Things* (New York: Vintage Books, 1973), p. xiii.
14. To some extent, it is useful to view the attempt to legitimize one's own

scholarly work as an attempt to establish "communicative competence" in opposition to an accepted consensus. See Jürgen Habermas, "Towards a Theory of Communicative Competence," *Inquiry* 13 (1970): 360–75.

15. Max Weber, *The Methodology of the Social Sciences* (Glencoe, Ill.: Free Press, 1949); *Critique of Stammler* (New York: Free Press, 1977); and *Roscher and Knies: The Logical Problems of Historical Economies* (New York: Free Press, 1975); Karl Marx, *Grundrisse* (New York: Vintage Books, 1973); Emile Durkheim, *Montesquieu and Rousseau* (Ann Arbor: University of Michigan Press, 1965).

16. The current revival in theoretical sociology, marked by such works as Anthony Giddens, *New Rules of Sociological Method* (New York: Basic Books, 1976), seems almost totally concerned with this level of positioning.

17. For the references to Eisenstadt's major writings, see the following bibliography.

18. Eisenstadt's usual method for introducing the literature on a topic is through footnotes. In the text, he will draw a brief analytic conclusion about a historical case or present a short summary of a historical period. He will then use a footnote reference to list books and articles concerning the case or period, often without citing the page numbers that correspond to his interpretation.

19. Eisenstadt writes very little about his methodological approach or about methodology in general. His clearest statement is found in *Essays on Comparative Institutions* (New York: Wiley, 1965), pp. 1–68. Hereafter cited as *Comparative Institutions*.

20. See in particular *Tradition, Change, and Modernity* (New York: Wiley, 1973) and *Revolution and the Transformation of Societies* (New York: Free Press, 1978).

21. Eisenstadt and M. Curelaru, *The Form of Sociology – Paradigms and Crises* (New York: Wiley, 1976). Hereafter cited as *Form*.

22. I will elaborate this linkage with Marxian sociology in the final section of this chapter.

23. Eisenstadt does not use the term *historicism*, but he clearly has this interpretive tradition in mind when he criticizes the ecological group approach, as I describe in my discussion of Reinhard Bendix. Also see note 32.

24. Eisenstadt, *Comparative Institutions*, pp. 7–8.

25. Ibid.

26. Ibid., p. 7; also see "Social Change, Differentiation and Evolution," *American Sociological Review* 29 (1964): 375–86.

27. Eisenstadt, "Social Change, Differentiation and Evolution," p. 376.

28. Ibid., pp. 375–76. Also "Institutionalization and Change," *American Sociological Review* 29 (1964): 235–47.

29. This critique is usually implicit in his writings, and usually occurs in the context of his defending parts of structural functional theory, as for example in *Tradition, Change, and Modernity*, pp. 1–20. Sometimes this criticism is more open, as it is in *Revolution*, pp. 65–68 and in *Form*, pp. 178–210.

30. In *Comparative Institutions*, p. 51, for example, he notes that "differentiation is . . . first of all a classificatory concept." Although he uses it as a criterion for classification, he clearly uses the term in theoretical ways as well.

31. For instance, in *From Generation to Generation* (Glencoe, Ill.: Free Press, 1956), pp. 22–24, Eisenstadt explains the pattern variables in a long footnote and obviously regards them as the state of the sociological art. Later works do not show this level of confidence in the fact that his readers will

accept structural functional theory without some persuasion. This does not mean, however, that he drops the Parsonian concepts entirely. They remain very prominent throughout his works.

32. This definition of historicism is from Hans Myerhoff, *The Philosophy of History in Our Time* (Garden City, N.Y.: Doubleday, 1959), p. 10. This meaning of the term is quite different from that used by Karl Popper in his book, *The Poverty of Historicism* (New York: Harper Torchbook, 1964). Popper uses it to mean historical determinism and equates this approach to Marxian analysis.
33. Eisenstadt, *Tradition, Change, and Modernity*, p. 31.
34. Ibid., p. 104.
35. Ibid., p. 109.
36. Eisenstadt, *Form*, p. 89.
37. Ibid., pp. 10–13.
38. Ibid., pp. 253, 180–83, 196–97; *Comparative Institutions*, pp. 9–11; *Revolution*, pp. 60–68.
39. Eisenstadt, *Form*, p. 202 (my emphasis). In this passage, as well as others, Eisenstadt also cites Bendix's student, Randall Collins, as a member of the ecological group. For short critiques of Eisenstadt's writings by Bendix and Collins, see Collins, *Conflict Sociology* (New York: Academic Press, 1975), pp. 349–50; and Bendix and Guenther Roth, *Scholarship and Partisanship* (Berkeley: University of California Press, 1971), p. 210. In this passage, Bendix mentions no names, but his target clearly includes Eisenstadt.
40. Talcott Parsons, *The Structure of Social Action* (New York: Free Press, 1968), p. 730. For a more detailed analysis of Parsons's reinterpretation of Weber within the context of historical analysis, see David Zaret, "From Weber to Parsons and Schultz: The Eclipse of History in Modern Social Theory," *American Journal of Sociology* 85 (1980): 1180–1201.
41. Ibid.
42. Ibid., p. 34.
43. Ibid., my emphasis.
44. Ibid., pp. 34–35.
45. Bendix, *Scholarship and Partisanship*, p. 212. Also see Bendix, "Concepts and Generalizations in Comparative Sociological Studies," *American Sociological Review* 28 (1963): 532–39.
46. Eisenstadt, *Revolution*, p. 337.
47. Eisenstadt, *Form*, p. 61.
48. Eisenstadt, *Comparative Institutions*, p. 47.
49. Eisenstadt, *Revolution*, p. 234.
50. Eisenstadt, *Political Systems*, p. 4; *Comparative Institutions*, pp. 44–47.
51. Eisenstadt, *Comparative Institutions*, p. 46.
52. Ibid.
53. Ibid., p. 47. My emphasis.
54. Eisenstadt, *Form*, p. 278.
55. Eisenstadt, *Political Systems*, p. 3.
56. Ibid.
57. Ibid., pp. 5–10.
58. Ibid., p. 9.
59. Ibid., p. 10.
60. Ibid., p. 10. The six other types are as follows: (1) primitive political systems; (2) patrimonial empires; (3) nomad or conquest empires; (4) city-states; (5) feudal systems; (6) modern societies of various types.
61. Ibid., p. 19. His emphasis.

Gary G. Hamilton

62. Ibid., p. 11. Included in this list are the Chinese Empire from the Han to the Ch'ing dynasties, the Roman and Hellenistic empires, the Byzantine Empire, and the Western, central, and Eastern European states from the fall of the feudal systems through the Age of Absolutism.
63. Ibid., p. ix.
64. "A closer analysis of the unsuccessful attempts may contribute to our understanding of the nature of the centralized bureaucratic empires." Ibid., p. 28.
65. Ibid., p. 29.
66. Eisenstadt, *Revolutions*, p. 52; also see "Institutionalization and Change," p. 236.
67. Eisenstadt, *Revolution*, p. 65.
68. Ibid., pp. 45–46.
69. Ibid., p. 46.
70. Ibid., pp. 73–80.
71. Ibid., pp. 74, 80–84.
72. Ibid., p. 161.
73. Ibid., pp. 74–75, 84–85.
74. Ibid., p. 173.
75. Ibid., p. 179.
76. Ibid., p. 177.
77. Eisenstadt, *Political Systems*, p. 12.
78. Ibid., p. viii.
79. Ibid., p. 26.
80. Ibid, p. 27.
81. Ibid.
82. Ibid.
83. Ibid, p. 361–62.
84. Ibid, pp. 33–49.
85. Ibid., pp. 50–68.
86. Ibid., pp. 115–22.
87. Ibid., pp. 123–28.
88. Ibid., pp. 130–31.
89. Ibid., pp. 137–40.
90. Ibid., pp. 156–221.
91. This term is so frequently used that it seems to appear on almost every page of his writings. The other ubiquitous term is *institutionalization*. For some explanation of these two terms see *Comparative Institutions*, pp. 1–55. His use of these terms clearly implies the creation and stabilization of social forms. A concise statement of this meaning is found in "Social Change, Differentiation, and Evolution."
92. Eisenstadt, *Political Systems*, pp. 303–5.
93. Ibid. For a clearer statement of contradictions in bureaucratic empires, see "Institutionalization and Change."
94. Eisenstadt, *Political Systems*, pp. 309–60.
95. Ibid., p. 370.
96. Eisenstadt, *Revolution*, p. xv.
97. See especially "Social Change, Differentiation, and Evolution"; "Institutionalization and Change"; *Political Systems*, pp. 300–60; and *Tradition, Change, and Modernity*.
98. The following is an interpretive summary of Eisenstadt's theory of change. He is less than clear about where the process of change is located. He always stresses the systemic quality of change. But he is reluctant to say

that change is a function of a configuration itself, because to do so would be evolutionist. At the same time, he is equally reluctant to have change be the outcome of purely situational factors. Typical of his many statements about the nature of change and transformation is the following: "The passage of a given society from one stage of differentiation to another is contingent on the development within of certain processes of change which create a degree of differentiation that cannot be contained within the pre-existing system." *Comparative Institutions*, p. 52.

99. Eisenstadt, *Revolutions*, pp. 65–68.
100. Ibid., pp. 198, 337.
101. Ibid., p. 196.
102. Ibid., p. 175.
103. Ibid., pp. 182–83; also see *Tradition, Change, and Modernity*, pp. 258–307.
104. Eisenstadt, *Revolutions*, pp. 273–310; this idea was elaborated earlier in *Traditional Patrimonialism and Modern Neopatrimonialism*, Sage Research Papers in Social Sciences, studies in Comparative Modernization, no. 90-003 (Beverly Hills, Calif: Sage, 1973).
105. Eisenstadt, *Political Systems*, p. 360.
106. Eisenstadt, *Tradition, Change, and Modernity*, pp. 47–72; see also his comments about breakdowns in *Modernization; Protest and Change* (Englewood Cliffs, N.J.: Prentice-Hall, 1966), pp. 129–61.
107. See the bibliography for a list of reviews of his major books.
108. Charles Tilly, "Review of *Revolutions and The Transformation of Societies*," *American Historical Review* 84 (1979): 412.
109. Ibid.
110. Ibid.
111. Eisenstadt, *Political Systems*, pp. 71–79.
112. Ibid., p. 79.
113. Ibid., pp. 392–93.
114. Ibid.
115. Eisenstadt does discuss the coding criteria (Ibid., pp. 375–86), but the use of these criteria to assign scores is of questionable value.
116. Ibid., p. ix.
117. Ibid., p. viii.
118. I would not want to suggest that all such specialists necessarily follow this mode of reasoning. Like any set of disciplines, biological disciplines have many orientations. But they do share the attempt to study naturally occurring forms. For a parallel treatment of biology and social systems, see Vernon Pratt, *The Philosophy of the Social Sciences* (London: Methuen, 1978), pp. 117–30.
119. Marjorie Grene, *The Knower and the Known* (Berkeley: University of California Press, 1974), p. 218. Double determinateness is a term that Grene takes from R. D. Kapp, *Mind, Life, and Body* (London: Constable, 1951).
120. This theory is used in most of Eisenstadt's books. For instance, *Modernization*, pp. 145–61; *Tradition, Change, and Modernity*, pp. 89–95, 335–39; *Revolutions*, pp. 102–6; 245–47, 279–98. Similarly, *Political Systems* is largely concerned with the entrepreneurial abilities of rulers. See Smith's discussion of the role of elites in Eisenstadt's theories in *Concept of Social Change*, pp. 81–83.
121. Eisenstadt, *Form*, p. 278.
122. Ibid., p. 264.
123. Ibid., p. 262.
124. See in particular the Preface to *Capital* for Marx's statement on his method

of analysis. Marx's more journalistic writings, such as *The Eighteenth Brumaire of Louis Bonaparte* (New York: International Publishers, 1963), concentrate on the situational factors influencing events within particular types of societies.

125. In particular, see Jürgen Habermas, *Communication and the Evolution of Society* (Boston: Beacon Press, 1979) and *Legitimation Crisis;* Claus Offe, "Political Authority and Class Structures – An Analysis of Late Capitalist Societies," *International Journal of Sociology* 2 (1972): 73–105.

126. Lewis Feuer, ed., *Marx and Engels* (Garden City, N.Y.: Doubleday [Anchor Books], 1959), p. 134.

127. Ibid., p. 135.

128. A number of critics of structural functionalism and Marxian sociology have made similar observations. In particular, see Smith, *Concept of Social Change;* Bernstein, *Restructuring of Social and Political Theory;* Anthony Giddens, *Central Problems in Social Theory* (Berkeley: University of California Press, 1979).

129. Eisenstadt, *Scholarship and Partisanship,* pp. 207–24. Also see Guenther Roth's essays in *Max Weber's Vision of History* (Berkeley: University of California, 1979).

130. On this point Weber writes in *Methodology,* p. 103: "All specifically Marxian 'laws' and developmental constructs – insofar as they are theoretically sound – are ideal types. The eminent, indeed unique, *heuristic* significance of these ideal types when they are used for the *assessment* of reality is known to everyone who has ever employed Marxian concepts and hypotheses. Similarly, their perniciousness, as soon as they are thought of as empirically valid or as real (i.e., truly metaphysical) 'effective forces,' 'tendencies,' etc. is likewise known to those who have used them."

131. Ibid., pp. 185–86. Here Weber adds, "In order to penetrate to the real causal interrelationships, *we construct unreal ones*" (his emphasis). Also see Zaret, "From Weber to Parsons and Schutz," for his suggestive comments on the use of ideal types and Weber's historical analysis.

132. Giddens in *Central Problems* also makes these same points, but without an appreciation for the use of ideal types to arrive at actor meanings.

Selected Bibliography

With this bibliography I make no claim of comprehensiveness. I have selected works that, to me, represent Eisenstadt's most important contributions to historical and comparative sociology, as well as some additional writings to show the breadth of his scholarship. Eisenstadt is a prolific scholar, who writes in both Hebrew and English on a wide range of topics and who publishes in many different locations. At the time of this writing no comprehensive bibliography of Eisenstadt's publications has been compiled, and Eisenstadt himself was only in the process of putting one together. Moreover, in this chapter I have discussed only a few of the works I list below. Because the chapter mainly concerns Eisenstadt's methodological approach to the analysis of history, I have dealt primarily with those books and articles having significance for this topic. Eisenstadt has made many substantive contributions that I could not touch upon in the space provided. As far as I am aware, the following list of books, in the language in which they were first published, is complete; the list of edited books and articles is selective; and I have not attempted to compile a list of Eisenstadt's book chapters or book reviews.

BOOKS

Hebrew

Kelitat Aliyah [The absorption of immigrants]. Jerusalem: Dept. of Absorption of the Jewish Agency and the Research Seminar in Sociology, Hebrew University, 1952.

Mavo lesociologia [Introduction to sociology], with J. Ben-David. Tel Aviv: Israel Institute for Adult Education, Mercaz Hatarbut, 1956.

Hinuch vanoar: yiunim sociologiim [Education and youth: sociological essays]. Jerusalem: School of Education, Hebrew University, 1965.

Perakim benituach tahalichei hamodernizacya [Chapters in the analysis of processes of modernization]. Jerusalem: Akademon, 1967.

Western Languages and Japanese

The Absorption of Immigrants. London: Routledge & Kegan Paul, 1954. New York: Free Press, 1955; Westport, Conn.: Greenwood Press, 1975.

From Generation to Generation. Glencoe, Ill.: Free Press, 1956. London: Routledge & Kegan Paul, 1956. Paperback edition, New York: Free Press, 1964. Second paperback edition, 1971, with new Introduction, "Sociological Analysis and Youth Rebellion."

Essays on Sociological Aspects of Political and Economic Development. Institute of Social Studies, Seria Maior, no. 1. The Hague: Mouton, 1961.

The Political Systems of Empires. New York: Free Press, 1963. Paperback edition with a new Preface, New York: Free Press, 1969.

Essays on Comparative Institutions. New York: Wiley, 1965.

Modernization, Protest and Change. Modernization of Traditional Societies Series. Englewood Cliffs, N.J.: Prentice-Hall, 1966. Editorial foreword by Wilbert E. Moore and Neil J. Smelser.

Israeli Society. London: Weidenfeld & Nicolson, 1967. Reprinted. 1969. New York: Basic Books, 1968.

Political Sociology of Modernization. Tokyo: Mizuto Shabo, 1968. (In Japanese.)

Modernizacao e mudanca social. Introduction and translation by José Clovis Machado. Belo Horizonte, Brazil: Editora do Professor, 1968.

Ensayos sobre el cambio social y la modernizacion. Translated by José Elizalde. Madrid: Editorial Tecnos, 1970.

Social Differentiation and Stratification. Glenview, Ill.: Scott, Foresman, 1971.

Traditional Partrimonialism and Modern Neopatrimonialism. Beverly Hills, Calif.: Sage, 1973.

Tradition, Change, and Modernity. New York: Wiley, 1973.

The Form of Sociology – Paradigms and Crises, with M. Curelaru. New York: Wiley, 1976.

Revolution and the Transformation of Societies. New York: Free Press, 1978.

EDITED BOOKS

Comparative Social Problems. New York: Free Press, 1964.

Essays on Comparative Institutions. New York: Wiley, 1965.

The Decline of Empires. Englewood Cliffs, N.J.: Prentice-Hall, 1967.

The Protestant Ethic and Modernization, a Comparative View. New York: Basic Books, 1968.,

Comparative Perspectives on Social Change. Boston: Little, Brown, 1968.

Max Weber on Charisma and Institution Building. Chicago: University of Chicago Press, 1968.

Gary G. Hamilton

Readings in Social Evolution and Development. Elmsford, New York: Pergamon Press, 1970.
Integration and Development in Israel. New York: Praeger, 1970.
Political Sociology. New York: Basic Books. 1971.
Intellectuals and Tradition, with S. R. Graubard. New York: Humanities Press, 1973.
Building States and Nations, with Stein Rokkan. Beverly Hills, Calif.: Sage, 1973.
Post-traditional Societies. New York: Norton, 1974.
Political Clientelism, Patronage and Development, with Rene Lemarchand. Beverly Hills, Calif.: Sage, 1981.

ARTICLES

"The Sociological Structure of the Jewish Community in Palestine." *Jewish Social Studies* 10 (1948): 3–18.
"The Perception of Time and Space in a Situation of Culture Contact." *Journal of the Royal Anthropological Institute* 79 (1949): 63–8.
"The Oriental Jews in Israel." *Jewish Social Studies* 12 (July 1950): 199–222.
"Delinquent Group-formation among Immigrant Youth." *The British Journal of Delinquency* 2 (1950–51): 34–45.
"Youth, Culture and Social Structure in Israel." *The British Journal of Sociology* 2 (1951): 105–14.
"Research on the Cultural and Social Adaptation of Immigrants." *International Social Science Bulletin* 3 (Summer 1951): 258–62.
"The Place of Elites and Primary Groups in the Absorption of New Immigrants in Israel." *American Journal of Sociology* 57 (November 1951): 222–31.
"The Process of Absorption of New Immigrants in Israel." *American Journal of Sociology* 57 (November, 1951): 223–46.
"Processe of Communication among Immigrants in Israel." *Public Opinion Quarterly* 16 (Spring 1952): 42–58.
"Conditions of Communicative Receptivity." *Public Opinion Quarterly* 17 (Fall 1953): 363–74.
"Analysis of Patterns of Immigration and Absorption of Immigrants." *Population Studies* 7 (November 1953): 167–80.
"Studies in Reference Group Behavior." *Human Relations* 7 (1954): 191–216.
"African Age Groups." *Africa* 24 (1954): 100–13.
"Political Struggle in Bureaucratic Societies." *World Politics* 9 (October 1956): 15–36.
"Ritualized Personal Relations: Blood Brotherhood, Best Friends, Compadre, etc., Some Comparative Hypotheses and Suggestions." *Man* 56 (1956): 90–95.
"Sociological Aspects of the Economic Adaptation of Oriental Immigrants in Israel: A Case Study in the Process of Modernization." *Economic Development and Cultural Change* 4 (April 1956): 269–78.
"Sociological Aspects of Political Development in Underdeveloped Countries." *Economic Development and Cultural Change* 5 (July 1957): 289–307.
"Bureaucracy and Bureaucratization." *Current Sociology* 7 (2) (1958): 99–124.
"Bureaucracy, Bureaucratization, and Debureaucratization." *Administrative Science Quarterly* 4 (December 1959): 302–20.
"Primitive Political Systems: A Preliminary Comparative Analysis." *American Anthropologist* 61 (1959): 200–20.
"Anthropological Studies of Complex Societies." *Current Anthropology* 2 (June 1961): 201–22.

"Religious Organizations and Political Processes in Centralized Empires." *Journal of Asian Studies* 21 (May 1962): 271–94.

"Breakdowns of Modernization." *Economic Development and Cultural Change* 12 (July 1964): 345–67.

"Institutionalization and Change." *American Sociological Review* 29 (April 1964): 235–47.

"Social Change, Differentiation, and Evolution." *American Sociological Review* 29 (June, 1964): 375–86.

"Modernization and Conditions of Sustained Growth." *World Politics* 16 (July 1964): 576–94.

"Transformation of Social, Political, and Cultural Orders in Modernization." *American Sociological Review* 30 (October 1965): 659–73.

"Development of Socio-political Centers at the Second Stage of Modernization – A Comparative Analysis of Two Types." *International Journal of Comparative Sociology* 7 (March 1966): 119–37.

"Israeli Society – Major Features and Problems." *Journal of World History* 11 (1–2) (1968): 313–28.

"Some Observations on the Dynamics of Traditions." *Comparative Studies in Society and History* 11 (October 1969); 451–75.

"Status Segregation and Class Association in Modern Societies." *Sociology and Social Research* 54 (July 1970): 425–40.

"Intellectuals and Tradition." *Daedalus* 101 (Spring 1972): 1–19.

"Post-Traditional Societies and the Continuity and Reconstruction of Tradition." *Daedalus* 102 (Winter 1973): 1–27.

"Some Reflections on the Crisis in Sociology." *Megamot* 21 (1975): 109–23 (in Hebrew).

"Divergent and Convergent Theoretical Perspectives in the Analysis of Social Change." *Cornell Journal of Social Relations* 11 (Spring 1976): 87–95.

"Anthropological Analysis of Complex Societies." *Cahiers Internationaux de Sociologie* 60 (January 1976): 5–41 (in French).

"Convergence and Divergence of Modern and Modernizing Societies: Indications from the Analysis of Structuring Social Hierarchies in Middle Eastern Societies." *International Journal of Middle East Studies* 8 (1977): 1–27.

"Macro-Sociology – Theory, Analysis, and Comparative Studies," *Current Sociology* 25 (2) (1977): 1–112.

"Sociological Characteristics and Problems of Small States." *Journal of International Relations* 2 (1977): 35–60.

"Sociological Theory and an Analysis of the Dynamics of Civilizations and of Revolutions." *Daedalus* 106 (Fall 1977): 59–78.

"Sociological Tradition, Its Origins, Limitations, Trends, and Forms of Innovation and Crises." *Cahier Internationaux de Sociologie* 65 (July 1978): 237–65 (in French).

"Patron Client Relations as a Model of Structuring Social Exchange," with S. N. Roniger. *Comparative Studies in Society and History* 22 (January 1980): 42–77.

"Some Reflections on the Dynamics of International Systems." *Sociological Inquiry* 49 (4) (1979): 5–13.

"Cultural Orientations, Institutional Entrepreneurs, and Social-Change: Comparative Analysis of Traditional Civilizations." *American Journal of Sociology* 85 (January 1980); 840–69.

"Comparative Analysis of State Formation in Historical Contexts." *International Social Science Journal* 32 (1980): 624–54.

Gary G. Hamilton

"The Schools of Sociology." *American Behaviorial Scientist* 24 (January/February 1981): 329–44.

"Cultural Traditions and Political Dynamics: The Origins and Modes of Ideological Politics." *British Journal of Sociology* 32 (June 1981): 155–81.

"Clientelism in Communist Systems: A Comparative Perspective," with L. Roniger. *Studies in Comparative Communism* 14 (Summer/Autumn 1981): 233–45

"Some Observations on Structuralism in Sociology, with Special Reference to Max Weber." *Megamot* 27 (1981): 115–23 (in Hebrew).

SELECTED REVIEWS OF *POLITICAL SYSTEMS* AND *REVOLUTIONS*

Political Systems

Almond, Gabriel A. *American Sociological Review* 29 (June 1964): 418–19.
Diamant, Alfred. *American Political Science Review* 57 (December 1963): 968–70.
Friedrich, Carl J. *American Historical Review* 69 (July 1964): 1028–30.
Roth, Guenther. *American Journal of Sociology* 71 (May 1966): 722–23.
Wolf, Eric R. *American Anthropologist* 67 (February 1965): 172–76.
Yang, C.K. *Journal of Asian Studies* 23 (May 1964): 457–58.
Zinnes, Dina A. *Journal of Politics* 27 (February 1965): 203–5.

Revolutions

Cassinelli, C.W. *American Political Science Review* 73 (September 1979); 898–99.
Coser, Lewis A. *Political Science Quarterly* 93 (Winter 1978–79): 723–24.
Goldstone, Jack A. *World Politics* 32 (April 1980): 425–53.
Leggett, John. *Social Forces* 58 (March 1980): 966–70.
Madsen, Richard P. *Journal of Asian Studies* 38 (August 1979): 735–38.
McNeill, William H. *American Journal of Sociology* 85 (March 1980): 1241–42.
Skocpol, Theda. *Contemporary Sociology* 8 (May 1979): 451–52.
Tilly, Charles. *American Historical Review* 84 (April 1979): 412–13.

5. Theoretical Generalization and Historical Particularity in the Comparative Sociology of Reinhard Bendix

DIETRICH RUESCHEMEYER

The work of Reinhard Bendix embodies a distinctive sense of the fundamental purpose of sociological work. In 1951, virtually at the outset of his scholarly career, in the programmatic essay "Social Science and the Distrust of Reason," he distanced himself from a conception of social science that acknowledges no other rationale for its pursuits than the validity of specific findings and their possible usefulness for varied social purposes. This common view, Bendix argued, makes a fetish of science and relinquishes belief in a reason transcending empiricism, which since the Enlightenment had shaped ideas of the good society and determined the significance of questions and findings in social investigation. Bendix understood the intellectual developments – from Bacon to Marx, Nietzsche, and Freud – that led to the destruction of this faith in reason, yet he was concerned that "we pay for the greater empiricism of modern social science with unconscious and uncritical subordination of intellectual endeavor to the social and political forces of our time."[1]

The critical position he advocates is not primarily defined in substantive terms. With Max Weber, Bendix views intellectual clarification, human enlightenment, as the central task of the social sciences. In a formulation reminiscent of German idealism of the late nineteenth century, he urges that we "take our stand on the ground that our intellectual life is enriched by worthwhile research in the social sciences. Such research is a token of high civilization, worth preserving as an integral part of our quest for knowledge."[2] His scholarly work as a whole shows that two substantive concerns primarily inform Bendix's conception of a humane social science: the conditions of political freedom and the role of ideas, both in persistent tension with the realities of inequality, political and economic power, and the exigencies of organizing collective human endeavors. The critical position from which he writes, then, can perhaps be defined as that of a liberal intellectual committed to informed realism and humane reason.

Bendix's Work in the Context of Contemporary Sociology

Superficially, this position may seem similar to that held by many American social scientists in the 1950s and 1960s. It was consistent with the political attitudes and ideological outlook prevailing among them, but it was thoroughly at odds with the dominant intellectual orientations informing theory and research. Insistence on critical reflection about the purpose of social research beyond utilitarian and potentially manipulatory scientism was only one unusual conclusion Bendix drew from a continuing commitment to a more embracing idea of reason. He also registered grave reservations about the assumptions made by modern social science about the inherent ordering of social reality and the closely related views on the role of rationality and reason in human affairs, which emerged with the abandonment of a broader conception of reason:

> The older writers always thought of knowledge (or science) as enabling men to aid in the emergence of an order which already existed, "potentially," as it were, in society and history. Thus knowledge or "human reason," even to the most optimistic, was always accessory or auxiliary to the "inherent reason" which could be discovered in nature or society. We may ask whether many social scientists have not come to see in science the only ordering or reason which exists, in the sense that they equate science with prediction and with deliberate "social control." And another question is posed, when social scientists attempt to define their assumptions concerning an existing and discoverable order in society. This frequently seems to result in views which, on their face, rule out the possibility of a deliberate control over social forces. Two currently popular assumptions are the notion that society is a "social system" and the related view that the only regularities to be found in society are statistically significant correlations between various "social factors." These assumptions lead to the view that "whatever is, is necessary" (although not "best," as Pope would have it), and hence in all probability unalterable.[3]

These reservations accord with methodological considerations about fundamental differences between the natural sciences and the study of human affairs.[4] The strong version of the argument for a methodological dualism separating the study of nature from the study of human affairs holds that theoretical generalization, and thus causal explanation, is impossible in the latter. The major reasons advanced are the following: Any underlying order that may exist in human affairs is itself subject to historical change. More specifically, individual and social life are to a large extent shaped by human choice, based on variable needs and wants as well as on variable knowledge and interpretation of situations. This subjective dimension of action is not amenable to objective external analysis in the same way as the objects of natural science, but requires a knowing based on intuition and imagination as well as experience, similar to what we use in personal relations in everyday life. Finally, and closely related to the previous point, observers and analysts are themselves human beings and their investigation and knowledge are therefore inevitably contingent on their particular relation to the equally human subject matter.

Bendix does not embrace this strong version of the argument for methodological dualism, which was developed in reaction to ideas of the Enlightenment, primarily in Germany. But, without ever fully resolving the issue, he remains sensitive to the problems identified by the dualist argument. As in many other respects, he takes a position similar to that of Max Weber, in which the goals of theoretical generalization and causal explanation stand in uneasy balance with an appreciation of the variability and particularity of historical phenomena and an insistence on the need for *Verstehen*, a relation of cognitive empathy between analyst and subject in response to the centrality of the subjective dimension of action.[5]

If in its intellectual roots and fundamental premises Bendix's scholarship differed from the orientations that prevailed in contemporary sociology, he nevertheless exerted a significant influence in the field's development after World War II. Historically grounded macrosociological studies, which now have gained high ground again, owe much to his early insistence on continuing the investigation of problems that were among the central questions of the great social theorists of the nineteenth and early twentieth centuries – Alexis de Tocqueville, Karl Marx, Emile Durkheim, and Max Weber. Here Bendix's major comparative historical works must be mentioned; later I will discuss them selectively in greater detail. *Work and Authority in Industry* (1956) was one of the first works of this kind after the war and became an exemplary model in the emerging paradigm of comparative historical work. It was followed by the wide-ranging *Nation-Building and Citizenship* (1964), which examined both private and public authority relations, and most recently by *Kings or People: Power and the Mandate to Rule* (1978), which may be seen as the culmination of the analyses begun in more essayistic form in *Nation-Building*. *Kings or People* has been called "the most significant work of comparative history since Barrington Moore's *Social Origins of Dictatorship and Democracy*."[6]

The extent of Bendix's work was not limited, however, to the comparative study of power and legitimation. It is fair to say that the analysis of class and stratification was elevated to a new level in America with the publication of *Class, Status, and Power*, which he edited with S. M. Lipset.[7] Bendix made a decisive contribution to the reception of Weber by American sociology, and contemporary sociology as a whole, with his *Intellectual Portrait* of Max Weber, emphasizing the wealth of Weber's empirical work as the context for his conceptual and theoretical ideas. "For decades we were faced with attempts at grasping this or that aspect of Weber's writings. His work as a whole became visible for the first time when Reinhard Bendix presented us with his intellectual portrait, in which he sketched the main ideas that permeate Weber's work."[8]

Drawing on his conception of Weber's sociology and on his own comparative studies, Bendix became a persistent and influential critic of attempts at comprehensive, and in his view unduly closed, theory building – an aspect of his work I will examine shortly. His position on these issues of general social theory was particularly critical of structural functional system theory, but it remained equally distinct from Marxist and neo-Marxist counter-positions. Bendix takes a Weberian position, focusing on authority and domination as conflict-laden relations between dominant and subordinate groups. This orientation also underlies his critique of modernization theory, a distinctive and authoritative contribution to a wide-ranging discussion, in which he attacks the unhistorical dualism of tradition and modernity, insists on the variety of traditional social orders, and points to the different paths societies have taken. Bendix also emphasizes the changing leader-follower relations among countries, which shaped processes of political and socioeconomic modernization.[9]

This chapter does not seek to review the whole of Bendix's work and to assess its significance. It will focus on one set of questions raised with particular acuity by Bendix's comparative historical studies. These works, as well as his related essays, show a persistent concern with the tensions and antinomies between the universalizating thrust of sociology and an appreciation of historical particularity. Foreshadowed in his early reflections on the "distrust of reason," muted in *Work and Authority in Industry*, more fully developed in his later work, an increasing skepticism about the possibility of theoretical generalization in historical sociology becomes apparent. In *Kings or People*, Bendix comes close to abandoning theoretical generalization on the issues he investigates, aiming instead to elucidate divergent responses to similar problems in different historical circumstances and seeking "to preserve the sense of historical particularity"[10] in each single context. Bendix's work thus challenges the optimism of modern sociology to be able eventually to develop systematic – if always partial – theoretical explanations of historical reality. At the same time, he does not close the door completely: "We do not know enough to be sure of what cannot be known."[11]

I intend to show that his work, rather than constituting convincing evidence for this skepticism, uses theoretical, conceptual, and methodological approaches that do not give alternative conclusions a reasonable chance. At the same time, I believe that the problems Bendix cares about are more real than most sociologists assume. While a radical premise of indeterminism signals little more than a failure to attempt the search for theoretical generalization ("the miserable vainglory," as Bacon, cited by Bendix, commented, "of making it believed that whatever has not yet been discovered and comprehended can never be discovered and comprehended hereafter"[12]), many such attempts did founder on the stubborn obstacles of historical variability and particularity. This seems especially true for the subjective aspects of human action – for ideas, values, attitudes, motives, intentions, and understandings of circumstance. As noted, this dimension has been of abiding interest to Bendix. Yet we cannot easily put this aside as one man's preoccupation. For most of us, the subjective dimension of individual and social action in society and history is of intrinsic interest, and a voluntaristic model underlies much of modern social theory and research.[13]

Metatheoretical Orientations

Bendix has sought to define his position on issues of general sociological theory through critical commentary on evolutionary theories, on social system theory as well as on Marxian perspectives.[14] These arguments remain on the level of metatheory. They represent what Merton has called "sociological orientations"[15] – considerations that guide the specific formulation of hypotheses as well as the interpretation of historical situations and that, not being directly testable themselves, are subject to judgments of intellectual utility rather than truth value. Bendix's critical reservations about evolution and system theories form the background against which he develops the metatheoretical perspectives informing his work. Although he often presents these critical comments as results of his comparative investigations, their connection to this research is more complex. Some precede the comparative historical studies; others constitute broad reflections occasioned by specific research. I will therefore discuss this critique of received metatheories and Bendix's own framework of orientation before I turn to more specific issues of method in his comparative historical work.

Older evolutionary theory was based on classification of more or less complex social structures and on the assumption that all societies have passed or will pass through a determinate sequence of steps and stages. Bendix rejects this as incompatible with elementary historical knowledge.[16] Even though neo-evolutionary theorists no longer identify increasing complexity with progress and allow for multilinear developments, breakdowns, and reversals of evolution as well as leaps in development, Bendix sees many vices of original evolutionary theory continued in less clear forms and argues that these problems are often, as in the work of Parsons, or Bellah, compounded by the flaws of system theory.

"To future historians it may appear as a touching if minor irony that an organic conception of society based on the idea of equilibrium is one of the major perspectives of our time."[17] This dismissal rests on a number of arguments. Bendix rejects the idea that social structures can usefully be viewed as natural systems – as "interrelated functional whole[s] with systemic prerequisites, properties, and consequences," because this conception reifies society and culture.[18] It also exaggerates the "strain toward consistency"[19] in complex social and cultural patterns and the tendencies toward a stable and more or less harmonious equilibrium.

In his own view, "culture and social structure . . . [are both] more or less enduring end products of past group conflicts."[20] Furthermore, all forms of social action as well as all components of social institutions have multiple and opposing consequences that stand in pervasive tension with each other. Both conflicting group interests and the simultaneous functional and dysfunctional consequences of any social pattern make institutional stability always problematic. To deal more adequately with persistent group conflict and pervasive tension in any institutional arrangement, Bendix advocates the use of polar concepts. Tradition *and* modernity, formal *and* substantive criteria of law, bureaucratic *and* traditional authority patterns, charismatic *and* routinized leadership, individuation *and* socialization as consequences of the impact of social life on the individual – all signify dual tendencies that always coexist, though in different balances that are dependent on the interests of dominant and subordinate groups in changing historical circumstances. While one of these paired concepts may be most useful in analyzing a given phenomenon, keeping its opposite in view will elucidate the analysis and make it more adequate.[21]

One might argue that this conception also underlies Parsons's system theory, especially after he introduced the idea of four systemic problems that all social – indeed all living – systems have to solve and the solutions of which inevitably stand in tension and conflict with each other. That these tensions are built into the center of Parsons's later sytem theory is typically overlooked in critiques of his work.

However, Bendix does not accept Parsons's theoretical perspective for a number of interrelated reasons. A fundamental one was already mentioned – his opposition to viewing patterns of social life, i.e., social systems, as the equivalent of actors. Furthermore, Bendix holds that Parsons's conceptions are far too general to be fruitful guides for historical interpretation and causal analysis. By contrast, Bendix's own work represents, as he puts it, "an attempt to develop concepts and generalizations at a level between what is true of all societies and what is true of one society at one point in time and space." In fact, says Bendix, "many sociological concepts imply such an 'intermediate level' of analysis, though frequently they are used as if they applied universally."[22]

Bendix believes that the unit of functional analysis – ultimately society – cannot be clearly delimited. To conceive of a society as a relatively self-contained entity with more or less clear boundaries is, in Bendix's view, an undue generalization from such historically particular cases as England and France, which led the political and economic transformation of Europe and the modern world. Instead of society, Bendix considers actual social groups and organizations as the most useful units of analysis. These may in significant cases extend beyond a country's borders, if such borders clearly exist, as in many historical conditions they did not. The degree to which groups and organizations are integrated within a country is always problematic.[23]

Functional analysis presupposes a knowledge not only of functional prerequisites and functional problems but also of the varied possibilities of solution, which Bendix argues we do not possess: "The burden of this discussion is to suggest that we cannot specify the limits of what is possible in a society, even though such limits probably exist."[24] What we do know about the interrelations among groups, organizations, and institutions, Bendix insists, stands against or at least severely qualifies the assumption of pervasive strains toward consistency among the components of social structures and cultural patterns, even if modified by a conception of system problems with partially incompatible solutions.

From these premises, Bendix developed the beginnings of his critique of modernization theory, which he sees as a not sufficiently modifed version of evolutionary theories. Development in his view has identifiable historical origins; it always occurs under varied conditions, again historically shaped; and all development is partial or uneven.[25] This last assertion rests on several theoretical arguments. First is the already familiar view that in all patterns of social life heterogeneous and contradictory social and cultural elements always coexist with one another, in large part because social and cultural forms are products of conflicts between groups with different and changing positions of dominance and subordination.

Bendix finds another important source of uneven development in the persistence of historical patterns once established. In the formulation of Joseph Schumpeter, which Bendix has developed into an axiom underlying all his comparative work: "Social structures, types and attitudes are coins that do not readily melt. Once they are formed, they persist, possibly for centuries, and since different structures and types display different degrees of ability to survive, we almost always find that actual group and national behavior more or less departs from what we should expect it to be if we tried to infer it from the dominant forms of the productive process."[26] A final argument returns to the impossibility of identifying self-contained social systems with clear boundaries, and especially emphasizes the impact of developments in one country on change in another. This is set against the views of Veblen and Marx on long-term consequences of the transformation of the productive process:

> In the introduction to *Capital*, Marx points out that he had chosen England as his model, because it exemplified the "laws of capitalist development," which would govern by and large the future development of other capitalist countries. Thus, he felt that he could say to his German readers: *de te fabula narratur*. This position is, of course, based on the assumption of necessities emanating from the economic structure of societies, which – in the long

run – determine political change including international relations. We can now say, I believe, that the facts do not bear this out. Once industrialization had been initiated, no country would go through the same process in similar fashion . . .

What I said here with reference to the international repercussions of English industrialization, applies *mutatis mutandis* to the international repercussions of the ideas of the French revolution.[27]

These repercussions not only inevitably create different amalgams of indigenous and foreign, although adapted, social and cultural patterns, they also constitute for Bendix a major reason to view each instance of historical particularity as embedded in the historicity of world development. Even when dealing with similar issues – the legitimation of royal authority or ensuring compliance of workers in modern industry – the dominant groups in each society find themselves in particular historical circumstances partly determined by their place in the sequence of world history.

These metatheoretical considerations of Bendix, and in particular his view of the variability of historical constellations, set his position apart not only from functionalist system theory but also from much more limited and theoretically modest approaches which actually constitute the prevailing mode of research on social change.

> I refer to the social engineering approach, which is oriented toward planned social change. In this view analysis should aim at the discovery of critical independent variables, since control of these will entail predictable changes in the dependent variables . . . This approach is less classificatory than the older, evolutionary approach and less organicist than system theory proper. But like these theories, its simplifying assumptions and tests of truth depend upon a *ceteris paribus* treatment of historical constellations.[28]

A final element of Bendix's basic sociological orientations is his conception of the major determinants of social structure and social change. Here the opponents against which he defines his position are not evolutionary ideas and Parsonsian system theory, but monocausal determinisms and, in particular, Marxian views of historical materialism. Although Bendix refuses to be misled by the legitimation ideologies of dominant classes into overlooking the harsh pursuit of self-interest and the realities of inequality in economic resources, status, and power, he insists that ideas and ideals are not simply the outgrowth of material interests and that such cultural formations do make a difference. For instance, Bendix does not accept Wallerstein's view that "any complex

Dietrich Rueschemeyer

system of ideas can be manipulated to serve any particular social or political objective."[29] Material conditions; economic interests of different actors and groups; political interests, structures, and struggles; and fundamental cultural ideas and ideals – these sets of factors shape in varying patterns of interaction the outcome of a given process of social change. This position is similar to that of Max Weber. It is an agnostic position, except that it rejects materialist and idealist theoretical orientations as undue simplifications. We will see, however, that Bendix's practice of comparative analysis leans ambiguously toward a special emphasis on the role of ideas.

The framework within which Bendix approaches comparative historical analysis, then, is not a full-fledged theory of interrelated hypotheses, nor is it a systematic formulation of metatheoretical orientations guiding the formulation of hypotheses. Rather, it consists of an ensemble of loosely connected ideas, many of which are stronger in what they deny than in what they assert. His position is most sharply defined by the simultaneous rejection of system theory, evolutionism, historical materialism, and – perhaps least vigorously – idealism rather than by a theoretical program with its own weight and clear direction. Where these rejections converge, we can identify the ideas that are most central to Bendix's thought: Culture and social structure are the result of group conflicts however motivated; dual tendencies in social action and institutional forms are never completely resolved in one direction; historical legacies persist in social structure and culture; influences, dependencies, and interdependencies cut across political, cultural, and economic boundaries; varying historical constellations engender ever-changing responses to apparently similar issues of social structure and process; as a result, and finally, the historical structure must be viewed as essentially open.

Theory Building in Comparative Historical Analysis

The framework just sketched allows Bendix to approach historical materials with a maximum of openness and to "preserve a sense of historical particularity."[30] To do so is crucial for Bendix; but this approach involves a sacrifice of theoretical intent, as Bendix himself makes clear when he comments that

> comparative analysis of historical change attempts a closer approximation to the historical evidence than is possible either on the assumptions of evolutionism, or of system-theory, or of social engineering. As a result, it promises less in the way of prediction

138

and of guiding social action toward defined goals. Whether this sacrifice is permanent or temporary remains to be seen. Studies of social change in complex societies may hold in abeyance the tasks of causal analysis and prediction while concentrating on the pre-liminary task of ordering phenomena of social change to be ana-lyzed further.[31]

Bendix's open-ended agnosticism, however, may in fact close the door on advances in theoretical generalization. Whether the proposed sacrifice of causal analysis is permanent or temporary depends as much on the strategy of inquiry as on the presuppositions one holds about how causal analysis can be achieved. A preliminary ordering of the phenomena of social change cannot be divorced from the search for causal explanation if it is to make a contribution to that goal. In one strategy, this link to causal analysis – and the instrument of preliminary ordering – consists of a systematic conceptual framework based on arguments about the anticipated utility of the concepts in the formula-tion of powerful hypotheses. This is the strategy of Parsonsian struc-tural functionalism. Bendix's framework of basic sociological orienta-tions seems too loosely constructed to serve this purpose, and Bendix is explicitly skeptical not only of the utility of Parsons's version of a general conceptual framework but also of the promise of this strategy in general even though his metatheoretical arguments have this char-acter in fact. S. N. Eisenstadt's *Political Systems of Empires* is an example of comparative research that proceeds from conceptual bases provided by Parsonsian theory, develops broad yet specific hypotheses about feudal and premodern bureaucratic systems of rule, and then tests them against available historical evidence.[32] Critical for the success of this endeavor was the elaboration of theoretical propositions tran-scending, though suggested by, the conceptual framework Eisenstadt used.

A simple aggregation of thematically related phenomena of power struggles between kings and aristocracies, for example – clearly does not suffice to attain theoretical generalization. This empiricist strategy makes an assumption Karl Popper has discredited: that an examination of a set of particular instances will not only yield answers to particular questions but will also reveal causal patterns, even if these were not identified in general propositions or causal hypotheses. Induction is not led to determinate results by the historical evidence itself.[33]

Causal hypotheses do not have to be derived from a body of thought apart from the evidence examined. Such propositions may suggest themselves in the study of one historical process and then be used, and modified, in a succession of further case analyses. This may give the appearance of empiricist induction although logically it is different. Barrington Moore, Jr., warns in language similar to Bendix's against "too strong a devotion to theory," because it may do violence to the historical facts. Moore, however, along with others working in a similar mode,[34] searches for a theoretical explanation of the contrasting transformations he studies, identifying hypothetically causal variables in one case that are then explored in other cases with similar outcomes and, negatively, in yet others with different results. Such a procedure requires a sustained focus on the causal propositions employed, a focus that is easily blurred and possibly lost if preserving a sense of historical particularity and retaining the sequential character of each instance of historical change are overriding concerns. Bendix, as we shall see, first (in *Work and Authority in Industry*) followed a strategy similar to Moore's but later gave increasingly more weight to concern with historical particularities.

A related issue is the contention of some scholars that causal analysis is possible within the confines of a particular historical phenomenon. For instance, E. P. Thompson, arguing against Althusser and Popper in his brilliant essay "The Poverty of Theory," views "history as a process inscribed with its own causation" and historical explanation as a dialogue between reasoned expectations and evidence confined to "this particular social formation in the past, that particular sequence of causation."[35] If this view were correct, causal explanation of historical change could proceed without comparative analysis, and the tension between historical particularity and theoretical causal propositions would disappear.

Bendix does not hold this position, however. He adopts the conventional view of causal analysis as the identification of relations between dependent and independent variables, although he emphasizes that different historical circumstances may modify the effects of apparently similar causal factors. The identification of independent variables as well as of relevant historical contexts takes place through comparison. As historical reality cannot be varied for experimental purposes, this search requires the examination of many cases to avoid simplistic *post hoc ergo propter hoc* conclusions. Since comparative analysis of large-scale and long-term change typically "can deal only with a few cases," Bendix comes in his last major work to the conclusion that "comparative studies should not attempt to replace causal analysis."[36]

What, then, is the purpose of comparative studies? Bendix's various answers to this question are somewhat inconsistent with each other.

There is the long-term hope, framed by doubt and skepticism, that further analysis of phenomena of social change, which are ordered in a preliminary way by comparative history, may in the future yield causal understanding. A critical variant of this hope, and a more easily attained goal, is to expose the limited applicability or greater inadequacies of received general theories by confronting them with comparative historical evidence. A more limited goal is the contrasting identification of particular societal and cultural contexts in which specific explanations can be developed. Bendix's strategy is to "take a single issue which is found in many (conceivably in all) societies and seek to analyze how men in different societies have dealt with that same issue."[37] These issues or problems provide the organizing focus of comparative inquiry. The outcome of analysis may simply "exhibit the range of 'solutions' that men have found for a given problem in different societies"[38] or the analysis may seek to formulate the conditions under which one response or the other is more likely to emerge. Finally, comparative study provides the occasion for an integration of particular historical and general theoretical knowledge.

Comparative history, then, becomes a synopsis of our knowledge of social life: focused on important problems, enlightened by generalized theoretical propositions and guesses, but inevitably bound up with the historical particularity of divergent contexts and increasingly also with the historicity of worldwide interrelations between them. The actual methods used, as well as the more detailed methodological arguments advanced in Bendix's work, have to be judged in terms of these fundamental assertions about the goals and limitations of comparative historical sociology.

Four Cases Systematically Compared

Work and Authority in Industry is the most theoretically oriented comparative work of Bendix. It begins with the assertion that "wherever enterprises are set up, a few command and many obey"[39] and pursues the same question – how this authority is justified – in four historical contexts: early industrialization in England and Czarist Russia and bureaucratized industry in the United States and the German Democratic Republic. Case selection and basic research design approximate John Stuart Mill's "method of difference" and "method of agreement" in combination: Bendix compares two cases with an autonomous class of entrepreneurs or managers with two cases where authority relations in industry are subject to an overpowering system of political rule. At the same time, one case of both pairs lies before and the other after the historic divide that is defined by the societywide acceptance of industry as a mode of production and by bureaucratization of economic enterprise.

Ideologies of management justifying authority in industry are the dependent variable. According to Bendix's analysis, they reflect the necessity of justifying the industrial mode of production and the emerging forms of subordination in early industry, the widespread acceptance of industry and the bureaucratized forms of industrial work in the twentieth century, as well as the societal position of the entrepreneurial/managerial elite vis-à-vis dominant and subordinate classes and the different balances of incentives and control, trust and mistrust in contrasting political and cultural environments. The study transcends the confines of the sociology of work and industrial relations because Bendix sees the differences in labor relations as complexly related to – influenced by and in turn causing – variations in political freedom.

The mode of analysis follows functionalist logic: Bendix identifies problems to which he sees the ideologies as a response. Yet in contrast to naive functionalist arguments, Bendix neither assumes that the problems encountered determine by themselves the emergence and the content of such responses, nor that ideological suasion is necessarily successful – Czarist Russia, after all, was transformed by a revolution. Causation is a question separate from though related to functional problems.

Bendix formulates the problems to which management ideologies respond at different levels of generality. He begins with universal assertions: Authority relations between the few and the many are an ineluctable consequence of complex social organization. "The few, however, have seldom been satisfied to command without a higher justification . . . and the many have seldom been docile enough not to provoke such justifications."[40] "Men who are similarly situated socially and economically [tend universally] to develop common ideas and to engage in collective action."[41] A second level pertains to the common issues encountered in early industry or in large-scale bureaucratic enterprises by politically autonomous or subordinate industrial elites. For example, the public at large to which the justifying ideologies of early entrepreneurs are addressed "consists typically of two major groups, a politically dominant aristocracy and a newly recruited work force."[42] "As the delegation of authority and technical specialization have become more important for the successful functioning of modern enterprises, management has had either to rely upon, or to make sure of, the good faith of its employees."[43] Finally, these generic problems take particular shape in each historical context. For example:

It is necessary to identify who the early entrepreneurs were and what their relationship was to the "ruling classes" in the society in which industrialization was initiated. Relations between these entrepreneurs and their workers are strongly affected by the traditional master-servant relationships. It is necessary to characterize the latter before analyzing how the practices and ideologies of industrial management are differentiated from them and developed further. Moreover, the industrial entrepreneurs, the workers in their enterprises, and the ruling social groups are engaged in social and political interaction in their respective efforts to come to terms with the industrial way of life . . . It is necessary to characterize this interaction in order to understand the terms of the controversy in which the ideological weapons are fashioned by those who initiate the development of industry.[44]

The relation of ideologies to socioeconomic structures and processes constitutes an area of inquiry in which fascinating open questions abound, while plausible answers are few. Bendix argues that, in contrast to the "prevailing tendency to examine this interrelation where it was most elusive rather than where it was obvious," the study of management ideologies concerns a case where the relationship is "more or less apparent rather than a matter of inference," because these ideas are most closely related to self-interest and actual social practice.[45] Yet even here the matter is complex. To judge what is in one's interest requires an analysis of the situation that may be wrong or incomplete; different actors and groups with similar interests may develop divergent ideological responses; to be effective, an ideology must appeal to other groups with their own interests, mentalities, and ideas; and emergent ideologies in each case are shaped by the existing stock of ideas, including those that give full play to or restrict sharply the pursuit of self-interest.[46] Thus ideas, even those related to practical action, have to some extent a life of their own in relation to the underlying patterns of interest.

Arthur Stinchcombe has contended that theoretical generalization from historical studies best proceeds by the tentative identification of historical sequences that appear "causally analogous" after detailed investigation, an argument that agrees with the practice of analytic comparative history by Moore and others cited earlier. Stinchcombe illustrates his position with a careful exegesis of the actual procedures Bendix uses in studying entrepreneurial ideologies in nineteenth-century England. Although method and theoretical argument are much less explicitly stated in Bendix's within-country analyses, it is through these case studies rather than the overall design that Bendix's work impresses Stinchcombe as theoretically convincing.[47]

Thus Bendix formulated his questions about the justification of industrial authority through general theoretical argument and an analysis of the historical context in nineteenth-century England. Then he had to decide which of the many ideas expressed in treatises, pamphlets, or sermons from the period should be regarded as responding to actual problems of industrial authority. This question is crucial precisely because objective functional problems do not necessarily elicit any – and certainly not always identical or similar – ideological responses. Bendix's solution was, first, to concentrate on those ideas that constituted relatively complete intellectual arguments and at the same time had broad appeal among entrepreneurs. A second selection criterion was the commonality of problems addressed in different intellectual productions. Even with a reasoned guide for selection, another crucial question remained to be solved: In what sense do the diverse ideological arguments contribute to new, broadly accepted understandings, assessments, and evaluations? In what sense are they causally analogous? Expanding on Bendix's discussion of the interrelations between two books by Malthus and Ure, Stinchcombe answers:

> The analogy thus consists of two sorts of judgments. The first has to do with the similarity of function of the two books, that they divert blame for miseries in the mills from entrepreneurs. The second is a similarity in deep intellectual structure, that blame is connected with ideas of causality . . . and that there are various alternative causal ways to argue the same ideological point, that entrepreneurs cannot do better. Conversely, of course, there are various causal schemes that can argue the ideological point that workers can do better and hence that they are to blame for their poverty. For example, if workers did better, it would be in the entrepreneur's interest and within his capacity to reward them; they could live better if they did not spend their money on gin, if they had fewer children, if they had a philosophy of *Self Help*, and the like. If all these are similar, then we can understand why Bendix urges that the agitation of the Anti-Corn Law League was a fundamental ideological break. For the basic point of this agitation was that workers could help solve the problem of poverty by *civic and political participation* in the reform movement. This implied both that workers could be trusted (better than aristocrats)

with questions of public policy, and that the blame lay in political and legal arrangements, not in the vices of the poor.[48]

Both within each historical case and in the cross-national comparison, such analytic historical induction remains hypothetical in its causal results, and the theoretical generalizations developed through the identification of causally analogous sequences risk disproof when applied to new instances. Even with a careful selection of contrasting and similar cases, causal interpretation remains a mere *attribution* when this is not realized. Edward Gross argues, for instance, that the shift in American managerial ideologies from individualism to an emphasis on the virtues of cooperation, which Bendix demonstrates and explains primarily as due to increased bureaucratization, could equally well be attributed to "the labor union struggle and need for bargaining and diplomatic skills, the need for a favorable public opinion in view of the growth of large-scale semi-monopolistic enterprises, the limits imposed on the free-swinging entrepreneur by the government, the effects of the great depression, and many other possible factors."[49] A choice among these different though not necessarily incompatible hypotheses can be made only by testing them in further comparative study.

More than any other work by Bendix, *Work and Authority in Industry* aims to develop theoretical generalizations through systematic and at the same time historically specific comparative research. Yet in muted form we already find here – particularly *within* the four case studies – indications of the emphasis on historical particularity that was to lead Bendix toward increasing skepticism about, and ineffectiveness in, the theoretical identification of significant regularities. One such indication is an inclination toward historical narrative in which much of the more detailed theoretical reasoning is buried, if it is made explicit at all. Closely related to the importance of historical narration is the pervasive emphasis given to historical continuities in causal explanation. What we may call the "Schumpeter principle," the assertion that major facets of intercultural differences must be explained by the persistence of historical patterns crystallized in the past, even the distant past, rather than by the structural exigencies, conflicting group interests, and power struggles in the present and immediate past, will occupy us at length later. Here it is only to be noted that for exploring this notion the cases selected serve rather poorly, since the United States is by no means a historical extension of nineteenth-century English patterns, and East Germany can even less be seen in continuity with Russian civilization. In fact, if one searched for a case of a fairly radical break with the legacies of the past – a search mandated by Mill's method of difference – one might well end up with the German Democratic Republic.[50]

From Comparative Sociology to Juxtapositional History

If *Work and Authority in Industry* became for many a model of comparative historical sociology, Bendix himself moved toward an ever more historical mode of analysis, though it remained informed by sociological concepts and questions. In line with the skepticism of accompanying methodological and theoretical essays regarding the chances of theoretical generalization from historical materials, *Nation-Building and Citizenship* as well as *Kings or People* use a strategy of comparative history based on contrasts among cases. The search for new explanatory generalizations is avoided, and comparison is used to highlight the diversity of concrete historical experiences related to similar issues.[51]

Nation-Building and Citizenship extends the substantive and the historical scope of the inquiry in *Work and Authority in Industry*, but it is far less systematically designed, selecting several paired comparisons to elucidate specific issues. This work examines both private and public authority relations as they were transformed, directly or indirectly, by the industrial and democratic revolutions of Western Europe. Problems of legitimation remain a particular focus of these studies, but the analysis is not confined to them. The transformation of social structure and authority relations in Western European societies is discussed at length and then contrasted with patterns and developments in "Russian civilization," both Czarist and Communist. This comparison centers on the "historically new phenomenon of totalitarianism," which is viewed as an outgrowth of Czarist autocracy and the principle of plebiscitarianism orginating in Western Europe. The analysis moves beyond the European context by a comparison of the preconditions of nation-building and industrialization in Japan and Prussia – "both . . . latecomers, but both possess[ing] an effective, nation-wide public authority prior to the rapid industrialization of their economies."[52] The book concludes with an inquiry into the development of public authority in India, a country that attempts economic development and the establishment of nationwide political community and authority at the same time.

While *Nation-Building and Citizenship* might have been seen as an essayistic preliminary analysis to be followed by a more systematic and more theoretically oriented work,[53] *Kings or People,* which pursues the same themes more comprehensively, in fact moves more decisively in the direction of contrasting histories dealing with similar issues under divergent historical circumstances. The first part of the book deals with the authority of kings in agrarian societies. Bendix emphasizes religious legitimation as a crucial underpinning of that form of rule, and focuses on the tensions and power struggles between the royal center of power and the magnates and notables who seek to make their delegated authority more autonomous. The second part of the work traces the transformation of these varied patterns of domination and conflict toward an authority exercised in the name of the people. Although this transformation is common to all countries studied, Bendix concentrates on the differences in their experience. In each country the old order of authority was challenged by an "intellectual mobilization," but the challenge took place at different times in the overall historical sequence. The oppositional intellectuals thus took different, more advanced countries as their "reference societies." Furthermore, the contrasting legacies of the unique patterns of domination and conflict preceding the transformation also contributed to the outcome. Therefore, the experience of modernization was a different one in each case, and Bendix's analysis highlights the unique features of each pattern.

The cases studied – Japan, Russia, England, and France in the first part, with Prussia/Germany added in the second – are not selected as contrasting instances of hypothesized causes and phenomena to be explained, as they were in *Work and Authority in Industry*. This reflects the increased emphasis on the particularity of each historical development and the lesser confidence in the possibility of theoretical explanation. Even so, it is remarkable that deviant cases are neglected; for instance, the absence or weakness of royal rule in medieval Italy, the early modern Netherlands, or ancient Athens and Rome.[54] In Bendix's picture of the contrasting transformations toward rule in the name of the people it is difficult to speak of deviant cases, because the primary thesis is variability and there is no attempt to use contrasts and similarities to characterize systematically the different versions of new political orders. Here it is noteworthy that Bendix does not examine fascism. His analysis of the German case breaks off in 1871 with only brief allusions to later developments as "the liabilities of the German transformation."[55] Jon Wiener notes that

> Bendix's failure to examine fascism in relation to modernization leads to further problems concerning the politics of developing societies. Their leaders, he writes, choose between the models of development provided by the United States, the USSR, and China. Notably absent from this list is the "revolution from

above" model offered by fascist Germany and Japan. Franco
Spain, Brazil and South Korea have developed rapidly without
following the Soviet or Chinese routes, but does Bendix mean to
suggest that they are following the American path? Authority in
those countries is structured along the lines of "revolution from
above," rule by elites in the name of the people, not revolution
from below.[56]

In *Kings or People*, particularly in the first part, Bendix employs the
same strategy of analysis we found in *Work and Authority in Industry*: A
problem is formulated with which historical actors have to contend.
This may simply serve to demonstrate a variety of responses in several
historical instances that from time to time crystallize into different institutional forms. However, these responses and emergent institutional
patterns can be subjected to further analysis. The different paths of
action open to the actors, as well as the constraints under which they
pursue their goals, can be related to the similar functional problem
faced in all of the cases compared. At least implicitly, such further
analysis is inescapable, if only because of the exigencies of coherent
historical narrative. If such reasoning were made explicit and extended
from its original context to all other relevant instances, it could lead to
general propositions about the conditions that make one or another
outcome more probable.

This pattern of analysis bears closer scrutiny than we have given it so
far, especially since the issues Bendix must face in *Kings or People* are
far more complex than in *Work and Authority in Industry*. A crucial first
question is how the problems encountered by the actors are selected.
There is no doubt that even sheer description needs selective criteria
that derive from an implicit theoretical framework. This is even more
true for the identification of functional problems faced by actors in
certain specified situations. One can base such problem identifications
on prior theoretical argument, however derived, or one can make the
underlying reasoning itself problematic and conduct research on these
premises. In *Work and Authority in Industry* the fundamental conceptions of the inevitability of authority, of the near-universal need for
legitimation, of class, and of bureaucracy are introduced in the first
mode, from the "outside," as it were.

Bendix is well aware that these issues stand in tension with his
concern for historical particularity; he is concerned about using "inevitably arbitrary categories." A partial solution he favors is to be as true
as possible to the "terms in which the historical actors think about the
questions at issue."[57] Yet while insisting on the importance of the sub-

jective dimension of action, Bendix knows that an analysis of the problems he is concerned with requires more:

> [I]t is also necessary to go beyond that dimension and define the social structure which eventually results from all these contentions, and that cannot be done in subjective terms alone. Indeed some abstraction and arbitrariness will be unavoidable in order to "freeze" the fluidity of historical change for purposes of obtaining benchmarks . . . It may be that the deliberate employment of static and dynamic terms like bureaucracy and bureaucratization, democracy and democratization, etc., provides a way of conceptualizing both, the group contentions that are an essential part of change and the altered social structures which from time to time result from that change.[58]

This response still does not answer the issue, however. First, not only the outcomes but the problems, too, transcend the interpretations and intentions of the historical actors.[59] Furthermore, the use of dual concepts may be useful to sensitize the analyst to change and ambiguity, but such concepts remain part of the theoretical framework from which they sprang. Yet such conceptions are arbitrary in a peculiar sense; we may call them arbitrary if they are not made problematic and themselves exposed to testing and validation. Bendix, it seems, sees them as arbitrary because they transcend the subjective views of the actors studied. It is clear, however, that such a focus on the subjective dimension of historical action has itself theoretical consequences – it steers attention away from broader structural conditions and other hidden concomitants of the actors' options and decisions.[60] There is indeed no way to avoid arbitrariness in the choice of questions and, since questions are shaped by them, concepts and theoretical premises. The only way to control this arbitrariness is to make the presuppositions themselves – questions, concepts, and, above all, theoretical assumptions – problematic. Such reflexiveness is, ironically, harder to achieve in an approach that self-consciously abstains from theory building to preserve a sense of historical particularity than in one that explicitly and boldly searches for causal generalization through comparative history.

An example of a limited functional analysis, central to the first part of *Kings or People*, concerns the instability of royal rule in agrarian societies: "Different authority structures can arise in an agrarian economy with poorly developed techniques of transport and communication, ranging from federalist and even anarchic to absolutist and despotic tendencies" in the relations between sovereign and aristocracy, and "although king-

Dietrich Rueschemeyer

ship was sacrosanct and endured for long periods, the authority of any one king was always in jeopardy." How can a king secure his power and impose his will? He "has various means at his disposal, but each of them is flawed and none ultimately dependable."[61] Bendix discusses in a summary chapter the liabilities and advantages of different instruments for securing royal domination – the awesome display of sacrosanct majesty, the use of force, the bestowal of favors in the form of land grants, the assignment of rank or distribution of lesser honors, the employment of a staff in royal service, and the enlargement of the personal domain of the ruler.

There is little to quarrel about if one takes the goal of maintaining power and imposing the royal will for granted, though that, too, could be made problematic and examined for variation. However, a more systemic formulation of the explanatory propositions would have avoided several closely connected shortcomings of Bendix's analysis. In particular, it would have made clear that the argument is severely incomplete, made hidden assumptions explicit, and identified indeterminacies in the explanation as well as ad hoc explanations that are unrelated to the main analysis and perhaps only used once, thus remaining untested in repeated application. I will discuss these issues in turn.

Bendix pays little attention to the bases of power of kings *and* aristocrats in relation to the subject population. This is perhaps the largest omission of his analysis because it seems likely that here we would find the causes of the stability of the overall pattern of royal aristocratic rule. Only in relation to other problems is this question casually discussed:

> At the lower end of the social hierarchy, this defensive-offensive posture of the ruler was reflected in the efforts of weaker men, families, or communities to obtain the protection of a master, no doubt frequently a mixture of the desire for security and submission to brute force.[62]

> [P]olitical instability probably has coexisted with a marked degree of social stability. The bulk of the population lived in isolated communities and households. People could do little to change their condition. Most of the time, life near the level of subsistence discouraged even the most courageous from actions that would jeopardize such security as they enjoyed. Kings and their notables could fight their protracted battles for dominance at home and abroad only on the basis of this politically submerged but economically active population.[63]

150

How this ultimate foundation of rule in agrarian societies is related to conditions of communication and transportation and to the mode of production, how the legitimations of rule are related to the characteristic ethos of the subject population, and how both material conditions and prevailing cognitive and normative orientations shaped the (very limited) opportunities for effective organization among the bulk of the people – these questions are not explored, even though it seems that these relations in the substructure of agrarian polities are far less volatile and thus more open to systematic analysis.

Two remarks give a clue for the reasons. Bendix chooses "to look at social structures from the top down" because "the ideas and actions of those in positions of power or authority are the best documented part of the human record."[64] Second, by the time this record becomes realistic and reasonably detailed, "the distinctions between rulers and ruled, between rich and poor, are already well established."[65] Yet information on the life of peasants and other commoners does exist, and the second remark identifies causes with origins and neglects the possibility of comparative analysis of variations in these fundamental bases of rule in agrarian societies.

Hidden assumptions are a vice characteristic of much narrative historical writing. In any argument that makes group conflict and the pursuit of self-interest conceptually central, a crucial question is how the solidarity of groups and factions is established. This question is never specifically addressed, although one might take Bendix's discussion of the development of aristocratic culture,[66] his pervasive concern with religiously sanctioned obligation, and the discussion of changing feudal relations as partial, though largely implicit, answers. Solidarity based on family and marriage relations provides an example of a hidden assumption that remains theoretically unanalyzed in spite of the fact that it was by no means unproblematic, yet unquestionably had a tremendous significance for the power struggles of the royal and noble elite. Bendix even sees "the breakup of the fusion among family, property and authority" as the central process involved in the developments leading toward a "mandate of the people."[67]

Ad hoc explanations abound in Bendix's narrative, even where the argument turns to analytic reflection. The consequences of military conquest, for example, play an important role in his analysis of the relations between kings and notables. In the varied comparisons between England, Japan, Russia, and Prussia/Germany its effects are made dependent on conditions particular to each case: the internal hierarchy among the war leaders,[68] their interest in profiting from trade

Dietrich Rueschemeyer

or landed rule,[69] foreign or indigenous conquest,[70] the ability of rulers to ignore the hereditary rights of aristocratic landowners,[71] or the persistence of one pattern or another once established.[72] In countless other instances ad hoc explanations do not qualify the effects of one common factor but introduce new variables. For instance, in contrasting the "uneven seesaw between baronial interests *as represented in parliament* and the authority and power of the English kings" with comparable Japanese patterns, Bendix writes:

> The vitality of the English barons certainly compares with that of the Japanese gentry, but there are two marked contrasts between England and Japan. First, in England there was the early emergence of a quasi-parliamentary institution, a collective forum in which notables of the realm assembled to counsel the king and eventually to oppose him . . . Second, English kings intermarried with the French royal family and through inheritance of territorial possessions also become vassals of the king of France. These political ties with the Continent *involved the whole country* in the national defense, especially since France made periodic attempts to gain a foothold in Scotland. By contrast, Japan retained its isolation from the Asian mainland so that neither a common representative body nor a common political involvement overseas restrained internal strife.[73]

While such explanations can be fascinatingly suggestive of potential theoretical propositions, they often derive their plausibility from the retrospective certainty about how things turned out. One can certainly imagine that foreign involvement of kings and notables could fragment rather than unite the rulers of a given area, and institutions once established may fall into disuse or be abruptly discontinued as well as have lasting effects for the long-term future. The explanations Bendix uses in specific contrasts are typically not pursued beyond one or two particular comparisons, and thus run into the problem that "a particular causal judgment in historical work has no chance of being wrong." The theoretical proposition – implied or made explicit – thus turns into "the sort of sentence Hume worried about."[74]

This logical problem also stands in the way of Bendix's most limited goal of comparative analysis, to "sharpen our understanding of the contexts in which more detailed causal inferences can be drawn."[75] Causal explanation inevitably involves general theoretical propositions. If the context modifies the impact of an apparently general factor, such as military conquest, this modification either becomes part of a formulation applicable to other cases as well or it turns the causal judgment into a

self-validating exercise. Yet neither in analyzing specific historical sequences, nor in comparative contrasts, nor even in the overall thrust of
his work does Bendix pursue his causal explanations systematically. He
tends to alternate among historical narrative, relatively unsystematic
explanatory reflection, and broad metatheoretical assertions about, say,
the relative importance of ideas and material conditions.

The problems discussed are aggravated when the analysis is less
centered on a specific problem the historical actors have to deal with, but
is rather unified by broad themes only. The second part of *Kings or People*
is a case in point. Here the question is: Why and how was the authority
of kings transformed into different and broader-based structures of authority in one country after another, beginning in the sixteenth century
in England? Now the basic mode of analysis is causal rather than functional. Bendix formulates in advance of his analysis a theoretical or
interpretive framework that argues against giving too much emphasis to
urbanization and "the commercialization of land, labor and capital"[76]
(his phrase for the development of capitalism) and argues for a multicau-
sal explanation, which focuses in particular on the persistent effects of
earlier patterns, the impact of events in other countries, and the importance of ideas. The studies that follow give weight to Bendix's critique of
modernization theory, and he develops with the conceptions of "intellectual mobilization" and "reference society" important tools for comparative study of sociopolitical change in the modern world.

What remains ambiguous is whether his analysis is to be a full account of the transitions or whether it pursues only specific strands of
social change. On the one hand, he notes in a discussion of the intellectual antecedents and correlates of these transformations that "the
following chapters do not provide a comprehensive account, but focus
attention on those intellectual opponents of the status quo who propose a reconstitution of authority."[77] And he says of the role of an
increasing division of labor that "in the case studies which follow, this
agent is slighted in favor of the impact of external events on societies,
engendering ideas which have facilitated 'modernization.' "[78] On the
other hand, the broader program of a full explanation is never revoked,
the study is presented as shouldering the "burden of integrating
knowledge." He comments that "the risks of such integration are
great"[79] and defends the causal or interpretive emphases by an extended metatheoretical argument. With a broader and more diffuse
focus for the contrasting case studies and with an analytic program that
leaves ambiguous whether certain factors are asserted as causally predominant or whether their prominence is due to his special problem

Dietrich Rueschemeyer

selection, Bendix's analysis in the second part of *Kings or People* is particularly open to the charge of introducing an "idealistic Weberian explanation of 'modernizing' transformations of political authority structures," determining "what happenings and aspects of social life to include – or not – in his case histories in a manner appropriate to his implicit theoretical perspective."[80]

Since this is not really hidden by Bendix and is certainly plain to the theoretically aware reader, it is perhaps more troublesome that the ensuing case studies remain illustrations of interpretive themes rather than explorations of the explanatory power of the factors emphasized and attempts to specify theoretical propositions. The results of the case studies are interpretive synopses rather than tentative conclusions about the theoretical issues.

The Schumpeter Principle – Explanation by Historical Continuity?

What I have called the Schumpeter Principle, the assertion that the persistence of social structures, types, and attitudes once they are formed provides an explanation of different social and cultural patterns, is invoked in every work by Bendix. This centrality is no accident, since an inclination to search for causes in the distant historical past is endemic to many works that are concerned with preserving a sense of historical particularity and skeptical of cross-cutting theoretical explanation.

The persistence of institutional forms and cultural patterns formed in the past is an important obstacle to any functional analysis that seeks to understand social structures and cultural patterns in terms of interdependencies and the balance of forces in the present and recent past. This is an old metatheoretical argument.[81] Bendix invokes this principle not only in stating his overall strategy but also in causal explanations of historically specific patterns.

> The roots of historically developed structures, of the culture and political institutions of any present-day society reach far into the past. In studying these roots, I am striving to free our understanding of the stereotyped contrast between tradition and modernity.[82]
>
> Once the basic pattern of institutions (of royal rule) is formed under the circumstances of early kingship, it is difficult to change.[83]
>
> In each case, the institutionalization of popular sovereignty showed the effects of the way in which the authority of kings was left behind.[84]

154

The formative conditions of royal authority are of enduring importance. For example, Imperial Germany began with the legitimation of the Carolingian dynasty by an act of consecration and the subsequent involvement of the Frankish kings with papal political interests in Italy. Prussian kingship emerged much later, an outgrowth of efforts to overcome political fragmentation in a frontier province and a by-product of dynastic policies which utilized the devastations of the Thirty Years' War. Russian kingship began in two disconnected phases. Princely authority in Kievan Russia was established by armed merchants from Scandinavia, who chose certain towns as trading posts and attracted followers seeking protection and material advantage by organizing the defense against steppe nomads. In a second phase, the Muscovite tsars rose to preeminence under Mongol overlordship as collectors of tribute from other principalities and as a defense force against Lithuania; eventually they consolidated power by means of a systematic resettling of landed aristocrats from conquered territories like Novgorod.[85]

In the eighteenth and nineteenth centuries, successive reform efforts of the tsarist government revealed just how little Russian culture had prepared the aristocracy to act on its own initiative, and just how difficult it was for tsarist officials to allow local initiatives that were not controlled by the center.[86]

In Russia . . . (in contrast to England and the United States) historical legacies did not encourage management (under the Tsars) to presuppose the existence of a common universe of discourse between superiors and subordinates.[87]

The critical questions in fashioning specific explanations from the Schumpeter principle are ignored by Bendix. Even on the level of metatheoretical orientations, the principle conflicts with other strategic assumptions guiding his historical interpretation and the formation of propositions – the insistence on the pervasiveness of change, on group conflicts and the resultant instability of institutional forms,[88] and on the impact of events in one country on developments in another. What are the conditions under which institutional forms persist, and under which conditions do the various other forces pervail? Since "different structures and types display different degrees of ability to survive," as Schumpeter himself notes,[89] which patterns have a greater and which a lesser degree of this ability?

Bendix would certainly reject the "provisional assumption" Merton has advanced as a "directive for research" as far too narrow and too closely linked with a functionalism he rejects – namely, "that persisting cultural forms have a *net balance of functional consequences* either for the society considered as a unit or for subgroups sufficiently powerful to retain these forms intact, by means of direct coercion or indirect persuasion."[90] If the interests of and the conflicts between dominant groups determine structural persistence or change, not much is gained by the distinction between old and new institutional and cultural forms, except perhaps that it is often easier – and to the advantage of the interests in legitimation of powerful groups – to put new wine into old bottles than it is to create institutions and cultural patterns de novo. Bendix has more in mind, but aside from an implicit tendency to attribute special longevity to cultural and particularly religious patterns and their ramifications, he offers no ideas as to the types of sociocultural patterns or the other conditions that make persistence more likely. In his interpretive narrative he of course notes discontinuities as well, but there is no attempt to contrast the conditions and characteristics of these instances with those of persistence. Neither the selection of the historical cases nor the interspersed comparative reflections are designed in such a way as to explore, identify, and test the conditions for continuity and change in institutional forms and cultural patterns.

That the Schumpeter principle functions in Bendix's work in fact merely as a vague guide for interpretation and as an argument against competing general theoretical orientations is also demonstrated by the absence of detailed historical delineations of certain continuities crucial to his analysis. Thus, although one expects that *Kings or People* would give at least a detailed sketch of the continuous line of thought about the rights of the people against their royal rulers that begins in the Middle Ages, we have to content ourselves with a few brief and general remarks.[91]

General Concepts and Historical Particularity

It remains to discuss one last feature of Bendix's work that contributes to its lack of focus on the search for causal propositions and explanations – his ideas about the role of concepts in comparative historical analysis. Notice that he much more often speaks of "concepts" than of theoretical propositions and explanations. Concepts are, in his use of the word, more than defined terms that can enter descriptive, explanatory, or generalizing sentences. Concepts are not merely more or less useful for formulating adequate sentences about reality, but must themselves be judged by criteria of empirical adequacy and truth.

The reason for this is easily found: the word *concept* covers for Bendix both the identification of one class of phenomena and various approximations to Weber's ideal types. Bendix's use of "industrialization" in *Work and Authority in Industry* – "the process by which large numbers of employees are concentrated in single enterprises and become dependent upon the directing and coordinating activities of entrepreneurs and managers"[92] – is an example of the former, provided that not only "large numbers" but also "enterprise," "direction and coordination," and "entrepreneurs and managers" are unambiguously defined. An example of the second meaning of concept is his discussion of

> patrimonial and bureaucratic administration . . . [as] benchmark concepts of social structures [which] can encompass a range of historical experience. A given type of administration will retain its character as long as rulers and officials achieve some balance between that type's conflicting imperatives. The analytic task is to identify these imperatives and hence the issues or conflicts whose repeated resolutions define and redefine the attributes of that type. To avoid the reification of the type, that is the fallacy of attributing to a social structure a concreteness it does not possess, we must see these "attributes" as objects of action by specific groups.[93]

The failure to distinguish sharply between simple class concepts and theoretical arguments in the form of type concepts[94] seems at least partly responsible for a whole set of arguments about historicity and concept formation that mingle theoretical propositions and concepts and impede the search for theoretical hypotheses. The deficiencies of ideal types as incompletely specified theories are understood as problems of any definition of concepts in relation to the flux of historical change:

> Definitions of structures like feudalism, bureaucracy, etc., usually take the form of enumerating several, distinguishing characteristics. Such enumerations necessarily "freeze" the fluidity of social life, as Weber himself emphasized. They say nothing about the strength or generality with which a given characteristic must be present, nor do they say anything about structures in which one or another element of the definition is missing. The result has been uncertainty. Abstractions are needed to define the characteristics of a structure and thus they remove the definition from the

evidence. On the other hand, when we approach the evidence "definition at hand," we often find its analytic ultility diminished, because the characteristics to which it refers are in fact neither unequivocal nor general.[95]

From this derives the suggestion to use contrast conceptions as well as static and dynamic concepts in conjunction with one another:

> Implicitly or explicitly, we define such terms as feudalism, capitalism, absolutism, caste-system, bureaucracy, and others by contrast with what each of these structures is not. For example, fealty-ties are contrasted with contractual, absolutist centralized with feudal decentralized authority, caste with tribe or estate, impersonal with personalized administration, the unity of household and business with their separation, etc. My suggestion is that contrast-conceptions are indispensable as a first orientation (they serve a function as benchmarks), which introduces analysis, but should not be mistaken for analysis.[96]

> [W]e use "bureaucracy" when we wish to contrast one type of administration with another, and "bureaucratization" when we wish to emphasize that the new terms of reference like "depersonalized personnel selection" continue to be problematic, an issue whose every resolution creates new problems as well. Similarly one can distinguish between democracy and democratization, nation and nation-building, centralized authority and centralization of authority, etc.[97]

While these strategies are useful to exploit the sensitizing character of concepts and conceptual frameworks and to guard against pitfalls in their use, these strategies do not lead toward a fuller formulation of the implicit theoretical propositions. Instead, Bendix aims to achieve improved typological conceptions guiding historical interpretation.

The attempt to formulate universal concepts is rejected because they inevitably are either vacuous or at variance with the historical evidence.[98] But this argument, on which rests much of Bendix's thought about historicity and the problematic nature of theoretical generalization and explanation, also fails to distinguish between type conceptions and classificatory concepts. To take his own early definition of industrialization as an example of the latter, it is clear that the designated phenomenon is not found universally in history, but the concept can be applied universally, identifying the presence or the absence of the phenomenon. It is with these or equivalent concepts[99] that the more complex and quasipropositional type conceptions can be developed into full-fledged theories with explicit propositions that apply under similarly explicated circumstances. That such theories may be wrong or misstated can be found out best if they are thus formulated. If they are found wanting they can be discarded or amended; but this confrontation between theory and evidence is blurred if various balancing considerations are incorporated into not fully explicated types of conceptions.

This relates to the last issue, the skepticism about ethnocentric conceptualization:

> Weber's categoric distinction between legitimate authority and constellations of interests is itself a late outgrowth of our changing social order and intellectual development. In order to use such a distinction as an analytical tool, we must remain aware of its limited applicability, and this is best achieved by understanding its historical context. By learning how men come to think as they do about the societies in which they live, we may acquire the detachment needed to protect us against the unwitting adoption of changing intellectual fashions and against a neglect of the limitations inherent in any theoretical framework.[100]

A better safeguard than such anticipatory skepticism, which confounds the genesis and the validity of ideas, might be the testing of explicated theorems and their modification in continued use.

Conclusion

In his comparative historical work, Reinhard Bendix has moved – from *Work and Authority in Industry* to *Nation-Building and Citizenship* and *Kings or People* – toward a position intensely skeptical of systematic theoretical explanation. In my discussion I sought to show that the theoretical and methodological strategies he employs are such as to confirm his doubts. Bendix's own more limited goals the critique of received general theories, the specification of historical contexts in which more limited causal analysis may be achieved, and the integration of historical knowledge and social theory in the form of comparative-historical contrasts – run into difficulties in part due to the issues he rightly identifies and in part due to the problems of his approach. He contrasts received grand theories – system theory, evolutionary theories, and historical materialism – with his own metatheoretical guesses and assertions, rather than examining their varied applications in the light of historical evidence. Bendix misses opportunities to draw systematic delimitations and thus more specific causal propositions from

Dietrich Rueschemeyer

his analyses not only because of inherent difficulties but also because he does not really aim to develop propositions transcending historical particularity. Yet his own interpretive accounts of contrasting histories organized around common problems or themes abound with theoretical presuppositions that do not simply spring from the evidence.

With this said, however, it would be vacuous to dismiss Reinhard Bendix's achievement. His comparative historical studies of the interplay between power and legitimation include magnificently sensitive and imaginative interpretations of varied bodies of historical evidence and analysis. His work has done more than that of most leading sociologists to keep the historical dimension of all social structures and cultural orientations in the theoretical consciousness of contemporary social science.

The problems of theoretical explanation in history that Reinhard Bendix raises are real, even if his way of formulating and tackling them is open to criticism. They are especially real for those issues of special salience to Bendix – issues about the role of ideas in political legitimation. This points to a broader question for the future of social theory. The dominant strategy since the turn of the century has been to seek sociological explanation by focusing on the subjective dimension of action. Yet we encounter the most variability and historical particularity of human life precisely in the theories of historical actors about their world and their own needs and wants. If the focus on the subjective dimension remains central to our attempts at theoretical analysis, a strong component of historically bounded humanistic interpretation is likely to be inevitable, as well as desirable. Alternative, and possibly complementary, strategies may seek to bypass the subjective dimension and focus, for instance, on structural features of social life.[101] This may entail losses in problem-formulation as well as gains in explanatory power, however partial. Paradoxically, Bendix's work also contains many suggestive materials from which such explanatory arguments could be developed.

Notes

1. Reinhard Bendix, *Social Science and the Distrust of Reason*, University of California Publications in Sociology and Social Institutions, vol. 1, no. 1 (Berkeley: University of California Press, 1951), p. 41. Hereafter cited as *Distrust of Reason*.
2. Ibid., p. 42.
3. Ibid., pp. 23–24.
4. This concordance is the subject of a debate between Stuart Hampshire and Isaiah Berlin, in which Hampshire attacks the link as spuriously persuasive:

"one may so easily move from the moral proposition that persons ought not to be manipulated and controlled, like any other natural objects, to the different, and quasi-philosophical, proposition that they cannot be manipulated and controlled like any other natural objects. In the present climate of opinion a very natural fear of planning and social technology is apt to be dignified as a philosophy of indeterminism." See Isaiah Berlin, *Four Essays on Liberty* (London: Oxford University Press, 1969), p. xxiii.

5. Bendix has taken his guidance from Weber's work virtually to the point of identification, and many readers think of Bendix's work as an extension of Weber's. However, there are also important differences between their respective positions, partly occasioned by the different partners and opponents with whom the two scholars stood in dialogue. These differences pertain also to what will occupy us most in this chapter – how in scholarly practice the tension between historical particularity and theoretical generalization is handled; Max Weber was far more willing than Bendix to state causal generalizations. Since a detailed treatment of Weber's positions and a comparison with those of Bendix is a greater burden than I can assume in this chapter, I content myself with referring to Guenther Roth's introduction to the second edition of Reinhard Bendix's *Max Weber: An Intellectual Portrait* (Berkeley: University of California Press, 1977), pp. xiii–xliii, which discusses Bendix's work on Weber in relation to recent scholarship, to the body of that book itself, and to Reinhard Bendix and Guenther Roth's *Scholarship and Partisanship: Essays on Max Weber* (Berkeley: University of California Press, 1971).

6. Reinhard Bendix, *Work and Authority in Industry: Ideologies of Management in the Course of Industrialization* (New York: Wiley, 1956) (hereafter cited as *Work and Authority in Industry*); *Nation-Building and Citizenship: Studies of our Changing Social Order* (New York: Wiley, 1964) (hereafter cited as *Nation-Building and Citizenship*); *Kings or People: Power and the Mandate To Rule* (Berkeley: University of California Press, 1978) (hereafter cited as *Kings or People*). The assessment of the latter quoted in the text is Jonathan M. Wiener's; see his review of *Kings or People, New Republic* (December 2, 1978): 38. Another important contribution to comparative historical sociology is R. Bendix et al., eds., *State and Society: A Reader in Comparative Political Sociology* (Boston: Little, Brown, 1968, and Berkeley: University of California Press, 1973) (hereafter cited as *State and Society*), which represents one of the early initiatives for current concerns with the relatively autonomous role of the state in large-scale social change.

7. Reinhard Bendix and Seymour M. Lipset, eds., *Class, Status, and Power: A Reader in Social Stratification* (Glencoe, Ill.: Free Press, 1953; 2nd ed. 1966).

8. Friedrich H. Tenbruck, "Das Werk Max Webers," *Kölner Zeitschrift für Soziologie und Sozialpsychologie* 27 (1975): 663. See Bendix, *Max Weber: An Intellectual Portrait*.

9. Reinhard Bendix, "Tradition and Modernity Reconsidered," *Comparative Studies in Society and History* 9 (April 1967): 292–346; reprinted in revised form in R. Bendix, *Embattled Reason: Essays on Social Knowledge* (New York: Oxford University Press, 1970), pp. 250–314.

10. Bendix, *Kings or People*, p. 15.

11. Reinhard Bendix and Bennett Berger, "Images of Society and Problems of Concept Formation in Sociology," in *Symposium on Sociological Theory*, ed. L. Gross (Evanston, Ill.: Row, Peterson, 1959), p. 112.

12. Bendix, *Distrust of Reason*, p. 4.

13. I refer here not only to Talcott Parsons's influential reconstruction of a

conceptual and theoretical framework of social action, which, he argued in *The Structure of Social Action* (New York: McGraw-Hill, 1937), emerged from the work of Alfred Marshall, Vilfredo Pareto, Emile Durkheim, and Max Weber. Of equal importance for American sociology was the reception of Georg Simmel's social psychology (in contrast to his formal sociology) and its fusion with the approaches of Charles H. Cooley and George H. Mead in the Chicago school of sociology and the subsequent symbolic interactionism. The movements of Ethnomethodology and Phenomenology link this tradition, mediated through the work of Alfred Schutz, to Max Weber's interpretive sociology and phenomenological philosophy in Europe. Finally, one might point to the work of George Lukács and the even more influential writings of Gramsci in contemporary Marxian thought.

14. See, in addition to the substantive works cited in note 6, Bendix and Berger, "Images of Society"; Reinhard Bendix, "Concepts and Generalizations in Comparative Sociological Studies," *American Sociological Review* 28 (1963): 532–39 (citations in text are from the reprint in Bendix, *Embattled Reason*); "Concepts in Comparative Historical Analysis," in *Comparative Research Across Cultures and Nations*, ed. Stein Rokkan (The Hague: Mouton, 1968), pp. 67–81; "Tradition and Modernity Reconsidered."

15. Robert K. Merton, *Social Theory and Social Structure*, enlarged ed. (New York: Free Press, 1968), chap. 4.

16. For this critique and his own framework of analysis, see especially Bendix, "Concepts in Comparative Historical Analysis."

17. Bendix, *Nation-Building and Citizenship*, p. 301.

18. Bendix, "Concepts in Comparative Historical Analysis," p. 69.

19. The formulation is William Graham Sumner's, who saw among the components of social and cultural patterns "a strain toward consistency with each other, because they all answer their several purposes with less friction and antagonism when they cooperate and support each other." W. G. Sumner, *Folkways* (Boston: Ginn, 1940), pp. 5–6, quoted and discussed in Bendix, *Nation-Building and Citizenship*, pp. 209–10.

20. Bendix and Berger, "Images of Society," p. 110.

21. Ibid.

22. Bendix, "Concepts in Comparative Historical Analysis," p. 176.

23. See the introduction to Bendix et al., eds., *State and Society*, p. 10, and the first selection in that volume by Wolfram Eberhard, "Problems of Historical Sociology," pp. 16–28. The origin of conceptions of society as a self-contained unit in England and France is argued in Bendix, *Kings or People*, pp. 267–68: "The social theories of the nineteenth century were developed in societies that pioneered the industrial and democratic revolutions of the modern world. These revolutions occurred at the center of the British empire and in the great state of France, societies which could easily be considered in isolation. The theories developed in England and France depicted societies as self-contained units and focused attention on the major classes striving for social and political recognition." See also Bendix, "Concepts in Comparative Historical Analysis," p. 77.

24. Bendix and Berger, "Images of Society," p. 111. Bendix and Berger's formulations on this point are not unequivocal. For instance, a few paragraphs earlier, they discuss Tocqueville's view of the impossibility of prediction and refer to his conviction that the future of ever more egalitarian societies remained open as to servitude or freedom; yet they endorse his qualification "that the possible directions of social change were limited in number and that it was feasible to foresee them by means of 'speculative truths' which

extrapolated observed tendencies on the fictitious assumption that nothing would interfere with their ultimate realization" (p. 110). Since such extrapolation of trends is historically bounded and also "protected" by the *ceteris paribus* clause, it can be seen as compatible with the agnostic position on what is possible quoted. As we will see, it is the latter that informs much of Bendix's actual work in comparative historical analysis.

25. Bendix, *Nation-Building and Citizenship*, p. 9.
26. Joseph Schumpeter, *Capitalism, Socialism and Democracy* (New York: Harper and Brothers, 1947), pp. 12–13; see Bendix, *Nation-Building and Citizenship*, pp. 8–9.
27. Bendix, "Concepts in Comparative Historical Analysis," p. 76. In "Tradition and Modernity Reconsidered," Bendix extends this idea to a conception of different leader-follower relations between countries that define modernity. These causal relations are not uniform throughout world history. They are the more important the more different societies become dependent on or interdependent with each other in economic, political, and cultural terms. "Industrialization itself has intensified the international communication of techniques and ideas, which are taken out of their original context and adopted or adapted to satisfy desires and achieve ends in one's own country" ("Concepts in Comparative Historical Analysis," p. 76). Bendix acknowledges the relation of these ideas to Wallerstein's world system theory, but in discussing the emergence of "a world economy during the sixteenth century" (*Kings or People*, p. 253), he insists – as already adumbrated in the quoted reference to "the ideas of the French Revolution" – on "a greater emphasis on the political antecedents of the sixteenth century and on the role of ideas in the formation of the modern world" (note 8, pp. 629–30).
28. Bendix, "Concepts on Comparative Historical Analysis," p. 69.
29. Immanuel Wallerstein, *The Modern World-System: Capitalist Agriculture and the Origins of the European World-Economy in the Sixteenth Century* (New York: Academic Press, 1974), p. 152; see Bendix, *Kings or People*, note 2, p. 629.
30. Bendix, *Kings or People*, p. 15.
31. Bendix, "Concepts in Comparative Historical Analysis," p. 69.
32. S. N. Eisenstadt, *The Political Systems of Empires: The Rise and Fall of Historical Bureaucratic Societies* (New York: Free Press, 1963).
33. Karl R. Popper, *The Logic of Scientific Inquiry* (New York: Harper Torchbooks, 1965).
34. See Barrington Moore, Jr., *Social Origins of Dictatorship and Democracy: Lord and Peasant in the Making of the Modern World* (Boston: Beacon Press, 1966); the quote is from p. xiii. Other works using a similar approach are Theda Skocpol, *States and Social Revolutions: A Comparative Analysis of France, Russia, and China* (New York: Cambridge University Press, 1979); Frances V. Moulder, *Japan, China and the Modern World Economy: Toward a Reinterpretation of East Asian Development ca. 1600 to ca. 1918* (New York: Cambridge University Press, 1977); and Robert Brenner, "Agrarian Class Structure and Economic Development in Pre-Industrial Europe," *Past and Present*, 70 (February 1976): 30–75. See also the comparative discussion of parallel, contrast-oriented and macroanalytic comparative history by Theda Skocpol and Margaret Somers, "The Uses of Comparative History in Macrosocial Inquiry," *Comparative Studies in Society and History*, 22 (2) (April 1980); 174–97.
35. E. P. Thompson, *The Poverty of Theory and Other Essays* (London: Merlin Press, 1978), p. 226.
36. Bendix, *Kings or People*, p. 15.

37. Bendix, *Nation-Building and Citizenship*, p. 17.
38. Bendix, "Concepts and Generalizations," p. 180.
39. Bendix, *Work and Authority in Industry*, p. 1.
40. Ibid., p. 1.
41. Ibid., p. xx.
42. Ibid., p. 6.
43. Ibid., p. 10.
44. Ibid., p. 6.
45. Ibid., p. xxi.
46. See, for example, *Work and Authority in Industry*, pp. xix, xxif., 7–8.
47. Arthur L. Stinchcombe, *Theoretical Methods in Social History*. (New York: Academic Press, 1978), pp. 104–13 and 117–18. Stinchcombe observes: "The sort of theory we have been analyzing in the parts we have chosen from Bendix, Smelser, and the other analysts, comes in bits and pieces, rather than integrated systems of thought. This makes it hard to learn; to train oneself to be a 'theorist' of social change one has to read a great many monographs of theoretically oriented social historians, store analogies and distinctions in one's mind, and hope that some of them give theoretical handles on new situations" (p. 120).
48. Ibid., pp. 112–13.
49. Edward Gross, Review of *Work and Authority in Industry*, *American Sociological Review* 21 (December 1956): 790.
50. That Bendix in this remarkable way neglected his own commitment to preserving a sense of historical particularity, referring to the autocratic part of the modern comparison interchangeably as "Soviet Russia," "Russian Civilization," "Russia and the Countries in her Orbit," "The East" and the German Democratic Republic or, as he puts it, the "East Zone" of Germany, demonstrates the impact of Cold War definitions of the situation in the period in which he wrote. In his own words: "Two interpretations divide the contemporary world," and "this conflict is the point of departure for the present study" (*Work and Authority in Industry*, pp. 10 and 2).
51. Skocpol and Somers, in "Uses of Comparative History," speak of "contrast-oriented comparative history." I have borrowed the term *juxtapositional history* from Theodore Hamerow who makes a similar criticism of the second part of *Kings or People*: "What we have here intermittently is not comparative but juxtapositional history, in which the decisive national experiences of several countries appear side by side without an integrative principle to give them coherence." Theodore S. Hamerow, Review of *Kings or People*, *American Historical Review* 84 (4) (October 1979): 1018.
52. Bendix, *Nation-Building and Citizenship*, p. 3.
53. This expectation was expressed, for example, by T. H. Marshall, in his review of *Nation-Building and Citizenship*, *Political Science Quarterly* 80 (1965): 675.
54. For comments on these omissions see Bendix, *Kings or People*, pp. 14–15.
55. Ibid., p. 598.
56. Jonathan M. Wiener, Review of *Kings or People*, p. 39.
57. Bendix, "Concepts in Comparative Historical Analysis," p. 73. Bendix refers to the similar insistence of Otto Brunner in *Neue Wege der Sozialgeschichte* (Göttingen: Vandenhoeck and Ruprecht, 1956) and of E. P. Thompson in *The Making of the British Working Class* (London: Gollancz, 1963) and notes "that the same point is made despite the rather marked difference in political orientation of the two authors" (note 8, p. 80).

58. Ibid., pp. 73–74.
59. Thus, after listing a number of specific issues of baronial representation limiting royal authority, Bendix comments: "Problems like these can be formulated only in retrospect: therefore, to speak of opposition to royal prerogatives is only a convenient shorthand for the piecemeal process of delimiting the authority of the English king" (*Kings or People*, p. 189). And: "The English baronage managed to increase its power position vis-à-vis the English monarchy, though for a long time this was hardly a deliberate process" (p. 196). In *Work and Authority in Industry*, Bendix acknowledged explicitly that the formulation of problems historical actors respond to involves more than their subjective understandings and intentions: "I have taken care to interpret the evolving problems from their [the industrial leaders'] point of view. Yet sociological analysis also goes beyond the ken of the participants and other aspects of the empirical evidence. It must always make use of questions and concepts which are not themselves derived from the 'facts' " (p. xix).
60. Bendix is quite aware of this: "This study . . . differs from inquiries in economics, sociology, and psychology, which frequently examine the record of human behavior. Such inquiry into underlying structures has been a dominant theme in recent intellectual history. Marxists and Freudians are at one in their attempt to discern the underlying cause of manifest discontents, even if they differ in what they purport to find. Some anthropologists and psychologists have turned their attention from behavioral to the analysis of myths in searching for the underlying constants of the human condition. And some sociologists and political scientists engage in a search for universals when they analyze the functional prerequisites of all social and political structures. Such a search for structural forces can yield insights into motivation, ideological assumptions, and hidden interrelations. I am indebted to this intellectual tendency. But with so many scholars engaged in searching for underlying structures, there is space for an inquiry which focuses attention on structures that lie more open to view." *Kings or People*, pp. 13–14.
61. For the three quotes see *Kings or People*, pp. 227, 4, and 218, respectively.
62. Ibid., p. 222.
63. Ibid., p. 223.
64. Ibid., p. 14.
65. Ibid., p. 229.
66. Ibid., especially pp. 228–34.
67. Ibid., p. 249.
68. Ibid., pp. 197–98.
69. Ibid., p. 198.
70. Ibid., p. 198.
71. Ibid., p. 112.
72. Ibid., pp. 197–98.
73. Ibid., p. 195.
74. Stinchcombe, *Theoretical Methods in Social History*, p. 122.
75. Bendix, *Kings or People*, p. 15.
76. Ibid., p. 258 and note 20, p. 630.
77. Ibid., p. 271.
78. Ibid., p. 268.
79. Ibid., p. 15.
80. Skocpol and Somers, "The Uses of Comparative History," p. 193.

81. See Merton, *Social Theory and Social Structure*, pp. 84–86, for the problem's long history.
82. Bendix, *Kings or People*, p. 14.
83. Ibid., p. 3.
84. Ibid., p. 5.
85. Ibid., p. 197.
86. Ibid., p. 241.
87. Bendix, *Work and Authority in Industry*, p. 446.
88. Thus Bendix argues against systemic equilibrium notions that "men . . . by their actions (however conditioned) achieve a certain degree of stability, or fail to do so. Here the definition of social structure in terms of a set of issues helps, because it points to the contentions through which individuals and groups achieve a measure of accommodation or compromise between conflicting imperatives." And: "Stability of a social structure is . . . the end-product of always proximate efforts to maintain stability" ("Concepts in Comparative Historical Analysis," p. 73).
89. Schumpeter, *Capitalism, Socialism and Democracy*, p. 12.
90. Merton, *Social Theory and Social Structure*, p. 32 (Merton's emphasis).
91. A model of such a documentation in a related context is Benjamin Nelson's *The Idea of Usury* (Princeton, N.J.: Princeton University Press, 1949). One critic of *Kings or People*, Quentin Skinner, author of *The Foundations of Modern Political Thought: The Renaissance* (New York: Cambridge University Press, 1978), notes in "Taking Off," *New York Review of Books* 26 (15) (March 22, 1979): 16, that "the belief that the people's representatives have a right to set up and set down their rulers had already become a central feature of scholastic as well as civil law theories of political society in the course of the Middle Ages. And the same arguments were then adopted and carried to a new peak of revolutionary development in France and the Netherlands as well as in England as early as the middle years of the sixteenth century."
92. Bendix, *Work and Authority in Industry*, note 2, p. 2.
93. Bendix, *Nation-Buiding and Citizenship*, p. 113.
94. That type concepts like Weber's ideal types contain theoretical ideas and propositions, albeit insufficiently specified ones, is argued by Carl G. Hempel, "Problems of Concept and Theory Formation in the Social Sciences," in *Science, Language, and Human Rights* (Philadelphia: University of Pennsylvania Press, 1952), pp. 65–86. Most social scientists, though acknowledging the deficiencies of such embryonic theories in comparison to theory in the natural sciences and to the standards explicated in philosophy of science, are likely to appreciate more than Hempel the real advances such theoretical ideas represent.
95. Bendix, "Concepts in Comparative Historical Analysis," p. 70.
96. Ibid., p. 71.
97. Ibid., p. 72.
98. Ibid., pp. 74–75.
99. As we have seen, Arthur Stinchcombe argues in *Theoretical Methods in Social History* in favor of looking for analogies between different historical instances rather than using class concepts. This, it seems to me, is useful advice for the strategy of discovery and invention of theoretical ideas. It does not affect the logic of theory validation. If the search for analogies or equivalences in terms of causes and effects identifies precisely the relevant aspects, "the two methods of looking for analogies between cases of interest and looking for predicates of a class of interest [are indeed] logically . . . exactly equivalent" (p. 19).

100. Bendix, *Nation-Building and Citizenship*, pp. 23–24.
101. One example of such a strategy is found in Theda Skocpol's *States and Social Revolutions;* Skocpol argues against prevailing psychological approaches to the study of revolutions and for a structural perspective (pp. 5–18). Another, though much more formalist, example of a structural approach excluding the subjective dimension of action in a different area of inquiry is Peter M. Blau's *Inequality and Heterogeneity: A Primitive Theory of Social Structure* (New York: Free Press, 1977).

Bibliography

WORKS OF REINHARD BENDIX

"Max Weber's Interpretation of Conduct and History." *American Journal of Sociology* 51 (May 1946):518–26.

Social Science and the Distrust and Reason. University of California Publications in Sociology and Social Institutions, vol. 1, no. 1. Berkeley: University of California Press, 1951.

"Social Stratification and Political Power." *American Political Science Review* 46 (2) (June 1952): 3357–75.

"Karl Marx's Theory of Social Classes," with S. M. Lipset. In *Class, Status, and Power*, edited by R. Bendix and S. M. Lipset, pp. 26–35. Glencoe, Ill.: Free Press, 1953.

Class, Status, and Power: A Reader in Social Stratification, ed. with S. M. Lipset. Glencoe, Ill.: Free Press, 1953; 2nd ed. 1966.

Work and Authority in Industry: Ideologies of Management in the Course of Industrialization. New York: Wiley, 1956. Berkeley: University of California Press, 1974.

"Industrialization, Ideologies and Social Structure." *American Sociological Review* 24 (1959): 613–23.

"Images of Society and Problems of Concept Formation in Sociology," with Bennett Berger. In *Symposion on Sociological Theory*, edited by Llewellyn Gross, pp. 92–118. Evanston, Ill.: Row, Peterson, 1959.

Social Mobility in Industrial Society, with S. M. Lipset. Berkeley: University of California Press, 1959.

Max Weber: An Intellectual Portrait. Garden City, N.Y.: Doubleday, 1960; 2nd ed. Berkeley: University of California Press, 1977.

"Social Stratification and the Political Community." *European Journal of Sociology* 1 (1960): 181–210.

"The Lower Classes and the 'Democratic Revolution.' " *Industrial Relations* 1 (October 1961): 91–116.

"Concepts and Generalizations in Comparative Sociological Studies." *American Sociological Review* 28 (1963): 532–39.

Nation-Building and Citizenship: Studies of Our Changing Social Order. New York: Wiley, 1964; 2nd ed. Berkeley: University of California Press, 1977.

"A Case Study in Cultural and Educational Mobility: Japan and the Protestant Ethic." In *Social Structure and Mobility in Economic Development*, edited by Neil J. Smelser and Seymour M. Lipset, pp. 262–79. Chicago: Aldine, 1966.

"The Protestant Ethic Revisited." *Comparative Studies in Society and History* 9 (1967): 266–73.

"Tradition and Modernity Reconsidered." *Comparative Studies in Society and History* 9 (April 1967): 292–346.

State and Society: A Reader in Comparative Political Sociology. Edited in collabora-

Dietrich Rueschemeyer

tion with Coenraad Brand et al. Boston: Little, Brown, 1968, and Berkeley: University of California Press, 1973.

"Concepts in Comparative Historical Analysis." In *Comparative Research Across Cultures and Nations,* edited by Stein Rokkan, pp. 67–81. The Hague: Mouton, 1968.

Embattled Reason: Essays on Social Knowledge. New York: Oxford University Press, 1970.

Scholarship and Partisanship: Essays on Max Weber, with Guenther Roth. Berkeley: University of California Press, 1971.

Kings or People: Power and the Mandate to Rule. Berkeley: University of California Press, 1978.

REVIEWS AND DISCUSSIONS OF BENDIX'S WORK

Bottomore, Tom. "Has Sociology a Future?" *New York Review of Books* 16 (4) (March 11, 1971): 37–40. (Review of several books including Bendix, *Embattled Reason.*)

Dunn, John. Review of *Kings or People. History* 65 (February 1980): 67–68.

Feldman, Arnold. Review of *Nation-Building and Citizenship. American Journal of Sociology* 73 (March 1968): 637–38.

Gross, Edward. Review of *Work and Authority in Industry. American Sociological Review* 21 (December 1956): 789–91.

Gross, Llewellyn. Review of *Embattled Reason. American Sociological Review* 36 (June 1971): 528–29.

Hamerow, Theodore S. Review of *Kings or People. American Historical Review* 84 (4) (October 1979): 1018.

Janowitz, Morris. Review of *Max Weber: An Intellectual Portrait. American Political Science Review* 54 (1960): 1010–11.

Marshall, T. H. Review of *Max Weber: An Intellectual Portrait. British Journal of Sociology* 12 (1961): 184–88.

Marshall, T. H. Review of *Nation-Building and Citizenship. Political Science Quarterly* 80 (1965): 675–77.

Miller, Delbert C. Review of *Work and Authority in Industry. Annals of the American Academy of Political and Social Science* 310 (1957): 213–15.

Mueller, Hans-Eberhard. "The Role of Ideas in the Conditions of Backwardness." *Contemporary Sociology* 9 (May 1980): 333–36. First contribution in a review symposion on *Kings or People;* see Poggi for the second contribution and the answer of Reinhard Bendix, "Reflections on *Kings or People,*" ibid., pp. 339–41.

Nisbet, Robert A. Review of *Nation-Building and Citizenship. Annals of the American Academy of Political and Social Science* 359 (May 1965): 173–74.

Parsons, Talcott. "Max Weber." *American Sociological Review* 25 (October 1960): 750–52 (review of *Max Weber: An Intellectual Portrait*).

Parsons, Talcott. Review of *Embattled Reason. American Journal of Sociology* 77 (January 1972): 766–68.

Poggi, Gianfranco. "Stronger on Narrative than on Analysis." *Contemporary Sociology* 9 (May 1980); 336–38. Second contribution in a review symposion on *Kings or People;* see Mueller for the first contribution and the answer of Reinhard Bendix, "Reflections on *Kings or People,*" ibid., pp. 339–41.

Robertson, Roland. Review of *Nation-Building and Citizenship. British Journal of Sociology* 17 (1966): 325.

Simpson, Richard L. Review of *Work and Authority in Industry. Social Forces* 35 (March 1957): 288–89.

Skinner, Quentin. "Taking Off." *New York Review of Books* 26 (15) (March 22, 1979): 15–16.

Skocpol, Theda, and Somers, Margaret. "The Uses of Comparative History in Macrosocial Inquiry." *Comparative Studies in Society and History* 22 (2) (April 1980): 174–97.

Stinchcombe, Arthur L. *Theoretical Methods in Social History.* New York: Academic Press, 1978.

Wiener, Jonathan M. Review of *Kings or People. New Republic* (December 2, 1978): 38–40.

6. Destined Pathways: The Historical Sociology of Perry Anderson

MARY FULBROOK and THEDA SKOCPOL

The publication in 1974 of Perry Anderson's *Passages from Antiquity to Feudalism* and *Lineages of the Absolutist State* made quite a splash, sending ripples of appreciation through intellectual circles in Great Britain, the United States, and beyond.[1] Conceived in the grand tradition of classical social science and written in open dialogue with the ideas of Max Weber and Karl Marx, Anderson's two books offer a single, coherent overview of European civilization from the ancient sway of Greece and Rome through the last days of absolutist monarchies in early modern Europe. "A complex, beautifully interwoven and controlled" account, said Moses Finley in the *Guardian*, and Keith Thomas, reviewing *Passages-Lineages* for the *New York Review of Books*, seconded this enthusiasm: "The breath-taking range of conception and architectural skill with which it has been executed make [this] work a formidable intellectual achievement."[2] Tariq Ali called *Passages-Lineages* a "Marxist masterpiece."[3] Even D. G. MacRae, normally hostile to Marxist arguments, declared that these "two books are enormously pleasurable," and called them a "major contribution" to historical sociology.[4]

Anderson's books are not only brilliantly executed and intrinsically fascinating, they are also of unusual theoretical and methodological interest in a number of ways. For Marxists, perhaps their chief interest lies in Anderson's attempt to highlight the specifically political aspects of long-run social change. "One of the basic axioms of historical materialism," says Anderson in the Foreword to *Lineages*, is "that secular struggle between classes is ultimately resolved at the political – not at the economic or the cultural – level of society. In other words, it is the construction and destruction of States which seal the basic shifts in the relations of production so long as classes subsist."[5] Thus *Passages-Lineages* does "history from above," focusing especially on the rise and fall of empires in classical antiquity, the growth of monarchies in medieval Europe, and the life histories of absolutist states from Imperial Spain to czarist Russia. Furthermore, as we shall see, Anderson studies the political history of the past to elucidate political alternatives for Marxian socialists in the present. So not only does his emphasis on the political raise theoretical issues for Marxist scholarship, it also poses the question of how historical studies can speak to contemporary political understanding.

For all scholars (Marxist or not) interested in historically based studies of social change, Anderson's two books also raise methodological questions along several lines of long-standing concern. First, how are theoretical concepts and arguments used to make sense of societal arrangements and social change in history? Anderson himself understands this issue in terms of a challenge to "hold together two orders of reflection which have been unwarrantably divorced in Marxist writing": on the one hand, "laws of motion of whole structures," and on the other, "particular studies . . . confined to delimited areas or periods," studies referring to "the multiple empirical circumstances of specific events and institutions."[6] Second, how are comparisons across different societies and civilizations used to illuminate the individual cases and to develop an overall argument? Although Anderson says nothing explicit about comparative methodology, the architecture of *Passages-Lineages* is largely organized around juxtapositions of various historical case accounts, so comparative history is obviously an important part of Anderson's approach. Finally what status, if any, do evolutionist explanations of long-run social change have in Anderson's presentation? Evolutionist versions of Marxism and structural functionalism have long been influential in historical sociology. Both versions have attempted to identify necessary stages of social change through which individual societies are supposed to pass via endogenous mechanisms of transformation. In *Passages-Lineages*, Anderson rejects orthodox Marxist evolutionism, yet it remains to be seen how thoroughly he breaks with all features of evolutionist explanation.

Passages from Antiquity to Feudalism and *Lineages of the Absolutist State* thus offer rich material for theoretical and methodological probings. First, however, it makes sense to understand some basic things about Perry Anderson and his reasons for doing historical sociology at all.

Perry Anderson and the *New Left Review*

The work settings of scholars and the audiences for which they write profoundly influence the nature and purposes of their work. In the

171

Anglo-Saxon academic world, at least, professional historians almost never undertake broad, synthetic projects like *Passages-Lineages*. Historians become experts on delimited times and places, often specializing in particular kinds of subject matters within those limits: for example, early modern French political history; twentieth-century U.S. economic history; or Ming-Ch'ing Chinese intellectual history.[7] For the most part, historians address established problems, bringing to bear new sources of evidence, new arguments, or perhaps new methods of analysis; occasionally a professional historian may also redefine the key problems to be addressed in his or her specialty. As research proceeds, most professional historians must also teach established university courses and train graduate students within their specialities. At the peak of their careers, premier historians may write syntheses of existing scholarship, covering several countries and subject matters for a major epoch, or covering many centuries of one country's past. A project on the scale of *Passages-Lineages*, surveying over two millenia for all of Europe, with discussions of major non-European civilizations as well, would rarely make sense within the operating frame of reference and even of a premier professional historian.

Perry Anderson is not a professional historian – or a professional academic of any sort. He is free from the kinds of purposes and constraints embodied in professional roles and subject to those of a very different calling. As the editor of the *New Left Review*, a Marxist journal published in Great Britain, Anderson might best be described as a strategically located intellectual gatekeeper and promoter of scholarly production by and for Marxists in the English-speaking world. Anderson works with a small, self-selecting editorial board, many of whose members were associated with him as far back as his student days at Oxford on a leftist journal called *New University*. The *New Left Review* appears six times a year, and there is also an affiliated publishing operation, New Left Books, which puts out a steady stream of original books as well as translations of non–English-language Marxist classics and contemporary European neo-Marxist works. Virtually all of Anderson's own essays and books are published "in house" by *New Left Review* and New Left Books. Indeed, he and his associates see their editorial enterprise not as an opportunity to judge books and articles submitted by intellectuals outside their circle of acquaintance but as a way to develop Marxist intellectual life, both through the presentation of their own work and through the solicitation of work from others they know or come to know in extensive traveling and correspondence.

To a remarkable degree for the contemporary intellectual world,

Perry Anderson's activities are autonomous and self-defined. Yet his own scholarship is still influenced by the audiences, at once intimate and amorphous, toward which he is oriented. Anderson addresses a small group of like-thinking, albeit rigorously critical, peers, those involved with him in the immediate affairs of the *New Left Review*. In addition, he addresses the broad aggregate of leftist intellectuals – within Great Britain and the United States, and also on a European and worldwide scale – who follow the contents of the *New Left Review* and read the various New Left Books publications. From both directions Anderson's historical work is constrained to fit into the overall program defined and pursued by the *New Left Review* as a politically ambitious intellectual journal.

The *New Left Review* as it has operated since 1963 under Perry Anderson's leadership has to be understood both in terms of its continuities with, and its reactions against, the first New Left in Britain. The *New Left Review* was born in 1959 as the intended flagship for this socialist-humanist movement that flourished in the late 1950s. The first New Left was an attempt to re-inspire socialist political commitment among British intellectuals, freeing leftist cultural debates from the dogmas of Stalinist communism and from the "philistinism" of a Labour Party lost in day-to-day practical maneuverings.[8] Although most of the first New Leftists were educated middle-class people, there were ties to mass-based politics in two ways. Many of the original New Leftists operated within, or critically addressed, the left wing of the Labour Party, trying to reorient it into a vigorous democratic socialist movement. Others in the first New Left were intensely involved in the anti-Cold War "Ban the Bomb" politics of the Campaign for Nuclear Disarmament, a movement that fielded giant popular demonstrations for a few years after 1958. When the *New Left Review* was established, it was envisaged not only as a publication outlet for political commentary and cultural criticism along theoretically eclectic socialist-humanist lines, but also as a loose focus for a nationwide network of New Left Clubs, whose members were politically as well as intellectually engaged.

By the early 1960s, the first New Left in Britain was visibly faltering and the *New Left Review* was in serious trouble. In response, the journal as such was first separated from the associated network of clubs; then the old editors co-opted a young occasional contributor, Perry Anderson, to revitalize the *Review* as editor. Anderson took over decisively and turned the *New Left Review* into a very new and increasingly successful endeavor. Anderson and his friends scorned the vague populism and the lack of Marxist theoretical sophistication evidenced by their elders in the first New Left. What is more:

> Whereas the first New Left had tried to assimilate at least partially with the established labour movement, Anderson and his colleagues called for the creation of a new socialist intelligentsia in Britain, analogous to those of continental Europe, which would be detached from the concerns of everyday Labour politics, critical of past socialist traditions, and determined to work out a consistent and all-encompassing structural analysis of contemporary society.[9]

From the time of Anderson's advent as editor, the pages of the *New Left Review* boldly reflected the new priorities. Gone were short, heterogeneously focused articles about current events, contemporary culture, and the details of British politics. Instead there were major theoretical and historical essays consistently falling in recognizable key areas: commentary on classical Marxist texts; translations and discussions of contemporary continental Marxist writings; analyses of the sociopolitical contexts of contemporary political trends in Europe, the United States, and the Third World; and – last but perhaps of greatest importance to the editors – historical overviews of British society and of the failures of the British left down to the present day.

Unquestionably, the intellectual sophistication of this renovated *New Left Review* was very high, reflecting the fact that its self-declared mission was to create in Britain a true Marxist intelligentsia. In one sense, this mission can be seen as a fulfillment of one of the tasks the first New Left took upon itself – the furthering of socialist ideas among intellectuals. In another sense, it grew out of the failure of the first New Left to retain its relevance and orientation to ongoing mass-based politics in Britain. For, of course, the *New Left Review* under Anderson has been a self-consciously – willfully – elitist affair. True socialist politics, Anderson and his friends believe, comes where a socialist intelligentsia joins with a militant working class to bid for cultural and political hegemony in society, leading to the overthrow of capitalism. The first step on this road, they maintain, has to be the formation of a culturally autonomous Marxist-socialist intelligentsia. Only after it forms can the working class be weaned from reformist ideas and politics.

Depending on how one chooses to look at it, this has been either an orientation of great promise or one of growing political isolation for British Marxist intellectuals. Either way, it has provided a distinctive matrix for the pursuit of historical sociology by contributors to the *New Left Review*, including its illustrious editor.

Totalizing History and Contemporary Politics

In Perry Anderson's work, an integral unity is intended between historical argument and contemporary political strategy. This is most evident in some of Anderson's shorter theoretical, political, and historical analyses: in his survey of the themes and orientations of "Western Marxism,"[10] in his discussion of "Problems of Socialist Strategy,"[11] and, especially, in the first major piece of historical synthesis for which Anderson is widely known, a long essay on British history entitled "Origins of the Present Crisis."[12] An analogous unity of historiographical approach and political intent highlights the vast canvas painted in *Passages-Lineages*. Before delving into the methodological details of the greater work, therefore, it will be helpful to emphasize the basic orientation toward historical sociology that it shares with the "Origins" essay and, indeed, with all of Anderson's projects in this genre.

First published in 1964, "Origins of the Present Crisis" aimed, as its title suggests, to explain a contemporary situation. Anderson posited a two-pronged impasse in British society: first, a crisis of the dominant class, signaled by the inability of British capitalism to adapt to changing international conditions; second, a crisis of the socialist left, marked by its timidity and stasis even in the face of the faltering of the dominant capitalist class. To make sense of this "present crisis," Anderson turned to history, arguing that

> until our view of Britain today is grounded in some vision of its full, effective past . . . we will continue to lack the basis for any understanding of the dialectical movements of our society, and hence – necessarily – of the contradictory possibilities within it which alone can yield a strategy for socialism . . . If the Left is to take advantage of the present situation, the first prerequisite is a serious attempt to analyse its real nature. To do this involves a consideration of the *distinctive total trajectory* of modern British society, since the emergence of capitalism.[13]

Anderson's essay undertakes a preliminary attempt at this ambitious task through a focus on "the gobal evolution of class structure," relating the cultural-political orientations of the dominant class and the proletariat to that structure. Anderson posits a "cumulative constellation" of "fundamental moments" in British history as sufficient to explain "the differential formation and development of British capitalist society" from the seventeenth century right down to the present crisis.[14] Crucial to an understanding of contemporary British politics are the nature, timing, and consequences of the seventeenth-century political revolution; the pioneering Industrial Revolution in England; the early seizure of a huge capitalist empire; and England's favorable experiences in the two world wars of the twentieth century.

Anderson argues that the orientations of the dominant and working classes were formed fairly early in the development of British capitalism and maintained thereafter by international circumstances that have only recently changed to the sharp detriment of traditional British capitalism. Because Britain never experienced a "pure" bourgeois revolution, and because the industrial bourgeoisie always remained culturally and politically subordinate to the landed aristocracy within the dominant capitalist class, the class never developed the modern technocratic institutions and outlook that are needed to deal with the present crisis. But neither is the working class, or the British Left, prepared at the moment to push toward socialism – again, due to the disabling political and cultural effects of cumulative past moments. The oldest industrial working class emerged "too early" to benefit from Marxist socialist theory and, later, the ideology of the British working class was "contaminated," via the Fabians, by the utilitarianism of the ruling class.[15] Thus, for Anderson, the key to grasping the opportunities presented to the Left by the present crisis lies in the development of "an authentic socialist movement," with an appropriate and genuinely revolutionary strategy.[16]

Anderson's bold survey of British history in "Origins" provoked considerable interest and debate among socialists and historians, and most notably aroused Edward Thompson, Marxist historian and well-known author of The Making of the English Working Class, to develop a lengthy critique and alternative analysis.[17] We shall return later in this chapter to points raised by this debate. But important for a general characterization of Anderson's work is the explicit justification that Anderson produced in the course of the controversy for his particular vision of the meaning and uses of history. Speaking for himself and for Tom Nairn (whose essays on the Labour Party in the New Left Review had also been an object of Thompson's critique), Anderson proclaimed:

> We were not . . . writing a contemplative history of the past for its own sake. We were trying to reconstruct it in order to understand the present.[18]

> The method we have chosen is . . . to analyse the present situation as a totality, in which the determination of the crisis in each sector is to be located within that sector, . . . while all the sectors together

are structurally integrated in a significant whole – founded by their complex social past.[19]

We tried to provide the elements of a *totalising* and not a *fragmentary* history of modern Britain . . . The whole of our work was structured towards an explanation of contemporary Britain; this was what determined its unity and form.[20]

These statements reveal basic features of Anderson's approach to historical sociology. The takeoff point for a historical analysis is some conception of realities in the present, understood in terms of the obstacles and opportunities these present for the Marxian socialist forces for whom and to whom the *New Left Review* speaks. Moreover, the kind of historical understanding sought is totalistic – in fact, doubly so: first, in that society is to be understood as a significant whole, and second, in that the complex social past is to be holistically encompassed as a centuries-spanning trajectory from an origin to an end point.

Certainly "Origins" reveals these characteristic features. It analyzes the deep historical roots of capitalist and proletarian class orientations in Britain, tracing British departures from continental European patterns back to the very beginnings of capitalism. In particular, "Origins" suggests that the long-standing "timidity" of British socialism has been due to the absence of a truly revolutionary ideology and intelligentsia. Historical analysis thus reveals the need and opportunity for exactly the sort of intellectual politics being pursued by the *Review* under Perry Anderson's editorship, for the *Review*'s self-declared mission is to acculturate British socialists to the intellectual traditions of continental Marxism. Both the present crisis and one possible crisis response to which *New Left Review* could strategically contribute are revealed by Anderson's totalizing historical sociology to be founded in the entire trajectory of modern Britain's social past.

Passages from Antiquity to Feudalism and *Lineages of the Absolutist State* constitute a historical sociology of much grander scope and greater depth than "Origins." Yet in both works Perry Anderson pursues historical understanding in similar ways and for similar ends. The characteristic concerns with totality are unmistakably present in *Passages-Lineages*: "Ancient society," "Germanic society," "Feudalism," "Western Absolutism" and "Eastern Absolutism" (concepts that Anderson regularly capitalizes in his text) – each is portrayed as a functional unity, a complex configuration of socioeconomic, political, and cultural patterns, all of which, taken together, constitute the given significant whole of the particular sociopolitical order. What is more, *Passages-Lineages* takes its comprehensive scope – its unusual coverage of epochs usually kept separate in historical writing – from Anderson's remarkable concern to encompass entire historical trajectories from beginnings to (given) end points.

Although he freely borrows the terminology of Althusserian Marxism, Anderson actually maintains that a purely analytic structuralism cannot grasp the basic causes of social change in history; cannot, for example, explain the transition from feudalism to capitalism in Europe. Instead, Anderson believes that genesis is at least as important as structure in the explanation of social change, and he discusses the unique trajectories of various civilizations not only in terms of one social structure giving rise to another, but also in terms of a series of overlappings and reactivations of earlier structures at later points in time. From this perspective, "what rendered the unique passage to capitalism possible in Europe was *the concatenation of antiquity and feudalism.*"[21] Furthermore, European feudalism itself cannot be understood except in terms of its own unique genesis out of the "catastrophic collision of two dissolving anterior modes of production – primitive and ancient."[22] Thus Anderson begins all the way back in classical antiquity in order to trace out fully the historical trajectories that will culminate, at the end of *Passages-Lineages*, in the emergence of absolutist states and capitalism in Europe. Not only do societal orders of given epochs have to be comprehended as totalities, so does the entire course of historical development in European civilization.

If Perry Anderson's concern with totalizing history is apparent in *Passages-Lineages*, what about the other characteristic feature, the concern to do historical analysis relevant to present-day politics? After all, *Passages-Lineages* posits no present crisis. It covers only events truly in the past, and it is presented as but a prelude to two more subsequent volumes intended to bring Anderson's coverage of Western politics up to the present day. Nevertheless, in our view, *Passages-Lineages* stands very much on its own, and like "Origins of the Present Crisis," this work is intended to elucidate patterns held to be of immediate relevance for the contemporary prospects and conduct of revolutionary socialism.

Passages-Lineages is oriented to two key explanatory tasks. In the first place, it aims to "situate the specificity of European experience as a whole within a wider international setting."[23] To this end, not only does Anderson encompass European history from Greece to Bourbon France and czarist Russia, he also contrasts European development to the histories of Byzantium and Turkey, China, and Japan. In the second place, *Passages-Lineages* attempts to explain the divergent yet inter-connected development of West versus East *within* Europe. This theme is present from the very opening pages of *Passages;* it figures in Anderson's discussion of the Roman Empire, and it forms the central axis of organization for his discussion of the emergence and dynamics of feudalism, the forms and times of feudal crisis, and the emergence after that crisis of separate types of absolutism in the two great halves of the European continent.

Why should any contemporary Marxian socialist *care* about such matters? In *Passages-Lineages* itself, Perry Anderson is not as explicit as he might be about why these issues have such importance for him, but the reasons are easy to find in his writings taken as a whole. Anderson is anxious to defend the truth and continuing relevance of the classical Marxian scenario of a working-class-based socialist revolution emerging within the heartlands of advanced capitalism. Europe, of all world regions, holds special fascination for him because he believes that classical Marxist ideas about capitalism, bourgeois revolutions, and proletarian socialism must apply to European history if they are to apply straightforwardly anywhere.

Anderson is also concerned to establish the fundamental importance of an East versus West division within Europe because he is a Western-oriented Marxist who, like Antonio Gramsci, calls for socialist revolutions in the West without believing that such revolutions would or should closely resemble the Russian Revolution – especially not its antidemocratic denouement in Stalinism. In his article "Problems of Socialist Strategy," Anderson distinguishes contrasting revolutionary strategies that, he argues, correspond to "different sides of the great geo-political divide which runs between Western and Eastern Europe; they correspond to two worlds and two histories."[24] In Eastern Europe, Bolshevik-style Leninism has been an appropriate socialist revolutionary strategy because Eastern societies have been (at the moments of their revolutionary transitions) relatively "backward," lacking fully developed capitalism and democracy. In the West, however, Bolshevik-style Leninism has not been, and will not be, an appropriate socialist strategy, because

> the societies of Western Europe constitute a wholly different universe from those of Eastern Europe, let alone Asia. Their highly advanced economies and their complex, dense, tessellated histories have created a social and cultural world entirely of its own. The great political achievement of this world has been democracy.[25]

In Anderson's view, no socialist revolutionary strategy can succeed in the West unless it builds upon, extends, and, of course, transcends the capitalist-imposed limitations of the Western democratic achievements. Mere imitation of "Eastern" revolutionary strategies is neither possible nor desirable.

No wonder, therefore, that Perry Anderson is prepared to write a vast historical overview devoted to situating Western uniqueness in world-historical terms, and devoted to tracing the intertwined but separate trajectories of East versus West within Europe. Just as "Origins" started with a conception of contemporary sociohistorical realities in Britain and present political challenges for the revolutionary-socialist Left and then sought to ground these in a totalizing overview of the entire, complex social past of modern British capitalism, so does *Passages-Lineages* take off from conceptions of present realities that in Anderson's view impor- tantly affect the situation and prospects of revolutionary socialism. Then it attempts to trace the historical foundations of these patterns right back to the very beginnings of Western history in antiquity. Perry Anderson is consistent in his refusal to undertake any "contemplative history of the past for its own sake" and in his determination to pursue, instead, "a unified theory of the past to comprehend the present."[26] Moreover, Anderson said of "Origins" that this overriding historiographical goal was "what determined its unity and its form."[27] As we now probe more deeply into *Passages-Lineages*, we will see that, analogously, the unity and form of this work are determined by Anderson's aim to establish the deep-rooted uniqueness and centrality of Western European history.

Concepts, Comparisons, and the Diversity of History

Passages from Antiquity to Feudalism and *Lineages of the Absolutist State* argue a theory of long-run social change in and through a complex set of historical narratives. "Marxism," Perry Anderson once declared, "is the only thought which has rigorously united developmental and structural analysis, it is at once pure historicity (denial of all supra-his-torical essences) and radical functionalism (societies are significant totalities) . . ."[28] *Passages-Lineages* embodies this understanding of *Marxism as theorized history*, in contrast to any notion of Marxism as an order of theoretical reflection separate from empirical historiography. Anderson believes that the latter view is all too prevalent in contempo-rary Marxist writing:

> On the one hand, "abstract" general models are constructed, or presupposed . . . without concern for their effective variations; on

the other hand, "concrete" local cases are explored, without reference to their reciprocal implications and interconnections. The conventional dichotomy between these procedures derives, doubtless,
from the widespread belief that an intelligible necessity only inhabits the broadest and most general trends in history, which operate
so to speak "above" the multiple empirical circumstances of specific events and institutions, whose actual course or shape becomes
by comparison largely the outcome of chance. Scientific laws . . .
are held to obtain only for universal categories: Singular objects are
deemed the domain of the fortuitous.[29]

This "conventional" division of theory and history is rejected by
Anderson. "The premise of this work," he says of *Passages-Lineages*, "is
that there is no plumb-line between necessity and contingency in historical explanation, dividing separate types of enquiry – 'long run' versus 'short run' or 'abstract' versus 'concrete' – from each other."[30] Thus
Passages-Lineages pursues, at once, theoretical knowledge – knowledge
of what Anderson labels the "pure structures" of modes of production
and of the absolutist state – and explanations of the diverse particularities of various times and places. This simultaneous pursuit of theoretical knowledge and the explanation of particulars informs all of the
methodological tactics employed in *Passages-Lineages:* the uses of theoretical concepts, the renditions of historical details, and the comparisons of different historical trajectories. What is more, both the special
strengths and the limitations of *Passages-Lineages* stem from its distinctive ways of combining theory and history and from its unusual effort
literally to fuse "necessity and contingency in historical explanation."

A Stylistic Success

One strength of *Passages-Lineages* is worth emphasizing at the outset.
Anderson's attitude toward theory and history certainly has allowed
him to produce a stylistically appealing pair of books. More than most
works of macroscopic historical sociology, *Passages-Lineages* makes vivid
and compelling reading. All too often, macrohistorical works seem
either mechanical or confusing. Sometimes abstract jargon dominates a
presentation, to the detriment of any sense of the varied specificities of
history; at other times, unassimilable historical details are extensively
recounted without any apparent connection to an overall argument.
Where Anderson errs, it is in the second of these directions. To a
surprisingly pleasant degree, however, *Passages-Lineages* avoids both
potential pitfalls.

181

Every part of Anderson's presentation conveys a rich texture of historical detail. To be sure, virtually all of the material comes from secondary sources, the published works of specialist historians. In some places, Anderson actually weaves a highly original argument out of a great density of secondary sources; the chapter on England in *Lineages* is a case in point. More typically, though, Anderson relies on a handful of major authorities for both the overall framework and most of the facts in his discussions.[31] No matter how heavy his reliance on key secondary sources, Anderson invariably gives a dense account, saturated with specifics of institutional forms, rulers' names, and the twists and turns of particular chronologies. Because his purpose is to do historical sociology, not narratives of events or analyses of group actions and conflicts in delimited periods, Anderson surveys decades and centuries rapidly and panoramically. But diversities and complexities *are* evoked; the stuff of history is neither homogenized out of existence nor hidden by the application of theoretical abstractions.

Even so, the reader is not allowed to forget that Anderson is theorizing about history, arguing a logic of long-run social change and characterizing the significance of varied societal arrangements and sequences of events. Indeed, much of the appeal – certainly the compelling quality on a first reading – of *Passages-Lineages* comes from Anderson's systematic interweaving of theory and history. *Passages-Lineages* moves through three major phases in its overall account of Western development, looking first at ancient society, then at medieval feudalism, and finally at the absolutist states of mature feudalism in Eastern and Western Europe. In each major phase, the logic of presentation is similar. Anderson begins with a theoretical discussion, meant to highlight the important structures and dynamics at issue. Then he moves toward fuller and fuller presentation of the details of specific "social formations," such as empires, monarchies, or absolutist states. Before the reader arrives at the points of greatest empirical detail in *Passages-Lineages*, he or she knows what Anderson thinks is significant about the times and places in question. Thus it is possible for a book primarily devoted to covering the trajectories of many times and places also to be stylistically unified as a single coherent argument.

Holistic Concepts

Aesthetically speaking, therefore, *Passages-Lineages* is successful as a fusion of theory and history, in significant part because conceptual discussions precede detailed historical accounts in the exposition of the argument. However, it would be a mistake to conclude that Anderson uses analytically sharp theoretical concepts to gain explanatory leverage over the complexities of history. Concepts of sociopolitical totalities – the slave mode of production, the feudal mode of production, Western absolutism, and Eastern absolutism – play a prominent role in *Passages-Lineages*. It is important to be very clear about the nature and function of such key concepts. They obviously do not refer to universal dimensions that cut across all different times and places, as, for example, the theoretical concepts of a sociological structural functionalist such as Neil Smelser.[32] The resemblance to Max Weber's ideal types is much closer, because Anderson's concepts refer to concrete sociohistorical complexes. But Weberian (generic) ideal types, such as bureaucracy, are formal and "unreal," and are used as devices to explore the partial aspects of societies in many different times and places. In contrast, Anderson's key concepts are used to capture *all* of the essential structural and dynamic features of sociohistorical wholes. As a result, Anderson's concepts run the danger of being nothing more than economical devices for description, ways of highlighting multiple features of singular social orders and historical epochs. This tendency and some of the drawbacks it can have even within the bounds of Anderson's own argument are well illustrated by the definitions and uses of the concept of feudalism in *Passages-Lineages*.

Characteristically, Anderson situates his own approach to defining feudalism in contrast to an orthodox Marxist notion of feudalism as simply equivalent to any and all traditional forms of landlordism. "Feudalism, in this version of materialist historiography, becomes an absolving ocean in which virtually any society may receive its baptism."[33] Anderson finds this quite unacceptable because, in consequence, "all privilege to Western development is thereby held to disappear in the multiform process of a world history secretly single from the start."[34] If feudalism is mere landlordism, Anderson argues, the unique features of European history, including the birth of capitalism, can be explained only by superstructural factors such as politics or culture. Anderson wants, instead, a conception of feudalism that will pinpoint Western uniqueness. In the key conceptual chapter of *Passages*, "The Feudal Mode of Production," Anderson achieves this desired conception by covering in his definition virtually all of the major socioeconomic and political features that constitute medieval Western feudalism as "a complex unity": serfdom, manorialism, extraeconomic coercion of peasants by lords, vassal hierarchy among lords, and "parcellization of sovereignty." The last feature Anderson seems to consider most important of all: "The functions of the State were disintegrated in a vertical allocation downwards, at each level of which political and economic relations were, on the other hand, integrated. This parcellization of sovereignty was constitutive of the whole feudal mode of production."[35]

In fact, the chapter "The Feudal Mode of Production" could more appropriately have been titled, "Western Medieval Feudalism." At the relatively early point (in *Passages*) where the chapter appears, it does not seem to matter that a Marxist theoretical concept and an epoch of European history are so thoroughly fused. Eventually, however, it turns out that Anderson wants to use "feudalism" in ways that clearly reveal the awkwardness of his original definition. As soon as Anderson starts to use his concept in the construction of causal arguments, he is forced into implausible and self-contradictory assertions. This happens in different ways at two points in *Lineages*.

One place is Anderson's comparison of Europe and Japan. In Anderson's view, Japan historically knew an "authentic" feudalism,[36] which helps to explain why Japan "proved to be the only major region in the world of non-European derivation that was able to rejoin Europe, North America and Australasia on the march towards industrial capitalism."[37] Anderson also notes that Japan industrialized only after it came under pressure from capitalist Europe. This shows, he maintains, that feudalism alone was not enough to produce the original endogenous breakthrough to capitalism. Instead, capitalism first emerged in Europe not only because feudalism set Europe apart from most other agrarian civilizations, but also because there was an entire unique "genealogy" for European feudalism, which was born out of a synthesis of the ancient (slave) and Germanic modes of production. Because of its unique origin, European feudalism was more dynamic than Japanese feudalism, and European history retained cultural features, such as Roman law and an urban concept of citizenship, that eventually facilitated the birth of absolutist states and capitalism out of the crisis of its feudal mode of production. As Anderson puts it in a strikingly idealist formulation: "The classical past awoke again within the feudal present to assist the arrival of the capitalist future, both unimaginably more distant and strangely nearer to it."[38]

Several things are worth noting about Anderson's conception of feudalism in this complex set of causal assertions. For one thing, the application of Anderson's concept to Japan strains credulity. We are forced to accept the assertion that two sociopolitical orders, medieval Europe and Tokugawa Japan, with many particular differences, were essentially the same as feudal orders, and we must do this on the basis of a concept of feudalism that appears very much a redescription of the highlights of medieval Western socioeconomic and political arrangements. What are we to make of the fact that Japan always differed from medieval Europe in a number of institutional respects, and how are we to regard the significant bureaucratization and regional centralization of political power that occurred under the Tokugawa hegemony?[39]

Because his concept of feudalism is so completely identified with the totality of medieval European institutions, Anderson cannot analyze the various dimensions of similarity and difference between preindustrial Europe and Japan; nor can he develop specific causal hypotheses about how the structures of Tokugawa Japan partly blocked and partly facilitated the emergence of industrial capitalism. Instead he offers the very gross assertions that the entire sociocultural trajectory of Japanese history prevented a fully endogenous breakthrough to capitalism, while Japan's experience of feudalism at one historical epoch somehow accounts for its ultimate capacity to "join" Europe in capitalist development. Anderson's insistence on a holistic, essentialist conception of feudalism forced him toward such vague, genetic-determinist assertions. Ironically, this conception also prompted him to attribute long-run social development in Europe and Japan to exactly the sorts of superstructural causes that he originally tried to avoid by defining feudalism not as landlordism but as a complex unity of many social and political features. Anderson's concept of feudalism cannot serve as an effective tool for causal analysis. Even when he tries to draw a causal analogy between Europe and Japan, the analogy becomes only a way station toward the overall conclusion that Europe and Japan are different because the former started in Western antiquity while the latter did not, with the cultural and political effects of the contrasting origins enduring ever since.

The second place where Anderson's concept of feudalism runs into difficulties is in the discussion of absolutist states in the *Lineages* volume. Anderson counterposes his analysis of the absolutist state to other Marxist formulations, arguing against the view that absolutism was an early form of capitalist state and also rejecting the view that it was based on a balance of power between the declining feudal nobility and the rising bourgeoisie. On the contrary, says Anderson, absolutism was a "redeployed apparatus" of rule by and for the feudal nobility.[40] Western and Eastern variants of European absolutism were similar because they preserved noble class rule in societies where feudal relations of production remained predominant. As we have seen,

Anderson's basic definition of feudalism in *Passages* included parcellization of political sovereignty and the vassal hierarchy. Yet a major objective of *Lineages* is to argue that absolutist states were feudal even though they "represented a decisive rupture with the pyramidal, parcellized sovereignty of the medieval social formations."[41] Anderson develops this argument only by abandoning his original definition of feudalism – the synthetic highlighting of all the basic features of medieval feudalism – in favor of another approach that simply stresses private landed noble property and the use of extraeconomic coercion to appropriate peasant surpluses. Ironically, Anderson ends up equating feudalism with a type of landlordism, just like other Marxists of whom he is critical.

It is easy to see why Anderson resorts to a new, more analytic conception. As long as feudalism remains equivalent to the totality of medieval Western institutions, the concept has little scope to characterize and help explain social arrangements beyond that one epoch. But if Anderson wants, as he does, to argue that the "crisis of feudalism" caused the political transformation of medieval into absolutist Europe, then he needs a different conception of feudalism, one that refers to a *partial* complex of institutions and social arrangements, something less all-encompassing than the medieval social-economic-political arrangements as a singular functional totality. Political organization must be, to some degree, decoupled from socioeconomic relations and allowed to vary to some degree independently. In addition, Anderson's characterization of Western absolutism as feudal depends on treating serfdom not as a necessary, defining feature of feudalism, but as one possible alternative form within feudalism of extraeconomic relations between lords and peasants.

A tension therefore exists in *Passages-Lineages* between a synthetic, totalistic conception of feudalism, closely identified with medieval Europe, and a more analytic, partial notion that applies across epochs of European history. Anderson contradicts himself because he needs the different kinds of concepts to make separate parts of his overall argument – the part on the uniqueness of the West versus the part on the nature of absolutism. Anderson's lapse into a nonholistic definition of feudalism is, however, uncharacteristic. Synthetic, totalistic concepts, concepts meant to highlight the essential features of singular historical entities, predominate in the entire theoretical apparatus of *Passages-Lineages*. Although such concepts help Anderson to accentuate delimited configurations and trajectories in history, they provide little basis for pinpointing structural patterns that cut across epochs or typologically grouped societies. Nor do they provide a basis for teasing out causal generalizations across civilizations or within European history. Anderson's concepts confine *Passages-Lineages* primarily to historical re-description, allowing only limited space for the establishment of causal regularities.

From Concepts to Cases

The theoretical conceptualizations of *Passages-Lineages* are thus in a certain sense highly historically saturated. Nevertheless, Anderson, like all practitioners of historical sociology, faces challenges of mediating between his theoretical concepts and individual historical instances. Concepts like the feudal mode of production or Western absolutism refer, in Anderson's terminology, to pure types, while individual instances are, as he puts it, impure variants.[42] Throughout *Passages-Lineages*, detailed historical accounts normally refer to social formations that are politically sovereign entities. Any given type-concept always encompasses multiple social formations. Much of *Passages-Lineages* is devoted to discussing such individual social formations and relating them to the major pure type currently under discussion. Bridges from pure concepts to varied historical cases are partly built into the concepts themselves. Some key, defining feature of each major mode of production allows for, or even requires, variations among social formations.

The slave mode of production, which Anderson considers the basis for the civilizations of classical antiquity, was a mode focused on cities and commerce, yet productively based on slavery in agriculture. As a result of its ultimate basis in slave labor, Anderson argues, ancient civilization experienced "overall technological stagnation,"[43] and the

> typical path of expansion in Antiquity, for any given state, was . . . always a 'lateral' one – geographical conquest – not economic advance . . . Military power was more closely locked to economic growth than in perhaps any other mode of production, before or since, because the main single origin of slave-labour was normally captured prisoners of war, while the raising of free urban troops for war depended on the maintenance of production at home by slaves.[44]

When it comes to discussing individual social formations in antiquity, therefore, Anderson arrays them in time as successive waves of military expansion and conquest – the Athenian, the Macedonian, and the Roman. He discusses how each of the waves resulted in a political empire that "represented a certain solution to the political and organizational problems of overseas conquest." Each empire/solution was, in turn, "integrated and surpassed by the next, without the underlying bases of a common urban civilization ever being transgressed."[45] Thus Anderson asserts the ultimate unity of ancient civilization, identifies antiquity with his pure concept of the slave mode of production, and treats major individual social formations of antiquity (Greece, the Hellenistic world, and Rome) as variants on a key structural dilemma of the slave mode – the nexus between domestic sociopolitical relations and the conquest and control of foreign areas. The first major part of *Passages-Lineages* embodies a simple mediation between the pure concept and the impure variants because the very possibility of successive and varying social formations (here empires) is directly implicit in the logic of the concept of the slave mode of production.

The mediations work somewhat differently for the feudal mode of production. Anderson argues that European feudalism was a unique historical synthesis, born of the "catastrophic collision of two dissolving anterior modes of production – primitive and ancient," a collision that "eventually produced the feudal order which spread throughout medieval Europe."[46] Both the synthesis and the spread were, from the start, inherently uneven. From this unevenness Anderson derives, in *Passages*, regional typologies of European feudalism, and subsequently, in *Lineages*, the distinct ideal types of Western absolutism and Eastern absolutism.

Figure 6.1 summarizes Anderson's basic regional typology of European feudalism. Western Europe is the primary, core area of feudalism because that is where there were various full syntheses, more or less "balanced," of Roman and Germanic elements. In this zone, all of the defining features of Anderson's feudal mode of production – serfdom, manorialism, vassal hierarchy, and parcellized sovereignty – were to be found in medieval times. By contrast:

> There is . . . a curious inverse symmetry between the respective destinies of North-West and South-East Europe . . . Scandinavia was the one major region of Western Europe which was never integrated into the Roman Empire, and therefore never participated in the original "synthesis". . . . Nevertheless, . . . the far North eventually entered [through conquests and cultural diffusions] the orbit of Western feudalism, while preserving the durable forms of its initial distance from the common "occidental" matrix. A converse process can be traced in the far South of Eastern Europe. For if Scandinavia ultimately produced a Western variant of feudalism *without* benefit of the urban-imperial heritage

Figure 6.1. Regional Variations of European Feudalism

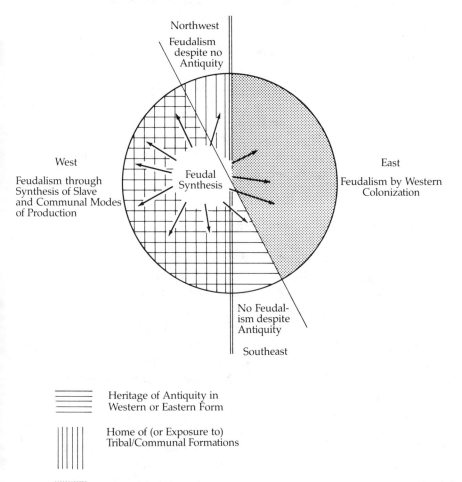

of Antiquity, the Balkans failed to develop a stable Eastern variant of feudalism *despite* the long metropolitan presence of the successor state to Rome in the region.[47]

Eastern Europe, beyond the River Elbe, also takes its fundamental identity for Anderson by stark contrast to the West:

> For our purposes, the most fundamental characteristic of the whole planar zone stretching from the Elbe to the Don can be defined as the permanent *absence* of that specific Western synthe-

sis between a disintegrating tribal-communal mode of production based on primitive agriculture and dominated by rudimentary warrior aristocracies, and a dissolving slave mode of production, with an extensive urban-civilization based on commodity exchange, and an imperial State system . . . This central fact [i.e., of absence] was the basic historical determinant of the uneven development of Europe, and of the persistent retardation of the East.[48]

For centuries, repeated invasions by nomadic-pastoral peoples from Central Asia interrupted the stabilization of primitive-communal social forms in the East. Then invasions ceased and regular arable farming and increased social and political stratification emerged. Ultimately, the East joined feudal Europe under the influence of colonization and military pressures from the West.

Despite the fourfold nature of his original regional typology, Anderson carries forward the main line of his argument from *Passages* into *Lineages* on the basis of the twofold West versus East division within Europe. Scandinavia conveniently becomes absorbed into Western Europe,[49] and the Southeast can drop out of the argument because no feudalism developed there either by synthesis or diffusion. But the West versus East division remains enduringly fundamental in European history. A "crisis of feudalism" emerges in different ways and at different times in the two regions. Although absolutist states ultimately crystallized out of the crisis in both areas, the underlying causes and the constitutive structures and dynamics were different, as summed up by Anderson's type-concepts in *Lineages* of Western absolutism and Eastern absolutism.

The basic and original form of absolutism was that which emerged in the West, where it served the nobility after the crisis of medieval feudalism as a *"compensation for the disappearance of serfdom,* in the context of an increasingly urban economy which it did not completely control and to which it had to adapt."[50] Yet absolutist states also emerged in the East, where towns were scarce and weak and where serfdom was mostly already established. To explain this, Anderson argues that Eastern absolutist states, which did of course become *"devices for the consolidation of serfdom,"*[51] nevertheless emerged not only because of the threat of peasant flight and resistance but also – primarily – because of military pressures from the more developed social formations of Western Europe. "It was the international pressure of Western Absolutism, the political apparatus of a more powerful feudal aristocracy, ruling more advanced societies, which obligated the Eastern nobility to adopt an equivalently centralized state machine, to survive."[52] Eastern absolutism, furthermore, was a distinct organizational type – more militarized and less venal than the absolutism of the more commercialized West. Western and Eastern absolutism were, in Anderson's view, fundamentally alike as devices for preserving noble class rule and feudal relations of production, yet he adds that Western absolutism simultaneously functioned to create conditions for the spread of commodity production and for the primitive accumulation of capital, thus objectively aiding the birth of capitalism in Europe.

Anderson's concept of the feudal mode of production, therefore, differentiates into type-concepts of regional variants, first into variants of the original European feudal synthesis (or its absence), and then into the two major variants of absolutism, Western and Eastern. Then, in the final movement from the pure concept of feudalism to historical instances, various individual social formations – either medieval European monarchies or absolutist monarchical states – are arrayed "under" each regional type-concept, just as in the simpler structure of the argument for antiquity the individual historical instances of Greece, the Hellenistic world, and Rome were arrayed "under" the concept of the slave mode of production. Comparative history as such – the juxtaposition of several historical trajectories – enters into Anderson's presentation especially at this culminating stage. But the purposes for which Anderson uses comparisons of multiple historical trajectories are especially complex and require a bit of untangling.

In macroscopic historical sociology considered as a whole, comparative history is used in three distinct ways.[53] Comparisons may be used to demonstrate the repeated applicability of a given theoretical argument to one case after another, with the repeated historical presentations serving to specify the general theoretical argument for different historical contexts. Comparisons may be used along with ideal types or conceptual themes to make contrasts among different historical instances, in order to bring out the unique features of each particular one. Finally, analytic comparative history may be used to validate causal hypotheses by comparing cases, or aspects of cases, in ways that approximate the logic of multivariate analysis. Each of these three types of comparative history has its own ways of relating historical trajectories to one another and to concepts or theoretical ideas. In *Passages-Lineages* Perry Anderson makes virtually no use at all of analytic comparative history, for he is hostile to the attempts at analysis and causal generalization that are entailed in this approach.[54] Instead, Anderson uses an inherently uneasy synthesis of the other two types of comparative history.

191

On the one hand, Anderson's juxtapositions of historical accounts for various social formations seem partly intended to illustrate repeatedly the dynamics of long-run social change posited for ancient (slave) society, feudalism, and Western and Eastern absolutism. Thus in Part One of *Passages,* the case accounts of Greece, the Hellenistic world, and Rome are used (in part) to apply and specify the theoretical characterization of the slave mode of production and its dynamics (see Table 6.1). In Part Two, once Anderson identifies each major regional type of feudalism, he launches into summaries of various social formations that "fit" the type. The same is true in *Lineages,* where the presentations of the defining features of each of the two major type-concepts, Western absolutism and Eastern absolutism, are illustrated by repeated examples referring to the various social formations of the relevant parts of Europe.[55]

Yet the plot thickens, because in no way are Anderson's cases simply or entirely repeated specifications of previously offered theoretical arguments. Rather, each case, especially when it is presented in full detail, is also played off against the defining features of "its" pure concept or regional type and also, frequently, played off against the other individual social formations with which it is grouped. In Anderson's discussion of the ancient world, this is especially true for the case account on the Hellenistic world, which turns out to share only urban civilization, not slavery, with Greece and Rome. The political-organizational peculiarities and failings of the Hellenistic instance are repeatedly stressed, especially in comparison to Rome. Anderson ends up calling this a "hybrid" between true ancient society and Near Eastern civilization. Indeed, one wonders as one reads whether Anderson means the case as a specification of, or a deviation from, his pure concept of antiquity (or the slave mode of production).

The same ambiguity arises in the parts of *Passages-Lineages* devoted to medieval feudalism. For example, within Anderson's Western zone of feudalism, there were a number of different medieval monarchies: England, France, Germany, Spain, Portugal, and Italy. When he gets down to these individual cases, however, it turns out that every one, except France, is in basic ways peculiar: "early" or "delayed" or "incomplete" or "set apart."[56] Certainly each is distinct from all of the others. France, too, is unique, yet it "conformed more closely to the archetypal feudal system than any other region of the continent."[57]

Finally, in the part of *Lineages* devoted to Western absolutism, the tension between using comparative history to apply a concept again and again and using it to draw contrasts among cases becomes espe-

Table 6.1. *Tables of Contents for* Passages *and* Lineages

Table 6.2. *The Pure Type and Specific Variants of Western Absolutist States*

	Case studies of Western Absolutist States				
Pure type	Spain	France	England	Italy	Sweden
Medieval heritage servile peasantry, parcellization of sovereignty	Separate kingdoms of Castile and Aragon; unified by marriage	Classic feudal synthesis; gradual concentric unification	Uniquely centralized medieval kingdom	Papal and imperial failure to establish unified monarchy	Incomplete feudalization of rural relations of production
Peasantry dissolution of serfdom: threat from below	Provincial variations; but no threat from below, except in Aragon (where no absolutism)	Dissolution of serfdom: threat from below	No great threat from below	Real serfdom only in Piedmont; no real threat from below elsewhere	Free independent small-holders
Towns growth of bourgeoisie in relatively autonomous towns	Variations: some towns in Castile; decline and expansion in Aragon	Rising commercial bourgeoisie and urban radicalism	Capitalist development, but towns not politically autonomous	Precocious mercantile capitalism in northern city-states	"Few and feeble" – no burgher challenge to noble power
Nobility venal centralization in face of peasant unrest and urban radicalism	Variations, but feudal local power of military orders remains; inadequate centralization	Venal centralization in face of peasant unrest and urban radicalism	Unusually civilian commercialized, regionally unified; no derogation	No cohesive feudal nobility (except in Piedmont); "illegitimate" personal adventurers	Small, compact nobility incapable of suppressing peasantry

State formation					
absolutism: army, state bureaucracy, national taxation, law, trade, diplomacy. Preserves noble rule while compatible with bourgeois interests	Imperial expansion and colonial wealth an early asset; failure to achieve aministrative and political unification at home. "Auxiliary determinant" of whole system, but felled by stronger French absolutism	Absolutism: army, state bureaucracy, taxation, etc.; classic sequence linking nobility and state for political preservation; overtaken by rising capitalist states and felled by classic bourgeois revolution	"Weakest and shortest" absolutism; no standing army, limited fiscality, no separate state bureaucracy; indigenous capitalist development "pushes beyond" absolutism; "premature" bourgeois revolution	Failure to develop national absolutism (belated absolutism in Piedmont); density and strength of city-states permit only local *signories* but cannot themselves achieve unification	Internally "under determined" absolutism emerges only in response to external military pressures; alternating royal and representative rule; contradictory combination of Eastern and Western forms

cially acute. The first two chapters of Part One lay out the pure type-concept of Western absolutism and illustrate its major features with examples from England, France, Spain, Sweden, and even parts of Italy. Then follow five individual chapters devoted to discussing the cases in detail. In these chapters the emphasis is on individuating each case, showing its peculiarities in contrast to the others and drawing implicit or explicit contrasts to the defining features of the pure type. Anderson apparently intends Italy (except for Piedmont) as a negative case, one where the deviations from the type were so great as to preclude the development of a Western absolutism. But the other cases are supposed to fit the type, and their long-run dynamics are somehow supposed to be elucidated by it. Nevertheless, as Table 6.2 shows, a cold-eyed juxtaposition of the defining features of the pure type of Western absolutism with the characteristics of all the various social formations presented as historical case studies in this part of *Lineages* reveals that *only* the French case really conforms to the pure type. *All* of the other cases differ from the type and differ among themselves in ways that lead one to wonder about their relation to the model of Western absolutism that Anderson propounds as applicable to the set as a whole.

Indeed, by now enough has been said about Perry Anderson's uses of theoretical concepts and comparative history to make it possible to conclude that the urge to differentiate, to subdifferentiate, and still further to distinguish various unique configurations in history thoroughly saturates all the levels of the argument of *Passages-Lineages*. Differences proliferate. Furthermore, each unique configuration is not only a sociopolitical structure, but also a chronological trajectory that stretches separately back in history to its origins, and forward in history from whatever present is under consideration. Thus Anderson characteristically says, when introducing the discussion of a new type or case, what he here says about Scandinavia: "It will suffice to say . . . that the *fundamental* historical determinant of Scandinavian 'specificity' was the peculiar nature of Viking social structure, which originally separated the whole zone from the rest of the continent."[58] Afterward came the "differential character and trajectory of the Scandinavian social formations, from the Dark Ages onwards."[59] In other words, earlier – original – differences beget later differences. This is true for Europe in contrast to non-European civilizations, and for West versus East within Europe. It is even true, as we have just seen, for varying social formations within each European type. The overall image is overwhelmingly one of history as an infinite series of separate pathways, each with its own unique origin and destiny.

196

Still, this proliferation of unbreakable differences is not all there is to Anderson's historical sociology in *Passages-Lineages*. A certain unity is also portrayed – and promised – for European and world history. To see the basis of this unity, let us move on to examine Anderson's ambivalent relationship to evolutionism.

Evolution Revisited: The West as Pure and Universal

In *Passages-Lineages*, Perry Anderson explicitly quarrels with many "orthodoxies" he associates with economic-determinist varieties of Marxism. One such theoretical tendency that he is especially determined to counter is Stalinist-style evolutionism, an approach to historical explanation according to which all societies develop along the same path, passing through a pregiven series of stages of development. Long-run change, in this view, is predetermined and driven by endogenous contradictions and class conflicts. Perhaps some societies lead while others lag, perhaps some transitions are more compressed than others, but all societies are following fundamentally the same path. The task of the historical analyst is simply to determine where in the given, universally applicable schema any given society or historical epoch fits.

Obviously *Passages-Lineages* directly contradicts any such evolutionist vision in many essential ways. Anderson refuses to believe that "an intelligible necessity only inhabits the broadest and most general trends in history." He eschews attempts to generalize, devoting himself instead to the ever-finer delineation of unique configurations. Anderson could not be further from believing that different civilizations, or even different zones and social formations within European civilization, have ever evolved along the same trajectory of long-run social change.

All the same, Perry Anderson's vision of the world is, in its own way, remarkably evolutionist.[60] Evolutionist forms of explanation vary, differing in degrees of qualification and sophistication. Nineteenth-century forms of evolutionism, which proceeded essentially by ordering societies into a hierarchical classificatory system according to a preconceived notion of progress, have generally been discarded by twentieth-century scholars.[61] Recently, however, serious attempts have been made, both within the Marxist tradition and among non-Marxist structural functionalists, to develop a more refined version of evolutionary theory.[62] When one closely examines Perry Anderson's interpretation of the development of Europe, one finds striking similarities to neo-evolutionary, functionalist approaches to the explanation of social change.

197

Contemporary neo-evolutionary theorists have criticized earlier stage models for not allowing a diversity of developmental paths and for not sufficiently explicating the mechanisms and processes of change.[63] Theorists such as Talcott Parsons and (at points in his work) S. N. Eisenstadt have sought to overcome these deficiencies by explaining substantive historical variations in terms of general evolutionary processes: differentiation, reintegration, adaptation. These describe the development of bounded entities or systems through internal specialization of function and the maintenance of dynamic equilibrium in the face both of endogenous development and of external environmental stimuli. "Progress" is measured in terms of increased differentiation and reintegration at higher levels of "enhanced adaptive capacity." Patterns of development vary. Thus the records of history are littered with "failures," paths that led nowhere, and "survivals" of older forms superseded elsewhere. But certain lines of development are (from a retrospective standpoint) "progressive." Parsons, for example, traces out the evolution of a "central stem" from the ancient Near East through Greece and Rome to contemporary occidental civilization.[64] Such an approach, distinguishing one privileged evolutionary stem as the most progressive through its enhancement of adaptive capacity as compared to alternative evolutionary branches, has been termed a "cladogenetic" rather than a "multilinear" form of evolutionism.[65]

The vision of history presented in *Passages-Lineages* corresponds in startling ways to this cladogenetic, functionalist form of evolutionary theory. For one thing, Anderson shares with non-Marxist functionalists an analytic focus on the functioning of a system, such that explanations are couched in terms of prerequisites for maintaining the stability of a system under changing conditions, irrespective of the conscious intentions of the actors involved. For Anderson, of course, the systems in question are defined in class terms; thus absolutism is functionally explained as a means for preserving noble class rule, "despite and against" the overt inclinations and wills of real members of the class whose "ultimate" interests it is in some way designed to protect. This systemic focus is linked to a reification of class, so that Anderson homogenizes out certain historical differences and treats classes as relatively fixed entities over vast spans of time and space. Evocative, anthropomorphic imagery can result: "The bourgeoisie won two modest victories, lost its nerve and ended by losing its identity."[66] This approach, however, leads to serious historical difficulties, as in the confusion between class and estate in Anderson's discussion of the supposed interests of the early modern English nobility. Moreover, Anderson's retrospective characterization of classes in functionalist terms means that he fails to connect the actual actions and strategies of groups to his grand descriptions or explanations of historical outcomes.[67]

The systemic focus and the reification of classes are in turn basic to Anderson's mode of depicting historical change. Here Anderson shares with non-Marxist functionalists a focus on a central stem of evolutionary progress in which endogenous, cumulative change occurs. According to Anderson, Western Europe and, in particular, France represent the central line of evolutionary advance. From antiquity onward, the histories of the West, and its French core, approximate most clearly the classical Marxist concepts of key modes of production and their progressive succession. This is where the political transformations making ascending transitions between modes of production have expressed themselves in purest form. Thus, in ancient times:

> The developed slave mode of production which powered the Roman imperial system was . . . from its birth naturalised mainly in the West. It was therefore logical and predictable that the endogenous contradictions of that mode of production should have worked themselves out to their uttermost conclusion in the West, where they were not buffered or checked by any antecedent or alternative historical forms. Where the environment was purest, the symptoms were most extreme.[68]

Further, the "original synthesis" of feudalism was centered in Western Europe, and especially in France, where a truly " 'balanced' synthesis generated feudalism most rapidly and completely."[69] "Northern France, in effect, always conformed more closely to the archetypal feudal system that any other region of the continent,"[70] and the "more organic character of Northern [French] feudalism ensured it the economic and political initiative throughout the Middle Ages."[71] In turn, European absolutist states developed endogenously and originally in the West, where they prepared the way for subsequent breakthroughs to capitalism. And, as we have seen, France developed the form of the absolutist state closest to Anderson's pure concept of Western absolutism.

Indeed, right down to the present – and into the projected future of a true socialist revolution led by a Marxist intelligentsia – the central line of world-historical development is still seen by Anderson to run through the history of Western Europe (and, again, especially France). For developments beyond the periods covered by *Passages-Lineages*, the debate with Edward Thompson over Anderson's "The Origins of the Present Crisis" is revealing. As Thompson pointed out in his critique, Anderson's discussion of British history and its modern political impasse implicitly relies on "an undisclosed model of Other Countries, whose typological symmetry offers a reproach to British exceptionalism."[72] Thompson correctly discerns that Anderson recurrently juxtaposed key moments of British history against a supposedly "normal" pattern of national political history under capitalism. The normal pattern is never explicitly discussed in "Origins," but it apparently corresponds to a notion of the French Revolution as the model for a pure bourgeois revolution, to a notion of classical Social Democracy as the model for an early Marxist-oriented proletarian movement, and to contemporary French Communism as the model for a mature Marxist-oriented proletarian movement. Only by assuming such a normal pattern of historical development, synthesized from continental European experience, can Anderson pronounce so definitely on the "paradoxes," "impurities," "prematurities," and "singularities" of British history.

Not only in "Origins" but also throughout *Passages-Lineages*, social formations and civilizations other than France, Western Europe, or Europe are measured against the norms of the more central areas. They are judged leading or lagging, expected or "bizarre," balanced or imbalanced, pure or "heteroclite" – always in relation to France or the West (Western Europe or Europe, depending on the scale of comparison). What is more, developments in the more central places are seen as disproportionately influencing developments in the less central places, either by cultural diffusion or by economic and military pressure. Thus within Western feudalism, the "balanced synthesis" in France "in turn had a great impact on outlying zones with a less articulated feudal system"[73] – zones such as England, Germany, and Spain. Western Europe, in turn, affected the East through colonization and intense military pressures. And Europe itself would eventually remake the world as a whole through the spread of capitalism and the force of arms.

When such impacts by more central on less central places have occurred they have never, in Anderson's scheme of past world history, actually obliterated the enduring differences between historical trajectories. In a particularly striking formulation, Anderson points out that despite the influence of the more advanced feudal and absolutist West on Eastern Europe, the latter could not be entirely deflected from its inherent backwardness. It entered European feudalism, but remained on its own destined path:

> Eastern European history was from the outset immersed in an
> essentially distinct temporality from Western European develop-

ment. It had "started" much later, and hence even after its intersection with that of the West, it could resume an earlier evolution towards an economic order that had been lived out and left behind elsewhere on the continent. The chronological coexistence of the opposite zones of Europe, and their increasing geographical interpenetration, creates the illusion of a simple contemporaneity of the two. In fact, the East had still to run through a whole historical cycle of servile development just when the West was escaping from it.[74]

Even when revolutionary breakthroughs have occurred in less central social formations, they have not in Anderson's view ever been able to leap ahead of the West or France. England's Civil War of the seventeenth century was premature and therefore impure compared to France's bourgeois revolution; Russia's revolution in 1917 was premature and imperfect compared to the future socialist revolutions that will come in the West.

Indeed, it is because Anderson has the most extravagant hopes for future socialist revolutions in the West that the centrality of the Western line of world history is so important to him. Not only has the West impinged one-sidedly – albeit with incompletely transformative consequences – on the non-West throughout prior world history, but more importantly, there is a promise that after a breakthrough to true democratic socialism in the West, the essential achievements of this particular historical trajectory will actually become *universalized*. Western socialist revolutions will have universally transformative implications, unlike previous revolutions in backward societies. With unblinking optimism, Anderson asserts: "Whatever its lacunae or limitations, . . . [Western] democracy represents a permanent achievement of mankind – an experience so important that it will eventually become democratized and cease to be the privilege of a region."[75] Unlike liberal evolutionists, Anderson does not see past Western breakthroughs to capitalism and bourgeois liberal democracy as the decisive telos of world history. If he did, his central stem of evolutionary progress would run through British and American history. Rather Anderson assumes that a future working-class-based socialist revolution will usher in a new epoch of full democracy for all humankind. Thus the *politically* most advanced area of the West – supposedly France – becomes the centerpiece of his evolutionary argument.

Methodologically, too, Anderson's evolutionism is crucial, for in *Passages-Lineages* he wants to bridge the gap between "necessity and contingency in historical explanation,"[76] yet without positing general laws to subsume and obliterate the particularities of history. Anderson's goal is achieved in a remarkable way: Many contrasting lines of history are explored, even as one in particular is elevated to a privileged status. Anderson thus turns Western Europe, and within it, France, into measuring rods, motors, and – prospectively – sources of salvation for world history as a whole, in all of its complexity and diversity.

Conclusion: The Limits of Totalizing History

Perry Anderson set out in *Passages from Antiquity to Feudalism* and *Lineages of the Absolutist State* to "situate the specificity of European experience as a whole within a wider international setting"[77] and to explore the roots of the division of East versus West within Europe. His unified theory of the past was intended to speak to the present,[78] contributing directly to the solution of theoretical and practical problems in the heritage of Marxist revolutionary socialism. It remains to assess the degree to which Anderson has been successful in his project and to highlight the ways in which his method lends his historical sociology distinctive weaknesses and strengths.

In a remarkably reflective and self-critical Afterword to his 1976 book *Considerations on Western Marxism*, Anderson himself raises issues that need to be faced not only for a reassessment of that short work but also for any critical examination of his more substantial contributions to historical sociology, including *Passages-Lineages*. Anderson notes the dangers of tying Marxist theory too closely either to present-day political assessments or to the received tenets of the classical Marxism of Marx, Lenin, and Trotsky. Despite "every laudable temptation," Anderson writes, "Marxist theory is . . . not . . . to be equated with a revolutionary sociology," restricted to the analysis of present conjunctures.[79] "The past, which cannot be amended or undone, can be known with greater certainty than the present, whose actions have yet to be done; and there is more of it."[80] Marxism entails, above all, a science of history. What is more, historical knowledge needs to be used to revise Marxian theory itself, not only to fill in its omissions but also to find and correct its outright errors. According to Anderson the "critical areas where the heritage of classical Marxism appears inadequate or unsatisfactory" include, especially, the received views (or lack of them) on the nature and function of states, nationalism, and imperialism, and on the past and potential workings of democracy and authoritarianism in capitalist and socialist contexts.[81] Faced with the need for better understanding of such obviously crucial matters, "the most important responsibility for contemporary socialists," suggests Anderson, "may be to isolate the main theoretical weaknesses of classical Marxism, to explain the historical reasons for these, and to remedy them."[82]

Insightful as are Anderson's charge and agenda for socialist theorists, it is difficult to read this 1976 Afterword without a sense of its ironic relation to Anderson's own historical scholarship. If our dissection is correct, *Passages-Lineages* exemplifies all too clearly some of the pitfalls emphasized by Anderson in his 1976 reflections. One difficulty appears in the overly close coupling of historical interpretation to an understanding of a "present political conjuncture." Now that French Marxists find themselves in disarray and retreat, we need not dwell on the awkwardness, evident within less than a decade after the publication of *Passages-Lineages*, of the francophilia so obvious in this work as well as in Anderson's earlier "Origins of the Present Crisis."

More important, however, is the overall relationship of theory and history in *Passages-Lineages*, where unfortunately Perry Anderson makes insufficient use of historical evidence to rework classical Marxist theory. To be sure, Anderson concentrates on the political level of long-run social development in order to address important lacunae in the classical corpus. But states and political struggles remain, in his rendition, inherently coupled to modes of production and class relations. And Anderson identifies his political reworking of the classical Marxist stages of history, from antiquity through feudalism to capitalism, with a single, privileged though peculiar line of the past. The selection of the Western European (and French) pathway as privileged, coupled with the firm genetic-determinism of Anderson's explanatory approach, means that alternative trajectories in history – especially those of Eastern Europe or Asia that, according to Anderson's own descriptions, fit Marxian theory poorly or not at all – can only be *contrasted to* the West, with their very "impurities" or "absences" supposedly proving the rules of classical Marxist normality exemplified by the privileged Western line of history. The variations of history so vividly surveyed in *Passage-Lineages* are thus not used as a basis for the generation of basically new causal insights. Instead, history is written to reassert the fundamental fruitfulness of classical Marxism, even at the rather ironic expense of admitting that Marxism's major modes of production, and its vision of progressive historical change through endogenous contradictions and class struggle, may directly fit only a single narrow band of the entire past.

203

Interestingly, much of the value of Anderson's books lies in the possibilities that skeptically minded readers can find within them for answering Anderson's own basic questions – about the rise and fall of states in relation to economic orders and social conflicts – in more analytically powerful ways than Anderson himself answers those questions. For example, in a thoughtful essay on *Passages-Lineages*, W. G. Runciman suggests various ways in which Anderson could have used comparisons of the cases he actually surveyed to construct or test causal explanatory hypotheses. A comparison of Rome and late Han China would, argues Runciman, have called into question Anderson's argument that the Western Roman Empire collapsed when imperial expansion halted largely because slavery sapped its political structure. "China from A. D. 25 to 311 is surely a relevant example of an empire which was fatally weakened by the systematic evasion of fiscal and military responsibility by its large semifeudal landowners irrespective of the fact that slavery was, at the most, marginal in the composition of the productive work-force."[83] Later in his essay, Runciman goes on to sketch hypotheses about the role of slavery in agrarian states that could be drawn out of explicit comparisons of Anderson's Roman, Ottoman, and Scandinavian case histories.[84]

On another, even more relevant subject – the causes and nature of absolutist monarchies in Europe – Runciman suggests conclusions that Anderson could have drawn by contrasting the failure of English absolutism to the success of French absolutism, and by underlining the similarities of Russian to French absolutism.[85] Just as Anderson is precluded from fully exploring the effects of slavery by his reluctance to compare directly cases that he narrates under very separate typological categories, so is he unwilling to emphasize contrasts between England and France, both of which are supposed to be Western absolutisms, or similarities between France and Russia, which are supposed to belong to the very separate worlds of Western versus Eastern Europe. As Runciman appropriately laments, "Comparisons do not constitute the organizing principle around which . . . [Anderson's] macrosociological explanations are constructed . . . Anderson's account of social evolution remains too closely constrained within a narrative framework . . ."[86] To Anderson, it is the very essence of a truly historical approach to draw firm distinctions between different types of sociopolitical orders and to insist on the holistic integrity, the functional systemicity, and the continuity over time of each separate type of order. The price Anderson must pay for *this* kind of historical and comparative approach is the failure to notice causally pregnant analogies and contrasts, even when, as the French say, these "jump to the eyes."

Part of the trouble, of course, lies with the *content* of the causal analogies that occur to W. G. Runciman, and to us, when we survey the relations between monarchs and landed upper classes for the full range of the European and Asian case histories that Anderson presents. Most of these analogies are not in conformance with the class-determinist political sociology of classical Marxism. In fact, military power and interstate competition assume a much larger and more theoretically independent role when one approaches Anderson's case materials with an eye to wide-ranging causal generalizations. For example, Anderson's own detailed case histories in *Lineages* suggest that there was one major factor underlying all efforts at absolutist state building in early modern Europe. That factor was land warfare. In both East and West there were possibilities and exigencies for monarchs to create and deploy standing armies within the multicentered state system that arose out of the medieval European political parcellization. The successful consolidation of absolute monarchies – or the failure of such consolidation, as in England – was everywhere related to such possibilities and exigencies. Anderson could have systematically explained the rise of the full range of European absolutist states partly in terms of the interstate military competition and partly by exploring the varying initiatives of monarchs as autonomous actors in relation to dominant and subordinate classes. This approach, however, would have entailed setting aside the assumption that Eastern and Western Europe are, and ever have been, separate worlds, intertwined only by the impact of the advanced West on the lagging East. And this approach would have contradicted Anderson's theoretical inclination to derive absolutism directly from the dynamics of the feudal mode of production and the interests of its dominant class.

One cannot avoid suspecting that Anderson was unwilling, from the time he launched *Passages-Lineages,* even to entertain the possibility of either of these moves. Either one, and certainly both taken together, would contravene his – and the *New Left Review*'s – intrinsic theoretical and political commitments. To give up the basic tenets of class-determinist political sociology would be to call into question the socialist-revolutionary vocation of the Western proletariat. To give up the firm division of West from East within Europe would be to allow the implication that the fate of the Russian Revolution might reflect more than the burdens of backwardness, that it could, indeed, hold pessimistic forebodings – or at least highly relevant lessons – for any revolution that might eventuate in the West.

No doubt, Perry Anderson never would have carried through in any form the vast project embodied in *Passages-Lineages* had he not been comitted to doing total history relevant to his understanding of political possibilities in the present. There are intimate "elective affinities" between Anderson's political commitments and the methodological choices embodied in his historical sociology. But the readers of *Passages-Lineages*, many as they have been in the past and the still more to come in the future, fortunately need not be encumbered by any of Anderson's metacommitments. Readers from all theoretical and political persuasions can appropriate Anderson's fine books for purposes other than his own, taking him at his word when he says that they are "intended to propose elements for discussion, rather than to expound closed or comprehensive theses."[87] Whatever the shortcomings, Perry Anderson has produced in *Passages-Lineages* an extraordinary piece of historical sociology, breathtaking in scope and nuanced in detail. It remains for others to build upon his achievement, breaking through its theoretical preconceptions where they are unfruitful and overcoming its methodological limitations wherever they have prevented the full exploration of comparisons across the destined pathways of Anderson's grand past.

Notes

1. Perry Anderson, *Passages from Antiquity to Feudalism* (London: New Left Books, 1974) and *Lineages of the Absolute State* (London: New Left Books. 1974). The set of the two books together will be called *Passages-Lineages.*
2. Moses Finley, *The Guardian*, February 6, 1975, and Keith Thomas, "Jumbo History," *The New York Review of Books*, April 17, 1975, p. 27.
3. Tariq Ali, "Feudalism to Absolutism," *Books and Bookmen* 20(235) (April 1975): 21.
4. D. G. MacRae, "Chains of History," *New Society* 31 (January 30, 1975): 269, 270.
5. Anderson, *Lineages*, p. 11.
6. Ibid., p. 8.
7. A good discussion of historians' practice is to be found in Charles Tilly, "Sociology, Meet History," in *As Sociology Meets History* (New York: Academic Press, 1981).
8. This discussion draws on David Richard Holden, "The First New Left in Britain, 1956–1962" (Ph.D. diss., University of Wisconsin at Madison, 1976).
9. Ibid., p. 356.
10. Perry Anderson, *Considerations on Western Marxism* (London: New Left Books, 1976).
11. Perry Anderson, "Problems of Socialist Strategy," in *Towards Socialism*, ed. Anderson and Robin Blackburn (London: Collins, 1965): 221–90.
12. "Origins of the Present Crisis" first appeared in the *New Left Review* 23 (January-February 1964). It was reprinted in *Towards Socialism*, ed. Ander-

son and Robin Blackburn (London: Collins, 1965). Page references below
are to the reprinted essay, hereafter cited as "Origins."

13. Anderson, "Origins," in *Towards Socialism*, p. 12 (emphasis added).
14. Ibid., p. 13.
15. Ibid., pp. 36–37.
16. Ibid., p. 52.
17. E. P. Thompson, "The Peculiarities of the English," in *The Poverty of Theory and Other Essays* (London: Merlin Press, 1978): 35–91. The essay is reprinted from *The Socialist Register* 1965. All page references in this article are to *The Poverty of Theory*.
18. Perry Anderson, "Socialism and Pseudo-Empiricism," *New Left Review* no. 35 (January-February 1966): 32.
19. Ibid., p. 33.
20. Ibid.
21. Anderson, *Lineages*, p. 420.
22. Anderson, *Passages*, p. 128.
23. Ibid., p. 78.
24. Anderson, "Socialist Strategy," in *Towards Socialism*, p. 225.
25. Ibid., p. 230.
26. Anderson, "Socialism and Pseudo-Empiricism," pp. 32–33.
27. Ibid., p. 33.
28. Perry Anderson, "Portugal and the End of Ultra-Colonialism," *New Left Review* no. 17 (September-December 1962): 113.
29. Anderson, *Lineages*, pp. 7–8.
30. Ibid., p. 8.
31. P. A. Brunt, A. H. M. Jones, R. Syme, M. I. Finley, and Max Weber are the major sources on Rome. J. H. Elliot, J. Lynch, G. Parker, and A. Dominguez Ortiz are the key authorities on Spain. Hajo Holborn, F. L. Carsten, and Theodore Hamerow are cited repeatedly on Germany, as is Michael Roberts on Sweden. On Russia, finally, Anderson defers to Lenin on some major points, but otherwise cites such standard authorities as Richard Hellie, Hugh Seton-Watson, and Geroid Robinson.
32. See Neil J. Smelser, "Sociological History: The Industrial Revolution and the British Working-Class Family," *Journal of Social History* 1 (1) (Fall 1967): 17–35; and *Social Change in the Industrial Revolution: An Application of Theory to the British Cotton Industry* (Chicago: University of Chicago Press, 1959).
33. Anderson, *Lineages*, p. 402.
34. Ibid.
35. Anderson, *Passages*, p. 148.
36. Anderson, *Lineages*, pp. 412–14.
37. Ibid., p. 419.
38. Ibid., p. 422.
39. See part 3 of W. G. Runciman, "Comparative Sociology or Narrative History? A Note on the Methodology of Perry Anderson," *Archives Européenne de Sociologie* 21 (1980): 162–78 for a good discussion of the problems with Anderson's discussion of Japanese feudalism.
40. Anderson, *Lineages*, p. 18.
41. Ibid., p. 15.
42. Ibid., p. 7.
43. Anderson, *Passages*, p. 26.
44. Ibid., p. 28.
45. Ibid.
46. Ibid., p. 128.

47. Ibid., p. 265.
48. Ibid., p. 213–14.
49. It is, of course, absolutely essential to Anderson's argument that Sweden end up being classified as an instance of Western absolutism, because Sweden became the "hammer of the East," the catalyst through military pressure of absolutist developments in Eastern Europe. Anderson says that the "more advanced societies" of the West put pressure on the East, yet he also coyly admits that the "concrete form which the military threat from Western Absolutism initially took was . . . historically circuitous and transient" (*Lineages*, pp. 197–98). It was economically backward Sweden that delivered the "Western" pressures on the East, not the most economically advanced societies of the West!
50. Anderson, *Lineages*, p. 195.
51. Ibid.
52. Ibid., pp. 197–98.
53. This discussion draws on Theda Skocpol and Margaret Somers, "The Uses of Comparative History in Macrosocial Inquiry," *Comparative Studies in Society and History*, 22(2) (April 1980): 174–97. Further elaboration of these points also appears in the Conclusion to this volume.
54. Anderson's avoidance of comparative causal analysis and the costs this entails will be examined in the concluding section of this chapter.
55. See especially the first and second chapters in Parts One and Two of *Lineages*.
56. Anderson, *Passages*, pp. 154–72.
57. Ibid., p. 156.
58. Ibid., p. 173.
59. Ibid.
60. Especially in this section, but also for previous points in this chapter, we have drawn ideas from one of the most insightful commentaries on *Passages Lineages*: Paul Hirst, "The Uniqueness of the West," *Economy and Society* 4(4) (November 1975): 446–75.
61. See for example, Robert Nisbet, *Social Change and History* (Oxford: Oxford University Press, 1969); and S. N. Eisenstadt, "Social Change, Differentiation, and Evolution," *American Sociological Review* 29 (3) (February 1964): 373–86.
62. See, for example, the companion articles by Bellah and Parsons in the *American Sociological Review* 29 (3) (February 1964); and, in a Marxist tradition, Jürgen Habermas, *Communication and the Evolution of Society* (Boston: Beacon Press, 1979).
63. See Eisenstadt, "Social Change, Differentiation and Evolution."
64. Talcott Parsons, *Societies: Evolutionary and Comparative Perspectives* (Englewood Cliffs, N.J.: Prentice-Hall, 1966).
65. See Anthony Smith, *The Concept of Social Change* (London: Routledge & Kegan Paul, 1973), pp. 33–37.
66. Anderson, "Origins," in *Towards Socialism*, p. 29.
67. See Betty Behrens, "Feudalism and Absolutism," *The Historical Journal* 19(1) (1976): 245–50.
68. Anderson, *Passages*, pp. 97–98.
69. Ibid., p. 155.
70. Ibid., p. 156.
71. Ibid., p. 157.
72. Thompson, "The Poverty of Theory," in *Poverty of Theory*, p. 37.
73. Anderson, *Passages*, p. 155.

74. Ibid., p. 264.
75. Anderson, "Problems of Socialist Strategy," in *Towards Socialism*, p. 230.
76. Anderson, p. 8.
77. Anderson, *Passages*, pp. 7–8.
78. Anderson, "Socialism and Pseudo-Empiricism," p. 32.
79. Anderson, *Considerations on Western Marxism*, p. 110.
80. Ibid.,
81. Ibid., p. 113 for cited passage. See pp. 113–21 for Anderson's survey of the questions left open or inadequately answered by Marx, Lenin, and Trotsky.
82. Ibid., p. 113.
83. Runciman, "Comparative Sociology or Narrative History?" p. 165.
84. Ibid., pp. 172–74.
85. Ibid., pp. 169–70, 175–78
86. Ibid., p. 163.
87. Anderson, *Passages*, p. 9.

Bibliography

ANDERSON'S CONTRIBUTIONS TO HISTORICAL SOCIOLOGY

"Sweden: Mr. Crosland's Dreamland." *New Left Review* no. 7 (January-February 1961):4–12.
"Sweden II: Study in Social Democracy." *New Left Review* no. 9 (May-June 1961):34–45.
"Portugal and the End of Ultra-Colonialism." *New Left Review* no. 15 (May-June 1962):83–102; no. 16 (July-August 1962):88–123; and no. 17 (September-December 1962):85–114.
"Origins of the Present Crisis." *New Left Review* no. 23 (January-February 1964):26–53. Reprinted in *Towards Socialism*, edited by Perry Anderson and Robin Blackburn. London: Collins, 1965.
"Socialism and Pseudo-Empiricism." *New Left Review* no. 35 (January-February 1966):2–42. This is a critique of E. P. Thompson and other English historians.
"Components of the National Culture." *New Left Review* no. 50 (July-August 1968):3–58.
Passages from Antiquity to Feudalism. London: New Left Books, 1974.
Lineages of the Absolutist State. London: New Left Books, 1974.
Considerations on Western Marxism. London: New Left Books, 1976.
"The Antinomies of Antonio Gramsci." *New Left Review* no. 100 (November 1976–January 1977):5–80.
Arguments Within English Marxism. London: New Left Books, 1980. This is a more appreciative critical assessment of Thompson's historiography than the 1966 critique.

SELECTED REVIEWS OF ANDERSON'S WORKS

Aya, Rod. "The Present as 'Jumbo History': A Review Article." *Race and Class* 17(2) (1975):179–88.
Behrens, Betty. "Feudalism and Absolutism." *The Historical Journal* 19(1) (1976):245–50.
Gourevitch, Peter. "The International System and Regime Formation: A Critical Review of Anderson and Wallerstein." *World Politics* 10(3) (1978):419–38.

Mary Fulbrook, Theda Skocpol

Hechter, Michael. "Lineages of the Capitalist State." *American Journal of Sociology* 82(5) (1977):1057–74.

Heller, Agnes. Review of *Passages* and *Lineages*. *Telos* no. 33 (Fall 1977):202–10.

Hirst, Paul. "The Uniqueness of the West." *Economy and Society* 4(4) (1975): 446–75.

Johnson, Richard. "Barrington Moore, Perry Anderson and English Social Development." *Working Papers in Cultural Studies* 9 (1976):7–28.

MacRae, D. G. "Chains of History." *New Society* 31 (January 30, 1975):269–70.

Miliband, Ralph. "Political Forms and Historical Materialism." *The Socialist Register 1975*: 308–18.

Porter, R., and C. R. Whittaker. "States and Estates." *The Journal of Social History* no. 3 (October 1976):367–76.

Runciman, W. G. "Comparative Sociology or Narrative History? A Note on the Methodology of Perry Anderson." *Archives Européenne de Sociologie* 21 (1980):162–78.

Thomas, Keith. "Jumbo History." *The New York Review of Books*, April 17, 1975:26–28.

Thompson, E. P. "The Peculiarities of the English." In *The Poverty of Theory and Other Essays*, pp. 35–91. London: Merlin Press, 1978. The essay appeared originally in *The Socialist Register 1965*.

7. E. P. Thompson: Understanding the Process of History

ELLEN KAY TRIMBERGER

Most historical sociologists know E. P. Thompson as the author of *The Making of the English Working Class,* published in 1963. Most have probably read part, but not all, of this book, which they view as a superb work of social history and a welcome departure from a simplistic or economist Marxism. Widely praised for its contribution to the new "history from below," which in a sense the book itself helped to create, Thompson's masterpiece tells the story of the "blind alleys, the lost causes, and the losers themselves" that history usually forgets.[1] Yet, however much they might admire him as a social historian and a compelling literary stylist, most historical sociologists do not see theoretical relevance in Thompson's work.[2] A perceived lack of theoretical generalization and explicit methodology in Thompson's social history has been used to account for his meager impact on sociologists, despite his influence among historians.[3]

Embedded in *The Making of the English Working Class,* however, is an implicit theory and method that Thompson subsequently has explicated through criticism of, and lively polemics with, other Marxists. The publication in 1978 of four of these long essays in one book, *The Poverty of Theory and Other Essays,* facilitates access to Thompson's perspective. The assumptions underlying Thompson's theory and method, however, still make them difficult to assimilate within sociology. Thompson offers a fundamental challenge to the positivism and empiricism that have shaped Anglo-American sociology and that have also influenced a large part of twentieth-century Marxism.[4]

This chapter contrasts Thompson's interpretive theory, dialectical logic, and concrete historical method to the causal analysis, deductive logic, and empiricist methodology that characterize positivist traditions of social scientific inquiry. The discussion will highlight what I consider

Ellen Kay Trimberger

to be Thompson's unique contribution to historical sociology: a theoretical method intended to capture historical process and to integrate an analysis of culture and human agency into a macrostructural analysis of social change. I begin with the discussion of Thompson's political and intellectual biography and then proceed to explore how he develops his theory and method in *The Making of the English Working Class.* Finally, I shall draw out the more general implications of Thompson's approach, implications relevant for both Marxist and non-Marxist historical sociology and social theory.

The Formation of a Critical Marxist Intellectual

> The mediations between any intellectual or artistic work and one's experience and participation in society are never one-to-one; they are never direct. I mean, no painter can paint his political experience like *that*, and if he tries to do so he paints a poster, which has perhaps a good value *as* a poster.[5]

One can agree with Thompson that social experience does not straightforwardly determine intellectual production, yet one of the key arguments in his scholarship is that experience mediates between social being and social consciousness. Indeed, Thompson's own experiences as a participant in the politics of the British Communist Party in the 1940s and 1950s and then as a spokesman for the British New Left during the 1960s and 1970s had a profound impact on his intellectual work. For Thompson, political participation was not a barrier to intellectual development. Rather, both his positive and negative experiences in the British left were prods to the elaboration of his distinctive ideas as a social theorist and historian. Political debates with other leftist intellectuals led Thompson to articulate his theoretical and methodological position within Marxism far more fully than he would probably have done had he worked exclusively as an academic historian. Thus the following sketch of Thompson's political biography is more than merely interesting background material. It suggests the relevance of life experiences for the development of theory in a manner nicely captured by Alvin Gouldner:

> Much of theory-work begins with an effort to make sense of one's experience. Much of it is initiated by an effort to resolve unresolved experience; here, the problem is not to validate what has been observed or to produce new observations, but rather to locate and to interpret the meaning of what one has lived . . . Theory-making, then, is often an effort to cope with threat; it is an effort to cope

with a threat to something in which the theorist himself is deeply and personally implicated and which he holds dear.[6]

E. P. Thompson joined the British Communist Party in 1942 at the age of eighteen and resigned in 1956, after the Twentieth Party Congress in the Soviet Union exposed and denounced Stalinism. Both the populism of the British party in the war years that attracted Thompson and the Stalinism that later repelled him influenced the type of questions he asked in his subsequent historical studies. Thompson's visit to Bulgaria for a memorial service to his older brother, who was killed there in 1944 while fighting with Communist guerrilla forces, and his own participation with a youth brigade in Yugoslavia in 1946, made a lasting impact on him. As he said in a recent interview:

> One had this extraordinary formative moment in which it was possible to be deeply committed even to the point of life itself in support of a particular political struggle which was at the same time a popular struggle; that is, one didn't feel a sense of being isolated in any way from the peoples of Europe or the peoples of Britain. I suppose this does affect the way one was formed. I was of course very active in the Communist Party and remained so until 1956. This didn't mean that one didn't have many inner doubts and also wasn't guilty of many casuistries explaining away what one should have repudiated in the character of Stalinism . . . [But] my brother's surviving letters are totally at odds with the cardboard ideological picture of what Stalinism was. His commitment was to people and above all to the astonishing heroism of the Partisan movements of southern Europe.[7]

Thompson was a student at Cambridge during and after the war, but he never did graduate work. In the early 1950s he went to teach in an adult education program in northern England, where he was also active in party political work. During this period Thompson wrote his first book, a study of William Morris, the nineteenth-century English romantic poet and noted designer, who became an active socialist organizer and writer in the 1880s after he was fifty years old. Thompson never consciously or clearly decided to become a historian or even to write this first book. He remembers:

> I was preparing my first classes. I was teaching as much literature as history. I thought, how do I, first of all, raise with an adult class, many of them in the labor movements – discuss with them the significance of literature to their lives? And I started reading Morris. I was seized by Morris. I thought, why is this man thought to be an old fuddy-duddy? He is right in with us still.

And then I read one or two books *so* dreadful and so ideological about Morris that I thought I *must* answer these . . . Morris seized me. I took no decision. Morris took the decision that I would have to present him. In the course of doing this I became much more serious about being a historian.[8]

Thompson's historical studies were shaped not only by his experience in a populist left movement during the war and by his identification with the earlier English socialist, but also by his experience in the Communist Party Historians' Group, which met regularly after the war until 1956. Eric Hobsbawm, a prominent member of the group, has recently written a short remembrance from which I draw. This group of thirty or more historians – some teaching in universities, more in secondary and adult schools, as well as some nonacademics – created a Marxist tradition in British history. Hobsbawm, Thompson, Maurice Dobb, Dorothy Thompson, Christopher Hill, John Saville, Rodney Hilton, V. G. Kiernan, and others who no longer identify themselves as Marxists were prominent members. In 1953, this group started the now prestigious history periodical *Past and Present*, an independent journal that sought to build bridges between Marxist and non-Marxist intellectuals with common interests and sympathies.

Hobsbawm feels that except for the history of the British Communist Party itself, there were no constraints, direct or indirect, on the historians' work. Instead, the group widened rather than narrowed or distorted their understanding of history.[9] The group, or subgroups, engaged in ongoing debate on the following topics, among others: the breakdown of feudalism and the rise of capitalism, the nature of absolutism, the impact of agrarian change in sixteenth and seventeenth-century England, the significance of the English Revolution, the nature of the nineteenth-century working class (including debate about the aristocracy of labor), and the development of the modern state. As Hobsbawm summarizes this experience:

The individual and collective aspects cannot be separated, for the Historians' Group of 1946–56 was the rare, possibly unique, phenomenon in British historiography, a genuinely cooperative group, whose members developed their often highly individual work through a constant interchange among equals. It was not a "school" built around an influential teacher or book. Even those most respected in the Group neither claimed to be authoritative nor were treated as such . . . None of us enjoyed the authority or prestige which comes from outside professional recognition, not even Dobb whose position in the academic world was isolated.

Fortunately the Party invested none of us with ideological or political authority. We were united neither by common subject-matter, style nor set of mind – other than a desire to be Marxists. And yet it is certain that each of us as an individual historian, amateur or professional, as teacher or writer, bears the mark of our ten years' "seminar" and none would be quite the same as a historian today without it.[10]

In fact, these friendships and collegial relations survived the exit of many of the group's members from the party in 1956.

Thompson explains how this experience in the Communist Historians' Group created a model of ideal intellectual work:

The formal and informal exchange with fellow socialists helped me more than anything I had found in Cambridge University. This is not to say that one can't, fortunately, sometimes find something in a university, but it is to emphasize that socialist intellectuals ought to help each other. We should never be wholly dependent upon institutions, however benevolent, but should maintain groups in which theory is discussed and history is discussed and in which people criticize each other . . . What socialists must never do is allow themselves to become wholly dependent upon established institutions – publishing houses, commercial media, universities, foundations. I don't mean that these institutions are all repressive: certainly, much that is affirmative can be done within them. But socialist intellectuals must occupy some territory which is, without qualification, their own: their own journals, their own theoretical and practical centers; places where no one works for grades or for tenure but for the transformation of society; places where criticism and self-criticism are fierce, but also mutual help and the exchange of theoretical and practical knowledge; places which pre-figure in some ways the society of the future.[11]

This model of socialist cooperation was not carried over into the British New Left, in which Thompson played an important role after 1956. Instead, Thompson's participation in the New Left culminated in strife. Ironically, political conflict and debate, rather than cooperation, finally motivated Thompson to write the series of polemical essays in which he began to articulate his own theoretical interpretation of Marxism and historical method. Although I cannot fully explain how this combination of negative and positive experience is connected with Thompson's particular revision of Marxist theory, I can trace some of the important events.

In 1956, after Khrushchev's speech revealing Stalin's crimes and before the Soviet invasion of Hungary, Thompson and his friend in the party, John Saville, started to publish a mimeographed discussion journal, *The Reasoner*, independent of the party press, to stimulate debate about the implications of Stalinism. When they were met by party criticism and asked to stop publication, Thompson and Saville resigned from the party.[12] In 1957, they began to publish an independent left journal, *The New Reasoner*. The editorial board was composed of ex-party intellectuals living primarily in the northern industrial districts. Besides Thompson and Saville (a historian) it included Doris Lessing, a novelist; Ronald Meek, Ken Alexander, and Michael Barrett-Brown, economists; Randall Swingler, poet and literary critic; Ralph Miliband, political scientist; and Mervyn Jones and Malcolm MacEwan, journalists.[13] In the first issue of the *The New Reasoner*, Thompson propounded the concerns of a Marxist socialist humanism, indicating many of the issues that became central to his own historical and theoretical work; the inadequacies of a base/superstructure model of society; the importance of consciousness and human agency; and the need to incorporate a concern with moral choice into Marxist theory and politics. Thompson defined a quest for self-consciousness and a return to real people instead of abstract formulations as central to socialist humanism.

The editors and supporters of *The New Reasoner* had close ties to another journal founded at the same time, *Universities and Left Review* (*ULR*). This journal began at Oxford as a student publication, but soon moved to London. Although all the editors of *ULR* – Stuart Hall, Charles Taylor, Alan Lovell, and Allen Hall – joined the Labour Party in 1957, they did not have close ties to either labor or the old left. Younger than Thompson, their politics and intellectual work were shaped not by disillusionment with the Communist Party or labor politics but by a revulsion from postwar British society and culture. Even more than *The New Reasoner*, *ULR* stressed the search for a socialist view of culture.[14]

In December 1959, the two journals merged to form the *New Left Review*, with Stuart Hall as editor and a twenty-six-member editorial board. The editorial in the first issue was built around a quote from Thompson's hero, William Morris, and clearly expressed his politics:

> We are convinced that politics too narrowly conceived has been a main cause of the decline of socialism in this country, and one of the reasons for the disaffection from socialist ideas of young people in particular. The humanist strengths of socialism – which are the foundation for a genuinely popular socialist movement –

must be developed in cultural and social terms, as well as in economic and political.

The original *New Left Review* also sponsored clubs for political and intellectual education and discussion. By November 1960, there were forty-five clubs with 3,000 paid members, and the journal had a circulation of 10,000.[15] The journal and the clubs, along with the mass movement headed by the Committee for Nuclear Disarmament, formed the heart of the first New Left in Britain. The organization of the *New Left Review*, however, soon became problematic. The large number of board members, scattered geographically, proved unwieldy, and the editor, Stuart Hall, an activist and leader in the antinuclear movement, had too little time for the journal.

At the end of 1961, after several attempts at reorganization, Thompson was instrumental in appointing Perry Anderson, then the editor of an Oxford student journal, as the new editor of the *New Left Review*. Later, Thompson reported the reasons for this move, and the unsettling events that ensued:

> We reached a point of personal, financial and organizational exhaustion; and at this moment, the agent of history appeared, in the form of Perry Anderson. We were exhausted: he was intellectually fertile, immensely self-concentrated, decisive. We saw, in a partnership with him and his colleagues, an opportunity to regenerate the review and to recuperate our own squandered intellectual resources. We did not, as it happens, anticipate that the first expression of his decisiveness would be to dismiss the review's founders from its board.[16]

The April 1963 minutes of the last meeting of the original *New Left Review* board with the new editor read as follows: "After a number of possibilities had been explored, it was found that the Board had no clear function in the present situation and was felt by the Editor to be a constitutional built-in irritant and distraction."[17]

As is evident from his later writings, Thompson was outraged by Anderson's dismissal of him, especially since the journal subsequently moved in an intellectual direction of which he disapproved. More theoretical and less political, and based on French structural Marxism, the revamped *New Left Review* denigrated Thompson's work and that of his close associates as empiricist, populist, and insufficiently theoretical.[18] Rather than engage in a fight over the journal, Thompson retreated for several years. Later he launched a biting theoretical debate with Anderson and his associates on the *New Left Review*. Although the various essays later collected in *The Poverty of Theory and Other Essays* express strong political emotions and personal anger, it is to Thompson's credit that he chose to channel these feelings into theoretical debate. Indeed, the personal and political intensity of these debates helped Thompson to sharpen his own distinctive theoretical position.[19]

Thompson's life and work may yet come full circle. The political, personal, and intellectual comradeship that he found in the Communist Historians' Group is now being re-created in the European nuclear disarmament movement, in which Thompson plays a leading role. In early 1980, in response to the impending placement of American-controlled Pershing and Cruise missiles in Europe, Thompson drafted an appeal for European nuclear disarmament; helped found a new group, END, with the primary goal of making Europe a nuclear-free zone; and became a leading spokesman for a mushrooming international peace movement. Thompson's desire to inspire a movement uniting Eastern and Western Europeans rests on an intellectual analysis of the necessity to break out of Cold War logic, but it is also motivated emotionally by his brother's death as a partisan in Bulgaria.[20]

As we shall see more fully at the end of this chapter, Thompson's theoretical stance in his historical studies directly inspired his recent plunge into anti-nuclear politics; reciprocally, this political work leads to further theoretical innovations. Characteristically, Thompson's most recent phase of political activism has been accompanied by intellectual debate with Marxists. In a widely read and reprinted 1980 article in the *New Left Review*, "Notes on Exterminism: The Last Stage of Civilization," Thompson argues that Marxist theories of imperialism and international class struggle cannot adequately explain the Cold War and the escalating nuclear arms race. He chides the left for its political and intellectual neglect of the issue. In response, the editors of the journal solicited replies and published them as a book, *Exterminism and Cold War*. Their motivation now seemed far removed from the acerbic criticism of the past. They called Thompson's anti-nuclear work "an act of public service with few comparisons in the recent history of any country."[21] In turn, Thompson termed the responses to his essay "remarkable" for "the openness of tone and of terms, the reach for an international discourse, and the common pursuit of convergent analysis and strategies."[22]

Doing History and Reworking Marxist Theory

From the writing of his first major historical work, *William Morris*, until the present, Thompson has sought to work within the Marxist tradition and to fill the "silences" he finds there. As he puts it:

There is a "silence" as to cultural and moral mediations, as to the ways in which the human being is imbricated in particular, determined productive relations, the way these material experiences are handled by them in cultural ways, the way in which there are certain value-systems that are consonant with certain modes of production and productive relations which are inconceivable without consonant value-systems. There is not one which is dependent upon the other. There is not a moral ideology which belongs to a "superstructure"; there are these two things which are different sides of the same coin. This concern has been in my work all the time. It has made me explicitly reject the metaphor of "basis/superstructure" and to look for other metaphors. In my work I have been particularly interested in values, culture, law and in that area where . . . [what] is normally called moral choice evinces itself.[23]

In his more recent theoretical essays, Thompson makes an additional criticism of Marx's theory, arguing that Marx's greatest work, *Capital*, did not fully develop a historical materialist theory:

It remains a study of the logic of capital, not of capitalism, and the social and political dimensions of the history, the wrath, and the understanding of the class struggle arise from a region independent of the closed system of economic logic . . . [*Capital*] is both the highest achievement of "political economy," and it signals the need for its supersession by historical materialism.[24]

Thompson is not content merely to criticize but has begun to articulate a new type of historical-materialist theory in the course of his own historical studies. His practice of creating theory through specific historical work, however, falls somewhat short of his own criteria for how the revision of Marxist theory should proceed. Through a comparison of Thompson's more general statements on how to integrate an analysis of culture and human agency into Marxist theory with his practice in his most important historical study, *The Making of the English Working Class*, we can proceed toward a more general presentation and evaluation of Thompson's theory.

Of central importance to Thompson's revisionist Marxism is his emphasis on "experience" as mediating "social being" (the determinate relationships of women and men in their material life) and "social consciousness" (the self-consciousness of these relationships). Culture – conceived of as a product of the human mind – enters into both social being and social consciousness. No mode of production, property relationship, or labor process is possible without human consciousness. Thompson's concept of social being also allows for those structured relationships that, despite their origins in intended actions, come to confront actors as limiting structures outside themselves. According to Thompson:

> Experience arises spontaneously within social being, but it does not arise without thought; it arises because men and women (and not only philosophers) are rational, and they think about what is happening to themselves and their world . . . . Changes take place within social being, which give rise to changed experience: and this experience is determining, in the sense that it exerts pressures upon existent social consciousness [and] proposes new questions.[25]

Experience is both structured and determining, but also shaped by human intervention:

> Men and women return [to theory] as subjects, . . . not as autonomous subjects, "free individuals," but as persons experiencing their determinate productive situations and relationships, as needs and interests and as antagonisms, and then "handling" this experience within their consciousness and their culture . . . in the most complex . . . ways, and then . . . acting upon their deterministic situation in their turn.[26]

In short, the new consciousness that arises out of new experience is shaped by human beings partly through their old consciousness – the cultural standards and values shaped by past experience. People may retain attachments to values and customs even as the economy is changing. In turn, they may use such cultural attachments to actively intervene in an attempt to alter economic conditions.

As a specific application of his emphasis on experience, Thompson used *The Making of the English Working Class* above all to rework the Marxist analysis of social class. In his own formulation of the concept of class, Thompson stresses the interaction of structure and agency, social being and social consciousness:

> Class happens when some men, as a result of common experiences (inherited or shared), feel and articulate the identity of their interests as between themselves, and as against other men whose interests are different from (and usually opposed to) theirs. The class experience is largely determined by the productive relations into which men are born – or enter involuntarily. Class-consciousness is the way in which these experiences are handled in cultural terms: embodied in traditions, value-systems, ideas, and institutional forms. If the experience appears as determined, class-con-

sciousness does not. We can see a *logic* in the responses of similar occupational groups undergoing similar experiences, but we cannot predicate any *law*. Consciousness of class arises in the same way in different times and places, but never in *just* the same way.[27]

Thompson's understanding of class seeks to tie together ideas about socioeconomic structure (Marx's concept of "class-in-itself"), consciousness ("class-for-itself"), and human agency. It rejects Marx's implicit assumption that class consciousness is primarily an automatic and rational response to given economic structures. Thompson also rejects Lenin's claim that class consciousness is consciously formulated by an elite based on a scientifically correct understanding of external objective conditions. Rather, Thompson sees class consciousness as collectively created by human actors using cultural resources inherited from a particular past to reflect on the way they experience the impact of larger social structures, i.e., "productive relations."

The theoretical frame of reference we have just explored, when applied to historical material, could produce an argument that is neither idealist nor economist, neither voluntarist nor structurally determinist. Such an argument could integrate an analysis of cultural (including ideological and moral) production with material (especially economic) production. It would grasp what Thompson calls "the crucial ambivalence of our human presence in our own history, part subjects, part objects, the voluntary agents of our involuntary determinations."[28] Unfortunately, however – perhaps because of its strongly polemic stance – *The Making of the English Working Class* develops an interpretation that swerves too far toward idealism and voluntarism while giving short shrift to material and structural analysis.

In the preface to *The Making of the English Working Class*, Thompson states clearly that his aim is twofold: as a historian, he seeks to write a narrative about the English working class from 1780 to 1832. As a theorist, he wants to contribute to the sociological understanding of class.[29] Moreover, Thompson formulates his analysis in specific opposition to theorists as well as historians. Thompson seeks to revise the interpretations of the older Fabian historians (the Hammonds and the Webbs) and the more recent economic historians (Ashton and Clapham). But he also presents an alternative to the theories of orthodox Marxists and to those of such functionalist sociologists as Neil Smelser and Ralf Dahrendorf. Thompson sets himself in opposition to these theoretical and historical positions because he feels that they all obscure the agency of working people and the degree to which working people contributed, by conscious efforts, to the making of history. In addition, Thompson holds that most other writers ignore the important contributions of cultural patterns to the shaping of social change during the English Industrial Revolution.

The organization of *The Making of the English Working Class* embodies the logic of Thompson's analysis. Part One of the book elucidates the political culture inherited by the English laboring classes at the time of the Industrial Revolution. Part Two analyzes how groups of working people experienced and evaluated the economic and political changes that constituted capitalist industrialization. Part Three depicts the way that laboring groups, in response to the experience of industrialization, forged an organized and conscious working class, aided by a creative use of their inherited cultural resources.

It is in Part Two of *The Making of the English Working Class* that we expect to find an extended presentation of social being – of the limits placed by the material relationships of the industrial-capitalist revolution on the English working class. Thompson does present a lot of historical data on economic productivity and labor relations, but this history is not analyzed in terms of the dynamics of capitalist accumulation or capitalist social relations. Rather, all the discussion is about experience and the degree to which this experience was *not* determined by economic circumstances. Here Thompson addresses the long debate among historians about whether the standard of living rose or fell during early industrialization in England. But Thompson is overridingly concerned with changing the very terms and premises of the debate. What he considers important is not the objective, quantifiable evidence about working conditions, wages, or levels of consumption, but how people *felt* about the huge transformations and disruptions they were experiencing.[30] Seemingly contradictory conclusions emerge from examining the economic data and the evidence on how people felt about and evaluated economic change:

> Over the period 1790–1840 there was a slight improvement in average material standards. Over the same period there was intensified exploitation, greater insecurity, and increasing human misery. By 1840 most people were "better off" than their forerunners had been fifty years before, but they had suffered and continued to suffer this slight improvement as a catastrophic experience.[31]

Thompson emphasizes this paradox about the Industrial Revolution in England to reject any and all economistic arguments (by Marxists and non-Marxists alike) that assert direct correspondences between the dynamic of economic growth and that of social or cultural life.

Workers' experience of exploitation was not directly the result of new technologies (steam power and the cotton mill) or standards of living. Nor was it the direct result of changes in the organization of production or of political institutions. Rather, values and expectations retained from particular precapitalist and pre-industrial ways of life shaped workers' sense of exploitation, because they provided the cultural lenses through which the technologies, factories, and living standards were interpreted and acted upon.

Thus Thompson stresses the continuity of cultural traditions in the making of nineteenth-century working-class communities. In turn, he discusses how specific aspects of eighteenth-century culture – religion, political theory, artisan traditions, local customs – were filtered through the experience of capitalist industrialization to produce a radical political culture that was the basis for working-class consciousness and political action. Far from implying a picture of pure working-class radicalization, however, the book (as we shall see later) also explores the ways in which the reactionary and nonpolitical responses of the working class to industrialization also drew on eighteenth-century culture by emphasizing aspects other than those that contributed to class consciousness.

The last third of *The Making of the English Working Class* is a rich narrative intended to substantiate Thompson's claim that by 1832 a working class had formed in England. Thompson believes that from 1790 to 1830 an identity of outlooks – and common forms of social and political organization – developed among what once were diverse groups of working people. Struggles against what were understood as the exploitative actions of the more privileged classes furthered this coming-together of the working class, as did the political repressions of trade unions and popular political clubs that accompanied and followed the Napoleonic Wars. By 1832, there were strongly based and self-conscious working-class institutions: "trade unions, friendly societies, educational and religious movements, political organizations, periodicals – working class intellectual traditions, working class community patterns, and a working class structure of feeling."[32]

Thompson's historical narrative provides many specific examples of the ways cultural traditions furthered class consciousness and political action. For instance, Thompson traces how the social egalitarianism and strong feelings of moral community among rural hand-loom weavers were transmuted into utopian notions for redesigning society, in turn inspiring political activities.[33] Similarly, according to Thompson, "one can see Luddism as a manifestation of a working-class culture of greater independence and complexity than any known to the eighteenth century, for it grew out of "the world of the benefit society, the secret ceremony and oath, the quasi-legal petition to Parliament, the craftsmen's meetings at the house of call."[34] The Luddites used cultural traditions to envision an alternative future, and they tried to revive ancient rights to establish new precedents. At various times their demands included a legal minimum wage; the control of the "sweating" of women or juveniles; arbitration; obligation of masters to find work for skilled men made redundant by machinery; the prohibition of shoddy work; and the right to organize trade unions. Such demands, according to Thompson, "looked forwards, as much as backwards; and they contained within them a shadowy image, not so much of a paternalist, but of a democratic community, in which industrial growth should be regulated according to ethical priorities and the pursuit of profit be subordinated to human needs."[35]

Analytically speaking, Thompson maintains that the new class consciousness and organization of British working people were not directly the result of the Industrial Revolution. The changing productive relations and working conditions of the Industrial Revolution were imposed

> not upon raw material, but upon the free-born Englishman – and the free-born Englishman as Paine had left him or as the Methodists had molded him. The factory hand or stockinger was also the inheritor of Bunyan, of remembered village rights, of notions of equality before the law, of craft traditions. He was the object of massive religious indoctrination and the creator of new political traditions. The working class made itself as much as it was made.[36]

It made itself by using its cultural inheritance to interpret and react to economic transformations and political events.

In sum, Thompson's argument in *The Making of the English Working Class* stresses the importance of cultural resources and human intervention for social change and class politics. But where is the reciprocal analysis of social change – the structured, material limits within which the English working class had to make itself? The absence of any systematic discussion of the ways in which English industrialization concretely affected the given patterns of class and community relations makes it appear that history did not in any way happen behind the backs of the English working class. In his zeal to correct the "objectivist" biases of economic historians and more orthodox Marxists, Thompson fleshed out only one side of the full dialectic of being and consciousness that he theorizes is central to historical process.

Without the structural side of a fuller analysis, moreover, Thompson's argument gives few insights into the weaknesses of the English working class after 1832. It fails to account for why class-conscious actors do not gain their ends, or why some working people may not become collectively conscious and may fail to act together.[37] Thompson gives insufficient attention to those factors that block people from making history as they please: the structural conditions of action, the unintended consequences of action, and the unacknowledged and unconscious factors of motivation.[38] Some of history does happen behind the people's backs, and Thompson's application of his frame of reference in *The Making of the English Working Class* is not helpful in ferreting out these hidden structures and unintended eventuations. Perhaps Thompson needs to be reminded of a quote from his favorite socialist, William Morris: "I . . . pondered how men fight and lose the battle, and the thing they fought for comes about in spite of their defeat, and when it comes, turns out not to be what they meant, and other men have to fight for what they meant under another name."[39]

The Interpretive Logic of Thompson's Historiography

Noticing the culturalist bias and the lack of a structural analysis in Thompson's historical work, some English Marxists have questioned the theoretical relevance and rigor of his contributions. Richard Johnson argues that Thompson's emphasis on experience and culture leads to a principled distrust of theory.[40] Similarly, Perry Anderson suggests that weaknesses in Thompson's method make it inappropriate for developing historical theory.[41] Anderson's judgment may rest on a view that theoretical work is necessarily aimed at establishing causal sequences in history.[42] Anderson is correct in perceiving that Thompson is little interested in causal analysis, but this is not a sufficient reason to dismiss his approach. Whatever the imperfections of *The Making of the English Working Class*, it provides an important example of an interpretive argument that is not causal but brilliantly illuminates the meanings of history in other ways.

The Making of the English Working Class does not in fact aim to explain any particular historical event or outcome. Although Thompson has some ideas about why no revolution occurred in England in 1832, these ideas are not systematically developed, and finding an answer to such a causal question is not the aim of his book. Nor does he seek to explain why Luddism (and other particular social movements) arose and fell in early nineteenth-century England. Thompson does see the spread of Methodism among the laborers after 1795 as related to the English counter-revolution. Yet in a 1968 postscript to the second edition of *The Making of the English Working Class*, Thompson says explicitly that he did not mean to present a causal hypothesis stating that Methodist expansion was the consequence of counter-revolution.[43]

Because he does not ask specific causal questions of the historical data, Thompson does not attempt to validate theoretical hypotheses about causes. The lack of such an explanatory approach hardly deprives Thompson's work of its own kind of theoretical significance. Rather than trying to explain actual historical events or causation, *The Making of the English Working Class* seeks to recapture lost historical possibilities. It starts from a premise that history is open and contingent, that the determining factors might have been different and could be changed in the future. Because the English working people did not make the history they pleased, Thompson believes we have lost any notion of how they did make history. As Eric Hobsbawm put it in an early review of *The Making of the English Working Class*: "Thompson's subject is the attempt of the pre-industrial laborers to remake their shattered world, and not the eventual results – not entirely intended – of their efforts."[44]

Thompson seeks to make sense of the *process* by which a conscious working class was formed in England and, by implication, could be formed elsewhere. Thompson indicates the significant parts of the process, the ways in which they are interrelated, and the ways in which they unfold over time. He does provide explanations but does not link concepts in a causal manner to predict events. Instead, concepts are related to other concepts to present a patterned meaning and to present a moving picture of a whole – whole class, group, or society – over a period of time.

As such, Thompson's discussion of the making of the English working class is an example of what Clifford Geertz calls an interpretive theory. Geertz maintains that this kind of theorizing is especially suited to the analysis of culture, where the essential task

> is not to codify abstract regularities but to make thick description possible, not to generalize across cases but to generalize within them. To generalize within cases is usually called, at least in medicine and depth psychology, clinical inference. Rather than beginning with a set of observations and attempting to subsume them under a governing law, such inference begins with a set of (presumptive) signifiers and attempts to place them within an intelligible frame . . . But the way in which the theory is used – to

ferret out the unapparent import of things – is the same. Thus we are led to the second condition of cultural theory: it is not at least in the strict meaning of the term, predictive . . . It is true that in the clinical style of theoretical formulation, conceptualization is directed toward the task of generating interpretations of matters already in hand, not toward projecting outcomes of experimental manipulations or deducing future states of a determined system. But that does not mean that theory has only to fit (or, more carefully, to generate cogent interpretations of) realities past; it has also to survive – intellectually survive – realities to come . . . The theoretical framework in terms of which an interpretation is made must be capable of continuing to yield defensible interpretations as new social phenomena swim into view.[45]

It is unfortunate that Geertz uses the term "thick description" to denote the central tasks of such theory building. Geertz recognizes that thick description is very different from mere description. Thick description is "really our own constructions of other people's constructions of what they and their compatriots are up to."[46] He also knows that interpretive theory goes beyond description to state "as explicitly as we can manage, what the knowledge thus attained demonstrates about the society in which it is found, and, beyond that, about social life as such."[47] Unfortunately, the term thick description has led those whose conception of theory is drawn exclusively from the causal-predictive model of science to dismiss such interpretation as mere description. Causal theorists charge that Thompson cannot provide hypotheses that can be applied to other working classes, or to the English working class at a different time.

In response to this kind of complaint, critical theorist Jürgen Habermas points out that an interpretive theory of history, like other critical theories, is *not* aimed at helping social scientists in their attempts at greater social control. Rather, it seeks to foster self-consciousness that will make humans into more conscious subjects who can actively affect the future. As Habermas says: "A study of history which restricts itself in a rigorously empirical-scientific manner to the causal explanation of individual events has immediately only retrospective value; knowledge of this type is not suited to application in practical life."[48]

An important key to Thompson's interpretive approach is his understanding of the relationship of historical facts to Marxist (or any other) grand theory. Thompson looks at history not to apply any pregiven theory or to produce a fixed general theory, but to use theoretical ideas in dialogue with the evidence to interpret particular historical processes. As he puts it:

History is not a factory for the manufacture of Grand Theory, like some Concorde of the global air; nor is it an assembly-line for the production of midget theories in series. Nor yet is it some gigantic experimental station in which theory of foreign manufacture can be "applied," "tested," and "confirmed." That is not its business at all. Its business is to recover, to "explain" and to "understand" its object: real history.[49]

Thompson criticizes and rejects those sociologists and historians who look at historical data only as facts to illustrate their theories. Here the theorist forgets that the historical subject has concepts and values that are also important. Thompson criticizes John Foster (a Marxist historian) and Neil Smelser (a functionalist sociologist) for having developed a model from contemporary theoretical concerns (Leninist and Parsonian, respectively), which they then imposed on the Industrial Revolution without dialogue with the cultural concepts held by those who actually lived through these historical changes. In Thompson's view: "Foster is a platonist Marxist; the model – of the 'true' or 'correct' formation of class organization, consciousness, strategies and goals – precedes the evidence and the evidence is organized in conformity with it."[50] For similar reasons, Thompson criticizes Perry Anderson for imposing the model of the French Revolution on nineteenth-century English history.[51] Criticizing other historians of eighteenth-century England, Thompson observes: "The error most common today is that of bringing to the definition of eighteenth-century popular culture, antitheses (industrial/pre-industrial; modern/traditional; 'mature'/'primitive' working class) inappropriate because they entail reading back into a prior society categories for which that society had no resources and that culture no terms."[52]

Thompson does not commit the opposite empiricist error of believing that the facts speak for themselves. He wants the historian to work hard to enable historical subjects to find their own voices, but he knows that "what they are able to 'say' and some part of their vocabulary is determined by the questions which the historian proposes. They cannot 'speak' until they have been 'asked.' "[53] Thompson also knows that the historians can never shed their own historically specific values and concepts. Historians can never completely escape their own world nor totally empathize with their subjects. Hence, Thompson continually stresses the necessity of dialogue with historical sources and subjects and with the interpretations of other historians. Thompson implicitly accepts Hans Gadamer's point that the meaning of a historical text does not reside in the communicative intent of its creator, but in the mediation between the text and those who understand it from the context of a different tradition.[54]

Thompson recognizes that most historical data or facts are themselves conceptual – people's ideas about themselves, their world, and its process. The social sciences, as Anthony Giddens emphasizes, involve a double hermeneutic, linking their theories and frames of meaning with those that are already a constituent part of social life. "Sociology, unlike natural sciences, stands in a subject-subject relation to its field of study, not a subject-object relation; it deals with a pre-interpreted world, in which the meanings developed by active subjects actually enter into the actual constitution or production of that world."[55]

Because of this dialogue between the theorist's concepts and those of the historical actor and because Thompson is investigating historical process, he emphasizes that theoretical concepts must be "elastic" – open to historical redefinition without becoming merged in the historically specific.[56] Only such elastic concepts are appropriate for "the scrutiny of 'facts' which, even in the moment of interrogation, change their form (or retain their form but change their 'meanings'), or dissolve into other facts; concepts appropriate to the handling of evidence not capable of static conceptual representation but only as manifestation or as contradiction."[57] Paul Feyerabend, the philosopher of science, agrees with Thompson that a researcher "must never try to make a concept clearer than is suggested by the material. It is this material and not his logical intuition that decides the content of the concepts."[58] Using such elastic theoretical concepts in dialogue with either the common sense concepts of historical actors or the theoretical concepts of another historical period, the historian comes to understand and interpret history. At the same time, the historian's own conceptual horizons are thrown into relief and come to critical self-consciousness.[59]

Thompson's antipositivism has much in common with other European thinkers who sought to revise Marxism, especially Sartre, members of the Frankfurt school (Adorno, Horheimer, Marcuse, and Habermas), and their younger followers in critical theory. Yet all these intellectuals have their roots in philosophy and in the "great tradition" of European culture. In contrast, Thompson's commitment to the "little traditions" of English popular culture and his practice as a historian make his work both more accessible and more relevant to historical sociologists.

To illustrate the nature of interpretive theory in action, we can look more closely at some of Thompson's interpretations in *The Making of the*

English Working Class. Many commentators consider Thompson's reinterpretation of the Luddite movement in early nineteenth-century England to be one of the most interesting and important parts of his
study. Thompson rejects the notion, widely accepted in both popular
and scholarly history, that the Luddites engaged in mob machine
breaking, reacting emotionally and irrationally to inevitable industrial
progress. Because the Luddites (like many other popular movements
and historical actors) did not leave good records of their motivations
and actions, Thompson and other historians have to sift through a host
of very inadequate source materials. To compensate for the lack of
direct historical evidence, Thompson looks at the economic and political context of those groups from which Luddites were drawn, and
inferentially reasons about how people with their traditions, values,
and context would have been likely to react to the experience of industrialization. Such an analytic procedure does not rest on the historian's
ability to empathize, but it does involve taking the culture of that
historical time seriously and attempting to understand how such
people evaluated and understood their life situation.

This method led Thompson to reject the conventional picture of Luddism as a blind opposition to machinery and to offer a new interpretation: Luddism rejected the social organization and values of emerging
industrial capitalism. As Thompson comments:

> We are so accustomed to the notion that it was both inevitable
> and "progressive" that trade should have been freed in the early
> 19th century from "restrictive practices," that it requires an effort
> of imagination to understand that the "free" factory-owner or
> large hosier or cotton-manufacturer, who built his fortune by . . .
> unrestricted competition, beating-down wages, undercutting his
> rivals, and undermining standards of craftsmanship . . . was re-
> garded not only with jealousy but as a man engaging in immoral
> and illegal practices.[60]

In a similar way, Thompson presents an interpretation of the meaning of Methodism for workers undergoing the Industrial Revolution.
He states: "Too much writing on Methodism commences with the
assumption that we all know what Methodism was, and gets on with
discussing its growth-rates or its organizational structures. But we
cannot deduce the quality of the Methodist experience from this kind
of evidence."[61] Thompson's interpretation of Methodism illustrates
another aspect of his methodological approach – its dialectical logic. To
understand this, we will look more closely at his explorations of
Methodism.

The Dialectical Uses of the Past

An interpretive argument does *not* relate concepts in a formal and hierarchical logic so as to deduce the more specific from the more general. Rather, an interpretive argument, especially one developed to fullest advantage, produces dialectical insights into the past. For example, in Thompson's view, Methodism had a dialectical relationship to class consciousness among English working people, for this religious movement had the contradictory potential both to foster and to block working-class consciousness. Interpretive theory traces out the dialectical relationship, but does not in itself explain why the dialectic was tipped one way or another in the past, nor predict which way it might work in the future. Thompson believes that such a dialectical logic is distinct from deductive logic and is especially appropriate to an analysis of historical process. It is

> a logic appropriate to phenomena which are always in movement, which evince – even in a single moment – contradictory manifestations . . . As Sartre has commented: "History is not order. It is disorder: a rational disorder. At the very moment when it maintains order, i.e. structure, history is already on the way to undoing it."[62]

In *The Making of the English Working Class* Thompson dialectically emphasizes both the liberating and reactionary potential of dissenting Protestantism, and especially of Methodism. He stresses the tensions in Methodist beliefs and practices between authoritarian and democratic tendencies. On the one hand, the early Methodist societies promoted genuine fellowship and found a place for humble men as local preachers and class leaders. Such experiences encouraged working-class people to learn to read and gave them self-respect and experience in speaking and in organization. On the other hand, Methodism was hostile to intellectual inquiry and to artistic values and channeled social energies denied an outlet in public life to emotional onanism. "Here was a cult of 'love' which feared love's effective expression, either as sexual love or in any social form which might irritate relations with Authority. Its authentic language of devotion was that of sexual sublimation streaked through with masochism."[63]

Even though some Methodists became Jacobins, Luddites, and working class activists of other sorts, Methodism also fostered the submission of many workers to the work discipline of the early factories and contributed to counter-revolutionary political movements in England after the French Revolution. Although Methodism started as a religion of the poor, its authoritarian church structure fostered submission and its Sunday schools imposed a discipline on children that Thompson labels "religious terrorism."[64] But Thompson does not believe that a doctrine can be imposed effectively only from above. Rather, he hypothesizes that Methodism had several positive appeals to the poor, which fostered its acceptance. Not only did it offer a new community to those whose traditional ties had been uprooted by the Industrial Revolution, but more importantly the extreme emotionalism of its revivalist meetings and preachers offered important psychological outlets in a sexually and emotionally repressive society.[65]

In a more recent analysis of eighteenth-century England, *Whigs and Hunters*, Thompson similarly analyzes the dialectical relationship of law to class power, developing in the process an interpretation that has general implications for social theory:

> We reach, then, not a simple conclusion (law = class power) but a complex and contradictory one. On the one hand, it is true that the law did mediate existent class relations to the advantage of the rulers; not only is this so, but as the century advanced the law became a superb instrument by which these rulers were able to impose new definitions of property to their even greater advantage, as in the extinction by law of indefinite agrarian use-rights and in the furtherance of enclosure. On the other hand, the law mediated these class relations through legal forms, which imposed, again and again, inhibitions upon the actions of the rulers . . . And the rulers were, in serious senses, whether willingly or unwillingly, the prisoners of their own rhetoric; they played the games of power according to rules which suited them, but they could not break those rules or the whole game would be thrown away. And, finally, so far from the ruled shrugging off this rhetoric as a hypocrisy, some part of it at least was taken over as part of the rhetoric of the plebian crowd, of the "free-born Englishman" with his inviolable privacy, his habeas corpus, his equality before the law.[66]

Interestingly enough, when Thompson wrote his first book on *William Morris,* he had not yet developed such sophisticated theoretical insight into the dialectical potential of cultural traditions. Even in his new postscript to the 1976 edition of the book, Thompson still does not realize the lack of a fully dialectical analysis. Here Thompson simply restates his thesis that Morris became an original socialist thinker who made an "independent derivation of Communism out of the logic of the Romantic tradition."[67] This tradition gave Morris aspiration, moral realism, and hope, which led to a critique of capitalism and a realistic, utopian vision of the future.[68] For Thompson, there is a one-way trajectory linking Morris's early romantic poetry and novels to his career as a designer, and finally to his socialism. Yet, in emphasizing this progressive transition, Thompson ignores some of the facts of Morris's life that he reports – the despair, escapism, and individualism he finds in Morris's early life and in the poetry and novels of this period. Nor does Thompson attempt to explain why nearly all of Morris's early circle of romantic artists and writers gave up in despair or became conservative rather than radical.[69]

While accepting the analysis by Thompson and others of the progressive potential embedded in the romantic rejection of capitalism,[70] we must remember with Karl Mannheim and those who analyze the roots of Nazi culture that there is also a reactionary potential in this tradition. Even though the reactionary potential in Morris's romantic poetry and novels did not become activated in his case, we must recognize its existence. One can see a contradictory trajectory of hope and despair – both a progressive and reactionary impulse – latent in Morris's romanticism. An awareness of this contradictory potential leads one to ask another question: What in Morris's experience led him to overcome despair and embody hope in political action? Using Thompson's own historical narrative, let me attempt to expand the explanatory potential of his analysis.

The distinction that Karl Mannheim makes between a "traditionalist" and a "conservative" is very useful in beginning to answer this question. Mannheim sees a traditionalist as someone who

> does not go back to the past, he lives in the remnants of the past which still exist in the present. He lives in them and his thought arises out of them. The past is not something that lies behind him; it is an integral part of his life, not as a memory and a return, but as the intensified experience of something that he still possesses and is merely in danger of losing.[71]

It is in Morris' career as a designer, interior decorator, tapestry weaver, and preserver of ancient buildings – and not in his writing of romantic poetry and novels – that he embodies a living past. In this work he keeps alive cultural values that are an alternative to those of capitalism.

Morris organized his decorating firm on the model of the artisanal shop. All workers were craftspeople and artists, and the master worked beside his apprentices. Although trying to maintain a precapitalist form of work, Morris's firm did not copy ancient designs but integrated traditional with innovative styles. In this firm the upper-middle-class Morris was able to break through the strict class segregation of Victorian society. The living craft tradition also provided him a standard for rejecting the shoddy product, the alienating and exploitative process of capitalist production, as well as Victorian social relations. Here Morris first developed his love for "living art and living history."[72]

The very success of his firm led Morris to see the impossibility of an individual solution to the despised characteristics of capitalist society. Morris started his firm not as a commercial venture, but as his

> holy crusade against the age: it was intended to fight the flood of philistinism in one field of Victorian life, to inject into the very sources of production, pleasurable and creative labor, to re-create conditions of artistic production found in medieval times. But the age had not flinched in the face of this form of attack. The slums grew, and the respectable suburban jerry-building thrived.[73]

Morris became enraged when he found commercial manufacturers turning out cheap imitation-Morris products.[74] As a result, he wrote to a friend in 1883:

> In spite of all the success I have had, I have not failed to be conscious that the art I have been helping to produce would fall with the death of a few of us who really care about it, that a reform in art which is founded on individualism must perish with the individuals who have set it going. Both my historical studies and my practical conflict with the philistinism of modern society may have forced on me the conviction that art cannot have a real life and growth under the present system of commercialism and profit-mongering.[75]

Morris's transition from political dissent to political action began with his founding of the Committee to Save Ancient Buildings, an organization he dubbed "Anti-Scrape." This activity brought him into direct conflict with capitalist society. Faced with the jealous property rights of capitalism, he had to argue that irrespective of their position at law, " 'our ancient historical monuments' are national property."[76]

Morris also embodies a "living past" in his utopian novel, *News from Nowhere*, written after he became a socialist and depicting life in the communist society of the future. As Thompson says: "Never for long in *News from Nowhere*, does Morris allow us to forget this sense of tension between the real and the ideal . . . We are made to question continually our own society, our own values and lives. This is why the story engages our feelings. We cannot sit back as spectators, looking at a pretty never-never land."[77] Moreover, in this utopia "Morris never proposes that men may live in any way they may suppose that they might choose, according to any value-system imaginable. The indications are placed within a firm controlling historical and political argument."[78] Thompson calls this "romanticism inverted," yet "it is still a Utopia which only a writer nurtured in the romantic tradition could have conceived – a writer ever conscious of the contrast between the 'ideal' and the 'real.' "[79]

In contrast to Thompson, I would argue that Morris's ability to fight as a socialist for the ideal in the real world was possible because his romanticism did not remain embodied in fantasy or in writing. Thompson's emphasis on the dialectical logic of historical process, which opens up history to indeterminate outcomes, does not preclude a more structural analysis – one like that sketched here on the specific conditions of Morris's life that led him to socialism, while many other English romantic intellectuals became conservative.[80]

Thompson's dialectical analysis of both the progressive and reactionary potential in nineteenth-century Methodism could also be combined with an analysis of why the reactionary structural potential was stronger in this period. But such an analysis might require comparisons with other periods or national cases to help tease out the structural conditions favoring or inhibiting alternative uses of the resources of Methodist religious culture. Thompson himself never makes such cross-national or cross-temporal comparisons for analytic purposes. Yet others could. A structural analysis, developed through historically grounded comparisons, could help us understand what types of people under what conditions we can "expect" to use cultural resources toward reactionary and not progressive ends. Too often followers of Thompson have looked in other historical contexts only at the positive ways that precapitalist culture has motivated anticapitalist class consciousness.[81] They have failed to grasp and imitate Thompson's best dialectical interpretations of cultural traditions, and they have failed to improve upon his approach through more thorough analyses of the relationships of structural conditions and contradictory cultural potentials.

Conclusion

Both in his historical studies and in his theoretical essays, Thompson has developed arguments polemically, in self-conscious opposition to the positions of other historians and theorists. In the preceding pages, I have presented and sympathetically criticized Thompson's arguments without elaborating those of his opponents. (See the selected bibliography for references to the series of debates with Perry Anderson, Leszek Kolakowski, and Louis Althusser.) Engagement in lively and often heated debates pushed Thompson to explicate his theory and method. In stressing the importance of historical process and human agency, Thompson breaks with the static and deterministic nature of structuralist Marxism. In discarding a base/superstructure model of society, Thompson integrates a consideration of culture and consciousness into material life.

In so strongly opposing economist and structuralist Marxism and in championing a theoretical method to analyze culture and incorporate human agency, Thompson fails sufficiently to integrate his own contributions with a properly reformed structural analysis. How do we engage in a dialogue between our theoretical concepts and those of our historical subjects while also trying to extricate the unintended consequences, unconscious or ideologically obscured motives, and hidden structural limits to historical actions? How does the theorist integrate a consideration of structural limits with an understanding of the logic of process open to human intervention?

Thompson begins to make this kind of integration in his most recent investigations of the logic of Cold War. Here he presents a structural analysis of the nuclear arms race between East and West, which he sees leading towards exterminism. In this examination of the deadly dynamic of the Cold War, Thompson breaks fully with Marxist concepts. He rejects class analysis, a theory of imperialism, or a theory of the dynamics of the capitalist economy as inadequate to explain the arms race. At the same time, Thompson makes compelling use of the interpretive principles developed in his previous work. He demonstrates how the material reality of nuclear holocaust is being structurally determined as much by our culture and language as by nuclear technology:

> The deformation of culture commences within language itself. It makes possible a disjunction between the rationality and moral sensibility of individual persons and the effective political and military process. A certain kind of "realist" and "technical" vocabulary effects a closure which seals out the imagination, and prevents the reason from following the most manifest sequence of cause and consequence. It habituates the mind to nuclear holocaust by reducing everything to a flat level of normality. By habituating us to certain expectations, it not only encourages resignation – it also beckons on the event.[82]

The anger and scorn that Thompson previously directed at the anti-humanism and scholasticism of structural Marxists he now turns more appropriately to dissecting the irrational logic of deterrence theory. Yet his belief in the ultimate importance of human agency and his historical studies of those who have summoned reserves of spirit to transcend material reality enable him to oppose, both intellectually and politically, what he theorizes is the structural probability of the destruction of Northern civilization.

Ultimately, Thompson may be most remembered for this current antinuclear work. Meanwhile, his contributions continue to have an impact on the academy. Applications of his ideas to U.S. history and to the study of women in history have already begun to rework his arguments about class consciousness and extend his theoretical method to new terrains of social experience.

Little has been said here about Thompson's explicitly political analysis in *The Making of the English Working Class*. Rereading the book from this perspective would highlight his repeated emphasis on the exclusion of the English working people from political rights and on the politically repressive reactions of the upper-class English to popular aspirations during and immediately after the French Revolution.[83] The most innovative theoretical developments made by American followers of Thompson develop further the explicitly political aspects of his approach to class consciousness. Eugene Genovese, in applying Thompson's method to the analysis of U.S. slavery, integrates Thompson's approach with a theory of hegemony borrowed from Antonio Gramsci.[84] And when Ira Katznelson uses *The Making of the English Working Class* as inspiration to study the development of working-class consciousness in urban America, it becomes clear how important political structures are in shaping the experience out of which workers construct the nationally specific meaning of class.[85] Further comparative, cross-national historical analysis could extend this potential for political analysis in Thompson's work.

Although women are historical actors in *The Making of the English Working Class* and in others of Thompson's historical works, including "The Moral Economy of the Eighteenth Century Crowd," gender never becomes a theoretical category in his work. There is no consideration of whether women in the early English working class had the same experiences and outlooks as working-class men. Nor does Thompson ever ponder how the existence of two genders in the working class might have affected its culture, consciousness, and struggles. Despite this absence of a feminist perspective, Thompson has had an important

Ellen Kay Trimberger

impact on the development of feminist history and theory in Britain. Sheila Rowbothom, Barbara Taylor, Anna Davin, Sally Alexander, and Judy Walkowitz all acknowledge their debt to Thompson.[86]

Thompson's emphasis on the centrality of experience and the model of his interpretive theoretical approach are indeed especially applicable to the study of women. For example, two American feminist historians (with no explicit recognition of Thompson) summarize a decade of developments in women's history with the observation that "the most striking and characteristic advances in the new women's history have occurred in the intersection of the themes of women's experience in the family, women's roles as economic producers, and the development of women's consciousness."[87] As we have seen, experience as mediating between social being and consciousness is at the heart of Thompson's distinctive approach to Marxist social history. Thus, a more explicit exchange between feminists and Thompson's interpretive approach could be very fruitful.

The legacies of E. P. Thompson's scholarship, like the legacies of the actors whose outlooks and activities he has so richly illuminated in his historical studies, remain open to development and change. "The past is not just dead, inert, confining; it carries signs and evidences also of creative resources which can sustain the present and prefigure possibility."[88] In these words, Thompson has made an important point that applies as well to both the strengths and the limitations of his own work in social history, Marxist theory, and methods of historical analysis.

Notes

I benefited greatly from comments by participants at the Harvard Conference in October 1979. I especially appreciated the postconference commentaries sent by Bruce Johnson and Theda Skocpol. Theda's detailed editing enhanced the coherence of the essay. In addition, the following colleagues and friends provided supportive enthusiasm along with helpful criticism: Paul Breines, Temma Kaplan, Naomi Katz, Tom Laquer, Mark Poster, Judy Stacey, and Alice Wexler.
  1. E. P. Thompson, *The Making of the English Working Class* (New York: Vintage Books, 1963), p. 12.
  2. It is threatening to many of us social scientists to have to admit that one can write as well as Thompson does and also be a theorist.
  3. In a recent article, Alan Dawley discusses Thompson's influence on American historians. See "E. P. Thompson and the Peculiarities of the Americans," *Radical History Review* 19 (Winter 1978–79): 33–59.
  4. Positivism implies that the study of society can be scientific, that social science can develop laws of prediction. The empiricist believes that facts create theory by disclosing their meanings independent of any rigorous conceptual work.
  5. Michael Merrill, "Interview with E. P. Thompson," *Radical History Review* 3 (4) (1976): 4.

238

6. Alvin Gouldner, *The Coming Crisis of Western Sociology* (New York: Avon Books, 1970), p. 484.
7. Merrill, "Interview with E. P. Thompson," pp. 10–11.
8. Ibid., pp. 13–14.
9. Eric Hobsbawm, "The Historians' Group of the Communist Party," in *Rebels and Their Causes: Essays in Honour of A. L. Morton*, ed. Maurice Cornforth (London: Lawrence & Wishart, 1978), p. 31.
10. Ibid., pp. 43–44.
11. Merrill, "Interview with E. P. Thompson," pp. 14, 25.
12. See John Saville, "The XXth Congress and the British Communist Party," *Socialist Register* (London: Merlin Press, 1976), pp. 1–23.
13. David R. Holden, "The First New Left in Britain, 1956–62" (Ph.D. diss., University of Wisconsin, 1976), p. 105.
14. Ibid., chap. 4.
15. Ibid., p. 262.
16. E. P. Thompson, "An Open Letter to Leszek Kolakowski," *The Socialist Register* (London: Merlin Press, 1973), pp. 9–10.
17. Holden, "First New Left in Britain," p. 341.
18. Perry Anderson, in a new book, apologizes for such inferences and gives his version of what happened in the break with Thompson. See *Arguments Within English Marxism* (London: New Left Books, 1980), chap. 5.
19. Thompson's personal intensity and emotion may also have helped polarize the British intellectual left, with less beneficial results.
20. Thompson refers to his brother as an inspiration in *Beyond the Cold War* (New York: Pantheon Books, 1982), p. 157.
21. Foreword to *Exterminism and Cold War* (London: New Left Books, 1982), p. ix.
22. Ibid., p. 329.
23. Merrill, "Interview with E. P. Thompson," p. 23.
24. E. P. Thompson, "The Poverty of Theory: Or an Orrery of Errors," in *The Poverty of Theory and Other Essays* (London: Merlin Press, 1978), p. 257. Please note that all references in this chapter are to the British edition of *The Poverty of Theory*. The American edition, published by Monthly Review Press, has different pagination.
25. Ibid., p. 200.
26. Ibid., p. 356.
27. Thompson, *English Working Class*, pp. 9–10.
28. Thompson, "Poverty of Theory," p. 280.
29. Thompson, *English Working Class*, p. 12.
30. Ibid., p. 232.
31. Ibid., p. 212.
32. Ibid., p. 194.
33. Ibid., p. 295.
34. Ibid., p. 601.
35. Ibid., p. 552.
36. Ibid., p. 194.
37. Perry Anderson makes similar criticisms, among others, in *Arguments Within English Marxism*, chap. 2. Craig Calhoun in *The Question of Class Struggle* (Chicago: University of Chicago Press, 1982) also emphasizes the lack of structural analysis in *The Making of the English Working Class*. In addition, he presents a sophisticated critique of Thompson's theoretical use of Marxian class analysis.
38. Anthony Giddens, *Studies in Social and Political Theory* (New York: Basic Books, 1976), p. 128.

Ellen Kay Trimberger

39. E. P. Thompson, *William Morris: From Romantic to Revolutionary* (New York: Pantheon books, 1976), p. 722.
40. Richard Johnson, "Thompson, Genovese, and Socialist-Humanist History," *History Workshop Journal* 6 (1978), p. 84.
41. Anderson, *Arguments Within English Marxism*, p. 58.
42. Ibid., p. 98.
43. This 1968 postscript to the second edition of *English Working Class* is only in the English edition, published by Penguin Books, and not in the American edition, published by Vintage. The citation is to page 919.
44. Eric Hobsbawm, "Organized Orphans," a review of *The Making of the English Working Class, New Statesman* 66 (November 29, 1963): 7.
45. Clifford Geertz, *The Interpretation of Cultures* (New York: Basic Books, 1973), pp. 26–27.
46. Ibid., p. 9.
47. Ibid., p. 27.
48. Jürgen Habermas, "The Analytic Theory of Science and Dialectics," in *The Positivist Disputes in German Sociology*, ed. Theodore Adorno et al. (London: Heinemann, 1976), p. 141.
49. Thompson, "The Poverty of Theory," p. 238.
50. E. P. Thompson, "Testing Class Struggle," review of John Foster, *Class Struggle and the Industrial Revolution, The Times Higher Education Supplement*, April 8, 1974, p. 1.
51. Thompson, "Peculiarities of the English."
52. E. P. Thompson, "Eighteenth-Century English Society: Class Struggle Without Class?" *Social History* 3 (2) (May 1978): 152.
53. Thompson, "The Poverty of Theory," pp. 222–23.
54. Editor's Introduction to Hans Gadamer, *Philosophical Hermeneutics* (Berkeley: University of California Press, 1976).
55. Anthony Giddens, *New Rules of the Sociological Method* (New York: Basic Books, 1976), p. 146.
56. Thompson, "The Poverty of Theory," p. 238.
57. Ibid., p. 237.
58. Paul Feyerabend, *Against Method* (London: Verso Editions, 1975), p. 201.
59. Gadamer, *Philosophical Hermeneutics*, p. xxi.
60. Thompson, *English Working Class*, pp. 549–50.
61. Ibid., Postscript to 1968 English edition, p. 918.
62. Thompson, "The Poverty of Theory," p. 230.
63. Thompson, *English Working Class*, pp. 40–41.
64. Ibid., p. 375.
65. Ibid., p. 380.
66. E. P. Thompson, *Whigs and Hunters* (New York: Pantheon Books, 1976), pp. 263–64.
67. Thompson, *William Morris*, p. 802.
68. Ibid., pp. 791–92.
69. Ibid., p. 86.
70. See Paul Breines, "Marxism, Romanticism, and the Case of George Lukács," *Studies in Romanticism* 10 (4) (Fall 1977): 473–89; and Alvin Gouldner, "Romanticism and Classicism: Deep Structures in Social Science," in *For Sociology* (New York: Basic Books, 1973), pp. 321–66.
71. Karl Mannheim, "Conservative Thought," in *Essays in Sociology and Social Psychology* (New York: Oxford University Press, 1953), p. 140.
72. Thompson, *William Morris*, p. 236.
73. Ibid., p. 248.

74. Ibid., p. 249.
75. Ibid., p. 98.
76. Ibid., p. 234.
77. Ibid., p. 694.
78. Ibid., p. 803.
79. Ibid., pp. 695–96.
80. Thompson himself has never repudiated causal theory. In the "Poverty of Theory," he says that the historian's "hypotheses are advanced to explain this particular social formation in the past, that particular sequence of causation" (pp. 238–39).
81. Three followers of Thompson who make this mistake are Calhoun, Scott, and Hearn. See Craig Calhoun, *The Question of Class Struggle*; James C. Scott, "Protest and Profanation: Agrarian Revolt and the Little Tradition," *Theory and Society* 4 (1, 2) (1977): 1–38, 159–210; Frank Hearn, "Remembrance and Critique: The Uses of the Past for Discrediting the Present and Anticipating the Future," *Politics and Society* 5 (2) (1975): 201–28. Judith Stacey, viewing traditional culture from a feminist perspective, has a more dialectical approach in "China's Socialist Revolution, Peasant Families, and the Uses of the Past," *Theory and Society* 9 (2) (1980): 269–82.
82. Thompson, "A Letter to America," in *Protest and Survive*, ed. E. P. Thompson and Dan Smith (New York: Monthly Review Press, 1981), p. 41.
83. Theda Skocpol made this point in a personal communication.
84. Eugene Genovese, *Roll, Jordan, Roll: The World the Slaves Made* (New York: Vintage Books, 1972).
85. Ira Katznelson, *City Trenches: Urban Politics and the Patterning of Class in the United States* (New York: Pantheon Books, 1981).
86. Sheila Rowbotham acknowledges her debt to Thompson in the introduction to *Hidden From History* (New York: Pantheon Books, 1974). In personal conversations, Judy Walkowitz and Sally Alexander stressed Thompson's positive influence on their work and on that of Barbara Taylor and Anna Davin. See Judith Walkowitz, *Prostitution and Victorian Society* (New York: Cambridge University Press, 1980); Sally Alexander, "Women's Work in Nineteenth-Century London," In *The Rights and Wrongs of Women*, ed. Juliet Mitchell and Ann Oakley (New York: Penguin Books, 1976); Anna Davin, "Feminism and Labor History," and Barbara Taylor, "Socialist Feminism: Utopian or Scientific," both in *People's History and Socialist Theory*, ed. Raphael Samuel (London: Routledge & Kegan Paul, 1981).
87. Nancy F. Cott and Elizabeth H. Pleck, eds., *A Heritage of Her Own* (New York: Simon & Schuster, 1979), pp. 18–19.
88. E. P. Thompson, "The Politics of Theory," in *People's History and Socialist Theory*, pp. 407–8.

Selected Bibliography

I have organized selected works by E. P. Thompson into several categories. A more complete bibliography can be found at the end of Perry Anderson, *Arguments Within English Marxism* (London: New Left Books, 1980). Thompson's books have been discussed in my text; all of them are important and interesting for the historical sociologist. Thompson's historical essays illustrate many of the same substantive historical and theoretical issues raised in the books, but in shorter texts. "Caudwell" is especially relevant to those interested in cultural theory and the study of ideology. "Eighteenth-Century English Society: Class

Ellen Kay Trimberger

Struggle Without Class?" is important for class analysis. As an oppositional thinker, Thompson often articulates important theoretical ideas in reviews, so a selection is listed here. Thompson's political essays are probably less relevant to the historical sociologist, but they could be of interest to scholars tracing the history of the British left or to anyone interested in a more in-depth study of Thompson's values and politics. Thompson's debates with other Marxists are extremely important for the articulation of his theoretical position. I have listed the most important works on both sides of these debates. Finally, I have included a short bibliography of additional commentaries on Thompson's work.

BOOKS BY E. P. THOMPSON

William Morris: From Romantic to Revolutionary. New York: Pantheon Books, 1976. Reprinted from the 1955 edition with a new postscript.
The Making of the English Working Class. New York: Vintage Books, 1963.
Whigs and Hunters. New York: Pantheon Books, 1976.
The Poverty of Theory and Other Essays. London: Merlin Press, 1978. New York: Monthly Review Press, 1979.
Writing by Candlelight. New York: Monthly Review Press, 1981.
Protest and Survive, edited with Dan Smith. New York: Monthly Review Press, 1981.
Beyond the Cold War. New York: Pantheon Books. 1982.

HISTORICAL ESSAYS BY E. P. THOMPSON

"Time, Work-Discipline and Industrial Capitalism." *Past and Present* (38) (December 1967):56–97.
"The Moral Economy of the English Crowd in the Eighteenth Century." *Past and Present* 50 (February 1971):76–136.
"Patrician Society, Plebian Culture." *Journal of Social History* 7 (Summer 1974):382–405.
"The Crime of Anonymity." In *Albion's Fatal Tree,* edited by Douglass Hay et al., pp. 255–308. New York: Pantheon Books, 1975.
"Caudwell." *The Socialist Register.* London: Merlin Press, 1977, pp. 228–76.
"Eighteenth-Century English Society: Class Struggle Without Class?" *Social History* 3 (2) (May 1978):133–65.

REVIEWS BY E. P. THOMPSON

"Anthropology and the Discipline of Historical Context." Review of Alan Macfalane, *The Family Life of Ralph Josseline,* and Keith Thomas, *Religion and the Decline of Magic. Midland History* 1(3) (Spring 1972):41–55.
"Testing Class Struggle." Review of John Foster, *Class Struggle and the Industrial Revolution. The Times Higher Educational Supplement,* March 8, 1974, p. 50.
"A Nice Place to Visit." Review of Raymond Williams, *The Country and the City. New York Review of Books,* February 6, 1975:34–37.
"On History, Sociology and Historical Relevance." Review of Robert Moore, *Pit-Men, Preachers and Politics. British Journal of Sociology* 27 (3) (1976):387–402.
"Happy Families." Review of Lawrence Stone, *The Family, Sex and Marriage in England, 1500–1800. New Society* 41 (77a) (September 1977):499–501.
"Sold Like a Sheep for £1." Review of George Rude, *Protest and Punishment. New Society,* December 14, 1978:645–48.

POLITICAL ESSAYS BY E. P. THOMPSON

"Socialist Humanism: An Epistle to the Philistines." *The New Reasoner* 1 (1) (Summer 1957): 105–43.

"Agency and Choice." *The New Reasoner* 1 (5) (Summer 1959):89–106.

"Commitment in Politics." *Universities and Left Review* 6 (Spring 1959):50–55.

"Revolution." *New Left Review* 3 (May-June 1960):3–9.

"Revolution Again." *New Left Review* 6 (November-December 1960):18–31. *Out of Apathy.* Ed. E. P. Thompson. London: New Left Books, 1960.

"The State Versus Its Enemies." *New Society,* October 19, 1978:127–30.

"The Secret State." *Race and Class* 20 (3) (1979):219–42.

"Notes on Exterminism: The Last Stage of Civilization." *New Left Review* 121 (May-June 1980):3–31.

"A Letter to America." *The Nation,* January 24, 1981:68–93.

THOMPSON'S DEBATES WITH OTHER MARXISTS

Anderson, Perry. "Origins of the Present Crisis." *New Left Review* 23 (1964):26–53.

Nairn, Tom. "The English Working Class." *New Left Review* 24 (1964):43–57.

Thompson, E. P., "The Peculiarities of the English." *The Socialist Register.* London: Merlin Press, 1965, pp. 311–63.

Anderson, Perry. "Socialism and Pseudo-Empiricism." *New Left Review* 35 (1966):2–42.

Thompson, E. P. "An Open Letter to Leszek Kolakowski." *The Socialist Register.* London: Merlin Press, 1973, pp. 1–100.

Kolakowski, Leszek. "My Correct Views on Everything." *The Socialist Register.* London: Merlin Press, 1974, pp. 1–20.

Thompson, E. P., "The Poverty of Theory: Or an Orrery of Errors." In *The Poverty of Theory and Other Essays.* London: Merlin Press, 1978, pp. 193–397.

Johnson, Richard. "Thompson, Genovese and Socialist-Humanist History." *History Workshop Journal* 6 (1978):79–100; and subsequent responses in issues 7, 8, 9.

Anderson, Perry. *Arguments Within English Marxism.* London: New Left Books, 1980.

Thompson, E. P.; Johnson, Richard; Hall, Stuart; and Samuel, Raphael. "Debates around the Poverty of Theory." In *People's History and Socialist Theory,* edited by Raphael Samuel. London: Routledge & Kegan Paul, 1981.

OTHER DISCUSSIONS OF THOMPSON'S WORK

Calhoun, Craig. *The Question of Class Struggle.* Chicago: University of Chicago Press, 1982.

Dawley, Alan. "E. P. Thompson and the Peculiarities of the Americans." *Radical History Review* 19 (Winter 1978–79):33–59.

Kazin, Michael. "European Nuclear Disarmament: An Interview with E. P. Thompson." *The Socialist Review* 58 (July-August 1981):9–34.

Merrill, Michael. "Interview with E. P. Thompson." *Radical History Review* 3 (4) (1976):4–25.

Palmer, Bryan. *The Making of E. P. Thompson: Marxism, Humanism and History* (Toronto: New Hogtown Press, 1981).

8. Charles Tilly's Collective Action

LYNN HUNT

There is always something foolhardy about analyzing the work of an author who is in the prime of productivity, but discussing Charles Tilly calls for more than the usual caveats. No single piece stands out as *the* representative Charles Tilly work, yet the size and rate of growth of his production makes any global treatment impossible. In their emphases, Tilly's books and articles range from the clearly delimited historical case analysis of *The Vendée* to the broad theoretical discussion of *From Mobilization to Revolution.*[1] Moreover, Tilly's impact on historical sociology is by no means limited to his published scholarly work, for he is unusually influential as a teacher and collaborator. Much of this influence can be attributed to Tilly's distinctive research style and in particular to his creation of a present-day atelier or historical-sociological workshop at the University of Michigan.[2]

The Center for Research on Social Organization has provided Tilly with a research format that is unique among historical sociologists. With extensive government funding he has been able to initiate long-term, quantitative projects that far exceed the resources available to scholars working in a more artisanal mode.[3] The Center framework fosters collaborative efforts, and in recent years Tilly has published the results of several such endeavors, e.g., *Strikes in France* with Edward Shorter and *The Rebellious Century* with Louise Tilly and Richard Tilly.[4] Each year the Center has formally brought together about seventy-five people – postdoctoral fellows, staff, research assistants, graduate students, and faculty – and informally it attracts many others. This beehive of activity has profoundly shaped Tilly's own work. The Center's research programs have been eclectic, ranging from experimental studies of encounters with unjust authority to historical investigations of tax rebellions in seventeenth-century France. Two features of the Center's diverse programs stand out, however: (1) the emphasis on problems of method and measurement, and (2) the importance of criticism, commentary, and synthesis as part of the Center's intellectual activity. Not surprisingly, it is in these two areas that Tilly has made his biggest mark on historical sociology, and the workshop format has been a continuing source of stimulation for his own work in these areas. Tilly has written on and influenced students in fields as diverse as American family history and the French Revolution, Durkheimian sociology and the rise of the nation-state (see Bibliography).

In addressing this exceptional range of interests and productivity, I have divided what follows into five sections. In the first one, on Tilly's agenda, I describe what I think are the main concerns informing Tilly's work. The second section, on theoretical orientations, places the agenda within the field of historical sociology. The third, on research strategies, focuses on Tilly's particular and often controversial historical method. The fourth section, on explanations, includes an examination of some of Tilly's substantive conclusions, and the final section more generally assesses Tilly's impact on historical sociology.

Agenda

"Agenda" is one of Charles Tilly's favorite words, and it is the key to understanding his approach. Tilly's agenda is always being revised. Thus, his preoccupation in *The Vendée* with urbanization was expanded in *Strikes in France* to include industrialization and national political organization. However much the topics, the methods, or the sources have been revised and updated, the central problem has remained much the same – how can we understand collective action. Fellow members of the Center for Research on Social Organization have looked at collective action in a variety of temporal and geographic settings: for example, professional socialization in medical schools, voluntary associations in contemporary Poland, and collective action in nineteenth-century French cities. Tilly's own agenda is definitely historical: How did collective action in Europe evolve under the influence of long-term structural transformations? Several kinds of transformation are at issue: urbanization, industrialization, statemaking, and the growth of capitalism. Within the broad category of collective action, Tilly focuses on contentious, and especially violent, public gatherings. Most of his articles and books concern strikes, food riots, tax rebellions, demonstrations against conscription, and the like.

There are two sides to Tilly's approach, which, though they are meant to be complementary, are at times in tension with each other. On the one side is Tilly's concern for "the ways that people act together in pursuit of shared interests."[5] Like E. P. Thompson and George Rudé, Tilly wants to rehabilitate the "mob" or what historians less pejoratively label the "crowd." Riots against tax collectors, attacks on grain merchants, and machine breaking are shown to have their own rationale and their own meaningful place in the polity; these are the means developed by local communities to express their outrage and demand justice when the political arena is structured so as to exclude the ordinary people. In *The Vendée* Tilly demonstrated that the apparently hopeless and atavistic uprising against the new revolutionary state made sense if you considered the social structure and political divisions of local rural communities. More recently, he has shown that European food riots in the seventeenth and eighteenth centuries can best be understood as a reaction of locals to the increasing demands of the centralizing state and of the expanding national market for foodstuffs.[6] By analyzing the actions of village communities, Parisian artisans or militant trade unions, Tilly emphasizes the creativity of the ordinary people, their ability to organize themselves and to defend their interests.

On the other side are the structural changes that have transformed the means and the ends of collective action. An event or series of events such as the Vendée rebellion or strikes in France may be the starting point of Tilly's analysis, but the real subject is long-run changes in collective action; Tilly examines large, continuous sets of descriptions of events (strikes, demonstrations) to trace the effect of structural changes. In *The Vendée* the process was urbanization: local peasants and artisans reacted against the revolutionary or "patriot" bourgeoisie, who were the agents of an expanding state and the representatives of encroaching urban markets. Several long-term structural changes are at work in *Strikes in France:* urbanization, the proletarianization of the workforce, the growth of large-scale associations or political organizations, and the nationalization of politics. Militant workers had to respond to these changes to compete effectively for political power. Thus, the ordinary people are continually confronting pervasive structural changes that often seem to have a life of their own. These hidden processes somewhat mysteriously rewrite the rules of collective action; peasants, artisans, and workers must constantly revamp their repertoire of responses to these changes. On the one hand, then, Tilly emphasizes the creativity of ordinary people, while on the other, he gives great weight to the impact of ineluctable, structural changes.

This tension in his agenda can be traced to Tilly's ambivalent relationship to modernization theory. Like other modernization theorists,

Tilly proposes an evolutionary scheme: In his earlier work, he described the fitful development from "primitive," to "reactionary," and finally to "modern" types of "collective violence."[7] In the 1970s Tilly modified his language:

> In the fifteenth and sixteenth centuries, competitive actions seem to have predominated. From the seventeenth into the nineteenth century, the reactive forms became much more widespread, while the competitive forms remained steady or perhaps declined. With the nineteenth and twentieth centuries, collective proaction began to predominate, the reactive forms dwindled, while new forms of competition came into existence.[8]

In this passage, the invidious language of modernization has yielded to a more neutral terminology: competitive replaces primitive, reactionary gives way to reactive, and modern becomes proactive.[9] Tilly recognizes the persistence of "old" forms and the difficulty of distinguishing one form from another. Still, even in its revised version, the schema implies an evolutionary or developmental model. The repertoire of collective action developed in successive, if overlapping, phases in response to underlying changes in the structures of economic, political, and social life. Proactive types of collective action appear superior to competitive or reactive types, since with proactive types of collective action such as strikes and demonstrations, ordinary people are able to assert new group claims through formal organizations that effectively compete in a national political arena.

Despite these structural similarities to other modernization theories, Tilly's work has also included forceful criticism of many varieties of such theorizing. Almost everything he has published since the early 1970s has been critical of the excesses of modernization theory. In a recent essay, he asked: "So is there anything wrong with summing up those changes as the 'modernization' of Europe? No, if the name is only nothing but a convenient name. The errors begin with the elevation of the idea of modernization into a model of change."[10] Tilly rejects the notion of general laws of development or timeless general models, yet does believe that sociological analysis can identify what he calls "master change processes" in particular historical eras. His aim is to connect specific transformations in particular times and places to the master processes of change.[11] To this end, he takes modernization and breaks it down into more precise, measurable categories, such as urbanization and industrialization. He uses his large, serial sets of data to test various modernization theories: How did the repertoires of collective action change over time? Is there any correlation between the pace of structural change and the extent of collective action and collective violence? In other words, Tilly does not assume that there is one universal model of the transition from tradition to modernity, but he does want to test the proposition that modernization breeds violence.

Theoretical Orientations

"Collective action" is a curious concept, and many aspects of Charles Tilly's theoretical position are implicit in his choice of this analytical category. Like Neil Smelser's "collective behavior," collective action is a broad, seemingly neutral or at least ideologically ambiguous concept. Collective action is certainly much less loaded than "class struggle," "mob violence," or "social deviance." Tilly defines collective action very broadly as "people acting together in pursuit of common interests."[12] There is no necessary reference here to mode of production or to social pathology. Tilly chooses collective *action* over collective *behavior* to emphasize the importance of agency: Acting together is not simply a response to changing conditions, for it can entail a purposeful shaping of conditions (e.g., the proactive type). In *From Mobilization to Revolution* Tilly describes collective action as a concept that straddles two major kinds of social analysis, the causal and the purposive. A causal explanation considers the action of an individual or a group "as the resultant of forces external to the individual or group." A purposive explanation considers the individual or group to be "making choices according to some set of rules, implicit or explicit." As he himself admits, it is difficult to synthesize the two kinds of explanation.[13] In other words, and as might be expected, the tensions inherent in collective action as an analytical concept are the same as those that inform Tilly's overall agenda. On the one hand, he wants to analyze the constraints set by structural conditions; on the other, he wants to investigate the choices people make among available courses of action.

This conceptual and theoretical predicament is hardly unique to Tilly, since it is one of the central problems of any social analysis. Still, Tilly has chosen to address the dilemmas of social analysis in certain ways. Briefly stated, Tilly's theoretical orientation is decisively shaped by a continuing dialogue with Durkheim and the Durkheimians, and it is secondarily pushed and pulled by conversations with the "Millians" and with Marx and the Marxists.

Tilly himself has described his original agenda as an endeavor to refute Durkheim on empirical grounds: "When I began my long inquiry into conflict, protest and collective action, I hoped to accumulate the evidence for a decisive refutation of the Durkheimian line." In Tilly's view, this agenda was necessary because "Durkheim and his successors are ever-present":

> Turn to the study of crime, and see the fundamental role of arguments treating it as a product of social disintegration. Turn to the study of urban disorganization, deviance, and social disorganization, and find the very definition of the problem based on a Durkheimian view of the world. Turn to the study of collective behavior, and discover a redefinition of important varieties of collective action as expressions of the gap between the level of social differentiation and the extent of shared consciousness.[14]

Tilly is especially critical of Durkheim's notion of anomie and of the way Durkheim derives from it undesirable social results. Tilly directs his heaviest fire, however, against American representatives of a more general Durkheimian tradition: Neil Smelser, Samuel Huntington, Chalmers Johnson, and Ted Gurr. His attack on this Durkheimian tradition has a political as well as a theoretical and empirical dimension.

Tilly's discussions of theory follow from his empirical investigations; thus he argues against the Durkheimian tradition by demonstrating the lack of fit between historical evidence and hypotheses derived from Durkheimian theory. In many different publications, Tilly argues on empirical grounds against the view that collective violence and especially revolution are the work of the masses uprooted by rapid social change. The people who fought against the government in the June uprising of 1848 in Paris, for example, were for the most part adult, married men employed in respectable trades with strong organizations. There was a large proportion of migrants among the insurgents, but probably no more than was true of the working population as a whole.[15] Tilly and Shorter make a similar claim about nineteenth- and twentieth-century strikes: "In our view, the motors of militancy are set in motion not by the marginal, the unintegrated and the recently arrived, but by workers who belong to firmly established networks of long standing at the core of industrial society."[16] His own historical studies have convinced Tilly of the importance of organization, not of social disintegration, in promoting collective action.

On the basis of such empirical tests, Tilly objects to the Durkheimians' theoretical neglect of organization and mobilization and to their accompanying psychologizing of interests; Durkheimians maintain that individual disorientation follows from social disequilibrium and leads in turn to violent protest. Tilly himself shuns all arguments about mental states. He does not try to maintain that strikers were happy and contented rather than hostile and frustrated, but rather argues that the explanation of collective action cannot be complete without reference to organization.[17] There is a significant political objection implicit here as well, for the psychologizing of protest usually discredits the motives of the protesters (Tilly calls them challengers); their acts reflect anxiety, panic, anger, in short, the dissolution of social control. By insisting on the importance of organization, Tilly concentrates on how people can act together to shape their world. In short, he is at pains to give collective actors an active and creative role.

Nonetheless, Tilly is in a sense the prodigal son of the Durkheimian tradition. He was fashioned in the Durkheimian mold, and even his efforts to break out of it are marked by that previous formation. Tilly rejects the Durkheimian language of social pathology and the corresponding breakdown theories of collective action. Still, his agenda is fundamentally similar to Durkheim's: How does structural differentiation (for Tilly, urbanization, industrialization, etc.) change the nature of collective action? The question itself implies that structural change must be a key variable. Over the years and as a result of various empirical studies, Tilly has self-consciously separated himself from the Durkheimian position. Yet, ironically, he has moved away from the Durkheim of *Suicide* and *The Division of Labour* only to find himself backed up against the Durkheim of *The Elementary Forms of Religious Life*. Durkheim himself was interested not only in the sources of social breakdown but also in the possibilities for solidarity and shared consciousness. In *The Rebellious Century*, the Tillys argue for a "solidarity" as opposed to a "breakdown" theory of collective action.[18] They associate solidarity theories with Marx and the Marxists, but Durkheim also wrote at great length on the same subject. By rejecting the obnoxious "psychologizing" consequences of Durkheimian breakdown models, Tilly ends up overlooking Durkheim's work on *conscience collective*. Indeed, to avoid psychologizing, Tilly avoids any kind of argument that hinges on mental state, consciousness, or even, strictly speaking, ideology. This orientation is a direct consequence of Tilly's ongoing tug of war with Durkheimian theory, and it has serious implications for his analysis of collective action.

In his effort to replace the Durkheimian model, Tilly borrows selectively from alternative traditions. From the Millians he takes an emphasis on the rational pursuit of interests. John Stuart Mill and the English utilitarians treated collective action as a calculating pursuit of individual interest.[19] Contemporary expressions of this view appear in models of collective choice that frequently employ the language of microeconomics or strategic interaction. The Millian influence can be seen in Tilly's "mobilization model" when he explicitly calls attention to the importance of interests and opportunity: People act collectively to maximize their collective gains, and they do so within the constraints set by the costs of such collective action.[20] On a more practical level, Tilly emulates what he considers a Millian emphasis on careful formalization and statistical estimation of arguments. This emphasis is especially apparent in *Strikes in France* and *From Mobilization to Revolution*, where scores of tables, maps, and figures buttress the exposition.

Tilly describes his analysis in *From Mobilization to Revolution* as "resolutely pro-Marxian."[21] He cites with approval the Marxist stress on interests rooted in the organization of production, and since his own empirical work has focused on conflict rather than on consensus, the Marxist emphasis on conflict is congenial to him. Despite this sympathy, Tilly is not commonly identified as a Marxist. This is true even though most of his empirical pieces conclude resolutely against a Durkheimian position and for one that is at least vaguely Marxist. In *Strikes in France*, for instance, Tilly and Shorter argue that factory proletarians used strikes to political ends and that this happened because industrial relations and relations of power overlapped.[22] In their analysis of the people of June 1848, Tilly and Lees concluded that Marx had been right: The central cadres of the National Guard were property owners, professionals, and shopkeepers and their employees; and the vast majority of men opposing the government "came from a specific social and economic milieu and were members of workers' organizations."[23] The Tillys similarly argue in *The Rebellious Century* "that as a general theory of collective action, the broadly Marxist formulation we have been following also holds up better than its main competitors."[24]

Tilly's evidence, however, often forces him to modify Marx's and Marxist propositions. This modification is especially apparent in discussions of who participated in collective action. Tilly and Shorter contend that skilled workers were in the forefront of militant strike activity long after mechanized factory production had become a reality in France's industrial life.[25] They also claim to have discerned the beginning of a new phase in labor militancy in which office workers and science-sector professionals predominate in contentious actions. In short, it is not the proletarians who inevitably lead the way in modern struggles; their militancy came later than predicted by Marx and has been superseded. Militancy depends on organization, and the most oppressed and mechanized workers were not necessarily the best organized. Many recent studies by affiliates of the Center for Research on

Social Organization have focused on this issue of industrialization and the organization of protest.[26]

More significant than these empirical differences are the theoretical ones. Tilly follows Marx in studying the effects of capitalist industrialization on collective action, but unlike Marx he is equally interested in urbanization and statemaking and treats them as potentially independent factors. Like Marx, Tilly consistently emphasizes the political dimension of collective action. For him the goal of collective action is political power, and alterations in the arrangement of power change the opportunities and threats confronting contenders. In Marx's analysis, political contests are always located in the context of changing social relations of production. Tilly considers changes in the *organization* of production, but this factor does not necessarily override statemaking and urban growth in his analysis. Even when Tilly examines the effects of capitalist industrialization, he focuses on long-term structural changes such as proletarianization of the work force rather than on social class relations themselves. Tilly's choice of language is crucial in this respect: In the place of classes struggling against each other, members and challengers in the polity engage in collective action to further their interests.[27] Class consciousness plays no role in Tilly's analysis, even though he calls attention to the importance of working-class interests and organization.

Tilly's relationship to Marx and Marxism has had something of the character of a dialogue manqué. Virtually every one of his recent publications makes some reference to Marxist positions, and almost always his reference is sympathetic. Nevertheless, the reader often comes away with the sense that Tilly is not fully engaging Marx or Marxism; Tilly usually comments on his empirical agreement or disagreement with Marx rather than on his theoretical position as such. To some extent, the difference here is one of focus: Tilly begins with collective action itself and analyzes in great detail the participants, i.e., those who were caught in the act. He does not devote as much attention to the statemakers, the capitalists, the factory owners, or the forces of repression. He frequently refers to the relative position of contenders within the polity, yet he does not explicitly root those positions in the relations of production. Still, even though Tilly is not strictly speaking a Marxist, it is nonetheless true that his recent work reveals a growing preoccupation with Marxist analysis. As he has moved further and further away from Durkheimianism, Tilly has worked his way closer and closer to Marxism and especially to Marx himself. As a result, his recent work has been increasingly concerned with proto-industrialization, "flows of capital," and proletarianization. He has concluded that "the analysis of capitalism and of statemaking," rather than vague notions of modernization, "offers a far more adequate basis for the understanding of change in nineteenth-century Europe."[28]

Tilly seems much less influenced by the third member of the sociological trinity, Weber. He makes no reference to charisma, and never uses the social movement as his unit of analysis. Tilly does concede that shared conceptions of rights and obligations serve as one of the bases of collective action, but he "assumes that beliefs, customs, world views, rights, and obligations affect collective action indirectly through their influence on interest, organization, mobilization, and repression."[29] Again, he is anxious to avoid the pitfalls of "magic mentalism."[30] Tilly does not subscribe wholeheartedly to Weber's characterization of bureaucratic rationalization, but his discussion of the growth of the national state and of large-scale organizations has some significant affiliation with that notion. Like Weber, Tilly emphasizes the importance of statemaking much more than do either Marx or Durkheim. But like Marx, Tilly stresses the political dimension of collective action much more than either Durkheim or Weber.

Tilly's own orientation can be situated in reference to the major theoretical traditions within sociology, but Tilly himself is not known primarily as a theorist. He draws inspiration, orientation, and conceptual categories from different traditions. Tilly starts with a problem – collective action – that can be addressed from various vantage points, and he does not identify himself as the representative of any one theoretical affiliation. His most prominent procedure is to derive hypotheses from different theoretical positions (or from the literature inspired by those positions) and to test them, before drawing theoretical conclusions. Tilly's agenda consequently emphasizes research and methodology, the "how to" of answering theoretical questions. The answers provided by research lead in turn to reformulation of theories of collective action. Thus Tilly's own theoretical position is always necessarily in the process of development and unusually concerned with the problems of research strategy.

Research Strategies

Although Tilly's basic agenda has retained its fundamental unity over the years, his research design has become more and more ambitious. From the beginning, he has used historical cases for his investigation of collective action, and France has been his most favored site. From one region within France (the Vendée), Tilly has expanded his analysis to include the nation as a whole, and on occasion he has used the French case for comparison with other European nation-states. Recently, he has initiated a large, detailed study of contentious gatherings in Great Britain, 1828–1834, which will no doubt eventually facilitate more in-depth comparisons with trends in France and on the European continent.[31] Yet, for the most part, Tilly's own focus has been and continues to be France.

Understanding collective action in France has both descriptive and analytical components: How has collective action changed over time, and why? The time periods considered by Tilly have varied enormously, from the June Days of 1848 in Paris, to a few years in *The Vendée*, to more than a century (1830–1968) in *Strikes in France*. Even when the analysis narrows in on a precisely delimited period, however, the aim is still to place that span of time within the larger framework of the changes in collective action between 1600 and the present. The first goal of Tilly's research strategy is to describe this transformation, and each investigation, whatever its time frame, fits into this overall strategy. Similar kinds of questions are posed again and again – what are the forms of contention or what is the repertoire of collective action available to the population; who are the contenders in the polity; who are the participants in collective action; and what are their claims?

Tilly's research strategy gives great weight to time as a variable; similar kinds of events (contentious gatherings) are compared over a long stretch of time within one country. Even in *The Rebellious Century*, where the Tillys discuss Italy and Germany as well as France, the explanations for collective action are primarily tested against the evidence provided by each separate national historical trajectory. The comparisons of contentious events over time in Italy and Germany confirm the results derived from the historical comparison with France, and the bulk of the book is devoted to establishing these *intra*-national comparisons. *Strikes in France* makes the reliance on the variable of time particularly clear; Tilly and Shorter build most of their arguments on the foundation of "correlates of year-to-year variation."[32] Such comparisons of configurations of variables in different periods of time enable Tilly to describe in detail the transformation of collective action in France.

Because Tilly, in addition, wants to test various explanations for the changes in collective action in France (and now also in Great Britain), he has devoted much time, money, and collaborative effort to the collection of large, continuous sets of data on contentious events.

Scores of coders, key-punchers, programmers, and data analysts have been set to the task of culling and processing quantifiable evidence from newspapers, political yearbooks, published series of government reports, and archival documents. Tilly and Shorter used evidence from approximately 110,000 strikes for their analysis of *Strikes in France.* In their article on the Parisian uprising of June 1848, Tilly and Lees investigated the social background of some 11,000 participants.

This style of research has made Tilly controversial, especially among historians. Some critics call it an entrepreneurial style of research, and they liken Tilly himself to a positivistic captain of scholarship, a Henry Ford directing the mass production of quantitative studies of strikes, food riots, and tax rebellions. Tilly and his colleagues are undoubtedly more comfortable with the image of French workers in the 1830s and 1840s; they are artisans by training, are technologically advanced by opportunity and necessity, and form cooperatives to meet the challenges of otherwise intractable research problems. It is in any case important to note that the Center for Research on Social Organization has fostered many individual pieces of scholarship, which have influenced Tilly's own analysis.[33] Tilly's projects at the Center have necessarily entailed collective and collaborative effort, but they have not precluded individual and artisanal modes of research.

Systematic comparison of contentious events over time requires considerable standardization of historical data. Since Tilly proposed to test the relationship between modernization and violence, he has been especially mindful of the problems of measurement. And well he might be, for such a massive attempt to quantify historical evidence is bound to stir up a hornet's nest of criticism. Tilly exposes himself to such criticism by forthrightly stating the assumptions that lie behind the procedures he has established. The validity of his analysis of collective action in France, for example, rests on the definition of violent event. How does the coder reading a French newspaper know that a violent event has occurred? When one formation of at least fifty persons is present during an instance of "mutual and collective coercion within an autonomous political system which seizes or physically damages persons or objects."[34] As Tilly himself admits, an exact or approximate number of participants is often not given in published accounts. As a result, he and his collaborators decided to assume that certain key words meant that such a large group of people was involved. This is just one example, albeit a significant one, of the kind of leap one must make to standardize recalcitrant historical information.

The risks of such an endeavor are apparent. How reliable are published sources that are most often controlled, censored, or even produced by government officials with a direct interest in the events? Is violence an adequate tracer of collective action? How can standardized historical evidence capture the vital, local particularities of events? Tilly himself criticizes the Millians for their tendency to stress variables that are easy to quantify, and he is subject to some of the same criticism.[35] Nevertheless, there are also considerable rewards attached to the use of quantitative evidence. Because he has large, standardized sets of evidence covering nearly four centuries of French history, Tilly can address problems of long-term change in a systematic fashion. He shares the interest in long-term, quantifiable evidence with the social historians of France who have used serial records of prices, vital statistics, and marriage contracts in much the same way that Tilly utilizes strike data.[36]

Tilly differs from the *Annales* school in one essential aspect, however: he seeks to establish serial sets of documentation about collective acts that are first and foremost political, whereas the *Annales* historians have almost always concentrated on evidence that is primarily social and economic. The problems involved in translating newspaper accounts of demonstrations, for instance, into machine-readable form are much thornier than those associated with price lists or baptism registers, for the latter are generally presented in quantified form by the original record keepers. As a consequence, Tilly has been forced by the nature of his enterprise to carefully define and refine, to explicate and justify, his various procedures. Unlike most historical sociologists, Tilly has not been content to simply "read" existing evidence from his own special armchair. He has struck out in search of new evidence, either by undertaking research into historical archives or by transforming already published data. The painstaking attention to procedure and the assembly of a prodigious collection of historical data have set Tilly apart from most historical sociologists. Thus the same ambitions that expose him to the critics' sting have also turned him into one of the leading practitioners and teachers of quantitative historical methods.

The enormous pool of systematic evidence that is gathered in this fashion serves in the first instance to establish the general contours and changing parameters of collective action in France. Tilly uses comparisons over time to support his assertion that communal, defensive, locally focused, and loosely organized collective acts of the past have increasingly given way to the more massive, associational, nationally focused and highly organized collective actions of the present. This is only the first part of Tilly's research strategy, however; the other part consists of developing explanations for this long-term change. Tilly has described his approach as consisting largely of hypothesis testing:

> We have recorded in machine-readable form standardized kinds of information on each of these thousands of strikes in order to construct from this massive base of evidence a kind of demolition platform for arguments about industrial conflict, politics and social change. Our exact procedure is to take ideas on these subjects, both our own and other scholars', and hurl them against this giant rock of strike statistics. The notions which survive this battering turn up as struts in the argument of this book [*Strikes in France*].[37]

It is not clear from this statement how new hypotheses might be generated; a trial-and-error method seems to be implied, but the authors do not spell this out. Since hypothesis testing is one of the key elements in Tilly's research strategy, it is worth discussing in some detail.

In developing his arguments, Tilly takes the following steps: (1) on the basis of suggestions made in the literature and his own hunches, he derives various hypotheses that might explain the durable features and long-term transformations of collective action; (2) he specifies the implications of these hypotheses (e.g., if structural differentiation dissolved traditional social bonds, then we ought to see a rise in the indicators of collective violence during the periods of accelerated urbanization or industrial growth); (3) he lays out "great slabs of data" concerning the durable features and long-term transformations of collective action in France; (4) he tests the fit between his data and the specific implications of the hypotheses; (5) he rejects or reformulates the hypotheses on the basis of the test results; (6) where hypotheses all seem to point in a similar direction, he derives a more universally applicable model (e.g., the mobilization model proposed in *From Mobilization to Revolution*).[38] Testing plays a decisive role in this program, and it usually takes the form of multivariate statistical analysis.

As a plan of action, this program is straightforward and in itself unobjectionable. Since it stresses data collection and the statistical testing of assorted hypotheses, it meshes well with Tilly's workshop setting of research, his theoretical eclecticism, and his aim to describe as well as explain French historical development.[39] By the very virtue of its clarity, however, it makes Tilly vulnerable to criticism at every step. These criticisms can be summarized according to the program Tilly has outlined: (1) Are the hypotheses correctly derived from the theoretical literature, e.g., is the breakdown theory of collective action a true derivation from Durkheim's social theory? (2) Are the implications correctly specified? (A sociologist contended that Tilly and David Snyder translated the "expectation-achievement gap hypothesis" into an inadequate regression equation.[40]) (3) Do the historical data provide information about the most important features of collective action? (4) What do the statistical tests actually demonstrate? (5) Is the new or reformulated hypothesis better than those it replaced?

It is impossible to review and comment on all of these possible points, most of which are applicable in some form to a wide variety of social science analysis. Suffice it to say that Tilly explicitly aims to satisfy the cardinal criterion of scientific method; by making plain his assumptions and procedures, he makes possible the replication, validation, and falsification of his conclusions. The various critiques of Tilly's hypothesis testing can perhaps best be summed up in one trenchant question: How far is it possible to duplicate scientific procedures when one is using historical materials? Any judgment of Tilly's substantive contribution must rest in large measure on the answer to that question.

If, however, we put the knotty problems of hypothesis testing aside, there still remain two sets of methodological issues that are of particular interest to historical sociologists: the problem of the developmental model and the critical choice of historical test cases. These two interlocking issues are fundamental because they shape and set limits on Tilly's overall research strategy. Tilly tests the effects of modernization (i.e., the consequences of urbanization, industrialization, growth of the market, and expansion of the nation-state) on collective violence with evidence that until now has been drawn almost exclusively from France. Obviously, this choice does not strike historians of France as particularly defective. For historical sociologists, on the other hand, the privileged focus on France carries with it certain consequences. It is difficult, for example, to *test* the effects of the rise of the nation-state with evidence from one of the more nationalized and most "statelike" of the modern nation-states. France was a paradigm of "stateness" for aspiring national leaders in the seventeenth and eighteenth centuries, and it is to this day one of the most bureaucratized states in the world.[41] As might be expected, most of the historical records for France reflect this centralization and bureaucratization. Record keeping was a function of the state, and the very manner and spirit in which it was performed tended to deemphasize local differences. Thus the evidence from France has built into it the very parameter under consideration.

In addition to state making, Tilly's research has emphasized the increasingly associational character of collective life, such as the growth of unionization discussed in *Strikes in France*. This factor is also difficult to incorporate into a research strategy. Is a national association more associational than local ones? How can you measure the trade-off between cohesiveness and size in an organization? Moreover, the inevitability of the trend toward national organization seems much less apparent now than it did a generation ago. Here too the hypothesis and the records available are intertwined; an important, virtually definitional, part of being an organization is the keeping of records, yet the records may inflate the level of organization while prompting the researcher to overlook forms of association that go unrecorded. These are the kinds of problems that beset any researcher who wants to use historical documents, and the difficulties are especially acute for those who seek to determine historical trends.

Every research strategy involves critical choices and has its own set of advantages or disadvantages. In most of his work, Tilly focuses on one developed country as an illustrative historical testing ground for the elaboration of general models of collective conflict. In *The Vendée*, Tilly systematically compared two sections of southern Anjou, one that supported the Revolution and one that actively participated in the counter-revolution. The selection of the entire nation-state France in his subsequent work gives Tilly a broader range and makes possible comparison with other states as well as comparisons of smaller units within France. Tilly and Shorter were able to include several different levels of analysis in *Strikes in France*: comparisons between departments, regions, and cities; the national level as a whole; and finally, comparisons to other Western nation-states. The choice of one nation-state is not unreasonable, since most collective action, outside of war, takes place within national arenas. At the same time, however, this choice precludes direct examination of any international system (e.g., the capitalist market) and deemphasizes the investigation of more local factors. The comparison of departmental trends in *Strikes in France*, for example, generally only substantiates the patterns detected on the national level.

Just as he has moved from more local comparisons to national ones, so too Tilly's type of comparative analysis has shifted from comparisons that stress differences to comparisons that emphasize similarities or parallels. In *The Vendée*, Tilly examined the "significant differences" that explained the varied responses to the Revolution in southern Anjou.[42] Since then, his work has drawn attention primarily to similarities. By putting French strikes in an international perspective, for instance, Tilly and Shorter attempt to "show how trends in French strikes reflect universal trends, movements running parallel in all western states during the last hundred years."[43] The study of parallel cases in *The Rebellious Century* also reveals similarities. Despite differences in the level and timing of collective violence, the same general conclusions apply to Italy and Germany as well as to France – all three began with reactive forms of collective action and ended with proactive ones. France is the paradigmatic case for collective action in the West, and comparisons usually serve to confirm this status.

Tilly's choices of unit and method of analysis reflect the often conflicting demands of historical and sociological audiences. Historians customarily want rich documentation of everyday social structure and politics; for them France is a broad category that threatens to mask all the interesting and relevant particularities in the French experience. Sociologists, in contrast, want the most general possible conclusions; for them France is after all just France. Tilly tries to resolve this dilemma by answering sociological questions with historical data. Cross-national comparisons are not central to his method. Rather than proceeding by extension across space, his comparisons run over the dimension of time within one well-defined place. He slices that time sociologically, but the central strand is still historical.

Explanations

Two kinds of explanation emerge from Tilly's research: (1) hypotheses that explain why changes in collective action took place in the way they did and what their specific, historical consequences were; and (2) general models of collective action. The two types represent different levels of generality, and the second depends on the first. Tilly has written about both, yet his main effort has been directed at the first level. The establishment of hypotheses rests in turn on Tilly's description of the historical transformation of collective action in France, for it is the particular form of the trajectory that calls out for explanation. Before proceeding any further, therefore, we must briefly consider Tilly's description of the long-term transformation of collective action.

Tilly has published descriptions of collective violence and of collective action more generally. With David Snyder, Tilly presented his data on disturbances and participants in disturbances from 1832 to 1958.[44] This information provides the essential measure of collective violence, and it shows very high levels of collective violence around the revolutions of 1830 and 1848, at the beginning of the twentieth century, and in the mid-1930s. Tilly's work with Shorter on strikes covers almost exactly the same time period, but it concerns events that were not necessarily violent. Tilly and Shorter claim that the number of strikes rose dramatically between 1830 and 1964, and that militancy took off in the early 1880s.[45] In the early industrial period strikes tended to involve few workers and last around four days. By the 1960s strikes characteristically involved more than 500 workers but normally lasted only one day. During the same time, from the July Monarchy to the Fifth Republic, strikes became ever less successful in achieving the strikers' stated demands, although they seem to indicate an emerging spirit of compromise in industrial relations.

Most of Tilly's quantitative series of data begin in 1830 because it was from that time on that the French government began to gather reasonably complete records, which can be complemented by equally full accounts in newspapers. For the preceding centuries, Tilly must rely on a motley patchwork of documentation that includes unpublished government correspondence, fitful runs of newspapers, and local police reports. His description of seventeenth- and eighteenth-century forms is consequently less systematic and detailed. A good example of this more general (and historical) approach is his chapter on "Food Supply and Public Order in Modern Europe" in *The Formation of National States in Western Europe*.[46] Here Tilly argues that food riots became a prevalent form of collective violence in France from the end of the seventeenth century and that they only faded after reaching maximum intensity in 1846 and 1847.

The two kinds of description – the quantitative, continuous picture of the post-1830 period and the snapshots taken of earlier centuries – both go into the establishment of Tilly's overall schema of the development of collective action. The competitive-reactive-proactive classification rests on the claims being asserted: Competitive actions lay claim to resources also claimed by rival or competing groups; with reactive forms people act in the name of threatened rights; with proactive forms they assert group claims that have not previously been exercised. The claims correlate in a general way with the forms of action: "The demonstration and the strike have been privileged vehicles for new claims, have risen in periods and places in which ordinary people were articulating new demands, and are peculiarly suitable to the effort to make gains rather than to forestall losses."[47] Similarly, the food riot and tax rebellion are well suited to the expression of reactive claims, and the charivari, student brawls, and village fights to competitive claims.

What are the reasons for these successive changes? For Tilly the pivotal period is 1600 to 1850, as it was during this time span that proactive claims and forms eventually replaced reactive ones. Tilly cites two major long-term causes for the shift:

(1) The agents of international markets and of national states were pressing their new (and proactive) claims on resources which had up to then been under the control of innumerable households, communities, brotherhoods, and other small-scale organizations. The small-scale organizations reacted repeatedly, fighting against taxation, conscription, the consolidation of landed property, and numerous other threats to their organizational well-being. Eventually the big structure won, the battle died down, the reactive forms diminished. (2) Increasingly, the pools of resources necessary to group survival came under the control of large organizations, especially governments, which only redistributed them under the pressure of new claims.[48]

In other words, the inexorable expansion of capitalism and of the nation-state forced ordinary people to establish their own large organizations if they wanted to contend in the new arenas. At this very general level, Tilly's explanation depends on its ability to make sense of the long-term historical record. Most of his statistical tests concern the succeeding period, when the shift had already taken place, though even these tests refer back in the end to the validity of the overall schema. Various tests of alternative explanations have convinced Tilly of the plausibility of his own general explanation.

Most of the hypotheses directly tested by Tilly are concerned with the consequences of the shift from reactive to proactive forms, that is, with the consequences of the modernization of collective action. In *The Vendée*, Tilly concentrated on the effects of urbanization. He found that the most urbanized sectors of the West gave the most uniform support to the Revolution, and that the most intense conflicts arose where urbanization was both vigorous and uneven – at the junctures of urban and rural life. Since then, however, Tilly has consistently criticized those who trace violence directly to rapid urban growth.[49] In a recent preface to *The Vendée* he admits that his own emphasis there on urbanization obscured the influence of capitalism (especially proletarianization) and statemaking.[50]

The conclusions that Tilly has drawn in recent years from his analysis of long-term changes are summarized most conveniently in *The Rebellious Century*: (1) the changes labeled modernization had no uniform effects on the level, focus, form, or timing of political conflict; (2) in the short run, rapid urbanization and industrialization generally depressed the level of conflict; (3) urbanization and industrialization could nevertheless stimulate conflict when they diverted resources from established groups (urban craftsmen, for instance) that retained their internal organization; (4) the emergence of industrial capitalism transformed the identities and the interests of the major contenders for power, as well as the form of their collective action; (5) the frequency and outcome of collective conflict depends on the operation of the state.[51]

Three central points stand out in these conclusions. First, Tilly's tests of various hypotheses demonstrate that the indices of social disorganization (e.g., food prices, real wages) do not correlate with trends of collective violence. Here Tilly claims to be refuting Durkheim and Durkheimianism. Second, Tilly argues that modernization did change the prevailing *forms* of collective action and collective violence *over the long run*. Thus Tilly contends that the results of his various tests of hypotheses are consistent with his more general description of changes in collective action, 1600 to the present. Third, and very much related to the second point, Tilly insists on the primacy of power and political process; the last three conclusions listed in the previous paragraph all refer in some way to this point. (It is at this point, moreover, that the ambiguity of Tilly's relationship to Marx and Marxism enters in.) Since the emphasis on political contention is an essential part of Tilly's own model building, it merits some extended discussion.

Tilly argues in many places that shifts in the struggle for political power explain trends in collective action better than hypotheses based on social breakdown or economic hardship. Tilly maintains, for example, that the major bursts of violent conflict accompanied the largest realignments of the French political system.[52] Strikes expressed economic demands, but their real objective was working-class political power; as a result, strikes and violent disturbances often peaked in the same years.[53] The competition for political power thus explains the timing and intensity of conflict: if new groups emerge to claim their rights; if older, well-established groups perceive their rights to be threatened; or if the state resists the bids of new contenders, violence is likely.

Closely related to this stress on political contention is Tilly's emphasis on organization. Contenders for power depend on organization; when the struggle is based in the community, local organizations are sufficient. When contention takes place in a national arena, only national (and formal) organizations will be successful. Changes in organization consequently have a vital impact on the structure of industrial conflict. The surge in the frequency and extent of worker involvement in strikes, for instance, is linked to the increase in unionization and membership in political parties.[54] Through organization, then (rather than social disorganization), modernization has transformed collective action. Urbanization channeled protest into the cities; the centralization and nationalization of politics shifted violent conflict to the national arena; and proletarianization created a new contender with new claims to press and encouraged the formation of centralized, bureaucratically integrated political and trade organizations.

Tilly's stress on political contention has several important corollaries. Primary among them is the attention to the role of the state in any political conflict. By their actions, agents of the state frequently turned collective actions into collective violence; demonstrations turned into riots, for example, when government troops attacked the participants. In the seventeenth and eighteenth centuries, the French government provoked collective violence when it attempted to levy new taxes, redistribute the grain supply, or organize conscription. Hence the state was not just the object of struggle, but itself one of the chief parties to it. Coupled with this observation is the recognition that repression often works – periods of strong repression and central control such as the early years of the Second Empire and the two world wars produced little or no collective violence in France.[55]

Another corollary is that most violence followed rather than preceded major shifts in power; the revolutions of 1830 and 1848 in France, for example, inaugurated periods of intense political competition in which rival coalitions fought each other for control.[56] Finally, Tilly's emphasis on political contention allows him to analyze revolution in much the same way that he analyzes action. According to Tilly, revolutionary situations occur when (1) contenders advance exclusive alternative claims to control; (2) a significant segment of the subject population commits itself to these claims; (3) the agents of the government prove incapable or unwilling to suppress the alternative coalition.[57] Since revolution is one kind of collective action, it is composed of similar elements, e.g., interests, organization, mobilization, and opportunity. It follows from this similarity that in Tilly's view revolution is not an abnormal or pathological phenomenon; it is one of the possible outcomes of the struggle for power.

Tilly has summed up the findings of his diverse tests and more general historical investigations under the rubric of the "mobilization model."[58] The elements of the model should by now be familiar: organization, interest, repression, power, opportunity (or threat), and collective action. According to the model, the main determinants of a group's mobilization are its organization, its interest in possible interactions with other contenders, the current opportunity for such interac-

Figure 8.1. Tilly's Mobilization Model.

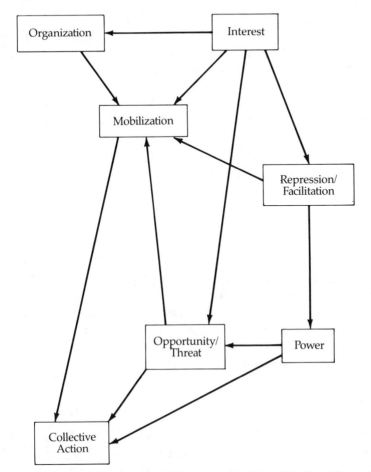

Source: Charles Tilly, *From Mobilization to Revolution* (Reading, Mass.: Addison-Wesley, 1978), p. 56.

tions, and the groups' subjection to repression. The extent of a contender's collective action is a product of its power, its mobilization, and the current opportunities and threats confronting its interests. The predominant parts of the model are mobilization, collective action, and opportunity (threat) – it is to these boxes that most of the directional arrows point (see Figure 8.1). These three elements have been the focus of Tilly's historical research; he has devoted much less attention to the determinants of power, repression, interest, or even organization. This difference in attention accounts in large measure for the ambiguity of his theoretical position, for the elements of power, interest, and organization have characteristically enjoyed prominence in Marxist analysis. Tilly explicitly recognizes their importance as factors (hence their inclusion in the model), yet he himself focuses on mobilization as a strategic interaction (a characteristically Millian approach) and on the forms and intensity of collective action itself.

This mobilization model is clear evidence of Tilly's theoretical ambitions. Yet, in some respects, it is very different from the rest of his work. The mobilization model can be viewed as a distillation of Tilly's various historical investigations; that is, as an economical way of expressing the relationships that he sees working again and again in the historical evidence. Although the model calls our attention to certain factors, it nevertheless operates in the most abstract fashion; hence a great variety of hypotheses might be specified under this model. Tilly himself points out many of its limitations: It makes no provision for time, and it is essentially quantitative – it concerns the amount of collective action, the extent of organization, etc.[59] In the latter respect, it is very much like Tilly's tests of hypotheses, but in the former (lack of time dimension) it is very unlike any of Tilly's other arguments. As a diagram of interrelationships, the model directs our attention to certain key, proven elements and to the probable direction of their influence. But unlike the models of Marx, Durkheim, and Weber, it provides no explanation for the historical appearance of new groups of contenders or new objects of contention.

Conclusion

More than most historical sociologists, Charles Tilly has a dual audience. Historians read him for his innovative, often highly technical, methods of analysis, and historians of France in particular read him for his arguments and analysis of French history. Among historians in general he is probably read most by students of the history of labor and of national revolutions. Sociologists can find in Tilly's work alternative models of collective action and an emphasis on elaborating historical research strategies that will produce answers to sociological questions. Historical sociologists aside, Tilly is of particular interest to sociologists of collective violence and revolution, the two major subsets of collective action with which Tilly has been most concerned.

A dual audience is not without its tensions. In *The Vendée* Tilly wrote primarily to historians; the task was "to put the Vendée in sociological perspective" and show that sociological questions, formulations, and methods could prove useful in analyzing a concrete historical situation.[60]

There is little explicit discussion of alternative hypotheses or models in *The Vendée*. *From Mobilization to Revolution*, on the other hand, is addressed to sociologists, or students of sociology; it argues that "historical analysis, taken seriously, will help us fashion more adequate models of power struggles."[61] Here, however, the historical materials are used only to illustrate the workings of the sociological models; most of the discussion is about the theories or models themselves, whereas in *The Vendée*, most of the discussion concerned the historical event.

As might be expected, criticism of Tilly varies depending on the specialization of the critic and on the critic's reaction to interdisciplinary work. Not everyone accepts E. H. Carr's dictum that "the more sociological history becomes, and the more historical sociology becomes, the better for both."[62] Some historians have taken Tilly to task for overloading or skewing his historical analysis with alien categories. Richard Cobb, for example, concludes his review of *The Vendée* on an ambiguous note: "This is a good and welcome book. It could have been so much better – and shorter – if Dr. Tilly could have been induced to forget his sociology, abandon his jargon, and show less desire to accommodate everything neatly."[63] In Cobb's view, the "complicated paraphernalia" of sociology leads to oversimplification and rigidity, yet he considers Tilly "such a natural historian" that "he still cannot prevent himself entirely from writing good history."[64] More recently, Tilly has been faulted for his use of modernization theory, even though he is less wedded to it than many other sociologists and social historians.[65] Yet historians never ignore Tilly's publications; whatever the reception given to them, they are taken seriously as contributions to the discipline. Sociologists have been on the whole more reticent. Tilly's more historical work, for example, is frequently reviewed in sociological journals by historians rather than by sociologists; in the *American Journal of Sociology* both *Strikes in France* and *The Rebellious Century* were reviewed by historians.[66] Specifically sociological criticism of Tilly usually concentrates on modeling and on the inadequacies of his testing procedures.[67] Thus, the very apparatus that offends some historians is found to be insufficiently developed by sociologists.

Most historical sociologists write for a rather special audience, one that intersects with but does not include the mainstream of either the historical or sociological professions. Indeed, most historians and sociologists remain skeptical of historical sociology. Tilly attempts to speak the language or argue in the terms of both disciplines, and he tries to speak to the skeptical center of each. His own professional situation reflects this duality; although he was educated as a sociologist (he received a Ph.D. in Sociology from Harvard University in 1958), he is a professor in both the Sociology and History Departments at the University of Michigan, Ann Arbor. The endeavor to speak two different types of professional discourse is fraught with difficulties, as the variety of criticism of Tilly's work demonstrates. To meet these difficulties, Tilly has until now periodically changed masks. The structure and language of *The Vendée*, for instance, is almost an academic world apart from that of *From Mobilization to Revolution*. Yet at least the intended audience of each of these books is evident and distinctly different.

Tilly has been much less successful, in my opinion, when he has tried to address both audiences at once, as he does in *Strikes in France*. Its relative failure is instructive, however. The structure of the book is clear-cut, and the presentation of evidence is lucid and to the point, but the prose is lackluster and the argument less than engaging. These problems do not seem to be the result of collaboration, since Tilly has written any number of collaborative pieces that have been more compelling. The disappointment is a consequence of the central duality in Tilly's approach.

When he tries to speak to both audiences simultaneously in *Strikes in France*, Tilly is forced to fall back on the one element that links the two disciplines in his agenda – research strategy or the testing of sociological hypotheses against new data generated by quantitative, historical methods. There is very little discussion of historical events (the actual strikes) and not much of broad theoretical positions, either. All of the attention is directed toward methods and test results, and the text consequently reads like a sourcebook or reference work. Such books can be useful, obviously, yet Tilly and Shorter surely did not intend to write that kind of book. Basically, neither historians nor sociologists come away satisfied. For example, various statistical tests of hypotheses show that labor organization was more directly significant than urban growth in promoting strike activity in France. But we do not know from such an analysis how, historically, or why, theoretically, labor organization fosters strike activity. Historians want to know more about the labor organizations themselves, for example, the kind of information presented by E. P. Thompson in his study of the English working class.[68] Social theorists want to know more about the possible theoretical explanations for the direction of the relationship.

Tilly is in a sense on the periphery of historical sociology precisely because he writes for the centers of the two disciplines of history and sociology. He addresses himself to the classic questions both in French history and in the sociology of collective action; he is as much at home with Georges Lefebvre and Michelle Perrot as he is with Mancur Olson and William Gamson. Yet because he attempts to speak to this dual audience using the language of each, no one of his books has been an entirely successful essay in historical sociology. Tilly himself rarely refers to historical sociology, except negatively:

> I am *not* talking about something called "historical sociology." I would be happier if the phrase had never been invented. It implies the existence of a separate field of study – parallel, say, to political sociology or the sociology of religion . . . I object to having sub-disciplines emerge from techniques and approaches rather than from theoretically coherent subject matters.[69]

Tilly's own arguments or discourses have been either predominantly historical, predominantly sociological, or caught uncomfortably between the two. Consequently, his various publications or his work as a whole has been Tilly's contribution, rather than his model or theory or paradigm or any one of his published pieces.

The same duality that creates tension in Tilly's work is also, paradoxically, the source of his influence on historical sociology. All historical sociologists use historical sources to construct their explanations. What is distinctive about Tilly is the way he uses those sources. He challenges the historical sociologists to leave their comfortable armchairs for the dust and exasperation of the archives, and he confronts them with research methods dependent on technology and teamwork. Tilly is both more like a historian and more like a sociologist than most historical sociologists. As a result, he has forcefully raised the issue of methodology by himself attempting to fashion a methodology at the interface of history and sociology. With this enterprise he has carved out for himself a singular position in historical sociology, one that makes him a leading teacher of historical-sociological methods. Tilly has helped push French history into new paths with his systematic tests of hypotheses, and he has shown how sociologists can seriously participate in historical research. At the same time, and by dint of both the successes and failures of this two-pronged attack, Tilly throws down the gauntlet to historical sociologists. Does historical sociology have a distinctive agenda, research strategy, or type of explanation? By pursuing the separate, frequently conflicting imperatives of history *and* sociology Tilly has made historians, sociologists, and historical sociologists more sensitive to the quandaries of historical methods of social analysis.

Lynn Hunt

Notes

It is not easy to write an essay of this sort about someone you know, respect, and like very much. Without helpful criticism from friends and colleagues I would have found a reasonable balance of critique and appreciation even harder to maintain. The conference with other authors of chapters in this volume provided an indispensable setting for thrashing out many of the perspectives presented here. Of those attending, I want to express my particular thanks to Victoria Bonnell and Theda Skocpol. I am also grateful to Lynn Eden for her perceptive comments. Finally, I want to thank Charles Tilly himself, who readily provided me with bibliographical and biographical information and documentation about the workings of the Center for Research on Social Organization.

1. Charles Tilly, *The Vendée* (Cambridge, Mass.: Harvard University Press, 1964; reprint ed., 1976) and *From Mobilization to Revolution* (Reading, Mass.: Addison-Wesley, 1978).

2. This chapter was written while Charles Tilly was still working at the University of Michigan. In 1984 he moved to the New School for Social Research in New York City. What this move will mean for his future work is not clear, but Tilly is starting a similar center for collaborative research at the New School.

3. Observations on the Center here and in the following pages are based on the annual reports of the University of Michigan's Center for Research on Social Organization. Funding for projects undertaken at the Center comes from a variety of government institutes, departments, and foundations. The Center publishes working papers written by its affiliates. These papers and lists of papers published in recent years can be obtained from the Center at 330 Packard Street, Ann Arbor, Michigan 48109.

4. Edward Shorter and Charles Tilly, *Strikes in France, 1830–1968* (Cambridge, U.K.: Cambridge University Press, 1974); Charles Tilly, Louise Tilly, and Richard Tilly, *The Rebellious Century, 1830–1930* (Cambridge, Mass.: Harvard University Press, 1975).

5. Tilly, *From Mobilization to Revolution*, p. 5.

6. Charles Tilly, "Food Supply and Public Order in Modern Europe," in *The Formation of National States in Western Europe*, ed. Charles Tilly (Princeton, N.J.: Princeton University Press, 1975), pp. 380–455. In his work on food riots, Tilly has been influenced by the work of his wife, Louise Tilly. See, for example, Louise Tilly, "The Food Riot as a Form of Political Conflict in France," *Journal of Interdisciplinary History* 2 (1971): 23–57.

7. See, for example, Charles Tilly, "The Changing Place of Collective Violence," in *Essays in Theory and History: An Approach to the Social Sciences*, ed. Melvin Richter (Cambridge, Mass.: Harvard University Press, 1970), pp. 139–64.

8. Tilly, *From Mobilization to Revolution*, p. 148.

9. This change in terminology is discussed in Tilly, Tilly, and Tilly, *The Rebellious Century*, pp. 49–55.

10. Charles Tilly, "Did the Cake of Custom Break?" in *Consciousness and Class Experience in Nineteenth-Century Europe*, ed. John M. Merriman (New York: Holmes & Meier, 1979), pp. 17–44; quote, p. 39.

11. See in particular Charles Tilly, *As Sociology Meets History* (New York: Academic Press, 1981), pp. 44–46.

12. Tilly, *From Mobilization to Revolution*, p. 7.

13. Ibid., p. 6.
14. Charles Tilly, "Useless Durkheim," in *As Sociology Meets History*, pp. 95–108; quotes, pp. 104, 107.
15. Charles Tilly and Lynn H. Lees, "The People of June 1848," in *Revolution and Reaction: 1848 and the Second Republic*, ed. Roger D. Price (London: Croom Helm, 1975), pp. 170–209.
16. Shorter and Tilly, *Strikes in France*, pp. 272–73.
17. Ibid., p. 338.
18. Tilly, Tilly, and Tilly, *The Rebellious Century*, p. 269.
19. For Tilly's description of the Millian tradition, see *From Mobilization to Revolution*, pp. 24–37.
20. Ibid., p. 56. See the later section, "Explanations," for a fuller account.
21. Tilly, *From Mobilization to Revolution*, p. 48.
22. Shorter and Tilly, *Strikes in France*, p. 349.
23. Tilly and Lees, "The People of June 1848," p. 201.
24. Tilly, Tilly, and Tilly, *The Rebellious Century*, p. 274.
25. Shorter and Tilly, *Strikes in France*, pp. 349–50.
26. See, for example, Ronald Aminzade, *Class, Politics, and Early Industrial Capitalism. A Study of Mid-Nineteenth Century Toulouse, France* (Albany: State University of New York Press, 1981); and Michael Hanagan, *The Logic of Solidarity, Artisans and Industrial Workers in Three French Towns, 1871–1914* (Urbana: University of Illinois Press, 1980).
27. The difference in language is most apparent in *From Mobilization to Revolution*. See in particular the polity model (p. 53).
28. Tilly, "Did the the Cake of Custom Break?" p. 39. See also Louise A. Tilly and Charles Tilly, eds., *Class Conflict and Collective Action* (Beverly Hills, Calif.: Sage, 1981).
29. Tilly, *From Mobilization to Revolution*, p. 48.
30. Tilly, "Did the Cake of Custom Break?" p. 48.
31. The Great Britain study is briefly described in appendixes 3 and 4 of *From Mobilization to Revolution*, pp. 274–306. See also Charles Tilly and R. A. Schweitzer, "How London and Its Conflicts Changed Shape, 1758–1834," *Historical Studies* 5 (1982): 67–77; and Charles Tilly, "How (And, to Some Extent, Why) to Study British Contention," in *As Sociology Meets History*, pp. 145–78.
32. Shorter and Tilly, *Strikes in France*, especially chap. 4, "Year-to-year Variation in Strike Activity," pp. 76–103.
33. A recent list of selected papers from the study of social change and collective action (1963–1983) at the Center includes over fifty individual authors. The papers cover countries from the U.S. to Finland.
34. Tilly, *From Mobilization to Revolution*, p. 248. The same or equivalent definition can be found in several other Tilly publications. See, for example, David Snyder and Charles Tilly, "Hardship and Collective Violence in France, 1830–1960," *American Sociological Review* 37 (1972): 520–32.
35. Tilly, *From Mobilization to Revolution*, p. 37.
36. The interest in long-run, serial documentation is particularly apparent in the pages of *Annales: Economies, Sociétés, Civilisations*. The *Annales* has given its name to the school of French historians associated with this kind of interest. Most of the French theses and books concerned with quantifiable historical documents have been devoted to the period 1300–1800. A humorous yet informative introduction to the *Annales* school can be found in J. H. Hexter, "Fernand Braudel and the *Monde Braudellien* . . . ," *Journal of Modern History* 44 (1972): 480–539.

271

37. Shorter and Tilly, *Strikes in France*, p. xvii.
38. My description of Tilly's method is based to a large extent on the account given in Shorter and Tilly, *Strikes in France*, p. 9. Some of these points are also developed in *As Sociology Meets History*.
39. I am indebted to Theda Skocpol for this observation.
40. Charles N. Halaby, " 'Hardship and Collective Violence in France': A Comment," *American Sociological Review* 38 (1973): 495–500, especially p. 496.
41. Tilly's most extensive discussion of the growth of the modern nation-state can be found in his "Reflections on the History of European Statemaking" and "Postscript: Western Statemaking and Theories of Political Transformation," in *The Formation of National States in Western Europe*, pp. 3–83 and 601–38.

    Recently, Tilly has focused more on regional differences within France. See, for example, "Statemaking, Capitalism, and Revolution in Five Provinces of Eighteenth-Century France," CRSO Working Paper no. 281 (January 1983).
42. Tilly, *The Vendée*, p. 340.
43. Shorter and Tilly, *Strikes in France*, p. 306.
44. Snyder and Tilly, "Hardship and Collective Violence," p. 523. A similar version appears in Tilly, Tilly, and Tilly, *The Rebellious Century*, pp. 51–77.
45. Shorter and Tilly, *Strikes in France*, especially chap. 3, "The Transformation of the Strike," pp. 46–75.
46. Tilly is now writing a general history of collective action in France from 1600 to the present.
47. Tilly, *From Mobilization to Revolution*, p. 148. The key chapter is 5, "Changing Forms of Collective Action," pp. 143–71.
48. Ibid., pp. 148–49.
49. See for example, A. Q. Lohdi and Charles Tilly, "Urbanization, Criminality and Collective Violence in Nineteenth-Century France," *American Journal of Sociology* 79 (1973): 296–318.
50. Pp. x–xii of the 1976 reprint edition.
51. Tilly, Tilly, and Tilly, *The Rebellious Century*, pp. 83–86.
52. Ibid., p. 56.
53. Shorter and Tilly, *Strikes in France*, p. 344.
54. Ibid., p. 348.
55. Tilly, Tilly, and Tilly, *The Rebellious Century*, p. 61.
56. This argument figures prominently in James Rule and Charles Tilly, "1830 and the Unnatural History of the Revolution," *Journal of Social Issues* 28 (1972): 49–76. A very similar version can be found in James Rule and Charles Tilly, "Political Process in Revolutionary France, 1830–1832," in *1830 in France*, ed. John M. Merriman (New York: New Viewpoints, 1975), pp. 41–86.
57. Tilly, *From Mobilization to Revolution*, p. 200.
58. Ibid., p. 56.
59. Ibid., p. 58.
60. Tilly, *The Vendée*, pp. 339–40.
61. Tilly, *From Mobilization to Revolution*, p. 231.
62. E. H. Carr, *What Is History?* (New York: Knopf, 1961), p. 84.
63. Richard Cobb, "The Counter-Revolt," in *A Second Identity: Essays on France and French History* (London: Oxford University Press, 1969), pp. 111–21, quote on pp. 120–21.
64. Ibid., pp. 118, 121.
65. Tony Judt, "A Clown in Regal Purple: Social History and the Historians," *History Workshop Journal* 7 (1979): 66–94. Judt's analysis of Tilly is in my

opinion often mistaken on many grounds. It should be evident that my analysis in this essay contradicts his on most salient points.
66. William M. Reddy reviewed *Strikes in France* in vol. 81 (1975): 187–88. George Rudé reviewed *The Rebellious Century* in vol. 82 (1976): 499–51.
67. Halaby, " 'Hardship and Collective Violence.' "
68. E. P. Thompson, *The Making of the English Working Class* (London: Gollancz, 1963).
69. Tilly, *As Sociology Meets History*, p. 100.

Selected Bibliography

WRITINGS BY CHARLES TILLY

Charles Tilly has authored or coauthored several books, edited a handful of others, and published scores of articles on topics as diverse as "Metropolitan Boston's Social Structure" and "Anthropology, History and the *Annales*." I present here the books, articles, and working papers that I found most representative of Tilly's central scholarly interests.

Books

The Vendée. Cambridge, Mass.: Harvard University Press, 1964; reprint ed. 1976.   His first book and still perhaps his best, despite overemphasis on urbanization. Demonstrates that sociologists can do precise, detailed research in historical archives and yet maintain their grasp on more general questions. Translated into French and Italian.
Strikes in France, 1830–1968, with Edward Shorter. Cambridge, U.K.: Cambridge University Press, 1974.   The single most important product of Tilly's long-term study of collective action in France yet published. Packed with quantitative analysis. Although generally well reviewed and nominated for a National Book Award, definitely my least favorite because I find it relatively lifeless.
The Rebellious Century, 1830–1930, with Louise Tilly and Richard Tilly. Cambridge, Mass.: Harvard University Press, 1975.   Presents in convenient, summary form most of Charles Tilly's main conclusions about collective action in France. The introductory and concluding chapters give a good sense of his theoretical orientation. Although each of the central chapters on France, Italy, and Germany is interesting in itself, I found the international comparisons predictable and less than exciting. A good place to start (along with *The Vendée*) any reading of Tilly because it is a much livelier book than *Strikes in France*.
From Mobilization to Revolution. Reading, Mass.: Addison-Wesley, 1978.   An explicit statement of Tilly's own theoretical orientations. Includes handy descriptions of both the France and Great Britain projects on collective action. A textbook on approaches to collective action that argues for the usefulness of historical research.
As Sociology Meets History. New York: Academic Press, 1981.   A collection of essays that presents both his theoretical orientation and his historical work on French peasants, proletarianization, and British contention.

Articles and Chapters in Books

"The Changing Place of Collective Violence." In *Essays in Theory and History: An Approach to the Social Sciences*, edited by Melvin Richter, pp. 139–64.

Cambridge, Mass.: Harvard University Press, 1970. A short, general statement of Tilly's classification scheme for collective violence.

"Hardship and Collective Violence in France, 1830–1960," with David Snyder. *American Sociological Review* 37 (1972): 520–32. Good example of attempt to build quantitative, sociological models out of historical materials. Discussion is very technical.

"Reflections on the History of European Statemaking," "Food Supply and Public Order in Modern Europe," and "Postscript: Western Statemaking and Theories of Political Transformation." In *The Formation of National States in Western Europe,* edited by Charles Tilly, pp. 3–83, 380–455, 601–38. Princeton, N.J.: Princeton University Press, 1975. Tilly's most general and historical reflections on the role of the nation-state in modern European history.

"Getting It Together in Burgundy, 1675–1975." *Theory and Society* 4 (1977): 479–504. Preview of Tilly's forthcoming general book on the "contentious French."

"The Historical Study of Vital Processes" and "Questions and Conclusions." In *Historical Studies of Changing Fertility,* edited by Charles Tilly, pp. 3–56, 335–50. Princeton, N.J.: Princeton University Press, 1978. Indicates Tilly's recent interest in European demography and proletarianization.

"Did the Cake of Custom Break?" In *Consciousness and Class Experience in Nineteenth-Century Europe,* edited by John M. Merriman, pp. 17–44. New York: Holmes & Meier, 1979.

CRITICISMS OF CHARLES TILLY

Many reviews of Tilly's books have appeared over the years, but there have been to my knowledge no thorough evaluations of his work as a whole. In my opinion (but this may be a historian's prejudice), the most useful reviews of individual books by Tilly are those that have been published in historical journals. Listed below are three of the longer reviews that have been written about individual Tilly pieces.

Cobb, Richard. "The Counter-Revolt." In *A Second Identity: Essays on France and French History,* pp. 111–21. London: Oxford University Press, 1969. Originally published as a book review of *The Vendée.* Perhaps the most antisociological critique of Tilly, yet still generally favorable to the book under review.

Halaby, Charles N. " 'Hardship and Collective Violence in France': A Comment." *American Sociological Review* 38 (1973): 495–500. A hard-line, quantitative sociological criticism of an article by David Snyder and Charles Tilly (see note 34).

Perrot, Michelle, and Claude Durand. "Débat." *Annales: Economies, Sociétés, Civilisations* 28 (1973): 888–94. Comments by a leading French historian and French sociologist on a Shorter and Tilly article that presented some of the arguments of *Strikes in France.* Charles Tilly and Edward Shorter, "Les Vagues de grèves en France, 1890–1968," *Annales: Economies, Sociétés, Civilisations* 28 (1973): 857–87.

WORK BY COLLEAGUES AND STUDENTS

Charles Tilly has influenced a variety of historians and sociologists. His direct influence can be seen in the large number of collaborative pieces that he has published. He has served on the editorial or advisory boards of many journals and institutions, and he is the coeditor of the Harvard University Press Studies in Urban History and the Academic Press Studies in Social Discontinuity. It is more difficult to document his impact as a reader of innumerable dissertations and manuscripts. In this section I have listed just a few recent examples of work by close colleagues and students, with the aim of indicating the breadth of Charles Tilly's interests.

Aminzade, Ronald. *Class, Politics and Early Industrial Capitalism. A Study of Mid-Nineteenth Century Toulouse, France.* Albany: State University of New York Press, 1981. A student in sociology at the University of Michigan, Aminzade now teaches in the Department of Sociology at the University of Wisconsin, Madison.

Hanagan, Michael. *The Logic of Solidarity. Artisans and Industrial Workers in Three French Towns, 1871–1914.* Urbana: University of Illinois Press, 1980. Hanagan wrote his doctoral dissertation in history and now teaches in the Department of History, Columbia University.

Roy, William G. "Inter-Industry Vesting of Interests in a National Polity over Time: The United States, 1886–1905." Ph.D. dissertation, University of Michigan, 1977. Roy teaches in the Department of Sociology, University of California at Los Angeles.

Tilly, Charles, and Louise A. Tilly. "Stalking the Bourgeois Family." *Social Science History* 4 (1980): 251–60. Louise Tilly is a historian at the University of Michigan. She wrote the chapter on Italy for *The Rebellious Century* and is the author with Joan Scott of *Women, Work and Family* (New York: Holt, Rinehart & Winston, 1978).

Zunz, Oliver. *The Changing Face of Inequality.* Chicago: University of Chicago Press, 1982. Zunz now teaches history at the University of Virginia.

9. The World System of Immanuel Wallerstein: Sociology and Politics as History

CHARLES RAGIN and DANIEL CHIROT

Few American sociologists have succeeded in forming academic cults around themselves, and until recently none had ever done so through the writing of social history. Yet this is precisely what Immanuel Wallerstein has done, and it is worth examining the reasons for this before discussing his intellectual biography and analyzing the substance of his work.

Although known as an Africanist in the 1960s and as the author of a provocative book about universities that was sympathetic to the student rebels of the late 1960s, Wallerstein did not achieve great prominence until the publication in 1974 of *The Modern World-System: Capitalist Agriculture and the Origins of the European World Economy in the Sixteenth Century*.[1] This book was an attempt to create a new grand synthesis of the economic and social history of European expansion from the fifteenth to the early seventeenth centuries.

The basis of Wallerstein's synthesis was the idea that whatever small technological and organizational advantage Western, particularly northwestern, Europe may have possessed at the end of the fifteenth century, it was turned into a much greater superiority by the West's exploitation of non-Western peripheries. Peripheral areas were primary product-exporting regions, at first in Eastern Europe and South America, whose economies and societies were subordinated by the power of the Western (or core) states' arms and markets. Drawing off the periphery's resources enriched the capitalist core and allowed it to increase its sphere of control throughout the world. This simultaneously retarded and impoverished the periphery and forced its development into social and political paths that made technological and economic dynamism difficult, if not impossible. To Proudhon's "Property is theft," Wallerstein added, in effect, that capitalist progress is theft on a global scale.

From this first principle followed a series of logical deductions and interpretations about historical and contemporary issues, which Wallerstein has elaborated in a staggering number of articles on a variety of issues ranging from the coming demise of NATO to the transition from feudalism to capitalism.[2] From this body of work a political perspective emerged that, in turn, has become the primary bond holding Wallerstein's followers together. It is a somewhat modified version of Marxism in which classes are viewed as transnational actors. The upper classes are situated primarily but not exclusively in the core, and peripheral societies contain the most exploited and the majority of the world's proletariat. The upper classes maintain their power by manipulating the core states to defend their control over the periphery.

Social change, in this view, is conditioned by changes in the world system as a whole, not by events in this or that country. Socialism can come only through a revolution in the entire system, not simply in one or several countries (much as this might help to create the conditions for an eventual world revolution). Perhaps most important in this world-system view is the notion that capitalism's wealth is critically dependent on its exploitation of the periphery, not simply the domestic proletariat of the major core states (which can be bought off with the surplus product taken from the periphery). As the most exploited part of the system, the periphery will be the locus of the future world socialist revolution.[3]

The political conclusions following from Wallerstein's perspective were very appealing to young American social scientists, particularly sociologists, in the early and mid-1970s. There were four reasons for this; some of them applied as well to the same categories of intellectuals in other advanced countries, and Wallerstein's fame spread well beyond purely American limits.

First, comparative and developmental social science in the 1950s and 1960s had been dominated by a melioristic, gradualistic explanation of the world called modernization theory.[4] According to this view all poor countries were promised eventual wealth as long as they stuck to the rules of liberal capitalism and allowed themselves to be exploited. Clearly, however, poor countries were not all willing to play their assigned roles, and some were, instead, revolting against the world capitalist system. Rather than behaving benignly, as liberal theory demanded, the United States was behaving like a fairly ruthless world police officer trying to force peripheral challengers of the system back into their proper subordinate place. Wallerstein's historical and political theory seemed to make much more sense of actual world events than did liberal modernization theory. Compared to the predictive failure and political hypocrisy of the prevailing theories about social and economic change, Wallerstein's was a clear and attractively radical position.

Second, the young scholars who embraced Wallerstein's ideas had lived their early university careers as students in the turbulent late 1960s. The domestic turmoil of that decade had awakened them to the imperfections of the view of American society as a happy melting pot without class lines or exploitation. Marxism seemed to be a theoretical solution, and Wallerstein presented it in an international context that addressed both foreign and domestic problems.

Third, Marxism, like all broad philosophies of history, needs to explain away unexpected developments, and Wallerstein dealt with Marxism's apparent predictive failures. He showed that the socialist revolution was still coming even though the proletariat of the industrialized countries was not behaving as predicted by Marx. This was because the proletariat was largely concentrated in the Third World. Thus, the failure of the original Marxist prediction was excused, but at the same time the original vision was reaffirmed. Moreover, the existence of a capitalist world system excused the most obvious failures of Communist countries. Socialism in one country is impossible, even if the attempt to create it is noble, for the entire global exchange system must be revolutionized. The stranglehold of capitalists on world markets and on most of the world's political systems has distorted the attempts at socialism made by the Soviet Union and others, and explains some of the unpleasant turns taken by Communist regimes trying to survive in a hostile world system. Many young scholars who were troubled by Marxism's failure to explain politics within industrial countries and by the abysmal record of Marxist states were attracted to Wallerstein's resolution of these problems.

The fourth reason for the acceptance of Wallerstein in the 1970s was that a significant minority of younger sociologists, discouraged by the functionalist positivism that had prevailed in the 1950s and 1960s, thirsted for concrete historical knowledge. To be sure, there had been some historical work by sociologists. But George Homans, as early as the 1950s, had turned from work on English social history toward ahistorical psychological behaviorism. S. N. Eisenstadt's attempt to synthesize functionalism with comparative history was politically discredited by the events of the 1960s, as was Seymour Lipset's political sociology. Reinhard Bendix, true Weberian that he was, presented far too complicated a picture of the world. He had no overarching model; each important country was discussed with the aid of particular ideal types. This style did not appeal to the students and young scholars who were trying to understand events at home and abroad in terms of a single perspective. Barrington Moore, alone of the major figures of the generation preceding Wallerstein, served as guide to some of the disaffected young scholars of the 1970s, but he never aspired to create a school of thought with an organized following.

That Wallerstein's success had something to do with his politics and with the political atmosphere in academia in the 1970s is not surprising or unprecedented in the world of scholarship. Nor is the fact that he explicitly identifies with an ideological stance. After all, Marc Bloch also became politically committed, both in his writing and his actions. And his martyrdom to what was a good and ultimately victorious cause was certainly manipulated by his followers to help them win academic power in France. But Bloch's politics surfaced in his writing only at the end of his life, in the crisis of World War II. They were not an important part of the work on which his scientific reputation rests. As for the political manipulation of his image to create a school, that was done after his death. Karl Polanyi and Barrington Moore wrote explicitly about their political positions, which were as central to their work as Wallerstein's are to his. Neither created a school of followers. Reinhard Bendix and S. N. Eisenstadt also have strong political beliefs. But they, like Charles Tilly (whose views are closer to Wallerstein's), have concealed their overt feelings under a cover of objective social science. Thus, more than for any other figure in this book except perhaps Perry Anderson and E. P. Thompson, an understanding of Wallerstein's explicit political aspirations is a vital key to the appreciation of his work and his impact.

The Discovery of a World System

Political interests were always at the core of Wallerstein's sociological work. His unpublished sociology master's thesis at Columbia University was on McCarthyism and American foreign policy.[5] There is little doubt that the smug antiintellectualism of America in the Eisenhower years contributed to his dislike of American capitalism. Perhaps, as Marc Bloch's love of his native countryside drove him to explore it in loving detail and develop a style of historical work based on its intimate knowledge, Wallerstein's distaste for the ideological climate of his country pushed him into a search for more important events and heroes outside its borders.

Nevertheless, the published version of Wallerstein's Columbia University sociology doctoral dissertation, "The Road to Independence: Ghana and the Ivory Coast," and his first published book, *Africa: The Politics of Independence*, do not openly declare their political commitments.[6] They are neither methodologically nor ideologically radical.

In his dissertation, Wallerstein compared the anticolonial nationalist movements of Ghana and the Ivory Coast. He interviewed various elite individuals about their attitudes and positions and set up a series of neat little tables in the best tradition of Paul Lazarsfeld. He looked at the role of voluntary associations as precursors of the independence parties. He cited the conventional modernization literature when he sought theoretical explanations, drawing on the ideas of Daniel Lerner, S. N. Eisenstadt, David Apter, even Talcott Parsons. When it came to African matters, however, the French sociologist Georges Balandier and the British leftist Thomas Hodgkin were obviously more relevant intellectual models. Although Wallerstein was not yet ready to proclaim it openly, functionalist social theory was of very limited utility in explaining Africa. The department from which he came, however, was still dominated by such theories.

In his more widely read text on African independence, *Africa: The Politics of Independence,* Wallerstein was closer to his later style. Sweeping generalization and broad comparisons made this one of the most useful early books about Africa, but his position remained conventionally left liberal. Wallerstein was, of course, anticolonial. He admired the intellectuals who were leading these countries' anticolonial struggles, and he excused their tendency to jettison democratic trappings soon after gaining independence by saying this was not as antidemocratic as it looked.[7] The book's theoretical base, however, was mainstream, which explains how it was possible for Wallerstein to quickly become one of the favorite Africanists of the modernization theorists he was to denounce a decade later.

In his edited work, *Social Change: The Colonial Situation,* Wallerstein gave the first published hints that his opinions were not exactly what they had seemed to be.[8] He included an excerpt from Franz Fanon, who was not yet well known in the United States. (Wallerstein played an important role in getting Fanon's work translated into English.) He also included a curiously wooden and explicitly Stalinist analysis of tribe, ethnicity, and nationalism by I. Potekhin. Most of the other selections were consistent with modernization theory and liberal anticolonialism, not with a radical anticapitalist analysis.

In 1967 Wallerstein published his third book, *Africa: The Politics of Unity.*[9] Although presented as a kind of second volume to his earlier book on African independence, this book was quite different. In the 1960s it had become painfully apparent to wiser Africanists that the optimistic expectations of the late 1950s concerning postindependence progress were not going to come true. Also, by the time *The Politics of Unity* appeared, one of Wallerstein's heroes, Kwame Nkrumah, had been overthrown. Some observers thought that this event had only exposed the emptiness of Nkrumah's "African socialism," with its overblown rhetoric and pandering to the ego of the so-called charismatic leader. Wallerstein's reaction was entirely the opposite. He blamed Western capitalist neocolonialism:

> It therefore follows that if the present world political and economic structure is disadvantageous to Africans and advantageous to others (say, collectively the Western developed nations or influential elements within them), it is natural that the former will work to change the structure and that the latter will oppose such attempts. The end-goal of change is equality – political, economic, and cultural – with the currently more developed regions of the world. Such equality can only be achieved by the modernization of African societies. The question then is: How is it possible to modernize such societies in the face of the expected opposition of developed countries? The movement toward African unity contends that continental unity is required before there can be successful modernization . . . Only with considerable self-discipline and self-denial can societies manage to place a sufficient amount of their current production income into the long-range investments which will multiply growth and hence enable these societies to "narrow the gap" with the developed societies . . . Massive investment . . . requires political self-control, and perhaps considerable social isolation in order to diminish the sense of relative deprivation among those who are asked to make sacrifices. It is further assumed that outside powers, for reasons of both short-term and long-run interests, will oppose, if they can, both self-discipline and isolation.[10]

To meet this outside resistance, African unity was important. Otherwise – and on this point Wallerstein quoted Julius Nyerere – Africans would be set against each other in the service of imperialism. Also, the larger the political unit, the more easily it could isolate itself. To carry out these goals, one-party states and nonalignment were necessary. However, "nonalignment, to be realistic, takes into perspective an over-all social accounting of outside influence. Hence at the present it leans more closely in Africa to the Communist world in order to counterbalance the effects of the network of inherited structures and relationships permeating contemporary Africa."[11]

These positions led to important methodological conclusions, both at the practical political level and for intellectuals committed to helping progress through their studies

> The field of action of the movement toward African unity was not Africa but the world, for its objectives were not simply to transform Africa, but to transform Africa by transforming the world. Its enemies were internal to be sure, but the internal enemies were seen as agents of foreign powers – the essence of the concept of "neocolonialism." We must accordingly analyze the emergence of the movement for African unity in terms of the world system, for it was the changing state of this system that made it possible for the movement to gain and then lose its freedom to maneuver.[12]

By world system Wallerstein did not yet mean a structure as broad as it was to become in his later writings. He was talking about the economic and political international system of the post–World War II world, which revolved around the United States, the dominant world power, and its enemy, the revolutionary world power, the Soviet Union. In an extraordinary final chapter, Wallerstein reviewed the history of this system and explained the vagaries of African politics almost entirely in its context. Development and domestic social change had become, in his opinion, entirely dependent on breaking away from Western, particularly American, hegemony. Clearly, then, it was the task of the sympathetic student to lay bare the underpinnings of the system.

To give himself and his readers hope, Wallerstein sandwiched his book between two telling quotes. Before the table of contents, he cited Georges Sorel: "The myth must be judged as a mean of acting on the present; any attempt to discuss how far it can be taken literally is devoid of sense."[13] The last paragraph of the book contains Modibo Keita's quote of Renan: "Nothing great is achieved without chimeras. Ah! Hope never deceives, and I am sure that all the hopes of the 'believer' will come to be more and more. Humanity achieves perfection in wishing for it and hoping for it."[14] African unity was the myth and the chimera. Wallerstein was too realistic to block all reality from his vision. (Soon after, Modibo Keita, another of Wallerstein's revolutionary heroes, was overthrown as president of Mali.)

There was more than a mere apology for having engaged in wishful thinking in these quotes. Wallerstein recognized that a solidly based myth could have considerable importance in its own right. Having recognized the importance of, first, the vision of African unity, and, later, the fact of neo-colonialism as the explanation of its failure, Wallerstein set himself the task of becoming the academic spokesman and promoter of the vision of world history that lay behind the Third World's revolutionary ideologies.

In 1968 Wallerstein was still at Columbia University, where he had begun as an undergraduate. He was Associate Professor of Sociology with tenure and was already working on his world-system ideas. The Columbia riots of the spring of that year caught him, as they did almost everyone else, by surprise. He and his friend and colleague Terence Hopkins befriended the student radicals and supported some of their demands in both public and closed meetings. Most of the Sociology faculty at Columbia reacted to the riots and to the questioning of their authority with fear, hostility, and complete rejection. Wallerstein wrote a quick book on the event that was not particularly extreme in tone, but that tied unrest in American universities to the larger problems of American life, and even to his emerging world-system perspective.[15] The book made sense of an exceptionally confusing and diverse period in American academia. It also advised student radicals to be realistic and moderate in recognizing that the American university was not the fulcrum of world power. Wallerstein was not condescending to the radicals. He understood their anger and put it in a broader perspective than most of them could. Of course, this did nothing to assuage his angry Columbia colleagues.

Association with Columbia University became increasingly unpleasant for both Hopkins and Wallerstein, and within a few years they abandoned their Columbia tenure. Hopkins went to the State University of New York at Binghamton. In 1970 Wallerstein went to the Stanford Center for the Advanced Study in the Behavioral Sciences, where he wrote the first volume of his world-system series. Then he went to McGill University in Montreal.

Although his stay at an elite English university in the middle of politically resentful French Quebec strengthened many of his ideas about the interaction between the world system, class, and ethnicity, Wallerstein did not get along with some of his McGill colleagues. Hopkins arranged for him to come to Binghamton, where an entire center for the study of the world system was established. This is the Fernand Braudel Center, whose journal, *Review*, and whose research activities, headed by Wallerstein and Hopkins, have been at the heart of Wallerstein's movement since 1975.[16]

Wallerstein's critical intellectual transformation, the realization that modern social change could be studied only in the context of a historically conceived world system, was essentially complete by the time the first volume of *The Modern World-System* was published in 1974. Since then, Wallerstein has continued to broaden his empirical base and to advance his enterprise, but his basic ideas have not changed.

The Selection of Units, Evidence, and Explanatory Concepts

Having decided that local, even continental, social science could not answer important questions about social change, Wallerstein had two choices: to remain an explicator of current events, as in his books on the problems of universities and on African unity, or to go further and explain how the capitalist world system came into being. He chose the latter in part because, as he put it, he did not want to continue "running after the headlines."[17] A more important reason was that he realized that the world system he was interested in had a beginning and a natural history of its own. He saw no way to understand it other than by tracing its history.

There are two general approaches to the explanation of social change. One is to assume that there are regular macrosociological laws that apply over all time and across all societies. Almost no one seriously accepts the total comparability of all societies because of the substantial differences in scale, technology, and geography among them. But most, perhaps almost all, social scientists outside of the discipline of history believe that if the variables of scale, technology, and geography are controlled, uniform laws of change can be discerned. Most assume, moreover, that geography is of decreasing importance as the scale and technological sophistication of societies increase. Time, then, becomes a contextual variable that can be decomposed into variables of scale and technology, and is unimportant for its own sake. If a sufficiently large number of cases can be studied, control of these confounding variables is possible, and the laws of social change can be established. History becomes nothing more than a field to be ransacked to increase sample size.

The other approach is to assume that each situation is explainable only by its history. There are no general laws, only one case after another, and history is the only explanation. Again, almost no one believes that it is totally futile to compare societies or to generalize, but there are historians who accept only commonplace psychological generalizations. They claim that each society contains so many important determining features shaped by its own unique history that the utility of comparison – beyond the construction of crude contrasts – is small.

Trained as a sociologist, Wallerstein found it difficult to take the second position. He had grappled with this question and related issues once before in a 1967 article coauthored with Terence Hopkins. The solution they offered was entirely consistent with the first position just described. Hopkins and Wallerstein delineated three types of comparative investigations and showed a strong preference for what is known today as cross-national study. Such investigations focus on what they called "national societies" as entities in their own right and examine a variety of types of variables characterizing these entities, including variables that indicate the place of national societies in international networks and systems. Hopkins and Wallerstein argued in the article that their favored strategy was well suited for testing any theory of modernization.[18]

This research strategy became unacceptable to Wallerstein for several reasons. First, he was no longer interested in the concept of modernization or in testing theories of modernization. Thus, the research strategy appropriate for testing such theories had, in his mind, become irrelevant. Second, this strategy was strongly associated with the group of social scientists whose theories and politics he had strongly rejected. Finally, Wallerstein believed that his world-system approach made it possible for him to dismiss this strategy altogether by negating the distinction between the two general approaches just described.[19] His world-system perspective dictated that the proper strategy was to identify the social system in which capitalism had grown as a single social system and to study that system as a totality.[20] By emphasizing the need to study a single system, Wallerstein hoped to end debates concerning both the comparability of societies and the degree to which social scientists could formulate generalizations about them.

The single social system Wallerstein identified was the capitalist world economy. It was not the loose collection of capitalist nation-states discussed by previous authors, but an economic entity spanning continents and polities, a unique and encompassing social system. To sharpen his imagery, Wallerstein contrasted his conception of the world economy with the more familiar concept of world empire. World empires are unitary political entities dominated by strong centers. Because they are unitary, they experience systemwide strains toward redistribution. World economies, by contrast, are integrated economically, not politically. While they lack political integration, the political entities embraced by a world economy constitute a single division of labor. This lack of political unity is one of the strengths of a world economy as a dynamic social system. Because of the absence of centralized control, economic actors have greater freedom of movement, which enhances their opportunities to amass wealth and promote accumulation on a global scale. These features of world economies also exacerbate the unequal distribution of wealth.

This focus on a single social system has important methodological implications. Because the capitalist world economy is defined as a single social system, its mechanisms cannot be discovered by comparing it to "other" capitalist world economies. If only one case exists, there is no choice but to establish its nature by knowing its history. Yet Wallerstein claimed that this is not a surrender to pure idiography. On the contrary, the distinction between nomothetic and idiographic social studies vanishes. According to Wallerstein, it was necessary to trace the history of the capitalist world economy from the sixteenth century because that was when the system was "born," its rules were established, and its conquest of the world began. Nothing that has happened since is comprehensible without knowing how it all began.

Wallerstein's reference to his enterprise as a type of astronomy, if disingenuous in its implied claim about the history of progress in that field, illustrates his feelings about the nature of social science: "I was inspired," he wrote, "by the analogy with astronomy which purports to explain the laws governing the universe, although (as far as we know) only one universe has ever existed."[21] By reaching for universal validity, too, Wallerstein knew that he could enhance his primary aim, to legitimize a version of world history favorable to the claims being made by the peripheral peoples of the world. Thus, his use of an astronomical analogy allowed him to justify his attempt to explain global inequality through historical analysis of the capitalist world economy.

This is not to say that smaller social units such as nation-states are irrelevant to world-system analysis. In fact, Wallerstein compares nation-states, regions, cities, and other units in a manner entirely consistent with the conventions of mainstream comparative sociology. What distinguishes his approach is the fact that these comparisons serve to illustrate general features of the world system. The similarities and differences between smaller units are not interesting in their own right. They are identified only as a way to demonstrate the nature of the world system as a whole.

Methodology involves more than defining the units and boundaries of the subject of study, though that is a critical first step. Evidence must also be gathered. Here Wallerstein faced another problem. No individual can master world history from primary sources. Nor can anyone even hope to read all the works based on primary sources. To gain enough expertise merely to judge the quality of the most important secondary sources would take scores of lifetimes. What Wallerstein needed, then, was a set of guidelines to help him select his secondary sources. A Marxist by political conviction, he might have limited himself to the well-worn paths of Marxist historiography. He certainly used this literature, but he also recognized that he had to broaden his intellectual base to make a more convincing case. He found what he was looking for in the French *Annales* school.

At the center of the *Annales* was Fernand Braudel, whose masterpiece *La Méditerranée et le monde Méditerranéen à l'époque de Philippe II* provided the raw material necessary for a detailed understanding of sixteenth-century economic history.[22] Even better, Braudel understood the notion of a system held together by geographic and commercial ties, not primarily by political unity. But the *Annales* offered more than this. Marc Bloch's work, and that of the medievalists he had inspired,[23] provided the information Wallerstein needed to get started with the "Medieval Prelude," the introductory chapter of the first volume of *The Modern World-System*. Pierre Chaunu, another of Wallerstein's favorite sources, was the preeminent historian of the Spanish colonial empire's economy in the sixteenth century.[24]

The *Annales* people were not dogmatic materialists, much less politically unified. But their work was consistent with a Marxist world view. They constituted a dense and disciplined network of researchers working on economic history, much of it written in or accessible through French, which Wallerstein knew fluently. They strengthened his hand in three ways. By using their journals and expertise he could tap a historical school that was highly respected by professional historians of all kinds and that was not tainted by ideological excesses. Moreover, despite the fame of the *Annales* school among specialized American historians, most American social scientists had never heard of them in the early 1970s. So, with legitimacy and easy access there was also novelty.

The comparison of Wallerstein with almost any of the *Annalistes*, however, reveals tremendous differences. They work with primary documents. Even Braudel in his old age continues to lean heavily on primary documents and illuminating anecdotes taken from original accounts.[25] Le Roy Ladurie has remained closely tied to documents even as he has become a writer of best-sellers.[26] Among lesser known *Annalistes* it is even more the case that history comes from documents of various sorts. Wallerstein's document, however, is the secondary work; in this respect, he is, like Reinhard Bendix, a user rather than a creator of historical work.

Why then do Wallerstein and Braudel admire and support each other? For Wallerstein, Braudel stands at the center of the raw material he needs to successfully produce his own brand of historical social science. On the other side, it is not difficult to imagine that it is gratifying to see one's work used and glorified

Yet this is probably not the whole picture. Wallerstein's use of illustrations and old maps in his volumes on the world system shows an affection for the grand sweep of history, for the romance of the great sea explorers, and for the daring of the cruel capitalist gangsters who made their fortunes from the misery of exploited peripheral populations. Braudel's work is unusual in being able to convey a sense of excitement and glamour while loading the reader with numbers and facts. If Wallerstein does not quite succeed in capturing this flavor in his own work, it may be because he has a theory to prove. Some of the sheer beauty and grandeur of global history does come through in *The Modern World-System*, which no doubt, is one of the things that has excited some social scientists bored by the emotional sterility of the usual academic fare. By associating himself with Braudel, Wallerstein could express a little of his own enchantment with history.

Wallerstein diverges profoundly from the *Annales* school in his choice of explanatory concepts. His central problem, to explain the origins and persistence of global inequality, dictates the use of explanatory concepts that are comparably global in scope. Wallerstein uses several explanatory mechanisms, all referring to the structure of the world economy itself.

The world economy is singular, yet it contains numerous political entities. This gives entrepreneurs a free hand to take advantage of the inequalities between areas, to use these inequalities to their economic advantage, without being subject to political pressures toward redistribution. International capitalists, in other words, are not politically accountable for the havoc they create in regions that were initially disadvantaged. This havoc usually takes the form of coercive labor systems in noncore, politically feeble areas. These coercive labor systems maintain low relative wages and thus deepen global inequality. Inequality persists as a system-level phenomenon because of the assignment of different regions of the world to the production of commodities using different systems of labor control. The economic stagnation of noncore areas and the growing gap between core and noncore areas are due ultimately to the political and economic advantages bestowed on core nations by virtue of their historical priority in the world economy. Wallerstein's most fundamental explanatory concept, therefore, is the composition of the world economy itself – the fact that it is a single economy containing many different political entities.

Wallerstein borrows other explanatory concepts and mechanisms from Lenin's theory of imperialism. These include (1) rivalry and competition between core powers, (2) inadequate demand, (3) wage pressure, and (4) the search for cheap raw materials.

The first explanatory mechanism Wallerstein borrows is geopolitical. Once the world capitalist economy was in place, countries dominated others as a way to insure their own survival. Peripheral countries came to be viewed as prizes necessary to the survival of core countries. Over time, as the technology of domination improved and as the stakes of the game increased, this system of competitive domination attained global proportions. The second explanatory mechanism argues that inadequate demand, especially in core areas, leads to recurrent crises of overproduction. Demand can be increased in two ways: by enlarging the system, that is, incorporating new areas, or by "deepening" the system, displacing competing forms of social organization in incorporated areas. The third explanatory mechanism argues that the demand for cheap raw materials provides further incentive for the incorporation of external areas and for the continued domination of peripheral areas by the core. Also, because the raw materials requirements of core countries shift with changes in technology, this mechanism also can be used to explain dynamic aspects of the world economy. Wage pressure as an explanation of global inequality focuses on the success of organized labor in core countries in securing higher wages. This reduces profitability and encourages a flight of capital to regions where wages are lower and workers less powerful – the periphery. International capitalists thus benefit from the uneven spread of development over the surface of the earth and support political actors in the periphery willing to keep wages down and labor docile.

These explanatory mechanisms are not entirely satisfactory to those who are not predisposed to accept Wallerstein's theory. Most economists, for example, adhere to some version of (or to some of the ideas contained in) the theory of comparative advantage, which argues that all countries, rich and poor, should benefit from the international trade. Since 1974, therefore, Wallerstein and associated scholars have been working on a more complete specification of the world economic mechanisms that maintain global inequality through the polarity of core versus peripheral areas in the modern world economy.[27]

289

An important part of this effort to explicate the world-system perspective has involved an attempt to specify in more detail how the world system is a system. For example, world-system scholars have attempted to demonstrate the existence of cycles and trends (short- and long-term) in the world economy as a whole. One manifestation of this effort is the rekindled interest in Kondratieff cycles.[28] An entire issue of *Review* and one of the annual meetings of the Political Economy of the World System Section of the American Sociological Association were devoted to the discussion of cycles and trends, with special attention to Kondratieff cycles.[29] Another indication of the interest in whole system cycles has been the attempt to link the periodic incorporation of external areas to economic cycles in the world economy. The goal of this effort has been to show that changes in basic features of the world system (for example, its size) result from its own internal dynamics, chiefly its economic cycles.[30] Finally, Wallerstein and his associates have also attempted to illustrate systemic properties by showing that the consequences of incorporation into the world system have been very similar for areas that differed markedly before incorporation. This effort has focused on postincorporation similarities among the Caribbean, the Ottoman Empire, and southern Africa.[31]

This recent interest in system-level cycles and trends, however, surfaced only after Wallerstein charted the emergence and the early history of the modern world economy and outlined the essentials of his world-system perspective. For this reason we must now turn to a detailed examination of his most important works.

From Theory to Interpretation: The History of the Modern World System

It would be neither useful nor possible to give full summaries of Wallerstein's volumes on the history of the capitalist world system. What can be done is to point to some of the solutions he offers to four major historical problems and to show how these solutions emerge from his theory.

The Problem of Western Development

At the outset, there is the old problem, probably the central issue of modern social science and history: Why Europe? What caused the West to progress faster than the rest of the world after about 1500? This was the question that lay at the center of Max Weber's work. Wallerstein found his answer in the interaction between politics and economics, not in the interaction between cultural and economic institutions, where Weber found his explanation.

As the European capitalist system emerged, it was never united politically. This meant that from its very beginning it was a world economy and not a world empire. This kept its merchant and manufacturing capitalists out of the confiscatory clutches of imperial rulers who would have destroyed profits and long-term investments by indulging in meaningless glory and trying to impose conformity over vast and unprofitable domains. Lack of unity in the West also allowed Atlantic rim societies to continue their long-range fishing, trading, and colonizing activities, unlike the Pacific rim regions of China, which were prevented from extending such activities by a center more concerned with the empire as a whole than with its troublesome coastal periphery. To enhance internal peace and stability, the Chinese Empire destroyed its chance to create a capitalist world system.

In Europe the Hapsburgs came the closest to creating a unified Western empire. In so doing they destroyed their own capitalists and condemned Spain and Italy to centuries of economic stagnation. The states that were successful in the long run were those that were unable to create continental empires and turned to overseas ones instead. They then used the complementary resources of their colonies to increase the economic division of labor in the world system. Spain failed to do this because it used its American resources simply to finance its European military and political enterprise.

If one of the reasons for the success of the capitalist system was its political disunity, how did its connective economic bonds grow? In part because of the mobility of capital afforded by the presence of competing states. If any state overtaxed its capitalists, they moved. In the second half of the sixteenth century, free Amsterdam replaced Hapsburg Antwerp as the financial and trading center of the system for precisely such reasons.

Economic strength allowed the areas at the core of the system to develop strong states. These became useful to defend mercantile interests. Why did these newly strengthened states not, in their turn, try to conquer European empires and overstrain their fiscal resources? France did, which explains its relative economic failure. England and the Netherlands did not because they lacked the size and centrality to continental affairs to try. As a result, their capitalists prospered and created state structures that served them instead of states that might crush them.

This very brief summary of the first five chapters of the first volume of *The Modern World-System* indicates some of the strengths of Wallerstein's approach. Through a series of paired comparisons that range from the Eurasian world as a whole to a little corner of Europe that lay at the heart of the developing world capitalist system, Wallerstein explicates both the origins and the modus operandi of the capitalist world economy. These contrasts provide a basis for illustrating and elaborating the conceptual terminology of the world-system perspective. The China-Europe juxtaposition shows the difference between world empires and a capitalist world economy. Comparing the Hapsburgs to the French, English, and Dutch explains Spain's failure to create a world empire as well as the ruin of those early capitalist centers that were controlled by or allied to Spain: Italy, Antwerp, and southern Germany. Finally, though this is only hinted at for later volumes, we are also given a framework for understanding why England and not France became the first industrial core nation.

At the same time we are led to conclusions that Wallerstein believes continue to hold today: Successful capital is mobile by its very nature. Capitalist states are not the ones that avoid interfering with the market but ones that help maximize profits. States that fail to protect their capitalists will lose their capital as long as they also remain part of the capitalist world system. Capitalism's success depends on the creation and maintenance of a division of labor between core and periphery. That Wallerstein makes it his task to point out these things even as he discusses history not only increases the scope of his work but also makes it appealing to a substantial number of readers who would not otherwise be interested in sixteenth-century economic and political history.

Many of Wallerstein's specific historical statements about the origins of the world system can be questioned.[32] But that is not entirely the point. His theory demands attention because it is so temporally and spatially inclusive and because, after all the historical quibbles are made, it has a plausibility shared by almost no other contemporary grand theory of social change.

Economic Backwardness

Wallerstein does not stop with his attempt to solve the problem of Western development. Other major issues and solutions follow. How and when did economic backwardness originate? The problem of Western economic success is widely posed, but the other side of the coin is not because most specialists of economic development and modernization simply assume that the reverse of progress is stagnation. In Wallerstein's opinion *active retardation* rather than mere stagnation is the fate of the periphery once it is incorporated into the world capitalist system.

Again, Wallerstein uses a paired comparison to illustrate his point; he contrasts Poland and Russia.[33] In the early fifteenth century both were vast states with thinly settled frontier zones. In most respects Poland was more advanced than Russia, but it was also closer and far more accessible to Western market forces. Poland was therefore "developed" as a cereal exporter to the West. Its peasants were turned into serfs in order to produce this grain. Its lords were strengthened by the wealth they received from the grain trade. Strong lords based on a strong export market worked against the interests of Poland's cities and putative manufacturing and mercantile capitalists. They imported finished goods from the West while their cities stagnated, and the central state, deprived of urban support and left to fight the large land magnates on its own, was demolished. Poland emerged in the seventeenth century as a thoroughly peripheralized weak state with a feeble domestic bourgeoisie, servile peasants, and no political future.

In Russia some of the same forces produced a different outcome because Russia stayed out of the capitalist system much longer. The growing demand for grain there was internal. It produced a tardy serfdom, too, because of the labor shortage, but it did not produce a strong nobility. On the contrary, the nobles became dependent on their growing state because they had no outside means of support. Although an independent bourgeoisie did not develop, neither did the cities decay. Russia in fact became a kind of "world economy" of its own, and had the time to develop a strong state autocracy that was to hold the country together in later centuries when it was penetrated by the Western market. The breathing space of several centuries provided by this development set Russia on a course quite opposite from Poland. Neither highly developed nor peripheralized, its strong state and relative economic autonomy allowed it to enter the world system as a semiperiphery and, eventually, to challenge the capitalist system itself.

For Wallerstein, the important lesson of this comparison lies in the demonstration of the effects of outside forces. The different fates of Russia and Poland come from their distinct histories of interaction with world capitalism rather than from purely internal factors. Of course, this illustrates the belief in the primordial nature of external as opposed to internal causes of change that lies at the core of Wallerstein's thinking.

Robert Brenner's criticism of Wallerstein, which was probably the most effective attack made after the publication of *The Modern World-System*, correctly takes him to task for neglecting the internal class relations of core and peripheral societies, chiefly England and Poland.[34] Brenner's criticism is based ultimately on his insistence on testing alternative causal arguments, especially about the origins of change. In a sense, however, the attack leaves the central structure of Wallerstein's argument unscathed because the question of internal versus external sources of change can turn into an endless debate about first causes. Wallerstein obviously has no interest in such a debate, and in subsequent publications he rests his case by continuing to emphasize the causes of change exogenous to individual countries and sticks to his position that the world system is the only proper basis for explaining major macrosocial changes. In short, he has persisted in his efforts to apply and elaborate his perspective, and has refrained from testing it against alternatives.

Nowhere is this clearer than in the discussion of the social effects of peripheralization. According to Wallerstein, the introduction of capitalist markets coerces the local peasantry into forced labor to extract primary products for the world system. It breaks the back of existing urban life. It impoverishes the masses so that their standard of living falls lower than before contact with the capitalist system. It fosters a parasitic local elite. This is not a reproduction of feudalism, or a petrification of tradition, but a devastating type of development whose consequences continue to be as catastrophic in the periphery of the late twentieth century as it was in Eastern Europe and Latin America in the sixteenth.[35]

Crises and Transitions

The concept of "crisis" is central to Marxist history because only out of the crises of various modes of production does the next mode emerge. Thus, feudalism was shaped by the lengthy crisis of slavery.[36] Capitalism was formed during the crisis of feudalism in the fourteenth and fifteenth centuries, and socialism will emerge from the crisis of capitalism that has begun in the twentieth century and will drag on into the twenty-first.[37] But a substantial number of economic historians do not accept the notion of periodic crises of capitalism, or of regular long cycles of expansion and contraction that produce adaptive reorganizations of the mode of production (much less the notion that capitalism is about to enter its ultimate cycle). At best, most economic specialists accept the idea of short-run business cycles that bear only pale resemblance to Marxism's grand swings and convulsive transitions. In this respect Wallerstein is in complete agreement with Marxism, so it is necessary for him to deal with the problem of cycles to build the foundation of a theory of transitions.

At the start of the second volume of the *Modern World-System*, which covers the years 1600 to 1750, Wallerstein justifies his position on crises by stressing their relative nature. He insists that a crisis may be brought on by a relative shift in the terms of trade of a key product, and that such a change will necessitate a series of readjustments, which then produce a new type of economy. Wallerstein saves the empirical historical base of his dialectic by spending a substantial portion of the second volume explaining the ramifications of the unfavorable terms of trade for cereals from the early seventeenth to the mid-eighteenth centuries. The point is not to find outright economic decline in the core (the Netherlands in the seventeenth and England in the eighteenth century) because that is not where it took place.[38] It is in the system as a whole that the crisis occurred, and it was the periphery that suffered while the core used this relative slowdown of growth to consolidate and improve its position.

He writes:

> What does a producer of export crops in the periphery do when there is suddenly an unfavorable market? There are two responses that make sense from his point of view. He can try to maintain his net income by expanding the volume of his export and/or by diminishing his production costs. Either or both often work in the short run for the individual entrepreneur, but they worsen the collective situation of peripheral producers in a given area in the medium run. Expansion of production of the export crop increases global production still more in a market where demand is already stretched. Diminishing production costs exhaust the potential of future production if it is achieved, as is most likely in peripheral areas, by intensification of exploitation of natural or human resources.[39]

Thus, adjustment and a kind of "retooling" to adapt to change in the core of the world economy becomes, in the periphery, yet another catastrophe. In the core the relative decline of the seventeenth century pushed countries toward greater nationalism and internal coherence to protect their domestic markets. This was the key to mercantilistic programs. In the periphery, the crisis was not merely relative, and it led to something quite opposite:

Charles Ragin, Daniel Chirot

While the period of world economic downturn led the core countries along the path of nationalism (mercantilism) and constitutional compromise within the upper strata, with the consequence of lowered ability of the lower strata to rebel, the weakness of the east European states meant that they could neither seek the advantages of a mercantilistic tactic nor *guarantee* any compromise within the upper strata. This led the peripheral areas in the direction of sharpening class conflict, increased regionalism and decreased national consciousness, the search for internal scapegoats, and acute restiveness of the peasantry. *Mutatis mutandis*, we shall see that the same thing was true of the old peripheral areas of southern Europe and the Americas. A rapid overview of the Christian Mediterranean shows that the same pattern prevailed for a seventeenth century that was characterized by "stagnation in business." The prices of primary exports fell.[40]

That the crisis was systemic and not local in character is an insight that comes from one of Wallerstein's major premises: The notion of a single world system is not meant to be taken as a metaphor or simply as an injunction to be comparative. Even though the capitalist world system has many different parts, an understanding of the whole provides a basis for interpreting the fate of each part.

What his theory can explain for the seventeenth century it can also predict for the late twentieth. In a book published in 1976 he foresaw the downturn of the world economy in the late 1970s and 1980s and predicted that the most peripheral parts of Africa would suffer most. This would prepare them for fuller incorporation into the world economy and more thorough exploitation at the end of the century, when the world economy will again turn up, probably for the last capitalist cycle before the arrival of world socialism.[41]

The Semiperiphery

One of the most original of Wallerstein's ideas is his solution of the problem of how to classify countries that are neither among the most advanced nor among the clearly peripheral. Some major examples are Venice and Spain in the late sixteenth century, Sweden in the seventeenth, Prussia in the eighteenth, Russia in the nineteenth and twentieth, Japan in the late nineteenth and early twentieth, and today, such countries as Brazil and South Africa. He labels them "semiperipheral," and they play a key role in his model.

Semiperipheral countries are engaged in the competition for core status, which keeps the world system in perpetual disequilibrium. Of the three categories of countries – core, periphery, and semiperiphery – only the third category always consists of specific states. The first two may be states, but they also refer to classes and ethnic groups that can be located among others of a different category. Indian laborers in 1600 in Potosi's silver mines, for example, were a coerced peripheral labor force living in an area ruled by the semiperipheral and declining Spanish state. African slaves in a seventeenth-century Dutch sugar plantation in the Caribbean were a peripheral labor force seized from an area external to the world system and working for core entrepreneurs. Semiperipheral cannot be used in this way and indicates neither a type of class nor subgroup within a state, but a kind of state itself.

In no other part of his theory does Wallerstein come so close to lapsing into the venerable historian's habit of anthropomorphizing countries as when he discusses the semiperiphery. As self-conscious actors attempting to enter the core, or trying to keep themselves from sliding into the periphery, semiperipheral states seem to develop motives and personalities similar to those that push ambitious people into career competition or into a search for personal wealth and power. In fact, some semiperipheral states become that way for precisely personal reasons. Wallerstein writes:

> When the first signs of economic downturn began to hit Europe in the seventeenth century, a strong personality like Gustavus Adolphus (1611–1632) was able to use the crisis to strengthen the Swedish state still further and launch an economic transformation. He mobilized Sweden's resources to fight the Thirty Years' War. He increased taxation . . . He instituted tax-farming.[42]

Sweden then proceeded to give Europe a bloody chase as it unsuccessfully scrambled for core status. Its motivation, presumably, was the ambition of its king and elite to be top dog.

Later it was Prussia's turn:

> The key to Prussia's development was that, from the perspective of the core powers, there was room for one major semiperipheral power in central Europe. When Sweden faltered, Prussia fit into that slot . . . But we cannot understand the process unless we realize in advance that *two* states in the same region could not simultaneously have succeeded in doing what Prussia did.[43]

Not only do semiperipheral states have personalities, but like individuals they compete for "slots" in an organization. Because core states do the same by competing for the position of "hegemon" in the system, the political mechanics of the world system correspond to Wallerstein's view of what capitalism is all about: a vicious scramble by tad-poles for the few available frog slots on shore. Wallerstein uses Tawney's scathing, contemptuous description of "tadpole capitalism," but for Wallerstein, states, not individuals, are the key competitors, and nowhere is the struggle more vicious than among semiperipheral states fighting to gain one of the few core positions.[44]

The semiperiphery does more. It acts as a kind of middle class in the system by doing the core's dirty work, being the focus of peripheral hostility, and also providing a home for core investments when wages rise too high in the old industrial centers. As Spain controlled Latin America for the core from the end of the sixteenth until the early nineteenth centuries, so did Sweden and later Prussia keep Poland in line in the seventeenth and eighteenth centuries. Brazil plays a similar role in contemporary Latin America and South Africa in Africa.[45]

The tensions caused by this ceaseless struggle are dangerous and may produce a genuine revolution, as happened in Russia in 1917 when the strains of fulfilling a semiperipheral role proved too much for the Czarist state to handle. As Russia was being pushed into the per-iphery, it reacted violently to avoid this, and by turning to communism it succeeded in making a strong claim for entering the core. In so doing, it is now in a position to threaten the entire system.[46]

There has long been agreement that countries at a middle stage of development are more prone to violent upheaval than either those above or below them. By placing this observation into a global context Wallerstein also explains the paradoxical interaction between such countries and the rich, well-established countries. The core needs a semiperiphery to balance the system, but it also fears the rivalry of advancing semiperipheral states. It thus encourages them but restrains them at the same time. This creates relatively strong state structures, aroused nationalism, and economic ambitions, which, if they are too successful, may be frustrated by core action.

It is possible to criticize this theoretical view as being too psychologi-cal and relying too much on old-fashioned diplomatic, balance-of-power reasoning. However, it does more. It satisfactorily handles such different but massively disruptive events as Sweden's attempt to con-quer northern Europe, Russia's love-hate relationship with the West from the seventeenth to the early twentieth centuries,[47] and Japan's behavior since 1868. Japan, of course, has now "made it" into the core, the only non-European state ever to do so, but at a substantial cost to everyone, not least of all because in reaching for a higher role it de-stroyed core control over most of East Asia.

In conclusion, Wallerstein's history of the world system, though far from complete (in 1983), has demonstrated its ability to handle both old and new problems and set them in a new, overarching theoretical framework. Whether he will succeed in extending his tour de force into the nineteenth and twentieth centuries remains to be seen. Hints of his planned volumes have been given in his essays, and there is no doubt that the entire body of his work still has a contemporary political thrust. So far, by writing in detail about the early stages of the capitalist world system but limiting his analysis of the late twentieth century to fairly cryptic essays, he has managed to balance the roles of social historian, social theorist, and political polemicist.

Issues of Theory and Method in World-System Analysis

To grasp fully the significance of Wallerstein's world-system perspective for historical analysis, it is necessary to contrast it with its main competition in the social sciences, the developmental perspective. The defining feature of the developmental perspective is its view of change as a societal-level endogenetic process. This view of change is present in almost every major sociological theory, in modern theories, such as functionalism, and in the writings of classical theorists such as Durkheim and Marx. The developmental view of change is seductive because it emphasizes social structural sources of change and thereby makes historical change seem sociological. When change is viewed as a process that is both natural and internal to "societies" – usually understood as coterminous with nations – it is possible to formulate general, abstract propositions about change. Each case is viewed as essentially independent so that quasiexperimental manipulations become possible and "scientific" requirements are met.

This idea of endogenetic change is often coupled in developmental thinking with a use of society as both an explanatory and an observational unit.[48] An observational unit defines the objects of a statement of empirical regularity; an explanatory unit defines the level of the causal mechanism specified in the explanation of an empirical regularity. Thus, the statement "Economic development is positively associated with representative democracy because developed countries have a more advanced level of structural differentiation and a consequent higher level of internal consensus" uses national societies as both observational and explanatory units. The empirical regularity is observed at the societal level, and the explanation of that regularity cites societal-level attributes. Although an endogenetic view of change does not necessitate using society in this way, the two metatheoretical ideas are highly compatible.

Also compatible with the developmental perspective is the use of explanatory units that are smaller than society. This practice is most common in social psychological modernization theory. Alex Inkeles and David Smith, for example, argue that large-scale social changes, such as economic development, are predicated on individual-level attitudinal change on a mass scale.[49] They believe that institutions such as schools and the media promote values that are internalized by members of society. Individuals who internalize what Inkeles and Smith call "modern values" are more likely to create and staff economic institutions (e.g., banks, firms, factories) central to large-scale change. This line of reasoning is entirely consistent with developmentalism. The original impetus for changing values may, in this case, come from the outside, but the mechanisms through which individual values are changed are internal. Furthermore, no limit on change is set by any exogenous constraints, but only whatever force endogenous tradition may exert. This has the effect of keeping social change well within the boundaries of single societies.

In *Social Change and History*, Robert Nisbet argues that the developmental perspective is based on a metaphorical way of thinking about social change that is deeply embedded in Western thought.[50] Traditionally, this metaphor has been used to describe changes in abstract entities, such as "Western civilization" or "capitalism," as though they were growth processes in biological organisms. The metaphor endows these entities with lives of their own: they emerge, grow, transverse stages, and terminate either by passing on or by transforming themselves into other types of social organisms. As long as the image remains purely metaphorical, Nisbet argues, it is useful; it aids in conceptualizing abstract entities. Unfortunately, the metaphor becomes reified as the basis of theories about empirical entities such as nation-states. Then it has failed because it has led to blatantly ahistorical explanations. One need not know the specific history of a place to understand how it came to be what it is now. Identifying it according to preconceived typology is sufficient to explain its direction and future. In this metaphorically laden perspective, Nisbet argues, change is seen as natural, immanent, and directional, when in fact it usually involves crisis, disruption, and discontinuity.

An understanding of developmentalism as a theory of change is important because Wallerstein developed his perspective as an explicit reaction against it. In fact, Wallerstein cites Nisbet's attack with approval.[51] He is especially supportive of Nisbet's contention that developmentalism is ahistorical to the point of being antihistorical, that it is incapable of explaining social change.

It is possible to conclude from Nisbet's statements about change (that it involves crisis and disruption and is typically exogenetic) that any attempt at social scientific generalization about macrosocial change is unwise. Nisbet apparently came to this conclusion, for he does not offer a coherent theoretical alternative of his own. Wallerstein, however, did not reach the same conclusion. In many respects his theory of the world system is an attempt to save the social scientific analysis of change from the clutches of both developmentalism and extreme historical specificity, for he repudiates both.

Wallerstein attempts this rescue by embracing the notion of change as exogenetic and building his theory around it. Note that this involves an inversion of normal practices. Typically, when American-trained social scientists are asked to explain an empirical regularity, they cite causal mechanisms that operate across multiple units, at the same level as (or on a smaller scale than) the observed regularity. The basic idea behind Wallerstein's perspective is that by constructing a theoretical model of the world system in which countries operate, it is possible to address exogenetic change scientifically. In short, the possibility of generalizing about the seemingly random crises and disruptions that constitute change is established by constructing a model of the larger system that produces such events. After all, that which is exogenetic to individual countries must be endogenetic to some larger entity, namely the world system that encompasses all of them. This gives his perspective a sense of closure that is absent in the developmental perspective. What developmentalists must treat as error induced by the vagaries of the historical record can be conceptualized in Wallerstein's perspective as the effect of world-system-level events and processes.

This solution to the problem of addressing historical change is not, however, without problems of its own. Nisbet's main objection to developmentalism is not simply its tendency to endow societies with the ability to change because of their internal dynamics, but also the next step, explanation by ontogenetic reasoning and organic analogy. If the potentialities and direction of development of any social system are inherent from its birth, there is little need to be historical. Wallerstein falls prey to this precise sin. His discussion of the world system is spiced with organic analogies. The modern world system was "born" in the long sixteenth century. It matured and went through stages of growth. Its aging and ultimate "demise" are predictable, and it will then turn into a new organism, the socialist world system. If there is nothing objectionable to making all sources of change in the world system endogenous, and then arguing through a biological metaphor (after all, astronomers do it when they talk about the births and deaths of stars, galaxies, and the entire universe), the problem comes when this is taken as a priori knowledge that is sufficient to understand all historical change. The concrete study of change no longer becomes necessary except as illustration. Endogenous causality transformed into ontogeny has become ontology. Knowing that there is a capitalist world system becomes, as it were, intuitively obvious for the true believer, and all reasoning flows from this. There is no need to waste effort on discovering the fundamental causes of change.

Many critics of Wallerstein have discussed his theoretical, concrete, and even logical lacunae.[52] All of them miss one important point. It is not possible to reduce his central theory to a set of logical propositions that can be proved or falsified; they are based on a political vision.

Nisbet, and his predecessor in the attack against "historicism," Karl Popper, understood perfectly well that the reason for the creation of deterministic laws of social change was political. For Popper, all laws of social change are either self-evident or false.[53] For Nisbet, all theories of stages of development that lead to some logical ultimate end are futile. More and more events intrude into the theoretical model until, finally, it becomes necessary to distort the record or make up events to save the theory.[54] Despite Nisbet's criticism, those who make politics the first order of their intellectual agenda know what they are doing. It is unlikely that anyone could attempt as grand an enterprise as Wallerstein's without a powerful ideological vision of the world.

To be more persuasive, Wallerstein borrows a page from Marc Bloch and turns it to his own purpose. Bloch showed that it could be useful to read history backward, to begin with such things as present field shapes and then to reason into the past to interpret otherwise obscure and misleading documents. Wallerstein has taken this a step further, as Aristide Zolberg points out:

> His [Wallerstein's] depiction of the world of the sixteenth century appears credible because it bears an uncanny resemblance to the familiar representation of the world of the late twentieth century in the literature on dependency; and the realism of the latter portrait is in turn vouchsafed by its resemblance to the ancestor.[55]

Not that this is surprising. It is precisely what Wallerstein claims to be doing.

What about the supposition that all social change comes from the world system and is not reducible to smaller-scale causes? If Waller-stein corrects prior overemphasis on endogenous causality and mechanisms of change, he gives no obvious reasons to accept a completely opposite emphasis. Acceptance of his view rests ultimately on simple appreciation of the breadth of its perspective. Yet, by making the world system almost the only meaningful source of change, except for the occasional "strong personality," Wallerstein is able to make a series of important historical evasions.

The most important is one that Marxist scholars have never been able to handle easily – culture. For Wallerstein no cultural differences between various peoples need be taken into account to explain different rates of development. To be sure, this is a conscious reaction against Weber, but it leads at times to some awkward reasoning.

One of the most glaring deficiencies of world-system theory is its inability to explain why economic development affects large areas with roughly similar cultural traditions in very similar ways, despite their profound differences in power or position in the world system. Thus, northwestern Europe industrialized before the rest of the world, but this included England, followed closely by Belgium, northern France, western Germany, Switzerland, and the Netherlands. Switzerland was a weak, internationally insignificant state, Belgium was not unified at all until well after industrialization, and western Germany was politically subordinated to the state that absorbed it. Later, industrialization spread to Scandinavia, an outcome that could not be anticipated at all in Wallerstein's theory. Sweden already had failed as a semiperiphery, as had Spain a century earlier, and neighboring Denmark had fallen into the periphery in the eighteenth century.[56] Why, then, do both Scandinavian societies, a century later, have such an easy time catching up to the core, while Spain does not?[57]

Another example of Wallerstein's neglect of culture is found in the treatment of the North American colonies of England. These colonies began as a periphery, but easily moved up to the semiperiphery because, according to Wallerstein, the English were too busy with their civil war in the 1640s to stop them.[58] Such remarks betray an unwillingness to consider the interaction between culture and economy. This neglect may be valuable in cases where the use of an exaggerated model can lead to important insights. For others, however, it leads to serious distortions of the historical record. In fact, Wallerstein's distortions have outraged some commentators.[59] The anomalous development of England's North American colonies is not surprising, any more than is the later success of Australia and New Zealand, despite their entry into the world system as primary exporters and their continued peripherality (in strict dependency theory terms). Some societies learn the culture of industrialization easily because they were very close to it from the outset.

In his first volume Wallerstein was at least willing to consider the importance of Western scientific progress and to tie it to the freedom from imperial censorship.[60] In his second world-system volume, however, even this has vanished, and the scientific and philosophical revolution of the seventeenth century receives only the following comment:

> Three dates, then for a rupture: around 1500, 1650, and 1800; three (or more) theories of history: 1800, with an emphasis on industrialism as the crucial change; 1650, with an emphasis either on the moment when the first "capitalist" states (Britain and the Netherlands) emerge or on the emergence of presumably key "modern" ideas of Descartes, Leibnitz, Spinoza, Newton, and Locke; and 1500, with an emphasis on the creation of a capitalist *world* system, as distinct from other forms of economies.[61]

The absence of culture also plays a major role in Wallerstein's theory of ethnicity. According to Wallerstein, ethnicity is a defensive reaction to the dynamic intrusion of the world system. It is a conscious reaction against the outside, orchestrated in large part by dominant strata of an emergent ethnic group. This means that fundamental differences of religion, language, and habit are irrelevant until they are activated in response to a change in the world system.[62] While this has major political implications for the present world, it can also produce unsatisfactory history.

For example, Austria's failure to become a power of the first order, especially when compared to Prussia, is explained with a cryptic sentence: "The key stumbling block to achieving such integration in the Habsburg Empire was Turkish military power."[63] While this is a doubtful but defensible proposition for the seventeenth century, it seriously contradicts the evidence for the early eighteenth century. Was it not, in large measure, the very fact that by European standards Austria was an exceptionally heterogeneous mix of peoples that blocked its integration? Certainly other countries in Europe had major, internal, culturally based differences, but none on the scale of Austria, whose Germanic center was overwhelmed by the provinces instead of vice versa. It is clear that Wallerstein's treatment of ethnicity is nothing more than a delineation of the subset of ethnicity-based phenomena that is relevant to the theory. In his perspective, ethnicity exists when it is clearly linked to world-system phenomena; otherwise, it is not ethnicity.

In many respects it is useless to raise these objections because the neglect of certain issues in Wallerstein's work is part of his grand design. His goals are to show that a world systemic interpretation works and to persuade readers that the basic theoretical premises are sound. Once these are accepted, a series of assertions about the contemporary world can be made. A large number of situations, from Stalin's excesses to the Cambodian tragedy and the rise of Solidarity in Poland, can be explained by the exploitative nature of the capitalist world system and its contradictions.[64] Some of Wallerstein's interpretations of current and past events are plausible; some are not. The perspective, however, is a given; Wallerstein's (and his followers') intention is to use the perspective to interpret events, not to test it in any way against alternative arguments. Wallerstein's perspective is the start of his long journey through history, and it will be his conclusion as well. It is not surprising, therefore, that the theoretical and methodological foundations of his work rest on assumptions consistent with such views or that they are designed to enhance their legitimacy.

Wallerstein's world-system perspective has both helped and hurt historical social science. Despite its shortcomings, it has generated considerable interest in historical and comparative sociology. Previously, sociologists especially seemed compelled to study abstract, universal features of societies and to refrain from studying particular historical chronologies. Wallerstein's work has helped to legitimate the study of concrete historical sequences and outcomes and has rekindled interest in understanding the historical origins of contemporary social phenomena. Yet the perspective also has posed obstacles to historical research. The historical record is complex, and much of this complexity cannot be grasped in a world-system perspective. While it is not necessary to surrender to complexity and to take the position that every historical outcome can be explained only in terms of its own history, slavish adherence to a monolithic theory of change such as Wallerstein's interferes with the task of historical explanation.

It is possible, however, to take advantage of the ideas and concepts that Wallerstein has introduced and resist the lure of his grand theory. The key is to use these concepts in the same manner as other social science concepts and models are used in historical research. Concepts are recognized as tentative from the outset, and there is no expectation that there will be a simple or straightforward correpondence between the conceptual model and the historical record.[65] Conceptual models should be seen as simplified exaggerations of social phenomena that help social scientists make sense out of the diversity and complexity they confront. Rather than ignoring or obscuring unsupportive evidence, social scientists engaged in historical research should see this lack of fit as a basis for interpreting significant unique features. In this way, interpretation is not strait-jacketed by theory, and the investigation remains focused on understanding the chronology, not on reaffirming a theory.

Conclusion: Wallerstein's Influence

Wallerstein's influence in macrosociology, historical sociology, and the study of social change has been substantial. He has produced a fairly long list of students who have written smaller but still macroscopic studies of various parts of the world system, and there have been others who, while not his students, have been inspired by his example. In the *New York Review of Books* in 1983 Geoffrey Barraclough began a review of a book by Eric Wolf with this statement:

> "Macro-history," so long discredited, is back in favor, but not the sort we used to associate with the name of Arnold Toynbee. Today it takes the form of long, sophisticated books, frequently with a distinctly Marxist flavor, tracing the story of the transformation of Europe from a marginal frontier of the Old World into a hub of wealth and power, and its impact on the non-Western world. "The Rise of the West," W. H. McNeill called it many years ago; but the new mode was really inaugurated by Immanuel Wallerstein with his "world system" analysis.[66]

Many of the first published books that followed Wallerstein's theories and style were produced by his Columbia University students. Michael Hechter argued that Wallerstein's core-periphery model could be used to explain the persistence of ethnic tensions in core societies. He attempted to show that the Celtic fringe had been turned into England's domestic periphery. Daniel Chirot analyzed a typically peripheral society, Romania, claiming that after a long exposure to capitalist market forces, it remained hopelessly poor and backward. Frances Moulder explained Japan's rapid development by its ability to shield itself from economic colonialism. She argued that Qing China, by contrast, had been penetrated by Western capitalism in the nineteenth century and has been peripheralized so that its development was blocked. Fred Block explained the modern capitalist banking and financial system in world-systemic terms.[67]

This kind of work has spread.[68] Peter Evans's book on Brazil combines a sophisticated use of Latin American dependency theory and world-system concepts to examine the role of the world economy and multinational firms in that country's spectacular but uneven industrialization in the 1960s and 1970s.[69] Eric Wolf's book is another example.[70] There will be other major books that, while they will accept some of Wallerstein's world-system perspective, will also criticize and expand it.

What explains this widespread emulation of Wallerstein? In many respects, it is his vision of social science more than his vision of the world system. Every aspect of Wallerstein's vision of social scientific work challenges social scientists to view social phenomena broadly, to examine seemingly isolated social phenomena as parts of a larger system. He encourages social scientists to locate the phenomena they study within "totalities" so that all possible influences can be identified. He states further that they should view social phenomena historically and that they should not let disciplinary boundaries between the social sciences constrain their investigations. Finally, he challenges social scientists to clarify their implicit political assumptions and not be deceived into thinking that they can conduct social science in a vacuum. They should recognize (and identify) the social and political origins and contexts of the questions they ask.[71] The effect of Wallerstein's presentation of this vision of social science has been amplified by the fact that he is the chief exemplar of the strategy he promotes.

While this vision of social science has inspired many, Wallerstein's vision of the world system continues to be a powerful draw, and he has carefully provided for the nurturance and propagation of this vision. With the help of Terence Hopkins, he has taken a long step toward institutionalizing his world-system view by creating a major center at the State University of New York at Binghamton to foster research and publications that will strengthen and increase his intellectual influence. The Fernand Braudel Center has its journal, *Review*, which has brought together a distinguished international collection of articles and comments on the history of the world system and its contemporary implications. The Center is engaged in some important work on such topics as the nature of Kondratieff cycles and the process through which the Ottoman Empire was turned into a peripheral area.

Ultimately, Wallerstein would like to create an American version of the *Annales* school. His version of it also has a complex and long-ranging political program, not merely a scholarly one. It will not only try to understand the history of the capitalist world system, but also attempt to prepare the intellectual ground for the coming of a world socialist system.

Charles Ragin, Daniel Chirot

Wallerstein's undertaking is mammoth. Even if he does not succeed entirely, he has already scored enough successes to insure that, at the very least, he will have an important impact on the historical work and on political intellectuals of the late twentieth century.

Notes

1. Immanuel Wallerstein, *The Modern World-System: Capitalist Agriculture and the Origins of the European World-Economy in the Sixteenth Century* (New York: Academic Press, 1974). Hereafter *The Modern World-System.*
2. Immanuel Wallerstein, "North Atlanticism in Decline," *SAIS Review* 4 (1982): 21–26; "From Feudalism to Capitalism: Transition or Transitions?" *Social Forces* 55 (1976): 273–83. A collection of Wallerstein's most important essays is presented in Immanuel Wallerstein, *The Capitalist World Economy* (Cambridge, U.K.: Cambridge University Press, 1979).
3. Immanuel Wallerstein, "The Rise and Future Demise of the World Capitalist System: Concepts for Comparative Analysis," *Comparative Studies in Society and History* 16 (1974): 389–415.
4. An overview of the recent history of sociological theories of development is presented in Daniel Chirot, "Changing Fashions in the Study of the Social Causes of Economic Progress," in *Sociology: Survey of a Quarter Century*, ed. James F. Short (Beverly Hills, Calif.: Sage, 1981), pp. 259–82.
5. Immanuel Wallerstein, "McCarthyism and the Conservative" (Master's Thesis, Columbia University, 1954).
6. Immanuel Wallerstein, *The Road to Independence: Ghana and the Ivory Coast* (The Hague: Mouton, 1964); *Africa: The Politics of Independence* (New York: Vintage Books, 1961). Hereafter *The Politics of Independence.*
7. Wallerstein, *The Politics of Independence*, pp. 153–67.
8. Immanuel Wallerstein, *Social Change: The Colonial Situation* (New York: Wiley, 1966).
9. Immanuel Wallerstein, *Africa: The Politics of Unity: An Analysis of a Contemporary Social Movement* (New York: Random House, 1967). Hereafter *The Politics of Unity.*
10. Wallerstein, *The Politics of Unity*, p. 223.
11. Ibid., p. 224.
12. Ibid., p. 237.
13. Ibid., p. vi.
14. Ibid., p. 253.
15. Immanuel Wallerstein, *University in Turmoil: The Politics of Change* (New York: Atheneum, 1969). Wallerstein also coedited a two volume work on the same topic with Paul Starr, *The University Crisis Reader* (New York: Random House, 1971).
16. Originally, *Review* was published by the State University of New York; Sage Publications, Beverly Hills, Calif., has published the journal since its third volume.
17. Wallerstein, *The Modern World-System I*, p. 5.
18. Terence Hopkins and Immanuel Wallerstein, "The Comparative Study of National Societies," *Social Science Information* 6 (1967) 27–58.
19. Wallerstein, *The Capitalist World-Economy*, pp. vii–xii.
20. Wallerstein, *The Modern World-System I*, pp. 347–48.
21. Ibid., p. 7.

22. Fernand Braudel, *La Méditerranée et le monde Méditerranéen à l'époque de Philippe II*, 2nd ed. (Paris: Armand and Colin, 1966).
23. Marc Bloch, *Feudal Society* (Chicago: University of Chicago Press, 1961). A good representative of later work on the Middle Ages inspired by Bloch is Georges Duby. See, for example, his *Rural Economy and Country Life in the Medieval West* (Columbia: University of South Carolina Press, 1968).
24. Pierre and Hugette Chaunu, *Seville et l'Atlantique (1504–1650)*, 8 vol. (Paris: S.E.V.P.E.N., 1955–59).
25. Fernand Braudel, *The Structures of Everyday Life*, vol. 1 (New York: Harper & Row, 1981).
26. Emmanuel Le Roy Ladurie, *Montaillou* (New York: Braziller, 1978).
27. Samir Amin, Giovanni Arrighi, Andre Gunder Frank, and Immanuel Wallerstein, *Dynamics of Global Crisis* (New York: Monthly Review Press, 1981).
28. N. D. Kondratieff, "The Long Waves of Economic Life," *Review of Economic Statistics* 17 (1935) 105–15. Kondratieff comments that when economists discuss cycles, they usually refer to cycles of three and a half to eleven years in length. Kondratieff proposes, by contrast, that there is reason to believe that there are much longer waves in capitalist economies, averaging about fifty years in length. Out of these fifty-year waves it is possible to construct still longer sequences of waves, spanning centuries.
29. Vol. 2, no. 4 of *Review* (State University of New York, 1979) is devoted to long waves. See also Terence Hopkins and Immanuel Wallerstein, eds., *Processes of the World-System* (Beverly Hills, Calif.: Sage, 1980).
30. Immanuel Wallerstein et al., "Cyclical Rhythms and Secular Trends of the Capitalist World-Economy: Some Premises, Hypotheses, and Questions," *Review* 2 (1979): 483–500.
31. See, for example, Immanuel Wallerstein, "The Ottoman Empire and the Capitalist World-Economy: Some Questions for Research," *Review* 2 (1979): 389–98.
32. A thorough review of Wallerstein's more debatable historical arguments is presented in Herman Kellenbenz's review of *The Modern World-System I*, *Journal of Modern History* 48 (1976) 685–92.
33. Wallerstein, *The Modern World-System I*, pp. 301–24.
34. Robert Brenner, "Agrarian Class Structure and Economic Development in Pre-industrial Europe," *Past and Present* 70 (1976): 30–75; "The Origins of Capitalist Development: A Critique of Neo-Smithian Marxism," *New Left Review* 104 (1977): 25–92.
35. Wallerstein, *The Modern World-System I*, pp. 87–100; *The Capitalist World-Economy*, pp. 119–31.
36. Perry Anderson, *Passages from Antiquity to Feudalism* (London: New Left Books, 1974).
37. Wallerstein, *The Capitalist World-Economy*, pp. 138–151.
38. Immanuel Wallerstein, *The Modern World-System II: Mercantilism and the Consolidation of the European World-Economy 1600–1750* (New York: Academic Press, 1980), pp. 37–125.
39. Wallerstein, *The Modern World-System II*, pp. 130–31.
40. Ibid., pp. 144–45.
41. Immanuel Wallerstein, "The Three Stages of African Involvement in the World-Economy," in *The Political Economy of Contemporary Africa*, ed. Peter Gutkind and Immanuel Wallerstein (Beverly Hills, Calif.: Sage, 1976), pp. 30–57.
42. Wallerstein, *The Modern World-System II*, p. 204.
43. Ibid., p. 225.

44. Wallerstein, *The Capitalist World-Economy*, p. 101.
45. Wallerstein, *The Modern World-System II*, pp. 95–118.
46. Ibid., pp. 30–31.
47. Theodore Von Laue, *Why Lenin? Why Stalin? A Reappraisal of the Russian Revolution, 1900–1930* (Philadelphia: Lippincott, 1971).
48. Charles Ragin, "Comparative Sociology and the Comparative Method," *International Journal of Comparative Sociology* 22 (1981): 102–20.
49. Alex Inkeles and David H. Smith, *Becoming Modern: Individual Change in Six Developing Countries* (Cambridge, Mass.: Harvard University Press, 1974).
50. Robert Nisbet, *Social Change and History* (New York: Oxford University Press, 1970).
51. Wallerstein, *The Capitalist World-Economy*, p. 2.
52. Major reviews of Wallerstein's work, especially of *The Modern World-System I*, are listed in the bibliography at the end of this chapter.
53. Karl Popper, *The Poverty of Historicism* (New York: Harper Torchbooks, 1964), p. 143.
54. Nisbet, *Social Change and History*, pp. 251–52.
55. Aristide Zolberg, "Origins of the Modern World-System: A Missing Link," *World Politics* 33 (1981): 253–81.
56. Wallerstein, *The Modern World-System II*, pp. 221–23.
57. Relevant economic data are presented in Paul Bairoch, "Europe's Gross National Product, 1800–1975," *Journal of European Economic History* 5 (1976): 273–340.
58. Wallerstein, *The Modern World-System II*, p. 237.
59. Arthur Stinchcombe, "The Growth of the World-System," *American Journal of Sociology* 87 (1982): 1389–95.
60. Wallerstein, *The Modern World-System I*, p. 53.
61. Wallerstein, *The Modern World-System II*, p. 7.
62. Wallerstein, *The Capitalist World-Economy*, pp. 184–91.
63. Wallerstein, *The Modern World-System II*, p. 232.
64. Wallerstein, *The Capitalist World-Economy*, pp. 239–41; "North Atlanticism in Decline."
65. Charles Ragin and David Zaret, "Theory and Method in Comparative Research: Two Strategies," *Social Forces* 61 (1983): 731–54.
66. Geoffrey Barraclough, "Return of the Natives," *The New York Review of Books* 30 (June 2, 1983): 33–35.
67. Michael Hechter, *Internal Colonialism: The Celtic Fringe in British National Development, 1536–1966* (London: Routledge & Kegan Paul, 1975); Daniel Chirot, *Social Change in a Peripheral Society: The Creation of a Balkan Colony* (New York: Academic Press, 1976); Frances Moulder, *Japan, China and the Modern World-Economy: Toward a Reinterpretation of East Asian Development ca. 1600 to ca. 1918* (Cambridge, U.K.: Cambridge University Press, 1977); Fred Block, *The Origins of International Economic Disorder* (Berkeley: University of California Press, 1977).
68. An important example of the increased popularity of world-system analysis is the Political Economy of the World-System Section of the ASA. This section holds annual meetings independent of the ASA and publishes its proceedings. Examples of the published proceedings include Barbara Kaplan, ed., *Social Change in the Capitalist World-Economy* (Beverly Hills, Calif.: Sage, 1978); Walter Goldfrank, ed., *The World-System of Capitalism: Past and Present* (Beverly Hills, Calif.: Sage, 1979); Terence Hopkins and Immanuel Wallerstein, eds., *Processes of the World-System* (Beverly Hills, Calif.: Sage, 1980); W. Ladd Hollist and Robert J. Boydston, eds., *World-System Structure*

(Beverly Hills, Calif.: Sage, 1981). Other examples of the spread of world-system analysis are John Meyer and Michael Hannan, eds., *National Development and the World-System: Educational, Economic and Political Change, 1950–1970* (Chicago: University of Chicago Press, 1979); and Albert Bergesen, ed., *Studies of the Modern World-System* (New York: Academic Press, 1980).
69. Peter Evans, *Dependent Development: The Alliance of Multinational, State, and Local Capital in Brazil* (Princeton, N.J.: Princeton University Press, 1979).
70. Eric Wolf, *Europe and People Without History* (Berkeley: University of California Press, 1983).
71. Wallerstein, *The Capitalist World-Economy*, pp. vii–xii.

Selected Bibliography

THE MOST IMPORTANT WORKS OF IMMANUEL WALLERSTEIN

"McCarthyism and the Conservative." Master's thesis, Columbia University, 1954.
Africa; The Politics of Independence. New York: Vintage Books, 1961.
The Road to Independence: Ghana and the Ivory Coast. The Hague: Mouton, 1964.
Social Change: The Colonial Situation. New York: Wiley, 1966.
Africa: The Politics of Unity: An Analysis of a Contemporary Social Movement. New York: Random House, 1967.
University in Turmoil: The Politics of Change. New York: Atheneum, 1969.
The Modern World-System: Capitalist Agriculture and the Origins of the European World-Economy in the Sixteenth Century. New York: Academic Press, 1974.
"The Three Stages of African Involvement in the World-Economy." In *The Political Economy of Contemporary Africa*, edited by Peter Gutkind and Immanuel Wallerstein, pp. 30–57. Beverly Hills, Calif.: Sage, 1976.
The Capitalist World-Economy. Cambridge, U.K.: Cambridge University Press, 1979.
The Modern World-System II: Mercantilism and the Consolidation of the European World-Economy 1600–1750. New York: Academic Press, 1980.
Dynamics of Global Crisis, with Samir Amin, Giovanni Arrighi, and Andre Gunder Frank. New York: Monthly Review Press, 1981.

BOOKS BY STUDENTS AND FOLLOWERS OF IMMANUEL WALLERSTEIN

Bergesen, Albert, ed. *Studies of the Modern World System.* New York: Academic Press, 1980.
Billings, Dwight. *Planters and the Making of the "New South": Class, Politics, and Development in North Carolina 1865–1900.* Chapel Hill: University of North Carolina Press, 1979.
Block, Fred. *The Origins of International Economic Disorder.* Berkeley: University of California Press, 1977.
Chase-Dunn, Christopher, ed. *Socialist States in the World System.* Beverly Hills, Calif.: Sage, 1982.
Chirot, Daniel. *Social Change in a Peripheral Society: The Creation of a Balkan Colony.* New York: Academic Press, 1976.
Chirot, Daniel. *Social Change in the Twentieth Century.* New York: Harcourt Brace Jovanovich, 1977.
Evans, Peter. *Dependent Development: The Alliance of Multinational, State, and Local Capital in Brazil.* Princeton, N.J.: Princeton University Press, 1979.

Hechter, Michael. *Internal Colonialism: The Celtic Fringe in British National Development, 1536–1966.* London: Routledge & Kegan Paul, 1975.

Meyer, John W., and Michael Hannan, eds. *National Development and the World-System: Educational, Economic, and Political Change, 1950–1970.* Chicago: University of Chicago Press, 1979.

Moulder, Frances. *Japan, China and the Modern World-Economy: Toward a Reinterpretation of East Asian Development ca. 1600 to ca. 1918.* Cambridge, U.K., and New York: Cambridge University Press, 1977.

Schneider, Jane, and Peter Schneider, *Culture and Political Economy in Western Sicily.* New York: Academic Press, 1976.

CRITIQUES OF IMMANUEL WALLERSTEIN'S WORLD-SYSTEM THEORY

Brenner, Robert. "The Origins of Capitalist Development: A Critique of Neo-Smithian Marxism." *New Left Review* 104 (1977): 25–92.

Chirot, Daniel. "Immanuel Wallerstein's *The Modern World-Economy.*" *Social Forces* 59 (1980): 538–43.

Chirot, Daniel. "Immanuel Wallerstein's *The Modern World-System II.*" *Journal of Social History* 15 (1982): 561–65.

Chirot, Daniel, and Thomas D. Hall. "World-System Theory." *Annual Review of Sociology* 8 (1982): 81–106.

Collins, Randall. *Sociology Since Midcentury.* New York: Academic Press, 1981, pp. 45–56.

Gourvitch, Peter. "The International System and Regime Formation: A Critical Review of Anderson and Wallerstein." *Comparative Politics* 10 (1978): 419–38.

Janowitz, Morris. "A Sociological Perspective on Wallerstein." *American Journal of Sociology* 82 (1977): 1090–97.

Kellenbenz, Hermann. "The Modern World-System: Capitalist Agriculture and the Origins of the European World Economy in the Sixteenth Century." *Journal of Modern History* 48 (1976): 685–92.

Skocpol, Theda. "Wallerstein's World Capitalist System: A Theoretical and Historical Critique." *American Journal of Sociology* 82 (1977): 1075–90.

Stinchcombe, Arthur. "The Growth of the World System." *American Journal of Sociology* 87 (1982): 1389–95.

Zolberg, Aristide. "Origins of the Modern World-System: A Missing Link." *World Politics* 33 (1981): 253–81.

10. Discovering Facts and Values: The Historical Sociology of Barrington Moore

DENNIS SMITH

It is difficult to do justice to Barrington Moore's approach to historical sociology within the limiting confines of a chapter.[1] One of the reasons for this is that the emphases within Moore's work have changed, albeit within the context of certain abiding concerns, in successive books published during a period of over three decades.[2] In *Soviet Politics* (1950), for example, functionalist styles of reasoning are drawn upon. Moore discusses the restrictions that the functional requirements of an industrializing society and its external relations imposed on attempts to realize a utopian ideology in postrevolutionary Russia. He also examines the functions that an ambiguous ideology could perform for a totalitarian regime in such a society and the nature of the dilemmas and penalties that were inevitably experienced by both the rulers and the ruled. These dilemmas are the subject of *Terror and Progress USSR* (1954), whose concern is the potential costs of the various strategies open to the regime after Stalin. In this work Moore pays particular attention to the psychological and social pressures of life within a totalitarian society and the consequences of such an existence for the development of ideas about truth and beauty.

In *Social Origins of Dictatorship and Democracy* (1966), Moore's interest in the costs and regularities of historical change is expressed in a scheme of "routes to the modern world," which has a strong evolutionary flavor. Comparative analysis plays a strategic role in the argument developed in that work. *Social Origins* had been preceded by *Political Power and Social Theory* (1958), in which Moore makes one of his rare forays into the discussion of methodology. It was followed by *Reflections on the Causes of Human Misery* (1972), in which Moore makes

Dennis Smith

an equally direct attack on moral issues, adopting a broadly utilitarian approach. Most recently, in *Injustice* (1978), Moore appears as a political theorist who attempts to use evidence from a specific historical study (the development of the German working class) as the basis for an approach to the understanding of political authority that draws on utilitarian, evolutionary, and functionalist perspectives and is sensitive to the complex interplay between culture, personality, and society. Another work by Moore has just been published (*Privacy: Studies in Social and Cultural History*), dealing with the social and cultural history of privacy. It is an indication of Moore's originality as a social analyst that neither his arguments nor his conclusions may be anticipated on the basis of his previous work.

Each of Moore's books has been organized around an attempt to answer a large and difficult question. The reader never gets the feeling that Moore really knows the answer before he begins his investigation. In that sense, his work consists of a series of genuine inquiries, in the course of which he advances under the banner of a very large interrogative. Because of Moore's confidence in starting out from a position of not knowing the answer, he has not felt the need to don the protective clothing of any particular theoretical scheme.

In fact, Moore is thoroughly at ease within the broad intellectual movement to which he belongs, whose origins lie in eighteenth-century Europe. James Sheehan is right to describe Moore as "an heir to the Scottish and English enlightenment," a tradition expressing the belief "that knowledge and reason, if rigorously pursued and honestly applied, can improve the quality of life."[3] From this tradition flow the two questions that, directly or indirectly, underlie all of Moore's writings. The first is, How much control can human beings have over their own destiny? The second is, Insofar as human action can influence processes of social change, which moral criteria are relevant to such action? These questions may be posed with respect to specific social situations occurring in the past and present as well as in the future. In Moore's words:

> The main structural features of what society can be like in the next generation are already given by trends at work now. Humanity's freedom of manoeuvre lies within the framework created by history. Social scientists and allied scholars could help to widen the area of choice by analyzing the historical trends which now limit it. They could show, impartially, honestly, and free from the special pleadings of governments and special interests, the range of possible alternatives and the potentialities for effective action. Such has been, after all, the aim of inquiry into hu-

man affairs since the Greeks. One may still hope that the tradition can survive in modern society.[4]

The penultimate sentence reminds us that Moore's own first degree was in the classics. In *Reflections* and *Injustice*, Moore's approach to the question of making moral judgments about social orders and human actions recalls an age when classical learning was not only central to European literate culture but also the staple diet of the leaders of the American Revolution. In *Injustice* Moore writes:

> Once upon a time in those happy days when students of human affairs were sure of their ground, it was possible to draw a sharp distinction between a political and social system based upon force and fraud and one based upon rational authority and justice . . . To recapture old certainties is . . . out of the question, at least in the form they once existed. Nevertheless, there are grounds for suspecting that the welter of moral codes may conceal a certain unity of original form, as well as a discernible drift in a single direction . . . It is at least just barely possible that human affairs do make sense after all.[5]

Moore's attempts to make sense of human affairs have focused on the political sphere, especially the relationship between the governing authority and the citizens within the specific societies. This preoccupation is based, in part, on practical experience. After studying sociology at Yale, Moore became a political analyst in the Office of Strategic Studies and also worked in the Department of Justice. This service was carried out during World War II. Subsequently, he taught at the University of Chicago before moving to Harvard in 1948. Three years later he took up a position at the Russian Research Center at that university. He has been there ever since.

Morality and Method

I am concerned with the methodology of Moore as a sociologist and historian and also his practice as a political theorist and moral analyst. In other words, I am interested in the kinds of knowledge Moore seeks, the techniques he applies in the attempt to acquire knowledge, and the relevance of this knowledge to Moore's efforts to define (or discover) the bases of a rational political or social order. The three issues just mentioned – the kinds of knowledge sought, the techniques considered appropriate for acquiring it, and the intellectual and moral relevance of the knowledge itself – are closely interrelated, as will be seen in the rest of this section of the chapter. The discussion in this section will in part be

Dennis Smith

based on the two collections of essays published in 1958 and 1972. Where appropriate, references will also be made to aspects of the major works, which will be considered directly in the three subsequent sections of the chapter devoted to the Soviet studies, *Social Origins*, and *Injustice*. In a final section, I will present an overall assessment of Moore's contribution to the enterprise of historical sociology.

Moore has been very reluctant to formalize his approach. It is necessary to refer back to essays that were published in 1958, in *Political Power*, to find anything resembling a set of rules for the researcher into society. In essays such as "The New Scholasticism and the Study of Politics" and "Strategy in Social Science," Moore itemizes a number of important goals. No detailed recipe book is to be found there, however. The tone is not so much "Take three eggs" as "Go West, young man" (or "young woman," as the case might be). If the discussion in the book just mentioned is considered alongside Moore's argument in *Reflections* (especially the chapter entitled "On the Unity of Happiness and the Diversity of Misery"), it is possible to itemize the practical objectives that Moore prescribes for himself and his students. Four may be identified.[6]

The first is to discover "principles of change that apply to more than a single series of events;" in other words, to identify general processes at work within specific events.[7] The second is to draw as accurately as possible the distinction between what is determined by historical or other constraining factors and what can be brought about by the deliberate actions of men and women at any particular stage of social development. The third is to distinguish those aspects of the social order that are constant or recurring through space and time from those aspects that are subject to cumulative growth and change. The fourth is to set out a workable procedure for making the moral choices facing people as they act within the limits imposed by history, social structure, and human nature.

In his pursuit of these objectives, Moore is necessarily concerned with the interrelationships among factual, counter-factual, and evaluative statements about social orders and human agents. One characteristic of a factual statement is that it conveys information whose accuracy may be assessed without reference to the existence or inclinations of the person making the statement. In Moore's view, facts are the objects of discovery in the social arena as in the natural world. Sociological facts and historical facts are not fundamentally different from each other. They have the same ontological status. In this sense, information about the characteristics of types of social structure belongs to the same factual order as information about the characteristics of particular individuals or groups

316

in the past or present. Furthermore, information about, say, material conditions has no more factual weight than information about forms of thought or the beliefs and motivations of specific people.

Which facts are relevant depends on which questions Moore is asking. These questions have included: How has the Bolshevik regime managed the conflict between its proclaimed ideological goals and the means it has employed to exercise power in an embattled and rapidly industrializing society (*Soviet Politics*)? How is the Soviet regime likely to develop in the wake of Stalin's death (*Terror and Progress*)? What forms of modernizing transformation in commercialized agrarian societies are favorable to democratic outcomes (*Social Origins*)? Under what conditions will members of a society perceive its political order as being unjust (*Injustice*)? Which elements of the social order in contemporary industrial societies are both unique and necessary to those societies (*Political Power*)? Which aspects of human misery are, in principle, unnecessary and what prospects are there, in fact, for eliminating them (*Reflections*)?

Moore typically employs two techniques to discover relevant facts. The first is detailed empirical study of specific cases with the object of obtaining all the evidence relevant to specifying causal chains. On the study of qualitative changes in this way, Moore writes "in principle, I think, it is possible, although shortcomings in the evidence and human failures in the historian mean that objectivity remains no more than an ever receding ideal."[8] It is an ideal that Moore has pursued most relentlessly in hard cases, such as the chapter on India on *Social Origins*. The Indian case does not fit easily into the theoretical framework of the book. Moore's response is to dig even further into the empirical evidence relating to that society, producing a chapter and attendant bibliography that are longer than any others in *Social Origins*. To cite another example, in his investigation of the "dog that failed to bark in the night," the nonrevolutionary German working class during the nineteenth and early twentieth centuries, Moore refers to a number of primary sources, including diaries and statistical materials, that have been relatively neglected by other scholars.[9]

The second technique employed by Moore as a way of discovering relevant facts is comparative analysis, the ordering and juxtaposition of specific facts drawn from particular societies to strengthen or weaken the claim to validity of generalizations about social structures or processes. Moore uses comparative analysis in at least three ways.

First, and least successfully, he attempts to derive generalizations about human nature and moral codes from wide-ranging surveys of data drawn from diverse societies. *Injustice* contains the most obvious

Dennis Smith

examples of this approach. Reading that work, one is occasionally reminded of William Graham Sumner's *Folkways* – its methodology, not its moral relativism. In this context, it is worth noting that Moore received his original training in the social sciences from Albert Keller who was "Sumner's greatest pupil and scholar."[10]

The second way in which Moore uses comparisons is as a means of testing and, if necessary, rejecting causal explanations that invoke generalizations to account for specific instances. For example, in *Social Origins* he responds to the suggestion that within a polity the opposing interests of industrialists exploiting a formally free labor force and great landowners with a servile labor force will lead to violent conflict between them, as in the American Civil War, by citing, as a contrary example, the peaceful accommodation between Junkers and the urban bourgeoisie that occurred in nineteenth-century Germany.[11] Similar antecedents may thus be associated with different outcomes. To cite another example, in the paper entitled "Totalitarian Elements in Preindustrial Societies" (in *Political Power*) Moore examines a series of repressive social orders, including the Chi'ing dynasty (221–209 B.C.) and Calvin's Geneva, as a means of contradicting the Marcusian generalization that totalitarianism is a distinctive product of industrial capitalism.

Third, Moore uses comparative analysis as a way of arriving at generalizations with respect to the range of variation possible within a given type of social structure or social process and the propensity for change in a particular direction associated with each variant. For example, in his "Notes on the Process of Acquiring Power" (in *Political Power*) Moore presents a series of generalizations that are, he believes, justified in the light of enquiry into the problems faced by "the Bolsheviks on the way to the Kremlin, the early Christians on the route that leads to Innocent III, the French kings on the road to Versailles [and] . . . the Moguls on the way to the splendours of Shah Jahan's reign."[12] This essay is an important bridge between Moore's Russian studies and his subsequent work for *Social Origins*. Rather than summarizing it all I will pick out one part of the argument.

Moore argues that three ways of controlling and coordinating power-seeking organizations (such as armies or political parties) may be distinguished. Each has its characteristic problems. For example, feudalism, a form of organization cohering through diffuse relationships of loyalty and personal obligation, does not allow a central policy to be enforced downward through the hierarchy. A second form, rational bureaucracy, overcomes this latter problem but at the expense of destroying the social order in which feudalism is embedded. Further-

318

more, bureaucracy develops its own rigidities. A third form, totalitarianism, acquires flexibility by dispensing with fixed rules and demanding complete commitment from subordinates. However, the burden of arbitration and monitoring placed on the totalitarian ruler is greatly increased. In brief, the three patterns manifest varying patterns of allocating and monitoring functions and resources. They do not represent historical stages but structural alternatives, each of which contains contradictions tending to transform it into one or both of the other forms.

Other, better known examples of this analytical strategy are the distinctions Moore makes among three possible "routes to the modern world" in *Social Origins* and his identification of a limited range of structural forms manifested by peasant communities and the commercialization of agriculture. These will be considered in a later section of this chapter. The second and third uses of comparative method are explicitly acknowledged by Moore in the Preface to *Social Origins* when he writes: "Comparisons can serve as a rough negative check on accepted historical explanations. And a comparative approach may lead to new historical generalizations." At the end of the same paragraph, he adds: "That comparative analysis is no substitute for detailed investigation of specific cases is obvious."[13]

For Moore's purposes comparative analysis and the detailed examination of specific cases are equally necessary. Knowing a great deal about a specific civil war or revolution will not, by itself, tell you what might have happened (as opposed to what did), nor allow you to assess the relative significance of various antecedent structural tendencies. On the other hand, by itself, comparative analysis may help identify a range of structural possibilities in a given type of society and the dilemmas and tendencies for change associated with each. It may also allow you to discard certain potential generalizations that, if true, would provide sufficient explanations of a series of specific instances. Furthermore, comparative analysis might suggest that in combination a series of structural tendencies, if found within a particular society, would strongly predispose it toward development in a certain direction and make other possibilities highly unlikely. Moore's discussion of tendencies "favourable to the growth of parliamentary democracy" is of this character.[14] However, explanation of specific social upheavals, such as a particular civil war, requires detailed examination of the actions and reactions of specific groups (and strategically located individuals) whose behavior is intrinsic to the processes of structural change. Human agency working through or tending to modify structure; the confining or facilitation of action by structure: this interplay

Dennis Smith

requires careful narrative presentation. Combining narrative history and comparative analysis within a single coherent argument is technically difficult and important to attempt. As will be seen, *Social Origins* constitutes one such attempt.

The two other kinds of statements with which Moore is concerned – counter-factual and evaluative – will be dealt with a little more briefly. When analyzing human choices and social transformations not only in the past but also in the present, Moore frequently asks (to paraphrase) either What is likely to have happened if certain antecedent conditions or specific human choices had been different? or What is likely to happen (in the future) if choice *A* as opposed to choice *B* is actually made or if structural outcome *X* as opposed to structural outcome *Y* actually occurs? An extended example of such analysis, which will not be considered in detail here, may be found in the essay entitled "Some Prospects for Predatory Democracy" in *Reflections*. Moore examines the possibility, likelihood, and costs of alternative types of political change leading toward or away from decent society, that is, one characterized by increased public services, reduced poverty, diminished consumerism and military spending, the dedication of science to humane ends, and an active debate about social goals. Specifically, he considers the potential for, and probable outcomes of, reactionary, reformist, and revolutionary political movements in the United States.

The most explicit account of the rules Moore follows in carrying out counter-factual analysis may be found in the chapter in *Injustice* entitled "The Suppression of Historical Alternatives: Germany 1918–1920." Moore's position is that, unlike factual statements, counter-factual statements cannot be verified, even in principle. In other words, we can never actually know for certain that a specific alternative outcome, which did not occur, was possible in a particular instance. However, rational and objective examination of available empirical evidence, including evidence derived from comparative analysis, makes it possible to subject counter-factual statements to the test of disproof. It is the responsibility of the scholar making such statements to couch them in terms that allow this test to be made.[15] Indeed, a strategy for testing counter-factual possibilities has many uses. For instance, it is useful when analyzing specific policy-making processes, such as the formation of Soviet economic policy, to know that certain options were not available to those concerned because of their likely consequences.

Just as factual statements are an important ingredient in the making and testing of counter-factual statements, so both factual and counter-factual statements are necessary for arriving at moral evaluations of human choices and structural transformations.[16] For example, with respect to the consequences of the French Revolution in terms of deaths and suffering, Moore points out that "in assessing it, one has to keep in mind the repressive aspects of the social order to which it was a response."[17] In other words, how many deaths and how much misery would have been produced by a continuation of the *ancien régime?*

A concern with moral issues underlies all of Moore's work and is implicit in the questions running through each of the large empirical projects; for example, how could a Soviet regime using immoral means in pursuit of unjustifiable ideological ends manage a complex industrial society? What forms of historical development have been conducive to the production of free societies in the modern world? Under what conditions do men and women rebel against injustice and demand a decent society? Such issues stimulate the very process of empirical enquiry and the discovery of facts. Indeed, Moore persistently seeks to derive a system of values about the social world from the factual substance of that world. He wants to discover not only facts but also values, to derive the "ought" from the "is."

In "The New Scholasticism and the Study of Politics" (in *Political Power*) Moore expresses the hope that "the concept of a perfect society" might eventually be defined, "taking off from real societies, to reach a critical standard."[18] Through the comparative and historical study of moral orders and forms of life it may be possible to derive an authoritative standard of truth and justice. When writing *Social Origins*, Moore seems to have been prepared to accept modern English society as a close approximation to a free and just society. The pressing moral issue in that work is, What forms and what degree of violence and repression are necessary to produce or maintain a given degree of human freedom? However, in *Reflections* and *Injustice* Moore shifts his focus from the promotion of freedom to the minimization of misery. In the first work he makes the central assumption that although definitions of happiness vary almost infinitely there is a broad, almost universal, consensus about the undesirability of specific forms of misery such as war, hunger, cruelty, and intolerance. Throughout those essays and, subsequently, in *Injustice*, the recurring moral question is, What combination of freedom and repression is necessary to reduce human misery?

Moore's essays in *Reflections* include discussions entitled "Of War, Cruelty, and General Human Nastiness," "Of Hunger, Toil, Injustice, and Oppression," and "Of Heresy, Intellectual Freedom, and Scholarship." Despite these portentous titles, Moore's discussions are diffuse and do not yield strong positive conclusions. Nevertheless, two messages do come through insistently. The first is couched in irony. On the one hand, Moore hopes that as human beings acquire greater rationality and moral awareness they will be more committed to reducing misery in societies. On the other hand, Moore fears that advances in rationality and moral awareness will coincide with the discovery that significant advances toward reducing misery might be intrinsically impossible within any feasible social order. The second message consists of Moore's belief that *moral* assumptions underlie all forms of political cohesion and conflict. This is because moral understandings about human nature and human purposes determine which kinds of social compromises are acceptable within the range of possibilities available at any given level of intellectual and technological development. This second message is, in fact, carried in all of Moore's major works, from *Soviet Politics* onward.

The Soviet Studies

Soviet Politics is about the management of structural dilemmas within an industrializing society, including those dilemmas that stem from specific ideological commitments. In particular, Moore deals with two related issues. One of these is the conflict between the Bolsheviks' ideological goals, including the achievement of social equality, and the imperatives flowing from the adoption of tyrannical and authoritarian means to achieve, exercise, and maintain power in Russia. The second issue concerns the need to maintain a complex and hierarchical division of labor within an industrial society and the consequences of that fact for political organization.

First, Moore studies the tactics used by the Bolsheviks to capture and secure control of the Russian state. Second, he examines the dilemmas faced by those exercizing political authority in the years leading up to Stalin's accession to power. Third, he looks at the period of Stalinist rule until 1950. Moore deals with three related issues in each of these phases: the dilemmas that are imposed on party leaders by a combination of ideological constraints, functional imperatives, and international relations; the costs and the benefits that flow from attempts to cope with these dilemmas by the party leadership; and the further structural problems that are brought into being by the attempted solutions themselves.

Moore argues that the Marxist-Leninist tradition has shaped the attitude of the party leadership to the exercise of power, an influence expressed in the importance to them of such questions as, How do economic and other social developments affect the distribution of power? How may these factors be manipulated to favor Communist interests? Within this context, ideologically acceptable means had to be found to solve problems that face all political regimes, Communist or non-Communist, in industrializing societies. First, how is industry going to be organized? How are the factors of production (materials, people, capital) going to be combined with each other? How are production goals to be specified? How is distribution to be organized? Second, how is the labor force going to be disciplined? How are the workers going to be organized? How will trade unions fit into the system, if at all? Third, how will the city and the countryside relate to each other? How will it be possible to ensure that the peasantry maintain the food supply to the cities and desist from political upheaval? Fourth, what form of status order, authority system, and disciplinary arrangements are to be maintained within the ruling groups and within society at large? Finally, how will relations with the rest of the world be managed?

The New Economic Policy (NEP) that was introduced in 1921 makes clear the importance of Marxist-Leninist ideology in shaping attempted answers to all these questions. The government had allowed private enterprise to continue in many spheres but had retained control over the "commanding heights" of the economy. In Moore's words: "If a group of Manchester Liberals had been in control of Russia at this time, they would not have perceived any dilemma."[19] Unfortunately, the very forces that were responsible for economic recovery in the early 1920s were actively or passively opposed to bolshevism. The tensions that resulted meant that an authoritarian response was bound to follow.

Moore traces implementation of such a policy through the 1920s and early 1930s. This policy had a number of characteristic features. Democratic sentiments were exploited by directing popular hostilities toward minor party functionaries and away from the leadership. Organized opposition was eliminated in the name of the "dictatorship of the proletariat." Soviets became little more than local administrative agencies for the leadership of the party. Bureaucratic means such as the secret police were developed to monitor the activities of administrators both locally and centrally and to maximize the amount of information available to the elite. A mythology of proletarian control was developed that justified the reduction of the independence of the trade unions (since class struggle was officially abolished) and permitted income differentials to be introduced within the labor force.

The largest part of *Soviet Politics* is concerned with exploring the inconsistencies and dilemmas of the Stalinist regime during the late 1930s and 1940s. The framework of the Soviet state was riddled with contradictions. Although class conflict had been officially abolished, classes continued to exist since they are (Moore argues) a consequence of the functional importance of status inequalities in an industrial society. Another conflict existed between the authoritarian organization of the society and the persistence of "a genuine residue . . . of democracy at the lower levels of the Party."[20] Even more fundamental was the contradiction between the desire of the ruler to maintain confusion and insecurity within the bureaucracy and the vested interest of the latter in predictability. "Protective alliances" at the lower levels of the bureaucracy were broken up through a complex system of monitoring. If they had not been feared as a source of political opposition such alliances could have been the basis for a more efficient coordination of bureaucratic effort.

In Moore's view, the regulation of the Soviet industrial order has been the product of a contradictory mixture of bureaucratic controls and market mechanisms. The latter have not been permitted in the field of labor, however, since that would have bolstered the power of the trade unions. The collectivization of agriculture reduced the role of the market in the countryside, but even in that sphere the importance of peasant production on private plots was evident. A final contradiction derives from the fact that, like American culture, Soviet culture is materialistic. It is able to exact obedience and effort from the subordinate population because it promises an improvement in material conditions. "On the one hand," observes Moore, "the system emphasizes the desirability of material goods; on the other hand, it is unable to satisfy this demand."[21]

Soviet Politics is an impressive synthesis of sociological and historical perspectives. Moore's achievement in this book, which was written at a time when clear thinking about Soviet Russia was a scarce commodity, is to have identified the intrinsic requirements that had to be satisfied and the intrinsic limits on the ambitions that could be realized in that society at that time. He shows that both the limits and the requirements were in part a consequence of the need to manage an industrial society within a given social structure and international setting. They were also in part a result of constraints imposed by an ideology that, while fulfilling the "apparent necessity" in all societies for a set of beliefs that were "in part above and beyond rational criticism," also imposed yet further demands, which had the effect of restricting the freedom of maneuver of the leadership.[22]

Above all, Moore demonstrates that a regime enforced through totalitarian techniques is perfectly able to meet the functional requirements of managing industrialization while at the same time maintaining itself in power. His analysis has a sharp cutting edge because, despite being an outsider, he is able to display empathy with the situation of his subjects. At the same time, in *Soviet Politics* Moore is beginning to explore in more general terms, applicable beyond the Russian case, some of the affinities and conflicts contained in the relations between patterns of human perception and practice, the constraints and potentialities of cultural symbols, the functional requirements of social life, and the political purposes of rulers.

In *Terror and Progress*, published four years after *Soviet Politics*, Moore presents a reasoned account of a number of possible ways in which the Soviet regime might develop after the death of Stalin. The logic he deploys is that of calculating the potential costs and benefits to strategic groups in Russia of types of structural change that are possible, given what is known about the constraints on action in that society. This form of reasoning is a variant on the strategy discussed in connection with counter-factual statements in the first section of this chapter. His organizing principle in *Terror and Progress* is "one of showing the kind of situation that confronts different people in Soviet society, the way in which they see their situation and respond to it, and how their behavior sometimes modifies it and sometimes perpetuates it."[23] An awareness of the interplay between structural constraint and human agency is clearly evident in this work. Through such an analysis Moore hopes to be able to assess, not the most "desirable" but the most likely future development of the Soviet regime. It is worth noting that at this stage of his intellectual career Moore had not yet fashioned a procedure for making moral evaluations other than intuitively. This hiatus in his methodology is not exposed insofar as the value system or ideology of the Soviet regime is treated as an objective datum, tied in with other relevant data, whose structural consequences are to be deduced.

Moore argues that the regime's freedom is restricted by a number of factors: previous decisions made since the Revolution; the internal structure of the system; and, not least, participation in "a larger system of world politics that has certain dynamic tendencies of its own."[24] Against this background, Moore specifies the instruments of control available to the regime. Apart from the existing indoctrinating mechanisms, two additional mechanisms are well established in Russia at the time Moore is writing. These are technical bureaucracies, staffed by experts as opposed to politicians, and bureaucracies specializing in repression, such as the military and the police. To some extent the overall analysis in *Terror and Progress* is similar to that carried out in

Soviet Politics, although a novel feature is Moore's preoccupation with the situation of Soviet intellectuals. However, I want to concentrate on what Moore perceived as the fundamental problem facing the Soviet leadership in the early 1950s – finding a balance between power, rationality, and tradition as a means of social coordination.

The totalitarian principle emphasized the principle of power above all else. Unfortunately, this approach suffered from the lack of any higher maxim of philosophy that could justify or guide the allocation of power. Under a totalitarian system it was necessary to distribute rewards and functions, which tended to create the conditions for the emergence of a stratification system whose effect was to undermine the freedom of action of the totalitarian ruler. This tendency toward stratification was also encouraged by the high degree of social separation between the political elite and the people and between the national groups of the Soviet Union. The emergence of a more highly developed stratification system would represent a move in the direction of the principle of tradition, argues Moore. Were such a principle to acquire prominence, groups would acquire significant amounts of autonomy and cultural distinctiveness as a result of their enjoyment of property and privileges that they could pass on to their children. A society of this kind would be difficult to regulate through a bureaucracy committed to innovation.

The allocation of functions to people whose authority is based on the principle of rationality is encouraged by the objective of organizing economic production and social coordination effectively. Such people may claim consideration on the basis of their capacity to operate procedures that produce desired effects within specific spheres. The problem with the extension of a system exhibiting rationality is that it weakens the ability of the totalitarian elite to deny the existence of clearly defined spheres of competence outside of the political realm of arbitrary command.

In Moore's opinion, a tendency toward tradition exists within the Soviet education system, with its elements of "ritual, etiquette, and the development of attitudes of veneration for the past."[25] However, there are also tendencies toward rationality within education, most obviously expressed in the emphasis on meritocratic values. The basic problem faced by the totalitarian leadership is that a strong tendency toward either rationality or tradition would place the control exercised by the party hierarchy over culture and values under serious threat. The problem is compounded by the fact that complete adherence to the power principle would engender cynicism about values among the population and this would also be damaging to the position of the party.

Moore's argument takes into account the important effects of the international climate within which the Soviet regime is operating. Any movement in a traditional direction, he notes, would depend on a relaxation of the pressure for industrial growth that stems from the need to support the military machine. Moore believes that totalitarian elements are very likely to persist in the Soviet Union of the 1950s and subsequently. Such elements, he argues, are not to be explained simply in terms of global pressures but are built into Marxist doctrine, the history of Russia, and the psychological makeup of the Russian people.

Social Origins of Dictatorship and Democracy

Social Origins is a more ambitious work than either of the Soviet studies in two senses. First, Moore deploys an argument that seeks to account for social change, especially political conflict and its outcomes, in not just one society but in six (England, France, the United States, Japan, China, and India), with frequent references to two others (Russia and Germany). Second, he attempts to provide not only causal explanations of processes of structural transformation in the societies concerned but also systematic moral evaluations of the consequences of these processes of transformation.

Moore is interested in the transition from commercialized agrarian polities to urbanizing, industrializing nation-states in the cases mentioned. His precise objective may best be described in his own words:

> This book endeavors to explain the varied political roles played by the landed upper classes and the peasantry in the transformation from agrarian societies (defined simply as states where a large majority of the population lives off the land) to modern industrial ones. Somewhat more specifically, it is an attempt to discover the range of historical conditions under which either or both of these rural groups have become important forces behind the emergence of Western parliamentary versions of democracy, and dictatorships of the right and left, that is, fascist and communist regimes.[26]

Moore argues that "in the range of cases examined here one may discern three main historical routes from the preindustrial to the modern world."[27] Later, he writes:

> To sum up as concisely as possible, we seek to understand the role of the upper classes and the peasants in the bourgeois revolutions leading to capitalist democracy, the abortive bourgeois revolutions leading to fascism, and the peasant revolutions leading to communism. The ways in which the landed upper classes and the

peasants reacted to the challenge of commercial agriculture were decisive factors in determining the political outcome.[28]

It is relatively easy to identify a number of factors that are treated by Moore as being relevant to all of his case studies and susceptible to comparative analysis. These include the degree of strength possessed by commercializing tendencies favoring capitalist groups benefiting from the operation of the market in town and countryside; the degree to which the forms of commercialized agriculture adopted by the land-owning upper classes depended on the backing of a repressive political apparatus; and the degree to which the structure of peasant society facilitated coordinated resistance from below to exploitation and repression.

It is also fairly clear from the text of *Social Origins* that the democratic route (England, France, United States) is characterized by the predominance of strong commercializing tendencies, encompassing the emergence of powerful bourgeois interests. In the case of the route leading to fascism (Japan, Germany), countervailing pressures from capitalist groups are insufficient to offset the political consequences of a labor-repressive form of agriculture backed by strong political controls, while peasant social structure is not conducive to effective resistance. In the case of the route leading to communism (China, Russia), commercializing tendencies are very weak, while labor-repressive forms of agricultural exploitation are ineffective either to resist the impact of an existing rebellious peasant solidarity (Russia) or prevent its subsequent growth (China).

These statements are analytical descriptions of certain features of the three routes and they fall far short of being systematic generalizations identifying antecedent structural factors whose presence or absence "causes" the particular political outcomes characteristic of each route. The absence of a succinct statement on this matter in *Social Origins* strongly suggests that Moore was not attempting to identify a distinctive set of causes appropriate to each route. His causal analyses are directed to the explanation of concrete structural transformations within specific societies (particularly civil wars, revolutions, etc.). These analyses may differ greatly among societies within the same route. This is very obvious when England, France, and the United States are compared. It is also evident when comparing the very different ways in which peasant revolution was brought about in Russia and China. In one case rebellious peasant solidarity contributed greatly to the collapse of the Russian Empire while in the other case the Chinese Empire disintegrated without much help from an atomistic and internally divided peasantry. The Chinese Communists had to forge a new solidarity among the rural labor force.

Moore does not attempt to iron out such differences in causal sequence. His routes are distinguished from one another not by sets of causes but by sets of consequences or outcomes. Broadly speaking, a strong bourgeoisie that exercises the lion's share of political power is the outcome favorable to democracy. Nondemocratic outcomes take two major forms. The Fascist form, whose values are an inversion of democratic ideology, is the expression of a dominant state, permeated with an agrarian upper-class tradition, engaged in incorporating the subordinate industrial classes within the polity. The Communist form, made possible by the eradication of the aristocracy, incorporates peasants and workers within an authoritarian polity legitimated in terms of a freedom supposedly "higher" than that offered by democracy.

It is worth paying some attention to the title Moore chose for his book. It is not entitled *Social Causes of Democracy, Fascism and Communism*, but *Social Origins of Dictatorship and Democracy*. Moore is not slapdash in use of words. The particular form of words chosen is significant in three ways. First, Moore refers to the "origins" of dictatorship and democracy and not to the "causes." This fact tends to support the argument just made to the effect that Moore's causal explanations are tailored not to general patterns specific to routes but aspects of specific national cases (although his explanations of particular cases certainly invoke generalizations). In referring to routes (e.g., that leading to democracy), Moore uses the looser term, origins. Where causes is appropriate – as in *Reflections on the Causes of Human Misery* – he uses it. Second, the juxtaposition of "dictatorship" and "democracy" emphasizes the moral or evaluative content of the two terms. Third, the use of dictatorship to cover both fascism and communism implies that the differences between these two forms are ultimately subordinate to their common denial of democratic freedoms within authoritarian polities.

Although Moore distinguishes three routes he does not give them equal attention. If the space devoted to the three democratic case studies is compared with that devoted to the case studies of fascist and communist routes (Japan and China, respectively), it will be seen that the latter two, taken together (152 pages), only just achieve equal rating with the chapters on England, France, and the United States (152 pages). Furthermore, the longest case study in the book (on India, entitled "Democracy in Asia: India and the Price of Peaceful Change") is primarily concerned with the reasons why India cannot easily be located in "the democratic route to modern society."

Dennis Smith

In the third part of his book Moore organizes his exposition on the three routes in a more balanced way, although in each of the three chapters ("The Democratic Route to Modern Society," "Revolution from Above and Fascism," and "The Peasants and Revolution") there are many references to societies lying outside the route being discussed. It is apparent that Moore regards the distinctions between the three routes as being very important. Each route, however, is characterized by a specific set of structural outcomes (and moral consequences) rather than by a specific set of causal antecedents, and the routes are located within a (largely implicit) dichotomous scheme distinguishing between democratic outcomes and nondemocratic outcomes (dictatorship).

The way the relationships among comparative analysis, generalization, and causal explanation in *Social Origins* are related expresses a complex and subtle dialectical process within the book. There are dialectics between negative and positive applications of the comparative method; between generalization and the identification of uniqueness; between the examination of specific concrete structural transformations within particular societies (civil wars, revolutions) and a consideration of the long-term developmental tendencies to which they contribute; and between causal analysis and the evaluation of consequences.

The third part of *Social Origins* contains a number of generalizations at which Moore arrives on the basis of comparisons drawn from the case studies in the first two parts of the book. Broadly speaking, these generalizations refer to two aspects of social structures (especially class relationships): the range of variation they manifest at a given stage of social development and the propensity of each variant to foster specific kinds of political arrangement. For example, Moore identifies a range of variation in agrarian societies with respect to the relationship of the landed upper class to the monarchy, the form of commercial exploitation of agriculture by the aristocracy, and the relationship between the latter class and the urban bourgeoisie. For each variable he identifies conditions that are favorable or unfavorable to democratic outcomes. In this case, a balanced relationship between crown and nobility, a form of commercialized agriculture that removes the peasantry from the land, and close collaboration between the urban bourgeoisie and the aristocracy, in the course of which the former gradually becomes dominant, are all, Moore argues, circumstances favorable to a democratic outcome.[29]

Another example may be taken from his discussion of the peasantry. With respect to the ties binding the peasantry to the upper classes, he suggests that a highly segmented society depending on diffuse sanctions for its coherence is more resistant to peasant rebellion than one in which a bureaucratic central authority carries out taxation. He argues that feudal arrangements fall between the two extremes, having more revolts than the former, fewer than the latter. In his discussion of the internal organization of peasant society, he distinguishes, first, weak and strong solidarity and then, within the latter, rebellious and conservative forms of solidarity. Moore adds that although the source of external support given to a peasantry in revolt has an important effect on the political outcome of such behavior, the peasantry themselves have seldom been "the allies of democratic capitalism."[30]

Comparisons are sometimes used to support generalizations within the particular case studies. For example, Moore argues that forms of feudalism with substantial bureaucratic elements were conducive to authoritarian modernization.

> The survival of feudal traditions with a strong element of bureaucratic hierarchy is common to both Germany and Japan. It distinguishes them from England, France and the United States where feudalism was overcome or absent and where modernization took place early and under democratic auspices – fundamentally and with all due qualifications those of a bourgeois revolution. In this respect, Germany and Japan also differ from both Russia and China, which were agrarian bureaucracies rather than feudal polities.[31]

Moore sometimes indicates unique characteristics of a specific society that are significant because they exclude from it other characteristics about which he is able to generalize on a comparative basis. Because characteristic X (unique to that society) is present, characteristic Y (common to some other societies) is absent. For example, "The special character of the Japanese feudal bond, with its much greater emphasis on status and military loyalty than on a freely chosen contractual relationship, meant that one source of the impetus behind the Western variety of free institutions was absent."[32]

Comparisons are employed in at least two other ways in the case studies. A proposed generalization that appears at first sight to explain a specific case may be shown through comparative analysis to be inaccurate. For example,

> One might start with a general notion to the effect that there is an inherent conflict between slavery and the capitalist system of formally free wage labor. Though this turns out to be a crucial part of the story [of the American Civil War], it will not do as a general

Dennis Smith

proposition from which the Civil War can be derived as an instance.[33]

Moore indicates not only that capitalists in the Northern states and in England were prepared to cooperate with Southern slavery but also that in nineteenth-century Germany advanced industry had coexisted very well with a form of agriculture based on a highly repressive labor system. In a brilliant passage of argument, Moore transforms the issue from being one of applying a particular general proposition to an exemplary instance to being one of discovering the unique circumstances that made the United States an exception from the contrary general proposition:

> We can answer our question with a provisional negative: there is no abstract general reason why the North and South had to fight. Special historical circumstances, in other words, had to be present in order to prevent agreement between an agrarian society based on unfree labor and a rising industrial capitalism.[34]

A further use of comparative analysis is as a means of producing evidence relevant to counter-factual argument. For example, would it have been possible in Imperial China for one section of society to detach itself from the rest, take over government, and launch a conservative version of modernization? Moore answers his own question as follows:

> If that had happened, historians might now be stressing the similarities between China and Japan rather than the differences . . . No flat answer is possible. Yet important factors were against it . . . [For example], in China's premodern society and culture there was little or no basis out of which a militarist patriotism of the Japanese type could grow. In comparison with Japan, the reactionary nationalism of Chiang Kai-shek seems thin and watery. Only when China began to make over her institutions in the communist image did a strong sense of mission appear.[35]

It is evident that Moore deploys comparative analysis as a means of both sustaining and dismissing specific generalizations. It is also clear, in the second type of dialectical interplay in his work, that Moore is as interested in those characteristics of particular societies that are unique as he is in those that they share with other cases. Indeed, there is a presiding sense of the uniqueness of the entire historical sequence that constitutes the democratic route to the modern world. Moore insists that "it makes sense . . . to regard the English Civil War, the French Revolution and the American Civil War as stages in the development of *the* bourgeois-democratic revolution."[36] The point

I am making is that Moore's careful fashioning of generalizations through comparative analysis is a method that is subordinate to his vision of the tidal flow of history, a flow that encompasses crucial passages of violent change in a number of societies. The comparative analysis of specific variants of human experience is, for Moore, an instrument for understanding the *unique* history of humankind. This sense of uniqueness lies behind his assertion that although "to a very limited extent [the three routes culminating in democracy, fascism and communism] . . . may constitute alternative routes and choices," this is not their most important characteristic:

> They are much more clearly successive historical stages. As such, they display a limited determinate relation to each other. The method of modernization chosen in one country changes the dimensions of the problem for the next countries who take the step, as Veblen recognized when he coined the now fashionable term, "the advantages of backwardness."[37]

Democracy made fascism possible, and if neither had appeared it is arguable that communism might not have come into existence at all.[38] Furthermore, "Indian diffidence is in good measure a negative critical reaction to all three forms of prior historical experience."[39] India's failure to follow England, France, and the United States in combining economic modernization with democracy makes this case not marginal but central to the underlying message of *Social Origins*. India provides a negative illustration of the tragic (or ironic) conclusion that the democratic route to modern society was a unique historical sequence that is probably now complete.

In effect, I am already to some extent discussing the third dialectical aspect of *Social Origins*, which concerns the interrelationship between long-term developmental tendencies and specific short-term transformations, such as civil wars and revolutions. Broadly speaking, Moore is interested in such events as the American Civil War, the French Revolution, the Meiji Restoration, and the Chinese Revolution because they obviously had a major effect on the occurrence of democratic or nondemocratic outcomes in the societies concerned. The events that have to be explained are indicated by Moore's broad sense of the violent movement of history toward democracy and dictatorship. At this point, the fourth dialectical aspect of his method also becomes relevant. Having turned to a specific event, Moore simultaneously considers it in two ways. On the one hand, he is interested in its causes, with reference both to the unique characteristics of the society concerned and the applicability of generalizations drawn from comparative analysis. On the other hand, he is interested in its consequences for subsequent political outcomes, its tendency to encourage good or evil in the state.

Moore nowhere provides a formal account of the logic of causal explanation that he uses in *Social Origins*. However, a careful examination of the work itself suggests that an adequate explanation of a specific structural change (such as a revolution) in a particular society would require answers to the following questions:

1. What were the potentialities for and limits on structural variations in a society at the stage of development, given the functional requirements that had to be met for it to continue in existence and the intrinsic characteristics of the organizational, technological, and intellectual techniques available to carry it out?

It is important to know what range of transformation is possible in principle without the society breaking down. These issues were important in a number of essays in *Political Power and Social Theory*, as has already been pointed out. On the basis of the comparative study of specific national cases, Moore is able to comment: "There . . . seems to be a rather wider range of choice than was once supposed in the political level at which a society organized the division of labor and the maintenance of social cohesion. The peasant village, the feudal fief, or even a crude territorial bureaucracy may constitute the decisive level under generally similar agrarian technologies."[40] More precise comparative statements are found in a number of the case studies. For example, as has been seen, by comparing Germany and the United States he shows that it was perfectly possible to combine an advanced industrial sector based on free wage labor and an agriculture to a great extent based on servile labor. Elsewhere, he points out that "all the main structural variables and historical trends in French society of the *ancien regime* differed sharply from those in England from the sixteenth through the eighteenth century."[41] The object of comparisons of this kind is to rule out possible arguments to the effect that structures of, say, type X are "in principle incompatible" with structures of type Y, or to the effect that structures of type X "could not possibly" produce political outcomes of type Z, and so on.

2. What tendencies toward cohesion and disintegration were actually present in the social configuration through which the division of labor and the coordination of social life were carried out?

A major example of this strategy of enquiry in *Social Origins* is Moore's discussion of peasant communities in different societies, including their relationship to the great landowners. A convenient case to consider is that of China. Moore finds that among the peasantry "the only frequently recurring activity that demanded cooperation was the management of the water supply. This was more a question of sharing a scarce resource than of working together on a common task and often resulted in fights within the village or between several villages."[42] Following an examination of "the system of sharecropping and the devotion of the upper class to stylized leisure, with its need for a labour force that it did not have to supervise directly," Moore concludes that "the political needs of the upper classes combined with agricultural practices to generate a combination of peasant individualism and surplus labour, leading to a relatively atomistic peasant society."[43] The significance of this conclusion (and others of a similar kind) derives from the relevant generalizations Moore produces on the basis of all the case studies taken together. For example, as has been seen, he distinguishes between weak and strong forms of peasant solidarity, and, within the latter, between conservative and rebellious forms of strong solidarity. Since only the strong, rebellious form of solidarity is likely to produce peasant revolution, the tendencies favoring this outcome under the Chinese Empire are not great. The situation changes, of course, after the effective work of the Red Army in rural areas, in conjunction with a variety of favorable factors.

3. What perceptions did members of this society located at various points within the societal division of labor and authority structure have of their own material and moral interests?

Apart from deploying relevant generalizations and specifying structural tendencies in particular national cases that have significance in the light of such generalizations, Moore also indicates ways in which the perceptions of participants in major events such as civil wars and revolutions have been molded by their experience of a variety of structural constraints in their past and present. Such perceptions play a part in shaping the ways in which classes and groups respond to challenges within the range of possibilities left open by history and social structure. It will, of course, be perfectly clear that although Moore – whose first book (*Soviet Politics*) was subtitled *The Role of Ideas in Social Change* – acknowledges the importance of "ways of seeing," he is far from regarding "culture" as an independent and overriding explanatory variable. However, he is aware that between people and an "objective" situation (as he puts it), there is always culture, an "intervening variable . . . made up from all sorts of wants, expectations and other ideas derived from the past . . . [which] screens out certain parts of the objective situation and emphasizes other parts."[44]

Examples of the significant part played by this intervening variable may be found by looking at Moore's discussions of the ambiguous attitudes toward capitalism and feudalism among the French upper class in the eighteenth century and of the nature of the Indian caste system.[45] He devotes an Epilogue to a discussion of "Reactionary and Revolutionary Imagery." The glaring omission, obvious from the title, is a discussion of democratic or liberal imagery. Indeed, Moore's uncritical approach to democratic ideology is a major weakness in the book.[46] Nevertheless, there are many examples of subtle analysis, since Moore is well aware that although values are to a great extent an expression of structures of economic and political domination it is not possible simply to "read off" a group's values with reference to its functional or class location. Moore gives examples of a "feudalized" bourgeoisie (France), commercially minded aristocrats (England), bureaucrats with considerable respect for familistic ties (China), and officials with powerful inclinations toward diffuse bonds reminiscent of feudalism (Japan).

4. What specific events occurred that presented a threat to these perceived material and moral interests suddenly or drastically enough to stimulate groups or classes into action?

One of the reasons why the enclosure movement did not stimulate more effective resistance from below in England was its very gradualness, a characteristic pointed out by Moore. The occasional acts of protest against this form of upper-class violence were unsuccessful. It is evident that Moore regards human action as being circumscribed by history and social structure (how closely circumscribed is an issue explored in *Injustice*) and that, in his view, much structural change is unattended by dramatic events.[47] However, in his treatment of serious short-term upheavals, such as the American Civil War and the Meiji Restoration, which decisively opened one door to the future and closed another in each case, Moore accords a significant role to the actions of groups or classes who suddenly perceived their established material and moral interests as being in danger. The crisis over "bleeding Kansas" and the arrival of Commodore Perry in Japan both caused groups strategically placed within the existing order to recognize that a way of life to which they were committed was in danger.[48]

5. In what ways did their perceptions of their moral and material interests and of a threat to such interests lead people to distinguish between potential allies and potential victims or opponents?

A convenient example may again be taken from the American case. Discussing the antebellum South, Moore emphasizes that "to grasp how a Southern planter must have felt, a twentieth-century Northerner has

to make an effort."[49] To explain the behavior of Southerners and, therefore, important aspects of the origins and course of the Civil War, this
effort is necessary. Moore writes, for example, "As industrial capitalism
took more and more hold in the North, articulate Southerners looked
about themselves to discover and emphasize whatever aristocratic and
preindustrial traits they could find in their own society: courtesy, grace,
cultivation, the broad outlook versus the alleged money-grubbing outlook of the North."[50] The North, it was believed, harbored the exploiters
and opponents of Southern civilization: "Shortly before the Civil War,
the notion took hold that the South produced in cotton the main source
of American wealth upon which the North levied tribute."[51]

6. What options in historical development had been cut off as a result of preceding sequences of structural change?

Again, the American Civil War provides a convenient example. Because the United States had developed in a way that precluded "any
strong radical working-class threat to industrial capitalist property in
the North" and since, also, "the United States had no powerful foreign
enemies," during the 1850s and 1860s "there was not much force behind the characteristic conservative compromise of agrarian and industrial elites."[52] Elsewhere, reflecting on the development of China,
Moore invites us to imagine the consequences that might have ensued
had one of the regional warlords active in the early part of the twentieth century been able to reunite that society and "inaugurate a politically reactionary phase with some degree of industrial modernization.
Chiang Kai-shek once seemed close to succeeding."[53] In Moore's view,
"If that had happened, historians might now be stressing the similarities between China and Japan rather than the differences."[54]

7. In what ways did people actually behave after the threat had been perceived
   and how is their behavior to be interpreted in terms of the answers to (3),
   (4), and (5) above?

Behavior in situations of crisis is profoundly affected by the perceptions of threat experienced by those involved. For example, during the
French Revolution the poorer peasantry were concerned with increasing their land holdings and were anxious to retain those local customs
at village level that served their interests. The richer peasantry were
largely concerned with establishing full ownership rights over land
they already largely possessed in fact. Once major obstacles satisfying
these interests to some extent had been overcome and new threats to
them were beginning to arise from urban radicals, the peasantry "refused to budge on behalf of Paris."[55] In many respects, concludes
Moore, "the peasantry was the arbiter of the Revolution."[56]

Dennis Smith

8. What were the outcomes of their behavior in terms of structural change, whether or not they intended such change, and how are these changes to be accounted for in terms of answers to (1), (2), and (6) above?

Ironically, to a considerable degree the consequences of human action in the midst of uprising and tumult are very different from those intended by the people concerned. The actions of the latter contribute to processes of structural transformation that have many other determinants. For example, although the peasants may have been the arbiters of the French Revolution, its consequences were, in Moore's view, ultimately favorable to urban bourgeois interests. To take another case, "As the dramatic events of the [English Puritan] Revolution unfolded . . . men were confronted by events they could not control and whose implications they could not foresee."[57] Although the English Civil War "did not result in the taking of political power by the bourgeoisie," its consequences included "an enormous if still incomplete victory for an alliance between parliamentary democracy and capitalism."[58] In the case of the United States, the victory of the North closed off at least one possible option in American development: "One need only consider what would have happened had the Southern plantation system been able to establish itself in the West by the middle of the nineteenth century and surrounded the Northeast."[59] The likely consequence of such an eventuality, suggests Moore, is that "the United States would have been in the position of some modernizing countries today, with a latifundia economy, a dominant antidemocratic aristocracy, and a weak and dependent commercial and industrial class, unable and unwilling to push forward toward political democracy. In rough outline, such was the Russian situation . . ."[60]

This formalization of Moore's strategy of causal explanation in *Social Origins* helps to emphasize a difference between his approach in this book and the Soviet studies and *Injustice*. In the Soviet studies, Moore explains the development of the Soviet state and the behavior of the Soviet elite by indicating that a specific range of strategies was available to the elite when confronting the structural dilemmas imposed by ideology, history, the tasks of industrialization, and the need for internal and external security. The structural dilemmas explain the elite strategies, which account for elite behavior, which leads to the appearance of new structural dilemmas. And so on.

In *Social Origins*, Moore interweaves two threads of argument. On the one hand, he explains the behavior of groups and classes during civil wars and revolutions with reference to their perceptions of their own material and moral interests. Almost without exception, the long-term (or even short-term) intentions expressed in such behavior bear little relation to the outcome of events. On the other hand, Moore also traces causal relationships of two further kinds: first, between antecedent structural tendencies (describable without reference to human intentions) and the processes of transformation in the dramatic social upheavals that follow, such as the overthrow of a regime or its challengers; and second, between these latter events and subsequent structural tendencies relevant to democratic or nondemocratic outcomes. The threads of causal explanation relating to human behavior and structural changes are juxtaposed in the narrative without being closely tied together. Moore explicitly denies that antecedent structural tendencies make any particular subsequent event (e.g., the French Revolution) inevitable.[61] However, he does not pay much attention in *Social Origins* to analyzing the interaction between structure and agency or between constraint and choice. This theme, which had been prominent in the Soviet studies, was to reemerge in *Injustice*.

It has already been noted that the structural consequences that concern Moore in *Social Origins* – the establishment of democratic or dictatorial polities – are identified in terms implying moral approbation and disapprobation, respectively. Furthermore, the structural transformations that are central to his analyses usually involve violent and disruptive behavior, producing misery and death. They impose massive penalties on many of those who participate in them.

What procedures does Moore use to assess the moral consequences of the wars, revolutions, and mutinies whose occurrence he has explained? Basically, he attempts to draw up a kind of "moral ledger." The costs in terms of human misery are set down on a balance sheet alongside the benefits, if any, obtained in terms of human freedom. Also relevant are the costs and benefits (again measured in terms of degrees of misery and freedom) that have *not* been incurred because of the failure of particular societies to develop in alternative ways that were genuinely in the cards. Moral assessment has to take into account the element of "opportunity cost." Moore does not make this procedure explicit. However, instances of its application may be found in sections of the chapters on France ("Social Consequences of Revolutionary Terror"), the United States ("The Meaning of the War") and Japan ("Political Consequences: The Nature of Japanese Fascism").

Moore emphasizes the importance of avoiding "a confusion between the causes of historical events and their consequences or meaning." The deeply ambiguous critical response to *Social Origins* suggests that he has not wholly succeeded.[62] He has not made sufficiently clear that his overarching typology of modernizing routes is based on an assessment of morally relevant outcomes rather than his analyses of causation. Even if the reader grasps this point, he or she is likely to be disappointed by Moore's failure to subject the claims of democratic ideology to the sharp critical appraisal that Marxist-Leninist ideology receives in the Soviet studies. In *Social Origins* Moore does little beyond itemizing the familiar list of legislative and judicial institutions, apparently assuming that the claim that these guarantee freedom may be accepted without serious questions. One has to conclude that his explication of historical and sociological causes is more impressive than his procedures for carrying out systematic moral evaluation.[63] Moore, of course, is likely to have been perfectly aware of the extent to which his self-imposed challenge had been unmet, and it is possible that the essays in *Reflections* were, in part, a response to the experience of writing *Social Origins*.

Injustice

In *Reflections* and *Injustice* Moore conducts a frontal attack on the problem of deriving the criteria for value judgments from objective knowledge about societies. In *Reflection*, he deduces from the application of quasiutilitarian moral calculus that rulers should govern in ways that minimize suffering within their societies as far as is humanly possible. In *Injustice* he tries to demonstrate that his own view of how rulers ought to behave, presented in *Reflections*, is in fact the expression of a universal consensus about the nature of political rights and obligations between rulers and subjects. The consensus, he argues, is based on the notion of reciprocity: "Obligations are accepted but should be reciprocal in nature; for the obligations of the subject there should be corresponding obligations for the ruler; and the whole should redound to the benefit of the community."[64] In practice, *Injustice* may usefully be considered as consisting of two books woven together. One book is a well-documented and self-contained analysis of the development of the German working class in the nineteenth and early twentieth centuries. The other is a transhistorical exercise in political theory.

The analysis of German materials focuses on the structure and consciousness of the German working class in the light of E. P. Thompson's suggestion that such workers were "capable of developing through their own experiences their own diagnoses and remedies for the ills that afflicted them."[65] Moore's approach, which entails study of a variety of primary and secondary sources, may be illustrated from his treatment of the crisis of 1848. He argues that this crisis stemmed from sudden economic failures in the context of a longer-run decline of guild organization under market and bureaucratic pressures. An estate system was gradually giving way before a strengthening industrial bourgeoisie. A new class of socially marginal unskilled workers was coming into existence.

The violence of 1848, however, did not signal support for revolution or even widespread strikes. The main demand expressed was for an elimination of the inhumane aspects of the rising capitalist order. There was also evident, Moore notes, a change in political awareness – an increasing recognition of the human capacity to reduce misery.

With respect to the subsequent period, Moore investigates three problems. First, was the German proletariat already "tamed" and integrated in the industrial order by the time of World War I? Why did neither a stable liberal-democratic regime nor a socialist revolution result from the political events of 1918–20 in Germany? To what extent do the answers to the above questions have a bearing on the rise of nazism in Germany?

Moore shows that the German working class before 1914 was divided between an intellectual elite and an inarticulate mass. The Social Democratic Party (SPD) was heavily influenced by the provincial and artisan origins of the former. On the basis of a working-class culture that emphasized craft pride there developed a demand for decent human treatment in the form of economic security and higher wage levels within the capitalist system. Although their demands included a reduction in the relative influence of Junkers and businessmen in the political sphere, the SPD and the working class were not revolutionary: "From the demand for acceptance in the social order it could only be a very short step to a positive willingness to defend this order when a foreign enemy loomed on the horizon."[66]

In the immediate postwar period, a crucial issue Moore confronts is the response of Ebert's SPD government to the uprising in the Ruhr. This occurred at a time when the old order appeared to be extremely unstable and the business elite was beginning to accept the need to work out some kind of accommodation with the trade union movement. Meanwhile, in the Ruhr a workers' Red army had been created, which for a while gained control in a number of towns. Its leaders claimed that the government was insufficiently radical, although the radical action they demanded was intended to maintain established standards, which were in danger of collapsing. Ebert brought in the conservative force of the army to put down the rising and in so doing chose to compromise with reaction rather than work toward a more liberal or even socialist political order.

In the chapter "The Suppression of Historical Alternatives," to which reference was made in the first section of this chapter, Moore asks what prospects there were in postwar Germany for the establishment of a liberal or democratic regime on a stable basis. To a significant extent, he concludes, Ebert could have helped to push change in a different direction by, for example, using the threat of unleashed radicalism as manifest in the Ruhr as a means of extracting more concessions from the reactionary old order. Moore argues that if there had been "slightly different changes in leadership and tactics all round," then "not only Germany but the rest of the world would have been spared enormous tragedies."[67]

The tragic and morally reprehensible outcome to which the choices of the SPD leadership contributed was nazism. Although this movement fostered a climate in which the only political choice in Germany appeared to be between anarchy and irrational obedience, in fact, "the choice . . . is between more or less rational forms of authority."[68] With this assertion, Moore's argument enters the realm covered in the second book to be found within the pages of *Injustice*.

This book has, in effect, two parts. The first part of the discussion concerns the existence of an implicit contract between rulers and ruled relating to universal problems of social coordination. This contract contains the norms of justice and, by implication, the criteria for identifying injustice. In a second, closely related part of this discussion, Moore looks at the circumstances in which social orders whose apparent effect is to produce unjustified suffering acquire moral authority. In this context, he also examines the factors – psychological, social, and cultural – that enable moral outrage against injustice to be expressed and facilitate action to eliminate the unjust exercise of authority.

Moore distinguishes between "predatory authority" and "rational authority." The former is typically based on a mixture of force and fraud and is rational only in an instrumental sense and not with respect to ends. By contrast,

> rational authority is a way of advancing individual or collective purposes by granting certain persons the right and in some cases even the obligation to execute specific tasks and give orders to other people in the course of so doing. For such authority to be rational the individual and collective aims must themselves be rational. I will define as rational any form of activity for which in a given state of knowledge there are good reasons to suppose that

it will diminish human suffering or contribute to human happiness without making other human beings miserable.[69]

Briefly expressed, Moore's explanation of the widespread acceptance of apparently "unjustifiable" suffering is that when misery is defined as being inevitable it becomes regarded as "just," as this is a strategy for making it seem bearable. Under what conditions, however, does resistance to repression as a source of misery develop within a society? Moore begins his answer to this question by pointing out that each major form of social order, such as a theocracy, military regime, or plutocracy, provides tests (successful invocation of the gods, military victory, economic criteria of various kinds) by which its claims to legitimacy may be tested. Because of the existence of such criteria the potential exists for opposition movements to exploit failures by rulers and propose new goals and values as having greater legitimacy. Resistance to unjust rulers depends on, first, a discovery and rejection of misery leading on to a disposition to act against its sources and, second, the development of social and political conditions that favor such action.

Successful resistance depends on changes in the spheres of culture, social structure, and personality. Moore's treatment of the first and last of these spheres is the most interesting and original part of his argument. He suggests, for example, that the self-control engendered by the effort to survive oppression has a potentially radical aspect. Subjection to industrial discipline, pursuit of individual social mobility, and engaging in political resistance all demand "a strengthening of the ego at the expense of the id, the taming of natural impulses, and the deferral of present gratifications for the sake of a better future."[70] A related consideration is that the processes of modernization, including industrialization, lead to a redefinition of the boundaries between those aspects of social life that are subject to human manipulation and those aspects that are beyond human control. The latter, but not the former, lie within the realm of inevitability, a realm whose extent, argues Moore, is being progressively diminished, and progressively perceived as diminishing, in the course of human history. In recovering our sense of moral outrage at the existence of injustice, the "intellectual liberation from the inevitable may be one of the most important next steps we have to take."[71]

Moore does not present his case simply, or mainly, as an abstract intellectual argument. He makes the suggestion that the implicit social contract with regard to the obligations of rulers and ruled is in fact accepted almost universally. However, while it is not surprising that Moore should encounter familiar social and political values in a German culture that did so much to nurture the Western philosophical tradition to which Moore himself belongs, he does not demonstrate that similar understandings of human relationships may be inferred from the evidence he produces on societies more estranged in time and space.

In the first section of this chapter I argue that one way in which Moore uses comparative analysis is as a means of deriving generalizations about human nature and moral codes from wide-ranging surveys of data drawn from diverse societies. A major weakness of this approach as applied by Moore throughout the transhistorical book within *Injustice* is that the author takes it for granted that the words and behavior of a variety of peoples derive from the same background assumptions as those of a mid-twentieth-century Western intellectual. There are powerful reasons why we should *not* take this for granted. As Clifford Geertz points out, common-sense assumptions are as subject to cross-cultural variation as religion and art. The content of the common-sense values expressed with the same "maddening air of simple wisdom" in different locales actually "varies too radically from one place and time to the next for there to be much hope of finding a defining constancy within it, an ur-story always told."[72] Steven Lukes makes a related point:

> Can we always assume that the victims of injustice and inequality would, but for the exercise of power, strive for justice and equality? What about the cultural relativity of values? Is not such an assumption a form of ethnocentrism? Why not say that acquiescence in a value system "we" reject, such as orthodox communism or the caste system, is a case of genuine consensus over different values?[73]

Lukes suggests some ways of investigating this problem, including the strategy of gathering evidence about the behavior of people when power is temporarily relaxed (for example, during revolutions) or that of contrasting their actual behavior in "normal" times with the content of the ideology they apparently accept. Moore indeed adopts similar strategies in his examination of German materials but neglects such procedures in the more wide-ranging survey being discussed here.

There are further difficulties associated with Moore's model of rational authority. There is no serious consideration of the problems associated with overlaps between competing realms of authority within complex nation-states: for example, those encompassed by the state, the company, the trade union, and the family. Another problem is the extent to which predatory authority tends to be treated by Moore as a very large residual category containing all forms of authority that cannot be described, in his terms, as rational. Since there are so few extant or historical examples of rational authority it would be useful if the residuum could be internally differentiated to some extent. The work of Richard Sennett is of some interest here. In his recent book, *Authority*, he distinguishes between forms of authority such as those characterized by paternalism or by autonomy on the part of the people who exercise command.[74] Like Moore, Sennett draws upon both Freud and Hegel in his analysis of the ways in which harmful forms of authority are enforced and may be transformed into more acceptable states. In view of Moore's emphasis on reciprocity, it is interesting to note that Sennett believes that "one of the most avoided subjects of modern society is the relationship between being controlled and being cared for."[75]

The significance of *Injustice*, with all its faults, may only be understood in the context of Moore's work as a whole. It is his culminating effort to answer the questions, What control can human beings exercise over their own destiny? And insofar as human action can influence processes of social change, which moral criteria are relevant to such action? Moore's argument in *Reflections* implies that the main hope for contributing to the reduction of human misery is the development of a model of rational authority whose parameters may be identified by a thorough empirical and theoretical exploration. *Injustice* contains an attempt to carry out that enquiry. It also focuses on an issue stemming from *Social Origins* and the Soviet studies. In *Social Origins* Moore establishes the framework of causes and consequences, processes and events, that constitute the various routes – partly successive and partly alternative – leading to the modern world. The regimes of Stalin (which Moore investigates in *Soviet Politics*) and of Hitler were responsible for a major part of the terror and misery associated with the passage of Russia and Germany along the Communist and Fascist routes to the modern world. To what extent were the excesses of these regimes inevitable? Could strategically placed individuals and groups have altered the course of history?[76] Moore's analysis in *Injustice* of the development of the German working class and the failures of its leaders to bring about either a stable liberal democratic government or a socialist revolution is directly relevant to those issues.

Injustice is essentially a long and complex working paper that tries to answer a number of questions that have troubled Moore throughout his career. In a sense, the text is overdetermined. It tries to do too much. Its various parts are related to earlier books by Moore rather

Dennis Smith

than being closely integrated with each other. I have little difficulty in agreeing with James Sheehan's verdict on the book:

> The various pieces of the book do not reinforce each other. Since the analysis does not cohere, some of its parts are strong *despite* rather than *because* of their place in the whole; the historical analysis is not strengthened by the theoretical, and vice versa . . . The questions Moore poses in *Injustice* are either too narrow or too broad; the answers he provides slip back and forth from specific historical explanations to diffuse theoretical reflections. In contrast to *Social Origins*, therefore, this book does not establish that middle range of analysis which rests upon a foundation of historical specifics and is illuminated by broader theoretical considerations. *Injustice* has many good things in it; it is clearly the product of a well-stocked and carefully-disciplined intelligence. But the book is not a success. If *Social Origins* qualifies as a "flawed masterpiece," *Injustice* can be regarded as no better than an interesting failure.[77]

An Evaluation of Moore's Work

On the evidence of Moore's work so far, it has to be admitted that he has made a greater contribution as a sociologist and historian than as a political theorist and moral philosopher. In the former guise, Moore has produced a corpus of work that displays remarkable unity of theme. In his very first major work, *Soviet Politics*, there are already passing references to issues to be dealt with at greater length in succeeding volumes. Mention may be found of the consequences of political systems for human happiness and misery, the nature of exploitation, the significance of reciprocity in relations between the people and their rulers, the importance of moral codes in relation to justice, and so on.[78]

The major works also complement each other in their subject matter. Whereas *Social Origins* is mainly concerned with the rural class structure, *Injustice* deals primarily with an industrial proletariat. The book just mentioned has as its subject matter currents of feeling and ideas among the lower orders; by contrast, the Soviet studies deal with similar topics in connection with a modernizing elite. In his Preface to *Social Origins* Moore mentions that he had originally intended to include chapters on Russia and Germany in that book.[79] To some extent, at least, the Soviet studies and *Injustice* help to make up for this lacuna. Taken as a whole, Moore's works may be treated as a prolonged inves-

346

tigation, approaching from successively different directions, of the development of relations between the masses and the elite, between rural and urban social orders, and between the exercise of political power and the constraints on its exercise flowing from political ideologies. In this context, an abiding concern has been the dynamics and consequences of the processes whereby workers and peasants have become participants in modern polities. In the course of these processes, they acquire, in one way or another, a stake in the new social order:

> By and large the industrial revolution has enormously increased the popular stake. The existing state has become the main agency, indeed the only agency, for the achievement of all purposes by all sections of the population . . . The modern citizen is caught in a web of beliefs, expectations, and sanctions that tie him to the existing regime far more tightly than was the case with most of his peasant ancestors.[80]

Misery, happiness, oppression, and liberty are the penalties and prizes at stake in the political arena; hence its abiding significance for Moore.

Barrington Moore's work in historical sociology has been the sustained enterprise of a lone scholar in determined pursuit of answers to some deceptively straightforward questions, such as What is a just society? Moore has been reluctant to formalize his approach. He has no taste for conceptual paradigms.

In spite of Moore's preference for engaging in sociology and historical study rather than writing about how to do it, it is certainly open to others to notice his strengths and his weaknesses. One methodological strength is Moore's skill in interweaving narrative history and comparative analysis, a strength most commandingly displayed in the particular case studies within *Social Origins*. Moore's discussion of each national case is punctuated with detailed and subtle cross-references to other societies. These references are brought in not as a mere adornment but as essential material for an argument being constructed before the reader's eyes. In the chapter on the United States, for example, there are at least two references to Russia, one reference to China, four references to France, three references to Germany, two references to Rome, one reference to Greece, and six references to England.[81]

A second strength is Moore's recognition of the mutual influence of culturally embedded meanings and the constraints imposed by the struggle for survival in society. The capacity to hold both aspects of human action and social order together in his work was displayed as early as the Soviet studies and continues to be evident in *Injustice*. In *Soviet Politics* a major issue was how have the Bolshevik elite been able both to act in ways that appear legitimate in terms of their ideology and also to survive as managers of an industrializing society under threat? Moore's general view is well expressed in the following quotation from *Injustice*:

> Poorly equipped for survival by their purely biological endowment, with the decisive exception of their brains, human beings are so constituted that they must cooperate somehow merely in order to stay alive. Survival, on the other hand, is no more than the absolutely minimal prerequisite for the other collective purposes served by moral rules. Apart from these purposes and the effectiveness or ineffectiveness that a moral code may have in both selecting and sustaining them, I see no criterion with which to pass judgment on any given form of morality.[82]

Moore's insistence on treating the struggle for survival and the search for meaning as intimately related is a valuable corrective to historians and sociologists inclined to stress either at the expense of the other.[83]

Before I consider some respects in which Moore has fallen short of his ambitions, it will be interesting to contrast his work with that of two scholars, E. P. Thompson and Immanuel Wallerstein, whose philosophical approaches to social analysis are very similar to that of Moore.[84] In view of these background similarities, their adoption of very different methodologies is fascinating.

The influence of Thompson's work on Moore's enquiry in *Injustice* has already been noted. Both men also share an interest in the relationship between forms of class domination and the norms of justice and reciprocity embodied in systems of rule.[85] Each writer is interested in identifying the potentialities in human nature and social arrangements. Each of them stresses the importance of assessing historical change in terms of the quality of life, especially its consequences for the extent of human misery. Thompson, like Moore, believes that "given societies at given technological levels and with given social systems simultaneously disclose and impose limits upon human possibilities."[86] The English historian is aware of the potential uses of counter-factual logic, of playing the "history-game in which we suppose that A did not happen and B (which did not happen) did."[87] He shares Moore's belief in the need to conquer the illusion of inevitability: "We *can* not impose our will upon history in any way we choose. We *ought* not surrender to its circumstantial logic."[88]

Immanuel Wallerstein agrees with both Moore and Thompson that the "concern with history, with social science and with politics . . . is a *single* concern."[89] Wallerstein does "not believe that there is or could be such a thing as value-free historical social science."[90] One is strongly reminded of Moore's own views when reading in Wallerstein's work that perceptions of truth alter as societies change and that although "we are irremediably the product of our background, our training, our personality and social role, and the structured pressures within which we operate," that is "not to say that there are no options. Quite the contrary."[91] Both Wallerstein and Moore have been more attracted by the contributions of C. Wright Mills, Herbert Marcuse, and Franz Neumann than they have been by the work of, say, Paul Lazarsfeld and Talcott Parsons. Both have written about the contribution to the shaping of the modern world made by forms of commercialized or capitalist agriculture. Neither can be labeled either a Marxian or a Weberian and both have responded sourly to the claims made by Communist and liberal regimes alike.

The similarities just mentioned coexist with important differences. Moore, Wallerstein, and Thompson may be contrasted with respect to their uses of narrative and comparative analysis and also with regard to their orientations toward meaning and values. Both Thompson and Wallerstein emphasize narrative in their presentation. Thompson has been preoccupied with the ways in which the English class structure was transformed during the nineteenth and twentieth centuries and the implications of this transformation for the possible achievement of a humane and just society. Wallerstein has been preoccupied with the ways in which the capitalist world system was transformed in the period since the fifteenth century and the implications of this transformation for the possible achievement of a socialist world system. He is dedicated to the task of "redoing our historical narratives, accumulating new world-systemic quantitative data (almost from scratch) and above all reviewing and refining our conceptual baggage."[92] To some extent his refined conceptual baggage, including the notions of core and periphery, provide convenient tools that allow his enterprise to be shared and imitated by others in a way that Moore's daunting questions (e.g., How may misery be reduced or abolished?) do not.

The main point to be made is that comparison is subordinate to narrative in the writings of both Thompson and Wallerstein. Comparisons are not absent from the work of either. For example, Wallerstein makes some very telling points about the similarities and differences between Europe and China in the fifteenth century. Thompson contrasts the communal experiences of field laborers, artisans, and handloom weavers in an illuminating way.[93] However, in both cases, the dominant tendency is to use comparisons as a means of illustrating an argument that is well established before such detailed contrasts are introduced. As has been seen, Moore to a greater extent uses comparative analysis as a means of producing and testing (as opposed to illustrating) his own or others' arguments. The similarities just mentioned between Wallerstein and Moore coexist with some important differences. For example, Wallerstein, to a much greater extent than either Thompson or Moore, expresses his argument in terms of an abstracted model based on distinctions between types of system. Furthermore, he pays less attention than either of the two other writers to the experiences of the human participants in the processes he describes.

Both Moore and Thompson are deeply concerned with the meaningfulness of social experience, the source of such meanings, and their implications for the processes of structural transformation. However, Moore is more ambitious than Thompson with respect to the possibility of evaluating human action and social change. Thompson accepts that writing history is a project in which making value judgments is an inevitable activity. As far as he is concerned, however, moral assessment entails an act of faith. Although the historian can acquire objective knowledge about what has happened and even make rational judgments about what is likely to happen under certain conditions, the values that underlie his moral evaluations can have no objective basis.[94] Thompson is more self-conscious about this issue than Wallerstein and less optimistic than Moore in his approach to it. In 1958 Moore accepted the same position as Thompson, believing that the intellectual would have to face the prospect of going "down with his ship, with all banners flying and steam hissing from the boilers, on behalf of principles about which absolute certainty is impossible."[95] However, as has been seen, Moore subsequently seeks to establish an objective basis for moral values in a quasiutilitarian psychology uneasily linked to a developmental view of human consciousness.[96] In Moore's view, there are grounds for believing that a social contract specifying the reciprocity that should exist between rulers and ruled is, in fact, widely accepted as the normative basis for the political order.

The central weakness of Moore's work is his failure to make this assertion plausible. His persistent attempts to pursue issues relating to evaluation at the same time as questions relating to causal explanation have sometimes blurred the outlines of his overall presentation, most notably in Social Origins, as has already been argued. In the case of Injustice this difficulty manifests itself in a geological fault-line running through the text. The most unified work is Soviet Politics, a study in the course of which Marxist-Leninist ideology is treated as an objective fact rather than a value system that has to be morally assessed.

Paradoxically, Moore's dogged pursuit of an objective basis for moral values has been a source of tremendous strength. It has meant that his work has been organized around a set of questions rather than a set of propositions. As I stressed in the first section, Moore has not sought intellectual protection from uncertainty by adopting any particular theoretical scheme, lock, stock, and barrel. He has been prepared to borrow from functionalism, for example, in his attempt to specify the minimum requirements of an industrial society; but this has not meant that he could not cope intellectually with the problems of social change. Moore has been very interested in the potentialities of evolutionary theory, including the idea that "stage-skipping" might be useful in analyzing the rapid progress of Asian societies;[97] but this has not meant that he has neglected the significance of certain persisting characteristics of recurrent organizational forms such as bureaucracy. On questions relating to the connection between economic and political change, Moore has drawn ideas from both Marx and Weber, yet he comments, in typical style: "Both Marx and Weber have led their followers, particularly those who try to be most literally scientific, thoroughly astray on certain of these issues, invaluable as their contribution certainly is on other scores."[98]

Above all, Moore has made it evident through his practice over several decades that our explanations of social order and social change can only benefit from systematically taking account of not only structural constraints but also the motivations, perceptions, and choices of human beings. His work provides a convincing demonstration of the proposition that the social processes that are most worth examining in detail and seeking to understand are those that have not only helped to shape the aspirations and values to which we are attached, but have also circumscribed the means and the opportunities that we have to pursue them.

Notes

1. Earlier versions of this chapter were read by Val Riddell and Theda Skocpol. I am grateful for their comments.
2. *Soviet Politics — The Dilemma of Power: The Role of Ideas in Social Change* (Cambridge, Mass: Harvard University Press, 1950) (hereafter *Soviet Politics*); *Terror and Progress USSR: Some Sources of Change and Stability in the Soviet Dictatorship* (Cambridge, Mass: Harvard University Press, 1954) (hereafter *Terror and Progress*); *Political Power and Social Theory* (Cambridge, Mass: Harvard University Press, 1958) (hereafter *Political Power*); *Social Origins of Dictatorship and Democracy: Lord and Peasant in the Making of the Modern World* (Harmondsworth: Penguin, 1969) (hereafter *Social Origins*); *Reflections on the Causes of Human Misery and upon Certain Proposals to Eliminate Them* (Har-

Dennis Smith

mondsworth: Penguin, 1972) (hereafter *Reflections*); *Injustice: The Social Bases of Obedience and Revolt* (London: Macmillan Press, 1978) (hereafter *Injustice*).

3. J. Sheehan, "Barrington Moore on Obedience and Revolt," *Theory and Society* 9 (5) (1980): 733.
4. Moore, *Political Power*, p. 159.
5. Moore, *Injustice*, pp. 3–4.
6. For a detailed discussion of the essays mentioned, see D. Smith, *Barrington Moore Jr.: A Critical Appraisal* (Armonk, N.Y.: M. E. Sharpe, 1983), pp. 43–67. This book is also published in Britain as *Barrington Moore. Violence, Morality and Political Change* (London: Macmillan Press, 1983).
7. Moore, *Political Power*, p. 152.
8. Moore, *Social Origins*, p. 521.
9. On the use of secondary (as opposed to primary) sources, Moore comments: "The real use of other people's research (as opposed to merely summarizing and reproducing it) sooner or later amounts to asking questions that go beyond their explicit answers. Their hard work is what makes it possible to perceive these questions." *Social Origins*, p. 94, n. 143.
10. W. G. Sumner, *Folkways*, with an introduction by W. L. Phelps (New York: Mentor, 1960), p. xi; Moore, *Soviet Politics*, p. xiii.
11. Moore, *Social Origins*, pp. 114–15.
12. Moore, *Political Power*, p. 2.
13. Moore, *Social Origins*, pp. x–xi.
14. Ibid., pp. 413ff.
15. Moore, *Injustice*, p. 380.
16. A more detailed discussion of this aspect of Moore's work may be found in D. Smith, "Morality and Method in the Work of Barrington Moore," *Theory and Society* 13 (2) (March 1984).
17. Moore, *Social Origins*, p. 103.
18. Moore, *Political Power*, p. 108.
19. Moore, *Soviet Politics*, p. 95.
20. Ibid., p. 276.
21. Ibid., p. 316.
22. Ibid., p. 409.
23. Moore, *Terror and Progress*, p. ix.
24. Ibid., p. 5.
25. Ibid., p. 209.
26. Moore, *Social Origins*, p. viii.
27. Ibid., pp. xi–xii.
28. Ibid., p. xiv.
29. Ibid., pp. 417–25.
30. Ibid., pp. 457–59, 467–70, 483.
31. Ibid., p. 253.
32. Ibid.
33. Ibid., p. 114.
34. Ibid.
35. Ibid., pp. 251–52.
36. Ibid., p. 427.
37. Ibid., pp. 413–14.
38. Ibid., p. 414.
39. Ibid.
40. Ibid., pp. 416–17.
41. Ibid., p. 40.
42. Ibid., p. 210.

43. Ibid., p. 211.
44. Ibid., p. 485.
45. Ibid., pp. 63–69, 334–41.
46. See D. Smith, *Barrington Moore*, pp. 103–7.
47. Ibid., pp. 89–90, 93–94; Moore, *Social Origins*, pp. 9–14, 20–29.
48. Moore, *Social Origins*, pp. 139, 251.
49. Ibid., p. 122.
50. Ibid.
51. Ibid.
52. Ibid., pp. 140–41.
53. Ibid., p. 251.
54. Ibid., pp. 251–2.
55. Ibid., p. 92.
56. Ibid., p. 77.
57. Ibid., p. 18.
58. Ibid., p. 19.
59. Ibid., p. 153.
60. Ibid.
61. Ibid., p. 108.
62. Ibid., p. 521; D. Smith, *Barrington Moore*, pp. 25–29.
63. For a more extended critique, see D. Smith, *Barrington Moore*, pp. 87–107.
64. Moore, *Injustice*, p. 510.
65. Ibid., p. 474; E. P. Thompson, *The Making of the English Working Class* (Harmondsworth: Penguin, 1963).
66. Moore, *Injustice*, p. 225.
67. Ibid., p. 397.
68. Ibid., p. 433.
69. Ibid., p. 440.
70. Ibid., p. 464.
71. Ibid., p. 500.
72. C. Geertz, "Common Sense as a Cultural System," *The Antioch Review* 30 (1) (Spring 1975): 17.
73. S. Lukes, *Power: A Radical View* (London: Macmillan Press, 1974), pp. 46–47.
74. R. Sennett, *Authority* (London: Secker and Warburg, 1980).
75. Sennett, *Authority*, p. 185.
76. See Moore, *Soviet Politics*, pp. 196–97; *Injustice*, p. 397.
77. Sheehan, "Barrington Moore," pp. 732–33. Italics in original.
78. Moore, *Soviet Politics*, pp. 38, 411, 245, 128.
79. Moore, *Social Origins*, pp. viii–ix.
80. Moore, *Reflections*, p. 35.
81. Moore, *Social Origins*, pp. 110, 114, 115, 212, 123, 140, 141, 152, 153, 154.
82. Moore, *Injustice*, p. 436.
83. For a relevant discussion dealing with the work of Norbert Elias and, more briefly, Richard Sennett and Clifford Geertz, see D. Smith, "Norbert Elias – Established or Outsider?" *Sociological Review* 32 (2) (May 1984).
84. The approaches of Thompson and Wallerstein are contrasted in D. Smith, "Social History and Sociology – More than Just Good Friends," *Sociological Review* 30 (2) (May 1982): 286–308, esp. pp. 291–92, p. 302.
85. Apart from *The Making of the English Working Class*, see also E. P. Thompson, *Whigs and Hunters* (London: Lane, 1975).
86. E. P. Thompson, *The Poverty of Theory* (London: Merlin Press, 1978), p. 155.
87. Ibid., p. 46.
88. Ibid., p. 186. Italics in original.

Dennis Smith

89. I. Wallerstein, *The Capitalist World-Economy* (Cambridge, U.K.: Cambridge University Press, 1980), p. vii. Italics in original.
90. Ibid., p. x.
91. I. Wallerstein, *The Modern World-System. Capitalist Agriculture and the Origins of the European World-Economy in the Sixteenth Century* (New York: Academic Press, 1974), p. 9.
92. Wallerstein, *Capitalist World-Economy*, p. 136.
93. Thompson, *Making of the English Working Class*, pp. 233–346; Wallerstein, *Modern World-System*, pp. 52–57.
94. Thompson, *Poverty of Theory*, pp. 148–56.
95. Moore, *Political Theory*, p. 196.
96. For an elaboration of this point, see D. Smith, "Method and Morality in the work of Barrington Moore."
97. Moore, *Political Power*, p. 153.
98. Moore, *Social Origins*, p. 49.

Bibliography

BARRINGTON MOORE'S MAJOR WORKS

Soviet Politics – The Dilemma of Power: The Role of Ideas in Social Change. Cambridge, Mass.: Harvard University Press, 1950.

Terror and Progress USSR: Some Sources of Change and Stability in the Soviet Dictatorship. Cambridge, Mass.: Harvard University Press, 1954.

Political Power and Social Theory. Cambridge, Mass.: Harvard University Press, 1958.

Social Origins of Dictatorship and Democracy: Lord and Peasant in the Making of the Modern World. Boston: Beacon Press, 1966.

Reflections on the Causes of Human Misery and upon Certain Proposals to Eliminate Them. Boston: Beacon Press, 1972.

Injustice: The Social Bases of Obedience and Revolt. White Plains, N.Y.: M.E. Sharpe, 1978.

SOME REVIEWS OF MOORE'S WORK

Almond, G. Review of *Social Origins. American Political Science Review*, 61 (3) (September 1967): 768–70.

Dore, R. P. "Making Sense of History." *European Journal of Sociology* 10 (2) (1969): 295–305.

Femia, J. V. "Barrington Moore and the Preconditions for Democracy." *British Journal of Political Science* 2 (1) (January 1972): 21–46.

Hobsbawm, E. J. Review of *Social Origins. American Sociological Review* 32 (5) (October 1967): 821–22.

Kumar, K. "Class and Political Action in Nineteenth-Century England; Theoretical and Comparative Perspectives." *European Journal of Sociology* 24 (1983): 3–43.

Lowenthal, D. Review of *Social Origins. History and Theory* 7 (2) (1968): 257–78.

Ness, G. D. Review of *Social Origins. American Sociological Review* 32 (5) (October 1967): 818–20.

Rubinstein, R. L. "Moral Outrage as False Consciousness." *Theory and Society* 9 (1980): 745–55.

Salamon, L. M. "Comparative History and the Theory of Modernization." *World Politics* 23 (1) (October 1970): 83–103.

Shapiro, G. Review of *Social Origins*. *American Sociological Review* 32 (5) (October 1967): 820–21.

Sheehan, J. "Barrington Moore on Obedience and Revolt." *Theory and Society* 9 (5) (1980): 723–34.

Skocpol, T. "A Critical Review of Barrington Moore's *Social Origins of Dictatorship and Democracy.*" *Politics and Society* 4 (1) (1973): 1–34.

Smith, D. *Barrington Moore Jr.: A Critical Appraisal*. Armonk, N.Y.: M. E. Sharpe, 1983. This book is also published in Britain as *Barrington Moore. Violence, Morality and Political Change*. London: Macmillan Press, 1983.

Stinchcombe, A. L. Review of *Social Origins*. Harvard Educational Review 37 (2) (1967): 290–93.

Tenfelde, K. "German Workers and the Incapacity for Revolution." *Theory and Society* 9 (9) (1980): 735–44.

Tumin, J. "The Theory of Democratic Development: A Critical Revision." *Theory and Society* 12 (1982): 143–64.

Wiener, J. M. "Review of Reviews." *History and Theory* 15 (2) (1976): 146–75. "Working-Class Consciousness in Germany, 1848–1933." *Marxist Perspectives* 5 (2) (1979): 156–69.

Zagorin, P. "Theories of Revolution in Contemporary Historiography." *Political Science Quarterly* 88 (1) (March 1973): 23–52.

Zelnik, R. E. "Passivity and Protest in Germany and Russia: Barrington Moore's Conception of Working-Class Responses to Injustice." *Journal of Social History* 15 (3) (1982): 485–512.

EXAMPLES OF WORK BY SCHOLARS INFLUENCED BY MOORE

Bonnell, V. *Roots of Rebellion. Worker's Politics and Organization in St. Petersburg and Moscow, 1900–1914*. Berkeley: University of California Press, 1983.

Castles, F. G. "Barrington Moore's Thesis and Swedish Political Development." *Government and Opposition* 8 (3) (1973): 1139–44.

Skocpol, T. *States and Social Revolutions*. Cambridge, U.K. and New York: Cambridge University Press, 1979.

Smith, D. *Conflict and Compromise. Class Formation in English Society 1830–1914. A Comparative Study of Birmingham and Sheffield*. London: Routledge & Kegan Paul, 1982.

Tilton, T. A. "The Social Origins of Liberal Democracy: The Swedish Case." *American Political Science Review* 68 (2) (1974): 561–71.

Wiener, J. M. *Social Origins of the New South Alabama 1860–1885*. Baton Rouge: Louisiana State University Press, 1978.

11. Emerging Agendas and Recurrent Strategies in Historical Sociology

THEDA SKOCPOL

Master agendas for historical sociology were first set back when Tocqueville, Marx, Durkheim, and Weber asked important questions and offered such fruitful, if varying, answers about the social origins and effects of the European industrial and democratic revolutions. During the twentieth century, the major scholars discussed in the essays collected here have been at the forefront of those carrying forward the traditions of historical sociology launched by the founders. At moments, to be sure, these men may have seemed rather isolated bearers of modes of scholarship that most sociologists considered part of the honored past rather than the vital present and future of the discipline. By now, however, it is clear enough that the stream of historical sociology has deepened into a river and spread out into eddies running through all parts of the sociological enterprise.

Until the 1970s, "historical sociology" was not a phrase one often, if ever, heard in conversations among sociologists in the United States.[1] Of course, major works of comparative history by the likes of Bendix, Eisenstadt, and Moore were widely known and respected. But these works were thought to be peculiar accomplishments. Only unusually cosmopolitan older men, operating in relative isolation from the mainstreams of empirical research in the discipline, were considered capable of producing such major historical works, while ordinary sociologists used quantitative or field-work techniques to study specialized aspects of present-day societies.

Then, from the mid-1970s onward, remarkable changes occurred. Partly these changes were due to the efforts of prominent institution builders like Charles Tilly and Immanuel Wallerstein. As I suggested in the introduction, they were also connected to shifting sensibilities about meaningful scholarship within and beyond academia, sensibili-

356

ties that revived long-standing historical orientations in sociology. Younger scholars increasingly posed historical questions and used historical evidence and modes of reasoning in their doctoral dissertations. Yearly sessions at the annual meetings of the American Sociological Association were given over to Historical Sociology or to Historical Methods. Many topical sessions, especially those on such macroscopic issues as the sociology of development or labor markets or the growth of the welfare states, began regularly to include historical papers. Graduate and undergraduate courses with historical labels or contents proliferated, and departments across the United States sought faculty members in comparative and historical sociology. Finally, even the major journals in the discipline opened their pages to historical articles by sociologists. By the mid-1980s, in short, historical sociology is no longer exclusively the province of the odd, if honored, grand older men of the discipline. Students and rising young sociologists, even women and middle-Americans, can and do make modest or major contributions to sociology through historical genres of research. Nowadays, historical questions or methods are the stuff of which conferences, courses, and sessions are made, and they orient the efforts of organized research groups as well as those of lone scholars in library studies.

Perhaps the surest sign that historical sociology is in a period not only of growth but of renewal lies in the changes one can see when the research agendas and methods of contemporary historical sociologists are compared to those of the founders of sociology. Where the traditional questions about the roots and consequences of the European Industrial Revolution, the rise of the working class, and the bureaucratization of states and democratization of politics are still being investigated, they are being pursued with more telling evidence and methods of analysis than those deployed by the founders. Excellent examples that come to mind are Jere Cohen's reexamination of Weber's thesis about rational capitalism through a close look at economic practices in Renaissance Italy;[2] Mark Traugott's reexamination of Marx and Engels's assertions about class and political conflicts in the French Revolution of 1848;[3] Jack Goldstone's careful probing of the demographic and institutional preconditions for the English Revolution considered in comparative perspective;[4] Victoria Bonnell's meticulous study of the roots of rebellion among Russian workers in the early twentieth century;[5] Mary Fulbrook's comparative historical analysis of the contributions made by Puritan and Pietist religious movements to struggles for and against absolutist monarchies in Prussia, Württemberg, and

England;[6] and David Zaret's original analysis of the social and religious conditions accompanying the emergence of contractarian theology within English Puritanism.[7]

Even more telling, perhaps, research agendas in historical sociology have broadened to encompass different times and places and new kinds of topics from those that preoccupied the founders. Think of Orlando Patterson's breathtakingly comprehensive comparative historical survey of the nature and internal dynamics of slavery.[8] Consider Daniel Chirot's very long-term study of the Romanian province of Wallachia between 1250 and 1970.[9] Consider as well studies by Elbaki Hermassi, Mounira Charrad, Ellen Kay Trimberger, and Michael Adas that pursue in-depth historical comparisons among non-Western countries or peoples examined in their own right.[10] All of these works break with the Western Eurocentric purview that has traditionally limited the questions asked and patterns explored by historical sociologists.

Industrial relations, welfare states, and ethnic patterns in the twentieth century have also become the objects of carefully designed studies by historically oriented social analysts. Important works about industrial relations include Ronald Dore's *British Factory, Japanese Factory: The Origins of National Diversity in Industrial Relations* and Charles Sabel's *Work and Politics: The Division of Labor in Industry.*[11] On welfare states, examples that come to mind are Francis Castles's *The Social Democratic Image of Society: A Study of the Achievements and Origins of Scandinavian Social Democracy in Comparative Perspective*, Peter Flora and Arnold Heidenheimer's collection, *The Development of Welfare States in Europe and America*, my own articles with John Ikenberry and Ann Shola Orloff on the United States in comparative perspective, and Gaston Rimlinger's *Welfare Policy and Industrialization in Europe, America, and Russia.*[12] Ethnic and racial relations have, finally, been the concern of some of the best historically oriented books recently completed by sociologists, including Michael Hechter's *Internal Colonialism: The Celtic Fringe in British National Development, 1536–1966*, William Julius Wilson's *The Declining Significance of Race: Blacks and Changing American Institutions*, Ivan Light's *Ethnic Enterprise in America: Business and Welfare Among Chinese, Japanese, and Blacks*, and Stanley Lieberson's *A Piece of the Pie: Blacks and White Immigrants Since 1880*, and Doug McAdam's *Political Process and the Development of Black Insurgency, 1930–1970.*[13]

Many of these works, along with other important studies in historical sociology by Robert Bellah, Joseph Ben-David, Fred Block, Morris Janowitz, Seymour Martin Lipset, Dietrich Rueschemeyer, Magali Sarfatti-Larson, Paul Starr, and Ellen Kay Trimberger, place developments in the United States in historical or comparative-historical perspective.[14] They thus provide the kind of full contextual basis for the better understanding of current American social relations and political events that C. Wright Mills advocated in *The Sociological Imagination* and attempted to provide in his own historical studies of class and power in the United States.[15] Were Mills still alive today, he would have much more reason for optimism about American sociology's historical imagination than he did in 1959. At that point, only a few sociologists, including Lipset and Bendix along with Mills himself, were placing American patterns in truly historical and comparative frameworks.

Of course, historical sociologists today are only part of a growing interdisciplinary community of historically oriented social scientists. The rise of historical work in sociology has happened in tandem with complementary developments in political science and anthropology, and it has come in a period when many scholars in the venerable and slowly changing discipline of history are unusually open to methods and theories from the various social sciences.[16] Historical orientations in the discipline of sociology have their own logic and contents, not always parallel to developments in other disciplines. That is why historical sociology deserves attention in its own right. Yet historical sociology certainly blends at its edges into economic and social history, and completely melds in one of its prime areas, political sociology, with the endeavors of scholars who happen to be political scientists by (original or adopted) disciplinary affiliation. Understood as an ongoing tradition of research into the nature and effects of large-scale structures and long-term processes of change, historical sociology becomes, in fact, a transdisciplinary set of endeavors that simply has always had one important center of gravity within the academic discipline of sociology.

Is Historical Sociology a Subfield?

Within sociology itself, historical sociology is not – and in my view, should not become – a subfield or self-contained specialty. To the glory as well as the despair of the discipline, sociologists have always been remarkably eclectic in the problems they choose to investigate, the research methods they use, and the styles of argument they develop. Today, historical orientations are on the rise in all of these aspects of the sociological enterprise, but in no instance are they necessarily exclusive orientations. Sociological research on historical problems, for example, may be research about past times and places, or it may be research on processes of change over time leading into and flowing through the present. In the realm of actual research practice, moreover, sociologists may borrow archival methods from historians, or they may use historians' works as "secondary sources" of evidence. Yet such historical techniques and evidence can readily be combined with other methods of gathering and analyzing evidence about the social world.

In fact, quantitative techniques traditionally identified with nonhistorical sociological research have been reworked to become relevant for the analysis of temporal processes.[17] Even more than has occurred so far, quantitative and qualitative approaches could be creatively combined in research.[18] Through quantitative and qualitative modes of analysis alike, sociological theorizing can become more sensitive to sequences over time and to alternative historical paths, without giving up long-standing concerns to explain the patterns and effects of social structures and group action in potentially generalizable terms.

Whenever a set of scholarly activities expands as remarkably as historical sociology has done since the 1970s, a sudden premium is placed on characterizing and classifying the phenomenon so it can be taught and properly pigeonholed in various institutional settings. Those historical sociologists who are currently attempting to link contemporary historical sociology closely to the epistemological, theoretical, and methodological legacies of Max Weber may be attempting a narrow and defensive approach toward carving out a secure place for historical sociology.

A recent article by Charles Ragin and David Zaret, "Theory and Method in Comparative Research: Two Strategies," cogently exemplifies this strategy.[19] In effect, Ragin and Zaret concede most of what has traditionally been understood as the sociological enterprise – the search for general explanatory variables, in large part through quantitative analysis – to a Durkheimian approach that they present as inherently antihistorical. In sharp opposition to this Durkheimian perspective, they define a Weberian approach dedicated to exploring the particular features of historical cases with the aid of ideal-type concepts. Ragin and Zaret downplay the ways in which quantitative methods can be adapted to the analysis of processes over time, or to the analysis of complex configurations of causes that may account in generalizable ways for particular cases. They drive a wedge between historical methods and others. They end up trying to force all practitioners of comparative history, from Reinhard Bendix and Perry Anderson to Barrington Moore and myself, into a single Weberian camp, ignoring the important differences between those who use comparisons essentially to sharpen particularistic descriptions and those who use them to explore or establish causal generalizations.[20]

Surely it is a mistake to tie historical sociology down to any one epistemological, theoretical, or methodological orientation. Such an attempt fails to do justice to the variety of approaches used by the nine major scholars discussed in this book. And it certainly fails to capture the *current* variety of historically oriented research proceeding in (and around the edges of) sociology. Both Charles Tilly and Immanuel Wallerstein have taken a different approach from Ragin and Zaret. In effect, both have refused to dally with defining historical sociology and have, instead, simply set wide-ranging agendas for research and theorizing about important substantive concerns. Using qualitative and quantitative approaches alike, Tilly and his students and co-workers have focused especially on describing and explaining historically changing forms of collective action in modern European history. Wallerstein and his adherents have taken a more theoretically oriented approach – positing a capitalist world system with certain structures and dynamics – and then doing many kinds of studies on a huge variety of times, places, and problems to demonstrate the cogency of the new perspective.

Beyond the research agendas set by Tilly and Wallerstein, we have also seen indications of the rich array of topics currently being addressed by historically oriented sociologists. Anyone who looks into the methods and ideas used by these many scholars will immediately perceive variety and fruitful eclecticism. Obviously, when substantive problems and perspectives, rather than preconceived epistemologies or methodologies, define the substance of historical sociology, research and arguments are free to develop in a variety of styles. Research strategies in historical sociology quite properly reflect all of the diversities, disagreements, and dilemmas that have always marked sociology and the social sciences as a whole. At the same time, historical questions and answers are left free to challenge nonhistorical approaches wherever they may be found in sociology. Intellectual competition can remain open, and historically oriented sociologists can gain ground wherever their ideas and research can do a better job than alternatives in accounting for the patterns and dynamics of social life.

Do we conclude, therefore, that nothing useful can be said about research strategies in historical sociology, broadly conceived? In fact, particular choices about research designs and techniques must always be made by individual scholars or groups of researchers who are addressing given problems in the light of specific concepts, theories, or hypotheses. There are no mechanical recipes for proper methods of historical sociology. Nevertheless, surveying the entire range of historically oriented sociological work, one can devise a "map" of alternative strategies for research and writing that have been, and are likely to continue to be, chosen. Such a map cannot provide methodological dicta for any given investigation. But it can sensitize both practitioners and audiences of historical sociology to the purposes, the advantages, and the disadvantages of alternative approaches.

I take for granted that sociologists always do historically oriented research with some sort of explicit theoretical or conceptual interests in mind.[21] Given this relatively neutral premise, one can readily identify three major strategies for bringing history and theoretical ideas to bear on one another. Some historical sociologists apply a single theoretical model to one or more of many possible instances covered by the model. Other historical sociologists want to discover causal regularities that account for specifically defined historical processes or outcomes, and explore *alternative* hypotheses to achieve that end. Still other historical sociologists, who tend to be skeptical of the value of general models or causal hypotheses, use concepts to develop what might best be called meaningful historical interpretations. Each of these strategies may be applied to a single historical case or to two or more cases through comparative historical investigations.[22]

The three major strategies are not hermetically sealed from one another; creative combinations are and always have been practiced. Still, many studies regularly cluster around each major strategy, and the strategies recur despite variations in the kinds of problems historical sociologists address, the precise ways in which they gather and analyze evidence, and the content of the theoretical ideas they bring to bear upon these problems. With the aid of the examples of published scholarship arrayed on Figure 11.1, let me now flesh out these assertions and explore some of the strengths and weaknesses of each of these major practical strategies within the full range of historically oriented sociological scholarship.

Applying a General Model to History

Back in the 1950s and 1960s, when sociology was comfortably – and imperialistically! – assumed to be a discipline capable of formulating a universally applicable general theory of society, and history was condescendingly assumed by sociologists to be a collection of archival researchers devoted to gathering "the facts" about particular times and places in the past, the application of a general model to one or more historical instances was the kind of historical sociology most likely to

Figure 11.1. Research Strategies in Historical Sociology:
The Uses of Theory, Concepts, and Comparisons.

	Apply a General Model to Explain Historical Instances	Use Concepts to Develop a Meaningful Historical Interpretation	Analyze Causal Regularities in History
Single Case	Erikson Schwartz	Thompson Starr	Skocpol article
		Wallerstein	Gouldner
Multiple Cases	Smelser	Bendix Geertz	Brenner Hamilton Skocpol book Moore
	◄─── Tillys	Anderson	Fredrickson	Tillys ───►

be recognized as empirically rigorous and theoretically relevant in mainstream disciplinary circles. A leading example of this approach is Neil Smelser's *Social Change in the Industrial Revolution,* a major structural functionalist work of historical sociology published in 1959 and appropriately subtitled *An Application of Theory to the British Cotton Industry.*[23]

The theory applied in Smelser's book is a supposedly universally relevant model of the logical sequences through which any and all evolutionary changes involving societal differentiation could be expected to proceed. This model is elaborated by Smelser in the form of elaborate sets of "empty theoretical boxes," which he then proceeds to "fill" and "refill" with two sets of facts from nineteenth-century British history: first, facts about changes in the structure of the cotton industry as a set of economic enterprises, and then facts about changes in the lives and activities of workers in the cotton industry. Precisely speaking, therefore, *Social Change in the Industrial Revolution* is a work of comparative history, in the sense that the same general model is successively applied to two analytically distinct (albeit empirically interconnected) cases of social differentiation. Smelser, however, is not interested in comparing his two sequences of change directly to one another. Nor does he present his application of theory to British history as anything more than incidental to his overall theoretical purpose. His structural functionalist theory of evolutionary differentiation could, in principle, be applied equally well to an infinite array of other instances across times and places.

Another example, this one published in the mid-1960s, further illuminates the intentions characteristic of historical sociologists who apply general models to history. Kai Erikson's appealingly written book, *Wayward Puritans: A Study in the Sociology of Deviance*, begins by elaborating a Durkheimian model of how any community might define and regulate deviant behavior.[24] Then it uses the Puritan community of Massachusetts Bay in the 1600s as a setting in which to examine several major ideas about deviant behavior derived from the Durkheimian model. Erikson acknowledges that he personally had an intrinsic interest in the historical case he chose to explore, and indeed he (like Smelser with the British Industrial Revolution) investigates his historical case by drawing on primary records much as a social historian might do. Nevertheless, Erikson stresses that his study "should be viewed as sociological rather than historical," and he offers a perfect statement of the logic of our first genre of historical sociology in support of this characterization:

> The data gathered here have *not* been gathered in order to throw new light on the Puritan community in New England but to add something to our understanding of deviant behavior in general, and thus the Puritan experience in America has been treated in these pages as an example of human life everywhere. Whether or not the approach taken here is plausible . . . will eventually depend on the extent to which it helps explain the behavior of peoples at other moments in time, and not just the particular subjects of this study . . .[25]

While Durkheimian and, especially, Parsonian structural functionalist ideas lend themselves with special force to this genre of historical sociology, very different kinds of theoretical ideas can also form the basis for general models to be applied to cases treated simply as one or more among many possible historical instances to which the model could be applied. No more determined critic of Smelser's views could be found, for example, than Michael Schwartz, who draws his arguments about subordinate classes and their experiences and behavior from Karl Marx, Nikolai Lenin, Mao Tse-tung, and Robert Michels. Yet, following a strategy of analysis that closely resembles Smelser's approach, Schwartz's book *Radical Protest and Social Structure: The Southern Farmers' Alliance and Cotton Tenancy, 1880–1890* elaborates a general model of the processes by which radical protest movements develop, and either succeed or fail in overturning an established power structure.[26] Then Schwartz applies the model to the historical example of the Southern Farmers' Alliance, which arose at the end of the nineteenth century in the United States to challenge oligarchies of cotton planters and merchants.

In assessing the strengths and weaknesses of this first strategy of historical sociology, we need to realize at the start that a practitioner of this approach is chiefly interested in demonstrating and elaborating the inner logic of a general theoretical model. For this purpose, the detailed application of the general model to a relevant historical case (or cases) is very valuable, because it prompts the theorist to specify and operationalize what would otherwise necessarily remain very abstract concepts and theoretical propositions.[27] Smelser, for example, must provide for each of his two sequences of change concrete referents for notions such as "structural differentiation" and "symptoms of disturbance," and he must give historical substance to his major proposition that seven analytically recognizable steps occur whenever "a division of labor becomes more complex."

Similarly, Erikson must pin down historically such ideas as "community boundaries" and "group norms" and he must show us how, in terms of the symbols and social practices of the Massachusetts Puritans, deviant persons and their acts supplied "needed services to society by marking the outer limits of group experience and providing a point of contrast which gives . . . [social norms] some scope and dimension."[28] Finally, Schwartz must specify and operationalize concepts like "structural power," "mass organization," and "parent structure," and he must try to convince us that "incorrect" demands and tactics, "structural ignorance," and failures to maintain "organizational democracy" can plausibly order the events of the history of the Southern Farmers' Alliance from its birth to its death as a radical protest movement.

Reference to plausibility brings us, however, to the possible pitfalls inherent in the genre of historical sociology practiced by Smelser, Erikson, and Schwartz: The application of the model to the historical instance or instances can seem very arbitrary, in at least two senses. First, the model itself has to be taken as given prior to its historical application. Indeed, the special givenness of the model is expressed in the very rhetorical structure of works in this genre, for they invariably devote entire chapters or sections to the logical elaboration of highly abstract concepts and propositions before using them to analyze the historical instance(s). For readers already sympathetically oriented to the kind of theoretical perspective at issue, this may not seem problematic. For those who find the model incomprehensible, incoherent, or questionable, a sense of arbitrariness can arise from the start.

Secondly, given the model, questions can also arise about its application to each case. Since highly general concepts and propositions are at

Theda Skocpol

issue, how are we to know that any two investigators would concretize them in the same way? Could some arbitrarily selected historical facts perhaps always be found to illustrate any conceivable general model? How do we know that the sociologist applying his or her favored model is not leaving out important facts that might tell against the model? Such questions are especially likely to arise when books or articles in this genre of historical sociology have a very high ratio of general theoretical elaboration to analytic presentation of concrete sequences of historical events. Especially to historians, the entire exercise can seem like a highly unaesthetic imposition of sociological jargon onto arbitrarily selected and arranged historical facts. Complaints along this line have certainly been directed against the Smelser book.[29] In contrast, books like those of Schwartz and especially Erikson, which spend much more space on description and reconstruction of historical events tied down to particular places and conjunctures, may arouse less criticism of this sort. Nevertheless, they could in principle be just as subject to charges of tailoring historical presentations to fit a preconceived theory.

Working within the confines of their genre, historically oriented sociologists who apply general models have moved in two diametrically opposite directions to break out of the trap of appearing to apply a theory to arbitrarily selected cases and facts. One solution used by the evolutionary theorist Gerhard Lenski is, in his own words, to "apply a general model to the universe of all known historical (including ethnographic) instances."[30] This approach has the advantage of avoiding the charge that cases are selected to fit the theory while others are ignored. The disadvantage, however, is that the investigator is driven so far away from intrinsic interest in *any* particular cases that the label "historical sociology" hardly seems appropriate for this kind of scholarship.[31]

A contrasting approach to modeling history is nicely exemplified by David Willer's attempt to use elementary formal models of social relationships and social conflicts to explore the adequacy of existing historical interpretations of the processes that led to the fall of the Roman Empire in the West.[32] Willer does not try to capture the entire historical case, in all of its complexity, in one pregiven model. Instead, he probes existing historical arguments about the case at selected, strategic points. His aim is simply to see if the processes being posited hold up in terms of his formal models, which have themselves been tested in controlled experimental situations. The results are merely suggestive and, as Willer himself emphasizes, do not substitute for more comprehensive arguments about the Roman case. Still, Willer's study does suggest useful tactics to sociologists who want to apply general models to historical instances.

Yet if problems of perceived arbitrariness can plague works in this first genre of historical sociology, would-be appliers of general models do not often back off to the more selective and partial tactics exemplified by Willer's study. More often, they combine the application of a general model with one of the other two major strategies of historical sociology to be discussed here. In their book *The Rebellious Century*, for example, Charles, Louise, and Richard Tilly apply a general "political conflict" model to account for the patterns of violent collective conflict in France, Italy, and Germany between 1830 and 1930.[33] They make their application of that model much more convincing by systematically confronting the historical patterns of each national history not only with causal hypotheses derived from their own preferred model, but also with causal hypotheses derived from a rival Durkheimian model that has often been used by laypeople and sociological theorists alike to account for collective violence. Interestingly enough, in a late chapter of *Social Change in the Industrial Revolution*, Smelser briefly engages in a similar strategy. He contrasts his approach to explaining working-class unrest in mid nineteenth-century Britain with hypotheses derived from Marxist or classical-economic premises. Not incidentally, perhaps, these passages provide some of the most vivid and convincing reading in Smelser's otherwise cumbersome book.[34]

An alternative strategy for shoring up the plausibility of a general model applied to history is best exemplified by the work of one of the major historical sociologists analyzed in the body of this book. Immanuel Wallerstein's *Modern World-System*, as we have seen, applies a model of world capitalism to the last five hundred years of world history. Complementary models – "world empire" and "mini-system" and "world socialism" – are also presented to cover all other, previous or subsequent, possibilities in world history. Wallerstein's enterprise, however, cannot be considered simply one of applying a general theory to history. He also offers a meaningful world view imbued with the political perspectives of Third World and American radical critics of the world capitalist system. As Ragin and Chirot stress, the plausible appeal of Wallerstein's approach depends very much on its resonance with the political sensibilities of many younger social scientists.[35]

In these concluding remarks about alternative ways in which the application of a general model to history can be made more plausible, I have assumed that the next two major genres of historical sociology to be discussed – using concepts to develop meaningful historical interpretations and exploring alternative hypotheses about causal regularities in history – typically deploy stronger rhetorical tactics than this first genre for convincing audiences that a plausible set of arguments is being presented. The reasons why this may be true should become more apparent as we now explore each of these other approaches in its own right.

Using Concepts to Interpret History

A second major strategy regularly employed by historical sociologists is one that uses concepts to develop meaningful interpretations of broad historical patterns. In some ways, this strategy can be considered a self-conscious critical response to the efforts made by structural functionalists, Marxists, and many others to apply putatively very general theoretical models to history. Works by Reinhard Bendix and E. P. Thompson exemplify our second strategy, and we have already seen how thoroughly the methods and contents of their scholarship have been shaped in reactions against the overgeneralizing and determinist tendencies they perceive in structural functionalism and in economistic readings of Marxism. Beyond its possible genesis in such critical responses, however, the strategy of using concepts to develop meaningful interpretations of historical patterns is a positive approach in its own right. As shown by Paul Starr's *The Social Transformation of American Medicine*, this is a strategy of research and rhetorical presentation that may be used straightforwardly, and not primarily in polemical opposition to arguments offered by general model builders.[36]

Interpretive historical sociologists – the label I want to give practitioners of this second strategy – are skeptical of the usefulness of either applying theoretical models to history or using a hypothesis-testing approach to establish causal generalizations about large-scale structures and patterns of change. Instead, these scholars seek meaningful interpretations of history, in two intertwined senses of the word meaningful.[37] First, careful attention is paid to the culturally embedded intentions of individual or group actors in the given historical settings under investigation. Second, both the topic chosen for historical study and the kinds of arguments developed about it should be culturally or politically "significant" in the present; that is, significant to the audiences, always larger than specialized academic audiences, addressed by the published works of interpretive historical sociologists.

Although interpretive historical sociologists are implicitly or explicitly skeptical of what passes for theory among scientifically oriented students of society and history, they certainly are not themselves antitheoretical. On the contrary, they pay careful attention to matters of conceptual reorientation and conceptual clarification, and they always use explicit concepts of some generality to define their topical concerns and to guide the selection and presentation of historical patterns from one or more case studies. For example, E. P. Thompson's *The Making of the English Working Class* puts forward (in polemical opposition to economic-determinist views) a concept of class as "an historical phenomenon," "an active process which owes as much as to agency as to conditioning,"[38] and then uses this concept to order selected narratives of events in early nineteenth-century British history. And Paul Starr's *The Social Transformation of American Medicine* reworks Weberian notions of authority and specifically dramatizes a conception of "cultural authority" to set the stage for a lengthy account of the rise of the American medical profession to a position of great prestige, power, and wealth.[39]

Similarly, Reinhard Bendix's major books in comparative political history, *Nation-Building and Citizenship* and *Kings or People*, do not simply plunge into historical narratives of each national case. First, Bendix draws themes and specifies concepts from the works of Max Weber, Otto Hintze, and Alexis de Tocqueville to direct his readers' attention to the questions about political authority and the varying patterns of political institutions that he chooses to discuss in the various cases he covers. Because Bendix's books are all comparative rather than single-case studies, he deploys his orienting concepts in two ways. First, like Thompson and Starr, he uses some of them – especially those posed as themes basic to organized political life in sets of polities of a certain type – to orient the narratives of events and patterns in each of his case studies. In addition, though, Bendix uses some concepts as benchmarks to establish the particular features of each case, either through contrasts of case patterns to a general concept or through contrasts of that case to others in terms of how it handles a certain basic issue (such as legitimating the authority of a king).

Indeed, whenever interpretive historical sociologists do comparative historical studies, rather than simply conceptually structured presentations of single histories, they use comparisons for the specific purpose of highlighting the particular features of each individual case. Comparative studies, according to Reinhard Bendix,

> increase the visibility of one structure by contrasting it with another. Thus European feudalism can be more sharply defined

by comparison, say, with Japanese feudalism, [and] the significance of the Church in Western civilization can be seen more clearly by contrast with civilizations in which a comparable clerical orientation did not develop.[40]

Elsewhere, Bendix further elaborates this way of using historical comparisons:

By means of comparative analysis I want to preserve a sense of historical particularity as far as I can, while still comparing different countries. Rather than aim at broader generalizations and lose that sense, I ask the same or at least similar questions of divergent materials and so leave room for divergent answers. I want to *make more transparent the divergence among structures* of authority and among the ways in which societies have responded to the challenges implicit in the civilizational accomplishments of other countries.[41]

Because interpretive historical sociologists use comparisons to highlight the particular features of each case, they are likely to choose cases for inclusion in their studies that will maximize the possibilities for drawing dramatic contrasts. If, like Bendix, they cover a range of cases, they will most frequently invoke the extremes, such as England versus Russia, in their comparative arguments. If, as often happens, they discuss only a pair of cases, they will select them according to the logic succinctly illustrated by Clifford Geertz's little book, *Islam Observed*. In a first chapter tellingly entitled "Two Countries, Two Cultures," Geertz tells us why, among the many possibilities, he selected Indonesia and Morocco for his study of religious development in modernizing Islamic countries:

Their most obvious likeness is . . . their religious affiliation; but it is also, culturally speaking at least, their most obvious unlikeness. They stand at the eastern and western extremities of the narrow band of classical Islamic civilization which, rising in Arabia, reached out along the midline of the Old World to connect them, and, so located, they have participated in the history of that civilization in quite different ways, to quite different degrees, and with quite different results. They both incline toward Mecca, but, the antipodes of the Muslim world, they bow in different directions.[42]

For Geertz Indonesia and Morocco are so promising to compare precisely because, through the sharp contrast they offer within Islam, "they form a kind of commentary on one another's character."[43] His choice of cases, along with his rationale for the choice, perfectly reflects the distinctive purpose for which interpretive historical sociologists use comparative history. The aim is to clarify particularities through contrasts, not to show the repeated applicability of a theoretical model as in the first genre of history sociology just discussed, and not to test or develop causal generalizations, as in the third strategy, to be presented subsequently.

If done well, interpretive works can be the most compelling contributions of any genre in historical sociology – certainly the most compelling for broad audiences that stretch beyond academia. The reasons why are simple. First, graceful writing can be deployed to fullest advantage in this genre. Orienting concepts can be presented briefly, and much of the argument can proceed through the common-sense device of narrative storytelling. There is no need to move from a highly abstract model to historical specifications that may appear arbitrary or artificially ripped out of context; nor do flows of description need to be repeatedly broken to examine alternative causal hypotheses. Second, works in this genre necessarily tap into vivid contemporary sensibilities, intellectual trends, and assumptions about how the world works. Interpretive works deliberately stress relevance to the meaningful world views of their intended audiences, whether they be establishment audiences (as for the Bendix and Starr books) or politically oppositional audiences (as for E. P. Thompson's book).

Finally, too, both single-case studies and comparative studies in this genre stress the portrayal of given times and places in much of their rich complexity, and they pay attention to the orientations of the actors as well as to the institutional and cultural contexts in which they operate. Consequently, interpretive works can seem extraordinarily vivid and full, like a good Flaubert novel. Of course, the whole story can never be told in any work of history or historical sociology. But interpretive works can convey the impression of fullness much more readily than works of historical sociology that aim to apply models or establish causal connections of relevance to more than one case.

From certain philosophical points of view, the kinds of understanding of social history that interpretive works seek to convey represent the most desirable, and perhaps the only really feasible, kind of knowledge available through historical sociology.[44] It follows that interpretive works can only be judged to be more or less successful at meeting the challenge they set for themselves: finding the most compelling conceptual lenses through which to mediate between meaningful happenings in the past and the concerns of present day audiences. From the perspectives of social scientists concerned with (any degree of) general theoretical knowledge about regularities in social structures and processes, however, interpretive historical sociologists can almost always be faulted for their insouciance about establishing *valid* explanatory arguments. Both the concepts deployed by interpretive historical sociologists and the descriptive narratives on which they rely so heavily assert or imply all sorts of causal connections. Yet these historical sociologists are not concerned to establish explanations that hold good across more than single cases. From the perspectives of those concerned with causal validity, therefore, interpretive works can be misleading even when they are compelling.

The danger is probably greatest for single-case studies in the interpretive genre. Comparative histories, especially wide-ranging works such as those of Reinhard Bendix, are likely to display inconsistent causal assertions and missed opportunities for exploring causal regularities in ways visible to any astute reader (as Dietrich Rueschemeyer's reflections on Bendix demonstrate!). For single-case explorations such as those of Thompson and Starr, however, a critic needs to call to mind potential new comparative cases to begin to perceive such causal inadequacies or missed opportunities.

Interestingly, for each of these examples one can wonder how the arguments presented for England or the United States might have held up if either author had extended his tentative causal assertions to the other nation. Recent work by Ira Katznelson suggests that E. P. Thompson might have developed a less cultural and more political argument about the structures, conjunctures, and activities that "made" the English working class distinctive, if only he had been willing to make careful comparisons to the United States and Western Europe.[45] Likewise, in a review of Paul Starr's book, Charles Bidwell questions whether British physicians enjoyed less "cultural authority" than their American counterparts. If the cultural authority and the economic demand for physicians' services were truly similar between Britain and the United States, Bidwell points out, other factors than those Starr highlights would be more important in accounting for the much greater professional power attained by the American medical profession.[46]

Bidwell characterizes the ideas that guide Starr's historical interpretations in *The Social Transformation of American Medicine* as "more metaphor than theory," and he concludes that "when the . . . metaphor is applied to a single case, it leads back into the particularity of the case itself" rather than yielding "a testable theory of professionalization." This is exactly the kind of criticism that can virtually always be made of a work of interpretive historical sociology from the vantage point of historical sociologists and others committed to developing causal generalizations and theoretical models. As long as interpretive historical sociologists remain within the confines of their own style of discourse, primarily committed to presenting meaningful social histories to others who share their sense of problems and their world views, they are not likely to find such criticisms compelling. They may even be prepared to assert, as E. P. Thompson has, that the most significant causal connections operate as complex configurations within a given national history and, in any event, are so intimately bound up with the meaningful orientations of past and present actors as to be inimical to causal generalizations that ignore or downplay those orientations.[47]

Like those of the other two major genres of historical sociology presented here, interpretive historical investigations can certainly be synthesized with elements of the alternative strategies. I have already argued that Wallerstein's world-system perspective combines the application of a general theoretical model to history with the development of a politically meaningful historical interpretation. Appliers of general models, I suggested, may find it helpful to make the kinds of appeals to current audience sensibilities that interpretive studies routinely embody. From the interpretive side, Perry Anderson's *Passages from Antiquity to Feudalism* and *Lineages of the Absolutist State* supplement comparative historical arguments devoted to highlighting particular historical trajectories with the application of a Marxist theory about the logic of long-run sociopolitical change to one historical lineage deemed more dynamic, progressive, and globally relevant than all other historical lineages. Anderson's pair of books could thus be considered an attempt to fuse the application of a general model with a primarily interpretive and particularizing study. But this kind of effort is unusual. Interpretive historical sociologists find it more congenial to move toward cautiously testing alternative hypotheses, since the application of truly general theoretical models violates their sense of historical particularity and variety.

Alvin Gouldner's "Stalinism: A Study of Internal Colonialism" is an excellent example of an interpretive case study that also moves in the direction of turning its favored interpretation into a cross-nationally testable causal hypothesis.[48] Most of Gouldner's essay is taken up with discussion of how Stalinism can be most meaningfully conceptualized, followed by a narrative presentation of the drama of Soviet history from the 1920s through the 1930s in terms of the "internal colonialism" conception that Gouldner favors. Briefly, however, at the very end of his essay, Gouldner considers whether this interpretation can also account for the different course taken by Communist domination in China, thus indicating a desire to test and refine an argument seen as potentially generalizable beyond the single Soviet instance.

An important work of comparative history that combines moments of explicit hypothesis testing with interpretation and telling contrasts is *White Supremacy: A Comparative Study in American and South African History*, by the historian George Fredrickson.[49] Each chapter in this impressive and beautifully written work slices comparatively into a different epoch and aspect of the relations between whites and nonwhites in South Africa and the United States from colonial to modern times. Fredrickson, like Geertz, primarily wants to let his two cases comment on each other's distinctive features. But here and there, at points where issues come up on which relevant bodies of theorizing are to be found, Fredrickson breaks his narrative to use approximations to controlled comparisons within or between his major cases to investigate which of various alternative causal arguments best accounts for the evidence. He does this, for example, with arguments about demographic ratios as possible explanations for the emergence of slavery or racial caste systems, and also with theories of the effects of industrial labor markets on racial segregation. The overall effect is to render crucial links of Fredrickson's argument more convincing to social scientists interested in valid causal generalizations than they would be if he remained solely oriented to highlighting concrete contrasts between South Africa and the United States. This is true, moreover, even though *White Supremacy* as a whole remains very much an interpretive work in all of the characteristic respects emphasized in this section.

Analyzing Causal Regularities in History

Practitioners of a third major strategy of historical sociology proceed differently from either interpretive historical sociologists or those who apply a general model to one or more historical cases. Here, as exemplified by some of the most important works of Marc Bloch and Barrington Moore, the focus is on developing an adequate explanation for a well-defined outcome or pattern in history. Neither the logic of a single overarching model nor the meaningful exploration of the complex particularities of each singular time and place takes priority. Instead, the investigator assumes that causal regularities – at least regularities of limited scope – may be found in history. He or she moves back and forth between aspects of historical cases and *alternative hypotheses* that may help to account for those regularities.[50]

Ideas about causal regularities may come from two or more preexisting theories that are brought into confrontation with the historical evidence. Or they may be generated more inductively from the discovery of what Arthur Stinchcombe calls "causally significant analogies between instances" during the course of a historical investigation.[51] The crucial point is that no effort is made to analyze historical facts according to a preconceived general model. Alternative hypotheses are always explored or generated. Ideas from apparently opposed theoretical paradigms may be combined, if that seems the most fruitful way to address the historical problem at hand. Or old theories may be entirely set aside, and a new explanation tentatively generated from the historical materials. The investigator's commitment is not to any existing theory or theories, but to the discovery of concrete causal configurations adequate to account for important historical patterns.

Indeed, in this analytic genre of historical sociology, research always addresses a clearly posed historical question. Where, how, and why did peasant-based revolts against the French Revolution occur, and what light can the answers shed on the general issue of collective protests in modernizing contexts? – as Charles Tilly asks in *The Vendée*. Why did some commercializing agrarian monarchies end up as democracies and others as fascist or communist dictatorships? – as Barrington Moore asks in *Social Origins of Dictatorship and Democracy*. What accounts for the similar causes and outcomes of the French, Russian, and Chinese Revolutions, and why did episodes of political crisis and conflict in other modernizing agrarian states not proceed in the same way? – as I ask in *States and Social Revolutions*.[52] Why did some regions of Europe experience the decline of serfdom and some the emergence of capitalist agriculture, while others did not? – as Robert Brenner asks in "Agrarian Class Structure and Economic Development in Pre-Industrial Europe."[53] Why were the nineteenth-century Chinese unusually resistant to buying foreign commodities? – as Gary Hamilton asks in "The Chinese Consumption of Foreign Commodities: A Comparative Perspective."[54]

The questions asked in such studies resemble the historically grounded kinds of questions posed by interpretive historical sociologists. "Why" questions, however, are posed more insistently by analytic historical sociologists, for their interpretive counterparts are more interested in a meaningful understanding of "what happened." Moreover, because analytic historical sociologists acknowledge the desirability of generalizable explanatory principles, they look much harder than would interpretive historical sociologists for answers based on valid causal connections – connections that either hold good across similar historical instances or else account in potentially generalizable terms for different outcomes across space and time in otherwise similar cases. Analytic historical sociologists avoid the interpretive tendency to attribute self-contained significance to each individual context.

At the same time, analytic historical sociologists also avoid what Samuel Beer once aptly called "the dogma of universality" – the notion that no theoretical hypothesis is worth exploring unless it can be stated as a universally applicable law. Instead, they are content to work with explanatory generalizations that are assumed to be "relative to a certain context or contexts."[55] In given studies, therefore, analytic historical sociologists may be willing to explore causal regularities within France conceived as an ensemble of communities, or within nineteenth-century world capitalism, or within the universe of agrarian bureaucratic states, leaving for another investigation the issue of how, if at all, to generalize an explanation beyond such contexts. Beer illustrates this point at some length through a careful analysis of the ways Charles Tilly (in the study that eventually became *The Vendée*) compared community and regional patterns in France with the aid of alternative explanatory arguments of delimited generality.

A hypothesis-testing version of analytic historical sociology can be done with only a single case. My own essay "Political Response to Capitalist Crisis: Neo-Marxist Theories of the State and the Case of the New Deal" is an example.[56] In this essay I juxtaposed several alternative theories about how capitalist states might be expected to respond to a major economic crisis, and I asked whether the causal connections implied by the various theories were borne out by the developments of American politics during the New Deal of the Great Depression of the 1930s. Finding none of the neo-Marxist theories entirely satisfactory, I sketched an alternative argument on the basis of the patterns I found in the history of the New Deal. But the terms of the alternative argument could not be adequately sharpened, nor its validity further explored, as long as my research remained concentrated on the single case. Normally, analytic historical sociology leads toward *comparative* studies, for these provide the most appropriate means to explore the validity of alternative explanatory arguments.[57] Single-case studies are far more typical for the first two genres of historical sociology than for the analytic strategy.

Comparative studies have a very different purpose for analytic historical sociologists than for interpretive historical sociologists. The latter, as we have seen, use comparisons to make contrasts among cases to highlight the features particular to each individual historical context. For analytic historical sociologists, differences among cases are also interesting – no less so than similarities. Yet these scholars examine the variations of history with the intention of establishing causal regularities, quite a different aim than that of their interpretive counterparts. To understand this difference, listen first to interpretive historical sociologist Reinhard Bendix, and then to analytic historical sociologist Barrington Moore, on the purposes of comparative history. According to Bendix, macroscopic comparisons have no role in establishing causal inferences, for such comparisons should be used only to contrast sociohistorical contexts to one another:

> Comparative analysis should sharpen our understanding of the contexts in which more detailed causal inferences can be drawn. Without a knowledge of contexts, causal inference may pretend to a level of generality to which it is not entitled. On the other hand, comparative studies should not attempt to replace causal analysis, because they can only deal with a few cases and cannot easily isolate the variables (as causal analysis must).[58]

Barrington Moore offers a very different perspective:

> Comparisons can serve as a rough negative check on accepted historical explanations. *And a comparative approach may lead to new historical generalizations.* In practice these features constitute a single intellectual process and make such a study more than a disparate collection of interesting cases. For example, after noticing that Indian peasants have suffered in a material way just about as much as Chinese peasants during the nineteenth and twentieth centuries without generating a massive revolutionary movement, *one begins to wonder about traditional explanations of what took place in both societies and becomes alert to factors affecting peasant outbreaks in other countries, in the hope of discerning general causes.* Or after learning about the disastrous consequences for democracy of a coalition between agrarian and industrial elites in nineteenth- and early twentieth-century Germany – the much discussed marriage of iron and rye – one wonders why a similar marriage between iron and cotton did not prevent the Civil War in the United States; *and so one has taken a step toward specifying configurations favorable and unfavorable to the establishment of modern Western democracy.*[59]

In this excerpt from Moore's Preface to *Social Origins of Dictatorship and Democracy*, one notices much the same suspicion of overly generalized theories as that which suffuses the scholarship of Reinhard Bendix. As Moore puts it, "too strong a devotion to theory always carries the danger that one may overemphasize the facts that fit a theory beyond their importance in the history of individual countries."[60] Yet Moore obviously cares more than Bendix about establishing causal generalizations, and unlike Bendix he believes that historical comparisons can be used both to test the validity of existing theoretical hypotheses and to develop new causal generalizations to replace invalidated ones. The flavor of the intellectual operation is effectively conveyed in the excerpted passage. Rather than contrasting whole histories in terms of pregiven concepts or themes, as interpretive historical sociologists do in their comparative studies, analytic historical sociologists like Moore think in terms of alternative hypotheses and comparisons across relevant aspects of the historical cases being compared. They thus try to specify in somewhat generalizable terms the "configurations favorable and unfavorable" to the kinds of outcomes they are trying to explain in their cases.

Research designs used in such comparative historical analyses share with other methodological approaches in the social sciences the aim of establishing controls over variation to distinguish valid from invalid causes.[61] In contrast to the probabilistic techniques of statistical analysis – techniques that are used when there are very large numbers of cases and continuously quantified variables to analyze – comparative historical analyses proceed through logical juxtapositions of aspects of small numbers of cases. They attempt to identify invariant causal configurations that necessarily (rather than probably) combine to account for outcomes of interest.[62] As originally outlined by John Stuart Mill in A System of Logic, comparative historical analyses can be done according to either of two basic research designs diagramed in Figure 11.2, or through a combination of them.[63]

Using the approach Mill labeled the "method of agreement," a comparative historical analysis can try to establish that several cases sharing the phenomenon to be explained also have in common the hypothesized causal factors, even though they vary in other ways that might seem causally relevant according to alternative hypotheses. Or, using the approach Mill called the "method of difference," a comparative historical analysis can contrast cases in which the phenomenon to be explained and the hypothesized causes are present to other ("negative") cases, in which the phenomenon and the causes are absent, even though those negative cases are as similar as possible to the "positive" cases in other respects. Taken alone, this second approach is more powerful for establishing valid causal associations than the method

Figure 11.2. Two Designs for Comparative Historical Analysis
(from John Stuart Mill).

The Method of Agreement

Case 1	Case 2	Case *n*
a	*d*	*g*
b	*e*	*h*
c	*f*	*i*
x	*x*	*x*
y	*y*	*y*

} Overall Differences (rows *a*–*i*)

} Crucial Similarity (rows *x*–*y*)

x = Causal Variable
y = Phenomenon to be
    Explained

The Method of Difference

Positive Case(s)	Negative Case(s)
a	*a*
b	*b*
c	*c*
x	not *x*
y	not *y*

} Overall Similarities

} Crucial Difference

of agreement used alone. Sometimes, however, it is possible to combine the two methods by using several positive cases along with suitable negative cases as contrasts.

A monumental work of comparative historical analysis, Barrington Moore's *Social Origins of Dictatorship and Democracy* primarily uses the method of agreement, yet also argues at times along the lines of the method of difference. With the aid of causal configurations referring to the strength of commercial bourgeoisies in relation to landlords, to modes of agricultural commercialization, and to the rebellious potential of different types of peasant communities and peasant/landlord relationships, Moore seeks to explain why the seven major agrarian states he compares traveled one or another of three alternative routes leading to democracy, Fascist dictatorship, or Communist dictatorship. Within each of his routes, Moore primarily argues along the lines of the method of agreement: Each route has two or three nations about whose development Moore makes a similar causal argument,[64] at times using the individual features or the differences of the cases to eliminate possible alternative arguments about the roots of democracy, fascism, or communism. Simultaneously, Moore makes some use of the method of difference at the level of comparisons across his three major routes. As he discusses countries within each route, Moore occasionally refers to relevant aspects of the histories of countries in one or both of the other routes, using their contrasting directions of development at similar junctures to help validate the causal argument he is currently making. Not only in terms of its substantive scope, therefore, but also in terms of the complexity of its explanatory design, *Social Origins of Dictatorship and Democracy* is a work of virtually unparalleled ambition.

My own book, *States and Social Revolutions,* is much less ambitious than Moore's masterpiece.[65] Yet, especially in its first part, "The Causes of Social Revolutions in France, Russia, and China," it also employs a combination of Mill's basic analytic approaches. I argue that, despite differences along many dimensions that certain theorists of revolution would consider decisive, Bourbon France in the late eighteenth century, Imperial China after 1911, and Czarist Russia from March 1917 all experienced social revolutionary crises because similar sets of causes came together. By thus stressing causal similarities in the face of other important differences, I reason according to the method of agreement. I also use the logic of the method of difference by introducing analytically focused contrasts between France, Russia, and China, on the one hand, and relevant moments and aspects of the histories of England, Prussia/Germany, and Japan, on the other. These other countries are suitable controls because, even at moments of revolutionary crises, they did not undergo successful social-revolutionary transformations, despite important structural and historical similarities to France, Russia, and China.

Contrasts to different sets of countries at relevant moments in their histories help to validate each specific part of the overall argument about France, Russia, and China. For causal arguments about crises in the relationships of states to landed upper classes or the agrarian economy as one configuration favoring social-revolutionary crises, I draw contrasts to the Japanese Meiji Restoration and the Prussian Reform Movement. For arguments about the contributions of certain kinds of agrarian structures and peasant revolts to social revolutions, I make contrasts to the English Parliamentary Revolution and the (failed) German revolutions of 1848–50. In *States and Social Revolutions,* the control cases are discussed much more briefly than France, Russia, and China. They are introduced not for the purpose of fully explaining their own patterns of political conflict and development, but instead for the particular purpose of strengthening the main line of argument about social revolutions in the three major cases.

Comparative historical analyses presented in article-length pieces, as opposed to books, can often range with greater flexibility across cases, especially when it comes to using relevant comparisons to call competing causal arguments into question. Two examples, both of which emphasize the method of difference in their research designs, nicely illustrate this point.

Robert Brenner's article "Agrarian Class Structure and Economic Development in Pre-Industrial Europe" seeks to explain long-term economic change in late medieval and early modern Europe, in particular "the intensification of serfdom in Eastern Europe in relation to its process of decline in the West" and "the rise of agrarian capitalism and the growth of agricultural productivity in England in relation to their failure in France."[66] Determined to debunk explanations of European economic growth that attribute it to market expansion or demographic trends, Brenner undermines such arguments by showing that similar market and demographic processes were associated with markedly different outcomes of economic development between Eastern and Western Europe, and also among regions within each of these broad zones. Then Brenner proceeds to argue that variables referring to class relations and the strength of peasant communities versus landlords can better account for the variations in economic development he wants to explain.

In his article "Chinese Consumption of Foreign Commodities," Gary Hamilton is concerned to sort out the factors influencing the use of Western commodities by people in non-Western civilizations.[67] The unwillingness of the nineteenth-century Chinese to buy very many Western textile products provides an especially intriguing concrete problem through which to address this broad issue. Why the Chinese reluctance? Hamilton suggests at the outset three alternative lines of explanation: faulty marketing and merchandising arguments; cultural explanations; and a Weberian "status-competition" hypothesis. Proceeding methodically, Hamilton makes ingenious use of comparisons across time and space to dispose of the first two explanations: Economic arguments cannot explain why China differed from certain other non-Western countries in the nineteenth century; and references to Confucian cultural values cannot explain why Chinese in earlier historical periods *were* willing to consume foreign products. Finally, Hamilton demonstrates that his preferred status-competition explanation can account for the temporal and cross-national variations that its competitors could not. All in all, therefore, Hamilton is able to make optimal use of comparative history as a tool of causal analysis, above all because he

ranges freely across countries and epochs to find the logically necessary comparisons to develop his explanatory argument.

Because wide-ranging comparisons are so often crucial for analytic
historical sociologists, they are more likely to use secondary sources of
evidence than those who apply models to, or develop interpretations
of, single cases. Secondary sources are simply published books and
articles by historians or by scholars specializing in the study of one
geocultural area of the world. Some people believe that such publications are automatically inferior to primary sources, the original residues
of the past that most historians use as their basic sources of evidence
about given times, places, and issues. From the point of view of historical sociology, however, a dogmatic insistence on redoing primary
research for every investigation would be disastrous; it would rule out
most comparative-historical research. If a topic is too big for purely
primary research – and if excellent studies by specialists are already
available in some profusion – secondary sources are appropriate as the
basic source of evidence for a given study. Using them is not different
from survey analysts reworking the results of previous surveys rather
than asking all questions anew, or students of comparative ethnogra-
phy synthesizing results from many different published field studies.

This said, however, it remains true that comparative historical sociologists have not so far worked out clear, consensual rules and procedures for the valid use of secondary sources as evidence. Certain principles are likely to emerge as such rules are developed. Comparative
historical sociologists who use secondary sources must, for example,
pay careful attention to varying historiographical interpretations, both
among contemporary historians and across scholarly generations of
historians. The questions that the comparative historical sociologist
needs to ask about every one of the cases included in his or her study
may not correspond to the currently fashionable questions historians
are asking about any given case. Thus, the comparativist must be very
systematic in searching through historical literatures to find evidence
for and against the hypotheses being explored. Perhaps the evidence
will be embedded in minor corners of publications, or in the work of an
"odd" historian out of tune with dominant historiographical trends.
Above all, the historical sociologist cannot let his or her findings be
dictated simply by historiographical fashions that vary from case to
case or time to time.

Secondary research can also be strategically supplemented by carefully selected primary investigations or reinvestigations, and I suspect
that comparative historical sociologists will increasingly converge on

the practice of starting with secondary analyses, but not stopping there. Targeted primary investigations can be especially useful for answering questions relevant from a comparative perspective that historical specialists have simply not pursued to date. In addition, comparative historical sociologists are well advised to familiarize themselves with at least some of the primary evidence on which the secondary sources have built conclusions. Such a practice may reconfirm confidence in the findings of the specialists. Alternatively, it may call particular secondary sources into question or open up the possibility for the comparative historical sociologist to build new findings out of primary sources previously inadequately analyzed.

Good comparative historical sociologists nevertheless must resist the temptation to disappear forever into the primary evidence about each case. Marc Bloch once made a statement that could be taken as a maxim for comparative history when done by analytic historical sociologists: "The unity of place is merely disorderly," Bloch declared. "Only a unified problem constitutes a central focus."[68] Analytic historical sociologists take this point very seriously, especially when they do comparative history. The temptation to narrate unbroken sequences of events, or to cover everything about a given time and place, is resisted. Instead, aspects of cases are highlighted according to the causal configurations currently under discussion. From the point of view of interpretive historical sociologists (and traditional historians), good analytic comparative history may seem rather unaesthetic. The unities of time and place must be broken for the purposes of drawing comparisons and testing hypotheses.

When analytic comparative historians sit down to write their books or articles, they face special challenges of integrating descriptive accounts for various cases with discussions of alternative hypotheses and with the coherent pursuit of the overall argument. Historical trajectories cannot simply be juxtaposed and contrasted, as in interpretive works of comparative history. Instead, the best approximations to controlled comparisons must be explicitly presented to carry off the logic of the analysis. Thus, effectively organized writings in this genre of historical sociology are difficult to prepare. When they are produced, however, they can rival interpretive works in rhetorical persuasiveness, not for sheer aesthetic reasons but through the force of an explanatory argument put forward as more able than plausible competitors to answer a dramatically posed historical question.

Because my own work in historical sociology falls within analytic historical sociology, it will come as no surprise to readers that I consider it the most promising strategy of the three I have discussed. Analytic historical sociology, I believe, can effectively combine the concern to address *significant* historically embedded problems – a concern that most of its practitioners share with interpretive historical sociologists – with ongoing efforts to build better general social theories, a concern shared with those who have applied general models to history. Analytic sociology can avoid the extremes of particularizing versus universalizing that limit the usefulness and appeal of the other two approaches.

Nevertheless, there are pitfalls and limits to the effectiveness of analytic historical sociology, especially in its strongest guise of comparative historical analysis. The search for appropriate controls to meet the logical requisites of comparative designs can become a dry and mechanical business, especially since the historical record does not always oblige in providing relevant comparative instances. Perhaps more serious, the assumption that independent units can be found for use in comparative assessments of causal regularities may be unfounded. This is especially likely to be the case if meaningful cultural wholes, or single systemic entities like a "world capitalist division of labor," are at issue. Immanuel Wallerstein, readers will recall, resists using comparative historical analysis precisely because he does not consider its logic applicable to partial and variously situated units (such as nations) within a capitalist world economy.

Even when they are more or less successfully accomplished, comparative historical analyses aimed at validating causal regularities in history cannot ever substitute for theoretical models or conceptual lenses in offering a meaningful portrait of how the world works. Obviously, some theoretical ideas always need to be used to set up the terms of a comparative historical investigation, even if an honestly even-handed effort is made to examine alternative hypotheses in the course of the investigation. In addition, when comparative historical analyses are completed and written up, they are often introduced and concluded with arguments that partake of the flavor of general model building or the provision of a meaningful view of the world. Charles Tilly's works invoke the tantalizing promise of general model building to convince readers that hypothesis-testing studies of French (and Western European) patterns of collective action offer a window toward a possibly much more widely applicable sociological theory. As Dennis Smith has argued, Barrington Moore's *Social Origins of Dictatorship and Democracy* relies on the taken-for-granted significance of "democracy" versus "dictatorship" in its sorting of the world's major polities into alternative, teleologically defined routes of long-term social and political development. Much of the power of the book's causal arguments comes from the reader's willingness to accept the alternative political routes of democracy, fascism, and communism at face value.

More than most social researchers, major historical sociologists end up with a hankering to develop grand maps of history. With considerable admiration, Charles Tilly has recently labeled these grand maps "encompassing comparisons."[69] Much less approvingly Arthur Stinchcombe calls them "epochal interpretations."[70] Analytic historical sociology as I have presented it does not in itself provide the wherewithal for creating such grand maps. So perhaps it should not be surprising that the most ambitious of comparative historical analysts end up borrowing emphases from our first two strategies of historical sociology to help them frame their questions and results in more encompassing or epochal ways.

In the final analysis, the theoretical skepticism that I have presented as intrinsically characteristic of good analytic historical sociology is simply a *practical* strategy for research and the presentation of arguments. Yet, for both the individual scholar and the community of historical sociologists, it is a practical strategy of immense value. This strategy of research cannot ultimately displace basic epistemological and substantive choices or render grand theories and meaningful world views superfluous. But using this research strategy makes possible lively debates about the regularities to be found in history and about the specific usefulness – or lack of it – of alternative theories and concepts for formulating valid causal arguments about those regularities.

The practice of analytic historical sociology forces a more intimate *dialogue* with historical evidence than either interpretive historical sociology or the application of a model to a historical case. However untenably in some strict philosophical sense, analytic historical sociology holds forth the possibility of constructing better social theories in a manner Arthur Stinchcombe has captured in a compelling metaphor: The analytic historical sociologist builds "as a carpenter builds, adjusting the measurements as he [or she] goes along, rather than as an architect builds, drawing first and building later."[71]

Ours is an era when no existing macrosociological theory seems adequate, yet when the need for valid knowledge of social structures and transformations has never been greater. Analytic historical sociology allows sociologists to move toward better theories through a full and detailed confrontation with the dynamic variety of history. Important questions about social structures and change can be continually raised

Theda Skocpol

and addressed by those determined to explore alternative hypotheses about causal configurations in history. To the extent that Marc Bloch and Barrington Moore find worthy successors today and tomorrow, the prospects are bright that historical sociologists can continue to illuminate the contours and rhythms of the changing world in which we live.

Notes

1. The focus here on developments in U.S. sociology is to some degree arbitrary. It is also partially warranted by the fact that in recent decades the United States has been the largest and most influential center of the academic discipline as such. Historical orientations, of course, have long had a more prominent place in other national sociological traditions.
2. Jere Cohen, "Rational Capitalism in Renaissance Italy," *American Journal of Sociology* 85(6) (1980):1340–55. A later exchange about this article is particularly interesting for the light it throws on how historical sociologists build conclusions out of varying interpretations of secondary sources. See R. J. Holton, "Max Weber, 'Rational Capitalism,' and Renaissance Italy: A Critique of Cohen," and Cohen, "A Reply to Holton," *American Journal of Sociology* 89(1) (1983):166–87.
3. Mark Traugott, *Armies of the Poor* (Princeton, N.J.: Princeton University Press, forthcoming). See also "Determinants of Political Orientation: Class and Organization in the Parisian Insurrection of June 1848," *American Journal of Sociology* 86(1) (1980):32–49.
4. Jack Goldstone, "Population and Revolution" (Ph.D. diss., Harvard University, 1981). See also "Capitalist Origins of the English Revolution: Chasing a Chimera," *Theory and Society,* 12 (1983):143–80.
5. Victoria Bonnell, *Roots of Rebellion: Workers' Politics and Organizations in St. Petersburg and Moscow, 1900–1914* (Berkeley: University of California Press, 1983).
6. Mary Fulbrook, *Religion and the Rise of Absolutism in England, Württemberg, and Prussia* (Cambridge, U.K., and New York: Cambridge University Press, 1983).
7. David Zaret, *The Heavenly Contract* (Chicago: University of Chicago Press, forthcoming).
8. Orlando Patterson, *Slavery and Social Death: A Comparative Study* (Cambridge, Mass.: Harvard University Press, 1982).
9. Daniel Chirot, *Social Change in Peripheral Society: The Creation of a Balkan Colony* (New York: Academic Press, 1976).
10. Elbaki Hermassi, *Leadership and National Development in North Africa: A Comparative Study* (Berkeley: University of California Press, 1972); Mounira Charrad, "Women and the State: A Comparative Study of Politics, Law, and the Family in Tunisia, Algeria, and Morocco" (Ph.D. diss., Harvard University, 1980); Ellen Kay Trimberger, *Revolution from Above: Military Bureaucrats and Development in Japan, Turkey, Egypt and Peru* (New Brunswick, N.J.: Transaction Books, 1978); and Michael Adas, *Prophets of Rebellion: Millenarian Protest Movements against the European Colonial Order* (Chapel Hill: University of North Carolina Press, 1979).
11. Ronald Dore, *British Factory, Japanese Factory* (Berkeley: University of California Press, 1973); and Charles Sabel, *Work and Politics* (Cambridge, U.K., New York: Cambridge University Press, 1982). Dore extends his compara-

tive analysis in "Industrial Relations in Japan and Elsewhere," in *Japan: A Comparative View*, ed. Albert M. Craig (Princeton, N.J.: Princeton University Press, 1979), pp. 324–70.

12. Francis G. Castles, *The Social Democratic Image of Society* (London: Routledge & Kegan Paul, 1978); Peter Flora and Arnold Heidenheimer, eds., *The Development of Welfare States in Europe and North America* (New Brunswick, N.J.: Transaction Books, 1981); Theda Skocpol and John Ikenberry, "The Political Formation of the American Welfare State in Historical and Comparative Perspective," *Comparative Social Research* (Special Issue on the Welfare State), ed. Richard Tomasson (Greenwich, Conn.: JAI Press, 1983), pp. 87–148; Ann Shola Orloff and Theda Skocpol, "Why Not Equal Protection?: The Politics of Public Social Welfare in Britain and the United States, 1880s–1920s" (Paper presented at the Annual Meeting of the American Sociological Association, Detroit, Mich., September 1983); and Gaston Rimlinger, *Welfare Policy and Industrialization in Europe, America, and Russia* (New York: Wiley, 1971).

13. Michael Hechter, *Internal Colonialism* (Berkeley: University of California Press, 1975); William Julius Wilson, *The Declining Significance of Race* (Chicago: University of Chicago Press, 1978); Ivan H. Light, *Ethnic Enterprise in America* (Berkeley: University of California Press, 1972); Stanley Lieberson, *A Piece of the Pie* (Berkeley: University of California Press, 1980); and Doug McAdam, *Political Process and the Development of Black Insurgency, 1930–1970* (Chicago: University of Chicago Press, 1982).

14. Robert N. Bellah, *The Broken Covenant: American Civil Religion in Time of Trial* (New York: Seabury Press, 1975); Joseph Ben-David and Awraham Zloczower, "Universities and Academic Systems in Modern Societies," *Archives Européennes de Sociologie* 3(1) (1962):45–84; Fred Block, *The Origins of International Economic Disorder: A Study of United States International Monetary Policy from World War II to the Present* (Berkeley: University of California Press, 1977); Morris Janowitz, *The Last Half-Century: Societal Change and Politics in America* (Chicago: University of Chicago Press, 1978); Seymour Martin Lipset, *The First New Nation: The United States in Comparative and Historical Perspective* (New York: Basic Books, 1963); Dietrich Rueschemeyer, *Lawyers and Their Society: A Comparative Study of the Legal Profession in Germany and in the United States* (Cambridge, Mass.: Harvard University Press, 1973); Magali Sarfatti-Larson, *The Rise of Professionalism* (Berkeley: University of California Press, 1978); Paul Starr, *The Social Transformation of American Medicine* (New York: Basic Books, 1982); and Ellen Kay Trimberger, "Feminism, Men, and Modern Love: Greenwich Village, 1900–1925," in *Powers of Desire: The Politics of Sexuality*, eds. Ann Snitow, Christine Stansell, and Sharon Thompson (New York: Monthly Review Press, 1983), pp. 131–52.

15. Relevant works by Mills include *The New Men of Power: America's Labor Leaders* (New York: Harcourt, Brace, 1948); *White Collar: The American Middle Classes* (New York: Oxford University Press, 1951); and *The Power Elite* (New York: Oxford University Press, 1956).

16. See Geoffrey Barraclough's "The Impact of the Social Sciences," in *Main Trends in History* (New York: Holmes and Meier, 1979), chap. 3.

17. Panel designs, time series analysis, and event-history analysis are among the quantitative techniques developed to handle over-time processes. A sophisticated recent discussion of quantitative techniques for analyzing sequential orderings appears in Andrew Abbott, "Sequences of Social Events: Concepts and Methods for the Analysis of Order in Social Processes," *Historical Methods* 16(4) (1983): 129–47.

18. Most primarily qualitative studies could benefit from the occasional presentation of graphs or models and from the use of statistical tables for key parts of the argument on which precise data are available. Two exemplary works in this regard are McAdam's *Development of Black Insurgency* and Richard Lachmann's "From Manor to Market: Structural Change in England, 1536–1640" (Ph.D. diss., Harvard University, 1983). Moreover, quantitatively oriented historical sociologists could often supplement their findings with appropriate qualitative investigations. For example, David Knoke's "The Spread of Municipal Reform: Temporal, Spatial, and Social Dynamics," *American Journal of Sociology* 87(6) (1982): 1314–39, would have added credence if its event-history analysis had been bolstered by a few qualitative case accounts to show that the posited "neighborhood diffusion" process actually happened historically.

19. Charles Ragin and David Zaret, "Theory and Method in Comparative Research: Two Strategies," *Social Forces* 61(3) (1983):731–54.

20. Margaret Somers and I discuss "contrast-oriented" versus "macroanalytic" strategies of comparative history in "The Uses of Comparative History in Macrosocial Inquiry," *Comparative Studies in Society and History* 22(2) (1980):174–97. Similar points are also elaborated in the following discussion.

21. Victoria Bonnell provides an especially clear discussion of this point at the beginning of her "The Uses of Theory, Concepts and Comparison in Historical Sociology," *Comparative Studies in Society and History* 22(2) (1980):156–73. Historians, of course, also draw upon concepts and theoretical ideas, but they often do so implicitly rather than explicitly, and they may orient their research to describing a time and place rather than to a conceptual or explanatory problem.

22. "Cases" need not be national societies, although they very often are. They may be civilizations, world systems, cultural systems, institutional sectors, groups, organizations, communities, or other units of analysis that are the sites of the processes or causal relationships under investigation.

23. Neil Smelser, *Social Change in the Industrial Revolution* (Chicago: University of Chicago Press, 1959).

24. Kai T. Erikson, *Wayward Puritans* (New York: Wiley, 1966).

25. Ibid., p. viii.

26. Michael Schwartz, *Radical Protest and Social Structure* (New York: Academic Press, 1976).

27. The following works included in the Annotated Bibliography at the end of this book elaborate this point and, in general, deal with methodological issues pertinent to the application of general theories or models to historical cases: Bellah (1967); Bonnell (1980); Davidson and Lytle (1982); Dray (1966); Nowak (1961); Ossowski (1964); Smelser (1967); Topolski (1972); and Willer (forthcoming).

28. Erikson, *Wayward Puritans*, p. 27.

29. For examples of reactions to Smelser's theorizing by historians, see A. E. Musson's mixed review in the *Journal of Economic History* 20(2) (1960): 497–99; Michael Anderson's probing review article, "Sociological History and the Working-Class Family: Smelser Revisited," *Social History* (3) (1976):317–34; and E. P. Thompson's scathing comments in *The Poverty of Theory and Other Essays* (London: Merlin Press, 1978), pp. 267–71.

30. Personal communication, October 11, 1983. Lenski has pursued this demanding strategy with distinction in *Power and Privilege: A Theory of Social Stratification* (New York: McGraw-Hill, 1966) and in *Human Societies: An Introduction to Macrosociology*, 2nd ed. (New York: McGraw-Hill, 1974).

31. For example, a book praised by Lenski, John H. Kautsky's *The Politics of Aristocratic Empires* (Chapel Hill: University of North Carolina Press, 1982) attempts to generalize about *all* known instances of a "premodern" type of sociopolitical order. Although the book is based on reviews of literatures about many historical cases, evidence about cases is presented in such fragmentary snippets that one cannot get a sure sense of what was really going on in any of the many particular times and places discussed.

32. David Willer, "Theory, Experimentation and Historical Interpretation," in *Social Theories in Progress, III*, eds. Joseph Berger, Morris Zelditch, and Bo Anderson (Pittsburgh, Penn.: University of Pittsburgh Press, forthcoming).

33. Charles, Louise, and Richard Tilly, *The Rebellious Century, 1830–1930* (Cambridge, Mass.: Harvard University Press, 1975).

34. Smelser, *Social Change in the Industrial Revolution*, chap. 14.

35. As in the Introduction, where references are made in this conclusion to arguments or major books discussed in the core essays, no citations will be given.

36. Paul Starr, *The Social Transformation of American Medicine* (New York: Basic Books, 1982).

37. The following works included in the Annotated Bibliography at the end of this book especially discuss the logic and methods of using concepts to develop meaningful interpretations of historical patterns: Bendix (1963); Dray (1966); Geertz (1973); Hexter (1971); Johnson (1982); McDaniel (1978); Ragin and Zaret (1983); Rock (1976); Stone (1979); Taylor (1979); Thompson (1978); Weber (1949); Wolff (1959); and Zaret (1980).

38. E. P. Thompson, *The Making of the English Working Class* (New York: Vintage Books, 1966), p. 9.

39. Starr, *Social Transformation*, pp. 9–17.

40. Reinhard Bendix, *Nation-Building and Citizenship*, new enlarged ed. (Berkeley: University of California Press, 1977), pp. 16–17.

41. Reinhard Bendix, "The Mandate to Rule: An Introduction," *Social Forces* 55(2) (1976), p. 247.

42. Clifford Geertz, *Islam Observed: Religious Development in Morocco and Indonesia* (Chicago: University of Chicago Press, 1971), p. 4.

43. Ibid.

44. See Charles Taylor, "Interpretation and the Sciences of Man," in *Interpretive Social Science: A Reader*, eds. Paul Rabinow and William M. Sullivan (Berkeley: University of California Press, 1979), pp. 25–71.

45. Ira Katznelson, "Class Formation and the State: Nineteenth-Century England in American Perspective" in *Bringing the State Back In*, ed. Peter Evans, Theda Skocpol, and Dietrich Rueschemeyer (Cambridge, U.K. and New York: Cambridge University Press, forthcoming); Ira Katznelson, *City Trenches: Urban Politics and the Patterning of Class in the United States* (New York: Pantheon Books, 1981); and Ira Katznelson and Aristide Zolberg, eds., *Working Class Formation: Nineteenth Century Patterns in Western Europe and the United States* (forthcoming).

46. Charles Bidwell, Review of Paul Starr's *The Social Transformation of American Medicine*, *American Journal of Sociology* 90(1) (1984).

47. The methodological statement of Thompson's approach appears in "The Poverty of Theory: or an Orrery of Errors," in *The Poverty of Theory and Other Essays* (London: Merlin Press, 1978), pp. 193–397.

48. Alvin Gouldner, "Stalinism: A Study of Internal Colonialism," in *Political Power and Social Theory*, vol. 1, ed. Maurice Zeitlin (Greenwich, Conn.: JAI Press, 1980), pp. 209–51.

49. George Fredrickson, *White Supremacy: A Comparative Study in American and South African History* (New York: Oxford University Press, 1981).

50. Works included in the Annotated Bibliography at the end of this book that deal especially with methods of analytic historical sociology, including comparative methods, are Beer (1963); Bloch (1967); Carr (1961); Fischer (1970); Hage (1975); Hopkins and Wallerstein (1967); Lijphart (1971, 1975); Linz and de Miguel (1966); Mill (1970); Moore (1958); Popper (1964); Ragin (1981); Sewell (1967); Skocpol and Somers (1980); Smelser (1976); Stinchcombe (1968, 1978); Thrupp (1970); Tilly (forthcoming), Walton (1973); and Zelditch (1971).

51. Arthur Stinchcombe, *Theoretical Methods in Social History* (New York: Academic Press, 1978), p. 7.

52. Theda Skocpol, *States and Social Revolutions: A Comparative Analysis of France, Russia, and China* (Cambridge, U.K. and New York: Cambridge University Press, 1979).

53. Robert Brenner, "Agrarian Class Structure and Economic Development in Pre-Industrial Europe," *Past and Present* no. 70 (1976):30–75.

54. Gary G. Hamilton, "Chinese Consumption of Foreign Commodities: A Comparative Perspective," *American Sociological Review* 42(6) (1977):877–91.

55. Samuel Beer, "Causal Explanation and Imaginative Re-Enactment," *History and Theory* 3(1) (1963):6, 9.

56. Theda Skocpol, "Political Response to Capitalist Crisis: Neo-Marxist Theories of the State and the Case of the New Deal," *Politics and Society* 10(2) (1980):155–202.

57. In fact, additional cases can be added one at a time, with each step leading toward a more pointed specification of a causal analysis. Thus, Margaret Weir and I followed up allusions in the above case study of the United States in the 1930s with a two-nation comparison in "State Structures and Social Keynesianism: Responses to the Great Depression in Sweden and the United States," *International Journal of Comparative Sociology* 24(1–2) (1983):4–29, and then with a three-nation comparison in "State Structures and the Possibilities for Keynesian Responses to the Great Depression in Sweden, Britain, and the United States," in *Bringing the State Back In*, eds. Peter Evans, Theda Skocpol, and Dietrich Rueschemeyer (Cambridge, U.K., and New York: Cambridge University Press, forthcoming).

58. Reinhard Bendix, *Kings or People: Power and the Mandate to Rule* (Berkeley: University of California Press, 1978), p. 15.

59. Barrington Moore, Jr., *Social Origins of Dictatorship and Democracy* (Boston: Beacon Press, 1966), pp. xiii–xiv; emphases added.

60. Ibid., p. xiii.

61. This is emphasized and repeatedly illustrated in Neil Smelser, *Comparative Methods in the Social Sciences* (Englewood Cliffs, N.J.: Prentice-Hall, 1976).

62. This important point is developed in Charles Ragin and David Zaret. "Theory and Method in Comparative Research: Two Strategies," *Social Forces* 61(3) (1983):743–44.

63. John Stuart Mill, *Philosophy of Scientific Method*, ed. Ernest Nagel (New York: Hafner, 1950; originally the 1881 edition of *A System of Logic*), pp. 211–33. See also the full elaboration of Mill's principles in Morris Zelditch, Jr., "Intelligible Comparisons," in *Comparative Methods in Sociology*, ed. Ivan Vallier (Berkeley: University of California Press, 1971), pp. 267–307.

64. Moore does not argue that cases within routes are exactly the same, and for the democratic route in particular he identifies alternative paths to the same end result. What the three cases in this route have in common are strong

bourgeoisies that become allied after revolutionary upheavals with triumphant commercial (i.e., non-labor-repressive) agrarian groups: the English gentry; the French propertied peasantry; and farmers in the American North. For a full discussion of Moore's causal analysis in *Social Origins*, see my "A Critical Review of Barrington Moore's *Social Origins of Dictatorship and Democracy*," *Politics and Society* 4(3) (1973):1–34.

65. See note 52 for full reference.
66. Brenner, "Agrarian Class Structure and Economic Development," p. 47. See note 53 for full reference.
67. See note 54 for full reference.
68. Marc Bloch, "Une Etude Régionale: Gëographie ou Histoire?" *Annales d'Histoire Economique et Sociale* 6 (1934):81; freely translated by me.
69. Charles Tilly, *Big Structures, Large Processes, Huge Comparisons* (New York: Russell Sage Foundation, forthcoming), chap. 8.
70. Stinchcombe, *Theoretical Methods*, p. 7.
71. Ibid., p. 122.

An Annotated Bibliography on Methods of Comparative and Historical Sociology

This selected and annotated bibliography includes a range of materials about logics of inquiry, problems of research design, and sources of evidence in historical and comparative historical sociology. Not included here are pieces that focus primarily on the substance of arguments in various bodies of historical and comparative research, or pieces featuring exegesis of the theoretical ideas of classical historical sociologists. The bibliography also omits many important works in the philosophy of social science and historiography, and has only a few selections from the voluminous literature on techniques for quantifying and quantitatively analyzing particular kinds of data about past times. The emphasis is very much on strategies for defining researchable problems and bringing evidence and theories to bear on one another in case studies or comparative historical investigations. Various programmatic statements by historical sociologists and social historians are also included to give a flavor of the changing ideas over the last several decades about relations between sociology and history as disciplines.

I am indebted to the following colleagues for suggesting appropriate entries for this bibliography beyond those with which I was already familiar: Ronald Aminzade, Diane Barthel, Victoria Bonnell, Sam Clark, Jack Goldstone, Seymour Martin Lipset, Jeffrey Prager, Charles Ragin, William Roy, Dietrich Rueschemeyer, Dennis Smith, Richard Tomasson, and Robert Wuthnow.

Abbott, Andrew. "Sequences of Social Events: Concepts and Methods for the Analysis of Order in Social Processes." *Historical Methods* 16(4) (1983):129–47. Using examples from social histories of the professions, this essay examines the theoretical and operational properties of conceptualizations of social processes in terms of sequences of events, and reviews mathematical and statistical techniques that are available for analyzing data where "order makes a difference."

Abrams, Philip. *Historical Sociology*. Ithaca, N.Y.: Cornell University Press, 1982. Abrams argues that good sociology and good history have the same goal: to unravel the relationships between structure and agency in processes of social change. This perspective reflects recent neo-Weberian thinking in Britain. Abrams dissects major sociological works from Marx, Weber, and Durkheim through the present, along with major works in social history, to show how, at their best, they converge methodologically and in terms of the kinds of knowledge they seek.

Aron, Raymond. "Evidence and Inference in History." Translated by Suzanne Keller and Judith K. Davidson. In *Evidence and Inference: The Hayden Colloquium on Scientific Concept and Method*, edited by Daniel Lerner, pp. 19–47. Free Press, Glencoe, Ill.: 1960. Historians, Aron argues, work toward "historical syntheses" by trying to "understand the human actors, explain the events, elaborate historical units consistent with the articulation of reality, and discover whether there are great lines of evolution which either humanity as a whole or each historical unit follows." Aron discusses issues involved in making each of these kinds of inferences from evidence.

Bailey, Kenneth D. "Document Study." In *Methods of Social Research*, chap. 12. New York: Free Press, 1978. A thorough discussion of the advantages, disadvantages, and techniques for using documents to find evidence about social life, this chapter includes a discussion of quantitative approaches for doing content analysis.

Barraclough, Geoffrey. *Main Trends in History*. New York: Holmes & Meier, 1979. This is a comprehensive survey of the concepts and methods used to structure debates and research in various fields of history, especially since World War II.

Beer, Samuel H. "Causal Explanation and Imaginative Re-enactment." *History and Theory* 3(1) (1963):6–29. Beer examines the methods used in the research for what later became Charles Tilly's *The Vendée* and Michael Walzer's *The Revolution of the Saints*. This is an excellent elucidation of the logic of hypothesis testing through comparative historical analysis. Interpretive and generalizing approaches to social-historical explanation are complementary, Beer maintains.

Bellah, Robert N. "Research Chronicle: Tokugawa Religion." In *Sociologists at Work*, edited by Philip E. Hammond, pp. 164–85. New York: Anchor Books, 1967. This is Bellah's frank account of the steps he took as a graduate student toward defining and researching his doctoral dissertation, which eventually was published as *Tokugawa Religion*, a theoretically structured historical case study.

Bendix, Reinhard. "Concepts and Generalizations in Comparative Sociological Studies." *American Sociological Review* 28(4) (1963):532–39. A cautious program is offered for comparative historical studies aimed at limiting the overgenerality of many theoretical concepts and explanations in the light of the variety of sociopolitical structures and processes of change that appear in the world's historical record.

Bloch, Marc. "A Contribution towards a Comparative History of European Societies." (1928). In *Land and Work in Medieval Europe: Selected Papers by Marc Bloch*, pp. 44–81. Translated by J. E. Anderson. New York: Harper & Row, 1967. This classic article is still unsurpassed for the subtlety and comprehensiveness with which it concretely illustrates the many contributions historical comparisons can make to the formulation of fruitful questions, the accurate characterization of historical patterns, and the development of valid explanations for one or more instances.

Bonnell, Victoria E. "The Uses of Theory, Concepts and Comparison in Historical Sociology." *Comparative Studies in Society and History* 22(2) (1980):156–73. Historical sociologists proceed, Bonnell argues, by asking questions and exploring evidence in relation to theories or concepts, and by seeking to explain phenomena in single cases, delimited classes of cases, or universally. Where comparisons are used, they may be "analytic" or "illustrative." Major works by Bendix, Moore, Smelser, Tilly, and Wallerstein are discussed to illustrate alternative research strategies.

Braudel, Fernand. *On History*. Translated by Sarah Matthews. Chicago: University of Chicago Press, 1980. This useful collection of some of the most important programmatic articles by a major social historian includes "History and the Social Sciences: The *Longue Durée*," dealing with the "times" and levels appropriate to social-historical studies. Braudel and the French *Annales* school are well known for breaking with political units of analysis and periodization to study the broader and longer-term geographic, cultural, economic, and demographic underpinnings of social life.

Burke, Peter. *Sociology and History*. London: Allen & Unwin, 1980. Burke discusses how to combine conventional sociological concepts with historical research.

Cahnman, Werner J., and Alvin Boskoff, eds. *Sociology and History: Theory and Research*. New York: Free Press, 1964. This is a wide-ranging collection of articles, some dealing with the historical validity of major macrosocial theories, including structural functionalism, and others reporting results of empirical research on scattered times and places. The editors assess the state of interchanges between sociology and history as of the mid-1960s.

Camic, Charles. "The Enlightenment and Its Environment: A Cautionary Tale." In *Knowledge and Society: Studies in the Sociology of Culture Past and Present*, vol. 4, edited by Robert A. Jones and Hendrika Kuklick, pp. 143–72. Greenwich, Conn.: JAI Press, 1983. Camic uses material from the Scottish Enlightenment to illustrate problems of relating cultural developments to historical social explanations. He argues against overdetermined models and advances the idea of seeking explanations within plausible sets of factors capable of actually influencing cultural activity.

Cantor, Norman F., and Richard I. Schneider. *How to Study History*. New York: Crowell, 1967. A basic handbook for students learning to be historians, this contains good chapters on "How to Use Primary Sources" and "How to Read Secondary Sources."

Carr, E. H. *What Is History?* New York: Vintage Books, 1961. This highly readable defense of historical work is unabashedly oriented to explanation and friendly to theoretical and methodological contributions from the social sciences. Carr provides a memorable discussion of why the search for "deterministic" historical explanations may not be such a bad thing.

Chirot, Daniel, ed. "The Uses of History in Sociological Inquiry." Special Issue of *Social Forces* 55(2) (1976). The issue brings together both methodological and substantive pieces, and Chirot's introduction surveys the state of research in historical and comparative historical sociology.

Clark, S. D. "History and the Sociological Method." In *The Developing Canadian Community*, pp. 238–48. Toronto: University of Toronto Press, 1962. Clark tellingly criticizes Park and Burgess's distinction between "history" and "natural history." Too often, Clark maintains, the sociologist "wants to use history without doing history." Instead, the sociologist must avoid merely applying preconceived grand theories to the past and be willing to engage directly in historical research.

Clubb, Jerome M., and Erwin K. Scheuch, eds. *Historical Social Research: The Use of Historical and Process-Produced Data*. *Historisch-Sozialwissenschaftliche Forschungen*, vol. 6. Stuttgart: Klett-Cotta, 1980. This important collection of articles about the uses of quantitative data in historical research touches on problems of theoretical inference and valid interpretation of sources as well as discussing such technical issues as how to merge different data files for computer analysis.

Davidson, James West, and Mark Hamilton Lytle. *After the Fact: The Art of Historical Detection.* New York: Knopf. 1982. Using vivid examples of actual studies by historians of the United States, this book explores various techniques and logics used to ferret out facts and patterns about the past, including psychohistory, pictorial evidence, quantitative data, oral history, documentary analysis, spatial patterns, and the application of grand theories or general models to particular cases. The book could be used either to give a feel for the variety of ways primary evidence can be found and analyzed or to illustrate fruitful uses of social-scientific ideas and techniques by historians.

Dibble, Vernon K. "Four Types of Inference from Documents to Events." *History and Theory* 3(2) (1963):203–21. Historians do not use documents only to find personal "testimony" to past events. They also use them as sources of "social bookkeeping" containing information about groups or organizations; or "correlates" of events; and as "direct indicators" of phenemona under investigation. Dibble's classification and discussion is especially useful for historical sociologists.

Dray, William H., ed. *Philosophical Analysis and History.* New York: Harper & Row. 1966. Dray's excellent collection of classic articles about the nature of historical explanation includes pieces by Isaiah Berlin, C. G. Hempel, Michael Oakeshott, and Ernest Nagel.

Eberhard, Wolfram. "Problems of Historical Sociology." In *Conquerors and Rulers: Social Forces in Medieval China*, pp. 1–17. Leiden: Brill, 1965. In this critique of the concept of "social system" from the perspective of the study of complex historical empires, Eberhard discusses the units of analysis appropriate for historical investigations and advocates attention to temporal contexts in comparative research.

Erikson, Kai T. "Sociology and the Historical Perspective." *The American Sociologist* (5) (1970):331–38. This book offers a thoughtful discussion of the contrasting "professional reflexes" of sociologists and historians and a series of suggestions about ways in which sociologists might profit from using historical methods to help analyze sociological data.

Ferrarotti, Franco. "Biography and the Social Sciences." *Social Research* 50(1) (1983):57–80. The possibilities of biographical methods for the social sciences need to be reexamined, argues Ferrarotti. Developing biographies of primary groups may be an especially fruitful way to mediate between social systems and individual experiences.

Fischer, David Hackett. *Historians' Fallacies: Toward a Logic of Historical Thought.* New York: Harper & Row, 1970. Readable and systematic, this book works its way through common pitfalls that plague historians – and not only them! – in posing research questions, developing explanations, and making arguments. Every point is entertainingly illustrated.

Fogel, Robert W. "The Limits of Quantitative Methods in History." *American Historical Review* 80(2) (1975):329–50. Fogel systematically addresses the quantitative methods applicable to certain kinds of historical problems and muses about the implications of quantification for the training of historians and for their ability to communicate with readers and with one another.

Fogel, Robert W. "Circumstantial Evidence in 'Scientific' and Traditional History." In *Philosophy of History and Contemporary Historiography*, edited by David Carr et al., pp. 61–112. Ottawa: University of Ottawa Press, 1982. This is a meticulous analysis by a leading "cliometric" historian of the kinds of evidence and inferential logic used in various styles of historical research and writing.

Fredrickson, George M. "Comparative History." In *The Past Before Us: Contemporary Historical Writing in the United States*, edited by Michael Kammen, pp. 457–73. Ithaca, N.Y.: Cornell University Press, 1980. The author of *White Supremacy*, a prominent comparative work in history, discusses the uses of comparisons, especially stressing how they can highlight contrasts and particularities more effectively then research confined to single times and places.

Furet, François. "Quantitative History." In *Historical Studies Today*. *Daedalus* 100(1) (1971):151–67. Furet presents a thoughtful discussion of various meanings of quantitative history and of the conceptual and research issues that need to be faced by those who use quantitative approaches and data to study historical processes.

Geertz, Clifford. *The Interpretation of Cultures: Selected Essays*. New York: Basic Books, 1973. This is an important collection of programmatic essays and case studies by a cultural anthropologist who has recently had enormous influence on historians, helping to generate a "new social history" devoted to cultural interpretation as a rival to social-scientific approaches oriented to socioeconomic explanation and the use of quantitative evidence. See Walters (1980) for a discussion of Geertz's impact.

Goldstein, Leon J. "Theory in History." *Philosophy of Science* 34(1) (1967):23 40. History is neither a mode of literary discourse nor an application of universal laws to particular cases. Agreeing with arguments such as those of Beer (1963) and Stinchcombe (1978), Goldstein examines good examples of the development of delimited theories through the testing of plausible hypotheses in the course of actual historical studies.

Grew, Raymond. "The Case for Comparing Histories." *American Historical Review* 85(4) (1980):763–78. Directed at historians, in the spirit of Marc Bloch's 1928 essay, this article is especially good on how comparisons can help in the formulation of interesting historical questions and research problems.

Habermas, Jürgen. "History and Evolution." *Telos* 39 (1979):5–44. Habermas makes a useful distinction between models of historical explanation that seek to present hypotheses amenable to empirical test versus models of cultural evolution that provide sensitizing concepts for the selection of problems, but are not in themselves subject to empirical verification.

Hage, Jerald. "Theoretical Decision Rules for Selecting Research Designs: The Study of Nation-States or Societies." *Sociological Methods and Research* 4(2) (1975):131–65. Reasoning by analogy from experimental rather than statistical research designs, Hage offers a series of valuable pointers on the selection of societies and time periods to include in comparative and temporally longitudinal research designs. He also suggests theoretically informed rules for choosing variables and measurements.

Hexter, J. H. "The Rhetoric of History." In *Doing History*, pp. 15–76. Bloomington: Indiana University Press, 1971. An antisocial-scientific historian analyzes and defends the special contributions of narrative writing to the communication of distinctly historical knowledge. The essay features a famous discussion of alternative ways of "explaining" how the New York Giants ended up in the 1951 World Series!

Historical Methods (formerly *Historical Methods Newsletter*). 1968–. Published quarterly by Heldref Publications, 4000 Albermarle Street, N.W., Washington D.C. 20016. This forum for the sharing of quantitative techniques in social and political history presents data sources, measurement issues, and analytic approaches in the context of short articles about actual, ongoing research projects.

Hopkins, Terence K., and Immanuel Wallerstein. "The Comparative Study of National Societies." *Social Science Information* 6(5) (1967):25–58. This methodological statement predates the emergence of Wallerstein's world-system approach, and he and Hopkins no longer advocate many of its positions. Nevertheless, this is a good discussion of the levels of analysis and inference used in comparative research, and it shows how world-historical, transnational, and international patterns can be incorporated as variables into cross-national research designs.

Johnson, Bruce C. "Missionaries, Tourists and Traders: Sociologists in the Domain of History." In *Studies in Symbolic Interaction*, vol. 4, pp. 115–50. Greenwich, Conn.: JAI Press, 1982. Johnson sharply opposes "positivist" and "interpretive" approaches in sociology, and advocates closer relationships between interpretive historical research, on the one hand, and ethnographic and field studies of meaningful social interactions, on the other. Johnson synthesized these styles of research himself in his *The Leader Must Not Fall: A Sociological Analysis of Mountain Climbing*.

Johnson, Richard, Gregor McLennan, Bill Schwartz, and David Sutton, eds. *Making Histories: Studies in History Writing and Politics.* Minneapolis: University of Minnesota Press, 1982. This collection was produced by radical British sociocultural historians associated with the Centre for Contemporary Cultural Studies of the University of Birmingham. As Mary Jo Maynes puts it in her Foreword, the essays "connect historical work with (Marxist) theoretical understanding and political practice."

Jones, Gareth Stedman. "From Historical Sociology to Theoretical History." Special Issue on History and Sociology. *British Journal of Sociology:* 27(3) (1976):295–304. Jones endorses the historical study of social structures and change under Marxist theoretical auspices, but warns against atheoretical interdisciplinary interchanges between conventional sociology and historiography.

Laslett, Barbara. "Beyond Methodology: The Place of Theory in Quantitative Historical Research." *American Sociological Review* 45 (1980):214–28. Laslett opposes sheer empiricism using individual-level data, and stresses the need for a structural theoretical perspective. Points are illustrated with evidence from Laslett's own quantitative research in U.S. family history.

Lijphart, Arend. "Comparative Politics and the Comparative Method." *American Political Science Review* 65(3) (1971):682–93. This is the best short discussion of comparative methodology in the political science literature. Lijphart assesses the strengths and weaknesses of the macroscopic comparative method as contrasted to experimental and statistical approaches, and he has especially insightful things to say about six different approaches to the study of single cases. Several kinds of single-case studies, he shows, are extensions of the comparative method.

Lijphart, Arend. "The Comparable-Cases Strategy in Comparative Research." *Comparative Political Studies* 8(2) (1975):158–77. A useful follow-up on Lijphart's earlier article, this one takes account of arguments by Przeworski and Teune (1970) and Smelser (1976).

Linz, Juan, and A. de Miguel. "Within-Nation Differences and Comparisons: The Eight Spains." In *Comparing Nations: The Use of Quantitative Data in Cross-National Research*, edited by R. L. Merritt and S. Rokkan, pp. 267–319. New Haven, Conn.: Yale University Press, 1966. Attention to regions within nations increases the overall number of units available for some comparative purposes. It can be very fruitful, Linz and de Miguel argue, to compare similar regions across nations rather than simply nations as wholes. This article dramatizes the need to consider units other than nation-states in comparative (and historical) research.

Lipset, Seymour Martin. "A Sociologist Looks at History." *Pacific Sociological Review* 1(1) (1958):13–17. Lipset briefly presents the themes developed at greater length in the next selection.

Lipset, Seymour Martin. "History and Sociology: Some Methodological Considerations." In *Sociology and History: Methods,* edited by S. M. Lipset and Richard Hofstadter. New York: Basic Books, 1968. This is one of the introductory essays for a volume that brought together historical sociologists and social historians using quantitative and comparative-historical approaches to study the United States. Lipset treats sociology as a "generalizing" discipline and history as inherently "particularizing," and points to ways in which the former can benefit from sound historical data and the latter can make better use of sociological concepts and analytic techniques.

Mariampolski, Hyman, and Dana C. Hughes. "The Use of Personal Documents in Historical Sociology." *The American Sociologist* 13(2) (1978):104–13. Drawing on writings by historians and historical sociologists to suggest methodological principles for the use of personal documents from the past to reconstruct events, this article essentially systematizes for sociologists things historians already know about interpreting this sort of primary source.

Marsh, Robert M. *Comparative Sociology: A Codification of Cross-Societal Analysis.* New York: Harcourt, Brace and World, 1967. Marsh catalogues the findings of comparative studies done by structural functionalists, anthropologists, and others into an overall scheme based on levels of societal differentiation. Of more contemporary interest, Marsh classifies the kinds of theoretically relevant knowledge comparative studies can yield: replication, universal generalization, contingency generalization, and specification. This book has extensive bibliographies on substantive studies and methodological writings from the 1950s and early 1960s.

McDaniel, Timothy. "Meaning and Comparative Concepts." *Theory and Society* 6(1) (1978):93–118. Taking very seriously the findings of anthropologists and historians about the diversity of cultures, McDaniel explores how "the comparison of meaningful social life" is possible.

Mill, John Stuart. *Philosophy of Scientific Method,* edited by Ernest Nagel. New York: Hafner, 1950 (originally the 1881 edition of *A System of Logic*), pp. 211–33. This is the classic statement of the logic of comparative analysis, and can be read along with Smelser (1976) and Zelditch (1971).

Milligan, John D. "The Treatment of an Historical Source." *History and Theory* 18(2) (1979):177–96. This highly readable presentation of the steps a good historian goes through to establish the authenticity, credibility, and implications of a primary document uses the concrete example of a letter from the time of the American Civil War.

Mills, C. Wright. *The Sociological Imagination.* London and New York: Oxford University Press, 1959. Mills assesses ahistorical "grand theory" and "abstracted empiricism" and offers an eloquent plea for a sociology devoted to grasping "history and biography and the relations between the two within society." Chapter 8, "The Uses of History," and the Appendix, "On Intellectual Craftsmanship," are especially relevant.

Moore, Barrington, Jr. "Strategy in Social Science." In *Political Power and Social*

Theory, pp. 11–159. Cambridge, Mass.: Harvard University Press, 1958. This is an apology for historical research in sociology and a careful discussion of how to situate an explanatory historical sociology between universalistic theorizing and idiographic historiography.

Nisbet, Robert A. *Social Change and History: Aspects of the Western Theory of Development*. New York: Oxford University Press, 1969. Instead of the developmentalist concept of endogenous, progressive, evolutionary social change that has dominated Western thought since ancient times and reappeared in structural functionalist theories of modernization, Nisbet advocates "a genuinely historical method, one which proceeds from social behavior, from events, from concrete circumstances," and pays careful attention to timing and to contacts and conflicts across societal boundaries.

Nowak, Stefan. "General Laws and Historical Generalizations in the Social Sciences." *Polish Sociological Bulletin* 1 (1961):21–32. Nowak advocates the ongoing conduct of theoretically relevant analyses at both general and historically bounded levels, along with recurrent efforts to look for "a better understanding of the . . . functioning of historically limited principles governing events."

Ossowski, Stanislaw. "Two Conceptions of Historical Generalizations in the Social Sciences." *Polish Sociological Bulletin* 3 (1964):28–34. This is very useful, along with Nowak's article, for thinking about general laws versus bounded generalizations in social-historical analysis.

Platt, Jennifer. "Evidence and Proof in Documentary Research: 1 and 2." *Sociological Review* 29(1) (1981):31–66. Platt's systematic survey of the issues that must be faced by researchers who draw upon documents to make social inferences includes discussions of establishing authenticity, sampling, interpreting meaning, and communicating findings from documentary research.

Popper, Karl R. *The Poverty of Historicism*. New York: Harper & Row, 1964. Popper decries the pernicious effects on sociology of determinist theories of history, including Marxism, and he offers alternative methodological prescriptions.

"Problems in Social History: A Symposium." *Theory and Society* 9(5) (1980):667–81. Have social historians bogged down in trivia, or become overly obsessed with quantification? Do they leave politics out of history? This symposium features Charles and Louise Tilly and others considering recent critiques of social history by Marxists and conservatives alike.

Przeworski, Adam, and Henry Teune. *The Logic of Comparative Social Inquiry*. New York: Wiley, 1970. Przeworski and Teune argue for a particular approach – the investigation of system level variables hypothesized to explain variations across systems in within-system relationships – as the optimal strategy for using comparative research to build general theories. "Most different systems" designs are advocated, with the aim of attributing effects to systematic factors only after individual-level possibilities are exhausted. This highly technical and idiosyncratic perspective would rule out most existing approaches in comparative-historical sociology.

Ragin, Charles C. "Comparative Sociology and the Comparative Method." *International Journal of Comparative Sociology* 22(1–2) (1981):102–20. Ragin argues that the distinguishing feature of comparative sociology is the use of "societies" as "explanatory units," even though "observational units" may vary. Because inferences are necessarily made from studies of relatively small numbers of units, the comparative method is case-based rather than variable-based like statistical approaches, and it develops "configurational" explanations of cross-societal similarities and differences. Comparativists also rely heavily on the use of "type concepts" to link theories to evidence.

Ragin, Charles, and David Zaret. "Theory and Method in Comparative Research: Two Strategies." *Social Forces* 61(3) (1983):731–54. Ragin and Zaret contrast the comparative strategies of Durkheim and Weber with respect to units of analysis, conceptions of causality, notions of adequate explanation, and logics of analysis. They identify historical methods with the Weberian tradition of research.

Rock, Paul. "Some Problems of Interpretive Historiography." Special Issue on History and Sociology. *British Journal of Sociology* 27(3) (1976):353–69. Rock critically examines historiographical methods from a radical phenomenological perspective and concludes that historians cannot really tap past meanings. At best, they can sketch only "skeletal portraits" of the past.

Schafer, Robert J., ed. *A Guide to Historical Method.* Rev. ed. Homewood, Ill.: Dorsey Press, 1974. This sophisticated handbook of historiographical methods is especially good on sources of primary evidence and rules for the effective and valid interpretation of documents.

Sewell, William H., Jr. "Marc Bloch and the Logic of Comparative History." *History and Theory* 6(2) (1967):208–18. This systematic gloss on Bloch's classic 1928 essay incorporates examples from Bloch's own use of historical comparisons in his various substantive studies.

Skocpol, Theda, and Margaret Somers. "The Uses of Comparative History in Macrosocial Inquiry." *Comparative Studies in Society and History* 22(2) (1980): 174–97. This article delineates and evaluates three different ways of doing comparative history: the "contrast-oriented" approach best exemplified by Bendix; the "macro-analytic" approach exemplified by Moore, Skocpol, and Hamilton; and the "parallel" approach exemplified by Eisenstadt and Paige. The approaches differ in their use of theories and concepts, as well as in the purposes for which they juxtapose two or more historical trajectories.

Smelser, Neil J. "Sociological History, the Industrial Revolution, and the British Working-Class Family." *The Journal of Social History* 1(1) (1967):17–35. Reprinted in Smelser, *Essays in Sociological Explanation.* Englewood Cliffs, N.J.: Prentice-Hall, 1968. Partly this is a synopsis of key arguments in Smelser's *Social Change in the Industrial Revolution.* It is also a careful methodological statement about how to apply a pregiven general theory to a historical case.

Smelser, Neil J. *Comparative Methods in the Social Sciences.* Englewood Cliffs, N.J.: Prentice-Hall, 1976. Smelser argues that the comparative method is but one variant of the scientific effort to control variation, logically akin to experimental and statistical approaches, but tailored to the special problems of comparing relatively small numbers of "historically given" cases. Smelser surveys a comprehensive array of issues about research design, classification, measurement, and analytic inference, using examples from the work of Tocqueville, Durkheim, and Weber, as well as from modern studies in sociology, anthropology, and beyond.

Smith, Dennis. "Social History and Sociology – More Than Just Good Friends." *Sociological Review* 30(2) (1982):286–308. Smith suggests that sociology and social history are experiencing a convergence of interests, although this may have been obscured by recent preoccupations with structuralism. He discusses works by Peter Burke, R. S. Neale, Anthony Giddens, E. P.

Thompson, and John Foster and suggests an agenda for research in historical sociology, with particular reference to the case of British society.

Stinchcombe, Arthur L. *Constructing Social Theories.* New York: Harcourt, Brace & World, 1968. This book contains very useful discussions of how to generate testable causal propositions from both "functionalist" and "historicist" perpectives in macrosociology.

Stinchcombe, Arthur L. *Theoretical Methods in Social History.* New York: Academic Press, 1978. A provocative argument that good theory is not "applied" to history but rather generated from efforts to explain detailed, analogous historical sequences. Stinchcombe's thesis is illustrated with idiosyncratic renderings of major works by Tocqueville, Trotsky, Smelser, and Bendix.

Stone, Lawrence. "Prosopography." In *Historical Studies Today. Daedalus* 100(1) (1971):46–79. Prosopography, also known as "collective biography" or "multiple career-line analysis," is "the investigation of the common background characteristics of a group of actors in history." In this essay, Stone discusses the origins, characteristics, and limitations of this approach.

Stone, Lawrence. "The Revival of Narrative." *Past and Present* 85 (1979):3–24. The leading historian who earlier helped move history toward social-scientific methods of analysis now pronounces a partial counter-revolution against quantification and "determinism," and endorses a return to interpretive "story telling," especially about culturally significant events in the past. Eric Hobsbawm replies to Stone in *Past and Present* no. 86.

Taylor, Charles. "Interpretation and the Sciences of Man." In *Interpretive Social Science: A Reader,* edited by Paul Rabinow and William M. Sullivan, pp. 25–71. Berkeley: University of California Press, 1979. While this essay is not directly about historical sociology, it cogently explains and defends hermeneutic social studies in contrast to generalizing social science, and so could be used to make intelligible the kinds of knowledge sought or advocated by some historical sociologists and comparative historians, such as Bendix, Johnson, Thompson, Zaret, and (in his latest incarnation) Stone.

Thompson, E. P. "The Poverty of Theory: Or an Orrery of Errors." In *The Poverty of Theory and Other Essays.* London: Merlin Press, 1978. In the course of this brilliant and amusing polemic against structural Marxists, Thompson lays out his own methodological prescriptions for conceptualization and the use of evidence in interpretive historical research, especially about classes, culture, and politics in Britain.

Thrupp, Silvia L. "Diachronic Methods in Comparative Politics." In *The Methodology of Comparative Research,* edited by Robert T. Holt and John E. Turner, pp. 343–58. New York: Free Press, 1970. Thrupp argues for greater historical depth in research about comparative politics and "rejects as a red herring the notion that the choice is between quantitative and nonquantitative methods. Rather, the choice is seen as turning on one's degree of sensitivity to the uses of differences for the purpose of generalization, as well as of similarities."

Tilly, Charles. *As Sociology Meets History.* New York: Academic Press, 1981. This is an important collection of substantive articles and methodological reflections. The lead essay, "Sociology, Meet History," introduces sociologists to the actual practice of historians' work and presents Tilly's view that sociological analyses of large-scale change need more historical grounding. Various topical essays give an excellent sense of Tilly's own past and present agendas for social-historical research and show how he collects and analyzes quantitative evidence.

Tilly, Charles. *Big Structures, Large Processes, Huge Comparisons.* New York: Russell Sage Foundation, forthcoming. This long essay does two things. It attacks the Durkheimian and structural functionalist approach to explaining social change and proposes, instead, a perspective highlighting state-making and the growth of capitalism as the intertwined large-scale processes that have reshaped Western countries in recent centuries. It also uses a simple scheme, based on generalizing versus particularizing and single versus multiple units, to distinguish four approaches to macroscopic analysis: individualizing comparisons; universalizing comparisons; generalizing comparisons; and encompassing comparisons.

Tomasson, Richard F. Introduction to vol. 1 of *Comparative Studies in Sociology* (later *Comparative Social Research*), a research annual. Greenwich, Conn.: JAI Press, 1978. Tomasson surveys the state and prospects of comparative cross-national or cross-cultural research in sociology.

Topolski, Jerzy. "The Model Method in Economic History." *The Journal of European Economic History* 1(3) (1972):713–26. Topolski explores issues in the use of general models to explain historical facts.

Topolski, Jerzy. *Methodology of History.* Translated by Olgierd Wojtasiewicz. Dordrecht, Holland: Reidel, 1976. This is a daunting overview of the logic of many kinds of historical and comparative-historical research.

Vallier, Ivan, ed. *Comparative Methods in Sociology: Essays on Trends and Applications.* Berkeley: University of California Press, 1971. Vallier presents an excellent collection offering perspectives from the 1960s. The essays range from discussions of the comparative methods of Tocqueville, Marx, and Weber, to discussions of methodological issues in cross-national survey research and in comparative studies inspired by structural functionalist theory. Lengthy annotated bibliographies are provided.

Walters, Ronald G. "Signs of the Times: Clifford Geertz and Historians." *Social Research* 47(3) (1980):537–56. This is an excellent discussion of the impact on contemporary social historians of Geertz's "thick description"–an approach to the investigation of meaningful orientations and symbol systems in human action. Walters explains why such borrowing from cultural anthropology is appealing to historians and offers thoughtful caveats about how far it should go.

Walton, John. "Standardized Case Comparison: Observations on Method in Comparative Sociology." In *Comparative Social Research,* edited by Michael Armer and Allen Grimshaw, pp. 173–91. New York: Wiley, 1973. Walton discusses the advantages and disadvantages of comparative case studies, comparative analyses using quantitative archival data, and studies that generate new data on a range of comparable cases. He advocates "standardized case comparisons," using cases selected with theoretically relevant comparisons in mind, and drawing on various sorts of systematically collected data.

Weber, Max. *The Methodology of the Social Sciences.* Translated and edited by E. Shils and F. Finch. New York: Free Press, 1949. These are classical methodological essays by Weber, covering such issues as the use of ideal types and the problem of "adequate causation" in sociological studies devoted to the interpretation and explanation of meaningful historical events and patterns.

Willer, David. "Theory, Experimentation and Historical Interpretation." In *Social Theories in Progress, III,* edited by Joseph Berger, Morris Zelditch, and

402

Bo Anderson. Pittsburgh, Penn.: University of Pittsburgh Press, forthcoming. Willer discusses the use of elementary formal models to mediate between experimental findings and the testing of key arguments from existing interpretations of historical social structures and patterns of change. Issues about the fall of the Roman Empire are explored to illustrate the method Willer advocates.

Wolff, Kurt H. "Sociology and History; Theory and Practice." *American Journal of Sociology* 65(1) (1959):32–38. Wolff advocates the self-conscious development of sociological theories based on "a historical diagnosis of our time."

Zaret, David. "Sociological Theory and Historical Scholarship." *The American Sociologist* 13(2) (1978):114–21. Sociologists have much to learn from new "analytic historiographies," Zaret argues. He advocates the reworking of sociological concepts and theories to become more historically grounded in problem-formulation and explanation.

Zaret, David. "From Weber to Parsons and Schutz: The Eclipse of History in Modern Social Theory." *American Journal of Sociology* 85(5) (1980):1180–1201. Zaret argues that any attempt by sociologists to dissociate general theorizing from historical research will produce only hollow results. He shows that Weber used historically grounded procedures for generating theoretical concepts, while Parsons and Schutz later tried, in different ways, to eliminate the historical components of Weber's thought.

Zelditch, Morris, Jr. "Intelligible Comparisons." In *Comparative Methods in Sociology*, edited by I. Vallier, pp. 267–307. Berkeley: University of California Press, 1971. Taking off from John Stuart Mill's logical rules for comparative analyses, Zelditch offers a rigorous and intelligent discussion of what comparativists try to do in their research and how they can proceed toward valid results. He concludes that theoretically relevant judgments and thorough knowledge of the subject matter are just as necessary for fruitful research as knowledge of methodological rules.

Notes on the Contributors

Fred Block first encountered Karl Polanyi's work as an undergraduate at Columbia College. While there, he studied with Immanuel Wallerstein and Terence Hopkins as they were beginning to formulate their analysis of the capitalist world system. He did his graduate work at the University of California, Berkeley, and afterward took a position at the University of Pennsylvania, where he is currently Associate Professor of Sociology.

Block's dissertation, later published as *The Origins of International Economic Discorder* (University of California Press, 1977), attempted to apply Polanyi's analysis of the contradictions of a self-regulating international monetary system to the post–World War II period. Block's work then turned to the analysis of the determinants of state policy. He has contributed to a reconceptualization of the relationship between state and society in a series of articles, including "The Ruling Class Does Not Rule" in *Socialist Revolution* (1977); "Beyond Relative Autonomy" in the *Socialist Register* (1980); and "Economic Instability and Military Strength: The Paradoxes of the 1950 Rearmament Decision" in *Politics and Society* (1981).

More recently, Block's work has focused on the political economy of advanced capitalist societies. One strand of this work continues a Polanyian theme by systematically criticizing the notion that economic imperatives "require" a rollback of the welfare state. Another strand seeks to develop a postindustrial analysis of employment trends.

Daniel Chirot attended Harvard College and graduated in 1964 in Social Studies. He then worked for the Ministry of Agriculture in Niger and found out that a sound knowledge of rural history, of field shapes, and peasant technologies leads to a better understanding of African countries than the study of their intellectuals' and politicians' ideologies.

He attended graduate school in sociology at Columbia University and obtained his Ph.D. in 1973. He studied with Immanuel Wallerstein and Sigmund Diamond. His doctoral research was in Romania, where

404

he worked with Henri H. Stahl, who, like Bloch, believed that it is important to combine current studies of agricultural practices and peasant habits with the examination of old documents to decipher the past. Chirot's dissertation, an attempt to put Stahl's knowledge into a Wallersteinian world-system framework, was published as *Social Change in a Peripheral Society: The Creation of a Balkan Colony* (Academic Press, 1976). In 1980, he published his translation of Stahl's *Traditional Romanian Village Communities: The Transition from the Communal to the Capitalist Mode of Production in the Danube Region*. It appeared in Wallerstein's Cambridge University Press series, *Studies in Modern Capitalism*.

Chirot's major work on world-system theory was *Social Change in the Twentieth Century* (Harcourt Brace Jovanovich, 1977). Although he has become skeptical about the utility of any grand theory, and about the political base of world-system theory in particular, he is working on a new edition of this book, and trying to incorporate his doubts into the revision.

Chirot now thinks that the best kind of social historical work, like Bloch's, combines an eclectic use of theory with intense regional specialization and love of detailed field work. He is studying Indonesian and preparing to work on contemporary Indonesian social history. He is Professor of International Studies and of Sociology at the University of Washington.

Mary Fulbrook is Lecturer in German History at University College, London. She was an undergraduate at Newnham College, Cambridge, where she studied Archaeology and Anthropology, and Social and Political Sciences, obtaining a First-Class Honours degree. She then did graduate work in the Department of Sociology at Harvard University, receiving her M.A. in 1975 and Ph.D. in 1979. In 1976–77 Mary Fulbrook held a Krupp Fellowship from the Harvard Center for European Studies. Following her lectureships at the London School of Economics and Brunel University, she held a Lady Margaret Research Fellowship at New Hall, Cambridge, from 1979 to 1982.

In her book *Piety and Politics: Religion and the Rise of Absolutism in England, Württemberg and Prussia* (Cambridge University Press, 1983), Fulbrook undertakes a comparative historical analysis of the different political contributions made by similar religious movements to the success or failure of attempts at absolutist rule in three early modern European states. She has also written articles on Max Weber, Christopher Hill, the historiography of the English Revolution, and aspects of religion and politics in England and Germany. Fulbrook is currently interested in problems of political development in postwar West and East Germany.

Gary G. Hamilton is Associate Professor of Sociology at the University of California, Davis. He received his Ph.D. in Sociology at the University of Washington, Seattle, in 1975. Having studied about and lived in East Asia for several years, he wrote his dissertation on the state and merchant activity in late imperial China. He has since published a variety of articles on historical and comparative topics in such journals as *American Journal of Sociology, American Sociological Review,* and *Comparative Studies in Society and History.* Included in these articles are analyses of adventurism in the California gold rush, the Chinese dislike of Western-made goods during the nineteenth century, and the commercial successes of marginal ethnic groups.

More recently, Hamilton has embarked on a series of studies examining historical and modern political organizations. One effort in this direction, supported by the National Science Foundation, has been to study the historical development and character of modern political authority. A monograph on this research, coauthored with Nicole Biggart, has just appeared: *Governor Reagan, Governor Brown: A Sociology of Executive Power* (Columbia University Press, 1984). He is currently working on a comparative study of the principles and organization of domination in late imperial China, a work whose purpose is to criticize and ultimately to revise Max Weber's analysis of China.

Lynn Hunt is Associate Professor of History at the University of California, Berkeley, where she has been teaching since 1974. She received her B.A. in History from Carleton College, and her M.A. and Ph.D. in History from Stanford University. After leaving Stanford, she spent three years at the University of Michigan Society of Fellows, where she participated in the weekly seminars of the Collective Action/Social History Group, led by Charles and Louise Tilly. Her first book, *Revolution and Urban Politics in Provincial France: Troyes and Reims, 1786–1790* (Stanford University Press, 1978) won a local history prize in France. She has published a comparative analysis of French towns in the Revolution: "Committees and Communes: Local Politics and National Revolution in 1789," *Comparative Studies in Society and History* (1976); and a geographically based analysis of the political differences between French regions: "The Political Geography of Revolutionary France," *Journal of Interdisciplinary History* (1984). The University of California Press will publish her *Politics, Culture, and*

Class in the French Revolution in 1984. In this book, she combines the techniques of literary criticism, art history, and political anthropology with quantitative studies of local and national political elites.

Charles Ragin received his Ph.D. from the University of North Carolina in 1975. He taught at Indiana University for several years before moving to Northwestern University, where he is currently an Associate Professor of Sociology and Urban Affairs.

Ragin has published in three major areas: political mobilization, economic dependency and development, and comparative and historical methods. His work on political mobilization includes analyses of quantitative data on Welsh and Scottish nationalism in an effort to assess the relative merits of different theories of ethnic mobilization, as well as analyses of historical data on the outcomes of major British labor disputes. Ragin also participated in the effort to use quantitative cross-national data to assess dependency theory and developed, with Jacques Delacroix, the "structural blockage" approach, which integrates several perspectives on comparative international development.

Ragin's recent work on comparative and historical methods deals with logical inconsistencies between quantitative techniques and the theories and interests of comparative and historical sociologists. Of special concern in this work is the problem of making holistic comparisons.

Dietrich Rueschemeyer is presently Professor of Sociology at Brown University. He studied sociology and economics in Munich and Cologne, Germany. His dissertation dealt with problems of the sociology of knowledge. He edited and introduced the first collection of essays of Talcott Parsons in German translation. In *Lawyers and Their Society* (Harvard University Press, 1973) he contrasted the state orientation of the German legal profession with the business orientation of the bar in the United States and sought to explain these differences as well as their change over time in terms of the role of the state in the modernization and industrialization of the two countries. In a number of subsequent essays he explored professionalization and the control of experts, joining theoretical and comparative historical problem formulations. The theoretical analysis of development and modernization has been an abiding concern of his since the late 1960s. In a series of essays, including "Partial Modernization," "Reflections on Structural Differentiation," and "Structural Differentiation, Efficiency and Power," Rueschemeyer has taken positions increasingly critical of consensual and functionalist models of social transformation. Currently he is working on a monograph on power and the division of labor and on problems relating to the sociology of the state.

Theda Skocpol first encountered comparative history when she read Barrington Moore's *Social Origins of Dictatorship and Democracy* during her senior year at Michigan State University, where she received her B.A. in Sociology in 1969. As a graduate student at Harvard from 1969 to 1975, Skocpol took seminars with Moore and also worked with S. M. Lipset, Daniel Bell, George Homans, and Ezra Vogel. Along with broad-ranging studies in social theory, social stratification, and political sociology, Skocpol used her graduate years to pursue questions about American society and politics and about the comparative history of revolutions.

After receiving the Ph.D. in 1975, Skocpol remained at Harvard from 1975 to 1981, and then taught in Sociology and Political Science at the University of Chicago from 1981 to 1985. In 1986, she returned to Harvard as Professor of Sociology. Skocpol is also the co-chair (with Peter Evans) of a new research planning committee on States and Social Structures organized under the auspices of the Social Science Research Council.

Skocpol's first book, *States and Social Revolutions: A Comparative Analysis of France, Russia, and China* (Cambridge University Press, 1979), was the recipient of the 1979 C. Wright Mills Award of the Society for the Study of Social Problems and of a 1980 American Sociological Association Award for a Distinguished Contribution to Scholarship. For the last several years, her research has centered on the New Deal, and, more broadly, on the development of American public social benefits from the nineteenth century to the present. The preliminary ideas for Skocpol's next book are sketched in a recent article (coauthored with John Ikenberry), "The Political Formation of the American Welfare State in Historical and Comparative Perspective," appearing in *Comparative Social Research* (1983).

Dennis Smith studied modern history at Cambridge University and sociology at the London School of Economics. He has taught at the University of Leicester and is currently Senior Lecturer in the Management Centre at the University of Aston in Birmingham. In 1980 he was an Associate of the Center for European Studies at Harvard University.

and a Visiting Scholar in the Department of Sociology. His previous works include *Conflict and Compromise. Class Formation in English Society 1830–1914. A Comparative Study of Birmingham and Sheffield* (Routledge & Kegan Paul, 1982) and *Barrington Moore, Jr.: A Critical Appraisal* (M. E. Sharpe, 1983). He has also published papers on various aspects of social theory, including the writings of Norbert Elias and Thorstein Veblen, the relationship between social history and sociology, and the intersocietal aspects of modernization.

Smith's current research is on the development of capitalist democracy in Britain and the United States, including its urban aspects. Forthcoming publications include a comparative study of Chicago and Birmingham from the late nineteenth century to the present, an examination of the Chicago School, and a textbook on the development of British society since 1745.

Margaret R. Somers is a research associate at Harvard University's Center for European Studies. She received her B.A. in Sociology from the University of California at Santa Cruz. Her doctoral dissertation in Sociology at Harvard is entitled "Collective Memory and the Claim to Regulative Liberty and Narrative Justice: Proto-industrialization, State Formation, and the Law in English Working Class Formation." Somers was an instructor at Boston University in 1981–82 and has taught tutorials at Harvard in social theory, political sociology, Western European comparative politics, and the history of the family. Her publications and papers include "Fascism – the Revolt of the Social: Karl Polanyi's Spiritual and Political Reality Principle," presented at the historical colloquium on German Social Science in America: The Interwar Migration and its Legacy, held at the Center for European Studies, Harvard University, in November 1983; "The Origins of the English Welfare State: A Re-examination," presented at the International Sociological Association Meetings, Mexico City, 1982; "The Family and the State in Early Industrialization: The Historical Fallacies of Class Analysis," presented at the Conference of Europeanists, Washington, D.C., 1982; "The Uses of Comparative History in Macrosocial Inquiry," *Comparative Studies in Society and History* (1980, co-authored with Theda Skocpol); "The Limits of Agronomic Determinism: A Critical Review of Paige's *Agrarian Revolution*," *Comparative Studies in Society and History*, (1979, co-authored with Walter Goldfrank).

Ellen Kay Trimberger is a historical sociologist who currently teaches and is the Coordinator of Women's Studies at Sonoma State University

409

in California. She has taught at Columbia University, Barnard College, Queens College (CUNY), the University of California, Santa Barbara, and San Jose State University. Her essay on the work of E. P. Thompson marked a transition in her own evolution as a historical sociologist from an analysis that was materialist and structuralist to one that incorporated culture and human agency.

Influenced by her experience as a teenager living in the Philippines in the 1950s, and by reaction to the Vietnam War in the 1960s, she focused her graduate research on social change in the Third World. Her teachers at the University of Chicago from 1962 to 1966 – especially Edward Shils and Morris Janowitz – introduced her to Max Weber, who provided a comparative method and an analysis of precapitalist, non-Western societies. However, she rejected the modernization theory prevalent at the University of Chicago and elsewhere in the early 1960s. Her doctoral dissertation became a book, *Revolution from Above: Military Bureaucrats and Development in Japan, Turkey, Egypt and Peru* (Transaction Books, 1978). It combined a Weberian analysis of the importance of state bureaucracies in non-Western societies with a Marxist analysis of the impact of class and imperialism on Third World development.

By the time the book was finished, however, Trimberger was dissatisfied with a framework that did not examine culture or gender. Moreover, her teaching and political interests had become increasingly focused on U.S. social change, and especially on the women's movement. In 1978 she began to focus her research on the changing culture of personal relations – intimacy, sexuality, and love – in twentieth-century United States. She has published two articles on this topic: "Women in the Old and New Left: The Evolution of a Politics of Personal Life," *Feminist Studies* (1979); and "Feminism, Men and Modern Love: Greenwich Village 1900–1925," in *Powers of Desire: The Politics of Sexuality* (1983). Currently, she is doing research for a book on the modernization of love in Greenwich Village from 1900 to 1925.